ROUTLEDGE LIBRARY EDITIONS:
SOVIET SOCIETY

Volume 3

CONTEMPORARY HISTORY IN THE SOVIET MIRROR

CONTEMPORARY HISTORY IN THE SOVIET MIRROR

Edited by
JOHN KEEP

with the assistance of
LILIANA BRISBY

Routledge
Taylor & Francis Group

LONDON AND NEW YORK

First published in 1964 by George Allen & Unwin Ltd

This edition first published in 2025
by Routledge
4 Park Square, Milton Park, Abingdon, Oxon OX14 4RN

and by Routledge
605 Third Avenue, New York, NY 10158

Routledge is an imprint of the Taylor & Francis Group, an informa business

© 1964 George Allen & Unwin Ltd

British Library Cataloguing in Publication Data
A catalogue record for this book is available from the British Library

ISBN: 978-1-032-86028-2 (Set)
ISBN: 978-1-032-87174-5 (Volume 3) (hbk)
ISBN: 978-1-032-87215-5 (Volume 3) (pbk)
ISBN: 978-1-003-53148-7 (Volume 3) (ebk)

DOI: 10.4324/9781003531487

Publisher's Note
The publisher has gone to great lengths to ensure the quality of this reprint but points out that some imperfections in the original copies may be apparent.

Disclaimer
The publisher has made every effort to trace copyright holders and would welcome correspondence from those they have been unable to trace.

Contemporary History in the Soviet Mirror

EDITED BY JOHN KEEP

WITH THE ASSISTANCE OF LILIANA BRISBY

LONDON: GEORGE ALLEN AND UNWIN LTD

FIRST PUBLISHED IN 1964

*Published under the auspices of
the Congress for Cultural Freedom*

PRINTED IN GREAT BRITAIN
in 10 on 11 pt. Times Roman type
BY C. TINLING AND COMPANY LTD
LIVERPOOL, LONDON AND PRESCOT

CONTENTS

Introduction   *page*   9
JOHN KEEP

I. Historiography and Change   19
MERLE FAINSOD
Discussion   34

II. Party Histories from Lenin to Khrushchev   43
BERTRAM D. WOLFE
Discussion   61

III. Continuity and Change in the new History of
the CPSU   69
LEONARD SCHAPIRO
Discussion   82

IV. Western Post-War History in the Soviet Mirror   92
JOHN KEEP
Discussion   109

V. Soviet Historiography after Stalin   117
S. V. UTECHIN

VI. Soviet Historical Sources in the Post-Stalin Era   130
GEORGE KATKOV
Discussion   144

VII. The National Bourgeoisie   155
WALTER Z. LAQUEUR
Discussion   169

VIII. Soviet Historians and the Sino-Soviet Alliance   177
MARK MANCALL
Discussion   192

IX. Socialism in Current Soviet Historiography   199
ADAM B. ULAM
Discussion   214

x. Trends in Soviet Historiography of the Second
World War   *page* 222
MATTHEW GALLAGHER
Discussion   236

xi. Diplomacy in the Mirror of Soviet Scholarship 243
VERNON V. ASPATURIAN
Discussion   275

xii. Soviet Historiography and America's Role in
the Intervention   286
GEORGE F. KENNAN

xiii. Soviet Historians and American History   306
MAX BELOFF

Index   315

Programme of the Conference Participants   328

INTRODUCTION

JOHN KEEP

How is the history of our rapidly changing world studied in the USSR today? What relationship does the Soviet historian's image of reality bear to the facts, and what can we learn from this about the way in which Soviet society is developing?

These were some of the principal questions discussed at a conference held in July 1961 at the Institut Universitaire de Hautes Etudes Internationales, Geneva, by courtesy of its Director, Professor Jacques Freymond. The meeting was sponsored jointly by this Institute and the editors of *Survey*, the British quarterly journal of Soviet and East European studies. The chair was taken by Sir Isaiah Berlin, Fellow of All Souls and Chichele Professor of Social and Political Theory at the University of Oxford.

This volume contains a selection of the papers presented at this conference and a summary of the discussions. The papers have been revised to take account of more recent developments. It is published in the hope that it will be of interest, not only to other students of Soviet affairs and professional historians, but also to everyone concerned with the problem of co-existence and the exchange of ideas between East and West.

Soviet historiography is a vast and complex subject, and no treatment of it can hope to be exhaustive. The contributors to this symposium are aware that they have only touched on certain aspects of the subject which they think particularly significant. Many of the themes discussed here could have been pursued further. A great deal is now being written by Soviet historians that deserves close study by their western colleagues—a study which, in view of the limited human and material resources available, it unfortunately does not always receive. As more qualified specialists enter the field, progress will no doubt be made in this respect. The day may yet arrive when each important Soviet historical work, whichever the period or area it covers, will be carefully analysed and evaluated by independent western experts. In the meantime this volume may help to clarify some of the basic issues involved.

One point needs to be stressed at the outset. This conference was not called in any militant 'cold war' spirit. The fact that no Soviet historians were invited to attend was not due to any reluctance to hear their point of view. The participants recognize that meetings between scholars from East and West can often lead to pleasant

A*

and fruitful discussions, particularly when views can be exchanged informally. Unfortunately, citizens of communist countries can only be invited to attend a gathering such as this by approaching them through official channels, whereupon a delegation may or may not be sent, armed with instructions to represent the official point of view. Experience shows that all too often this results in a formal confrontation of opposing ideologies, and sometimes degenerates into an exchange of polemics from which those involved derive neither pleasure nor profit. Naturally all the participants hope that this is a transitory state of affairs, and that one day it will be possible for western and Soviet historians to meet and discuss matters of mutual interest in a wholly academic setting, free from official or ideological pressure of any kind.

It is not the object of this volume to 'expose' sins of omission or commission by Soviet historians. The contributors make no secret of their opposition to the authoritarian aspects of the Soviet system, but seek to eschew emotional judgements. They do not share the view that any criticism of Soviet attitudes must necessarily indicate bias or hostility on the part of the critic. They are anxious to understand rather than to condemn. They know how important it is to keep an open mind, since so much of the truth must inevitably remain hidden from the view of outside observers.

In Soviet historiography, as in other fields of Soviet intellectual life, the year 1956 was something of a turning-point. The twentieth congress of the CPSU called upon Soviet historians, and particularly upon those concerned with the history of the party itself, to bring their studies 'closer to life', and to intensify their efforts to promote 'the building of communism'. This campaign was intimately linked with what was euphemistically called 'overcoming the consequences of the cult of the individual'. Stalin was toppled from the throne which he had occupied for thirty years, and his place was filled— rather inadequately, perhaps—by an anonymous collective, 'the party' as such. Some five years later, in October 1961, Stalin's posthumous reputation received a further blow from the twenty-second congress of the CPSU, when his physical remains were removed from Lenin's tomb to a humbler resting-place in the Kremlin wall. This gesture was accompanied by another directive to Soviet historians. Its practical effect was much the same as that of the first. They were expected to eliminate all those references to Stalin's activities which the present party leaders found unacceptable, and thereby to help strengthen the party's power and prestige. As we shall see in a moment, this was no easy task. It involved Soviet historians in a profound crisis of conscience, the effects of which are still felt strongly today.

First of all a word or two must be said about the external changes that have occurred in Soviet historiography during recent years.

That these represent progress—of a kind—no independent observer would deny. Four main developments may be noted, all of which deserve to be welcomed.

In the first place, there has been a considerable increase in the number of people actively engaged in historical research and teaching. New institutes and university faculties have mushroomed. Works by teams of authors, collections of documents, and individual monographs have flooded from the presses. This expansion is graphically illustrated by the development of historical journalism. Until 1956 *Voprosy Istorii* ('Problems of History') was almost alone in the field. It now presides over a whole cluster of periodicals devoted to various aspects of history (e.g. the history of Russia, of the communist party, of the international working-class movement, of science and technology, and many others). In December 1962 it was stated that there were eighty-one periodicals in which Soviet historians could publish their work, and this figure is soon likely to increase.[1]

In the second place, Soviet historians have been granted easier access to archive materials. During Stalin's lifetime work with original documentary sources virtually ceased. Today historians are not only permitted, but strongly encouraged, to search the archives for evidence with which to buttress their arguments. As Dr George Katkov points out in his essay, this has been something of a mixed blessing, for in Soviet historiography documentation plays a rather different role from that generally accepted elsewhere. But most independent observers will agree that there has been a significant improvement in the quality of Soviet scholarship during recent years. There is less dogmatic assertion and 'quotation-mongering'; reasoning is on a more sophisticated level; and greater care is taken with statistical and other evidence. There has also been a certain enlargement in the area of permitted debate among historians, although the limits are still extremely narrow by western standards, and the themes for discussion are normally selected from above.

In the third place, the scope of historical study has been greatly broadened. Books are now written on themes whose very existence was barely acknowledged until a few years ago (e.g. the philosophy of history). Modern studies receive greater priority than ever before. A powerful impetus has been given to the writing of military history, as well as to Oriental and African studies. As will be readily apparent, the choice of subjects reflects the interests of the politicians, who have a narrow and utilitarian view of the functions of scholarship. Nevertheless, many works now being published in the USSR make worth-while, and even notable, additions to historical knowledge. This is truer of some periods or aspects of history than others. As a general proposition it may be said that the value of a work stands in inverse proportion to the relevance of its theme to the preoccupations

[1] P. N. Fedoseyev, in *Voprosy Istorii,* 1963, No. 2, p. 22.

of the CPSU leadership. The more likely a subject is to affect the party's power or prestige, the less scope exists for a historian to make original judgements. In this connection it may be added that the contributors to this volume, by restricting themselves to contemporary issues, have voluntarily assigned themselves one of the least fertile fields of Soviet historical scholarship.

In the fourth place, closer links have been established between Soviet and non-communist historians. The USSR was represented at the tenth international historical congress in Rome (1955) and still more powerfully at the eleventh congress, held in Stockholm five years later. Numerous other conferences of more limited scope have been held, and academic exchanges at all levels have become more frequent. Since 1959 a special effort has been made in the USSR to keep up with current western historical literature. Each issue of the monthly journal *Voprosy Istorii*, for example, carries a special section entitled 'Historical Science Abroad', in which selected articles as well as books are reviewed. Soviet historians have become more sensitive about the impression their work creates in the outside world, and they are quick to counter criticism. However, as has already been noted, except on a very limited plane nothing resembling a genuine dialogue between East and West has as yet become possible. Indeed, the present official line in historiography is, if anything, even more militantly partisan and 'anti-bourgeois' than it was in Stalin's day.

And this, of course, is the root of the matter. Addressing the all-union conference of historians in December 1962 (reported in *Voprosy Istorii*, 1963, Nos. 1 and 2) party secretary B. N. Ponomarev spoke as follows:

Comrades! The struggle against the bourgeois falsification of history is a fighting and topical task for all Marxist historians . . . The basic content of anti-communism is slander against the socialist system, falsification of the policy and aims of communist parties, of Marxist-Leninist doctrine. In this 'crusade' to spread the most reactionary ideas no small role is allotted to historiography . . . The links between anti-communist historiography and the policy of the imperialist powers is at times truly striking . . .

After giving examples from the United States and West Germany, he continued:

Under the impact of the enormous successes of socialism in the Soviet Union and other countries . . . anti-communist propaganda and historiography are obliged to use more cunning and sophisticated techniques . . . At present one can say that bourgeois anti-communist ideology is making a frontal attack upon Marxism-Leninism, also in the historical sphere. . . . One thing is clear: we cannot allow the bourgeois falsifiers to darken the minds of the masses with impunity. We have to give them a decisive rebuff. And for this we have incomparably greater opportunities than ever before . . . By its character anti-communist historiography is completely outside science. An offensive unflagging struggle against every distortion of history—this is an important and honourable task for Soviet historians.

V. V. Mavrodin, another speaker at the all-union conference, noted that ideology, like nature, abhors a vacuum: if Soviet historiography were to weaken for a moment in its struggle against the class enemy, bourgeois ideology would at once penetrate and exercise its insidious effect. This is sound Leninist doctrine, epitomized in the principle of partisanship, or *partiinost*, according to which every disputed issue is seen as a point of conflict between representatives of antagonistic classes. Historians, according to this doctrine, cannot be impartial: their attitude is inescapably governed by their class allegiance. If a 'progressive' historian should seek to see both sides of a question, he would immediately expose himself to the error of 'bourgeois objectivism', thereby becoming an unwitting tool of the class enemy.

Now the significant point, it may well be thought, is not that these long-familiar views should be put forward by party spokesmen, or by historians anxious to show their loyalty to the party's teachings, but that some dissenting voices should be heard. The present editor of *Voprosy Istorii*, V. G. Trukhanovsky, complains that 'in scholarly circles one can sometimes hear the view expressed that there is no point in going on endlessly about the falsifiers of history, and that we should carry on the struggle against them solely by solving historical problems in monographs'—action which, he held, was far from sufficient to deal with the problem. Several other interesting points emerged at this conference. Ponomarev, for instance, lamented the fact that 'it is rare for theses to be written which unmask the reactionary internal policies of the ruling circles of the imperialist states'. One may perhaps be forgiven for supposing that such reluctance to 'prosecute the struggle on the historical front' is due, not simply to administrative oversight, but to a certain conscious act of choice on the part of the historians concerned.

What is involved here, as several contributors to this volume point out, is essentially a conflict between the professional interests of the historians and the political interests of the party. The various forms taken by this conflict are discussed below, where a good deal of attention is paid to the 'Burdzhalov affair' of 1955-7, the equivalent among the historians of the post-Stalin literary 'thaw'. As in other fields of activity, the relaxation of party controls led to a period of confusion in which there was no clear official 'line', and individual historians began, in Professor Fainsod's words, 'to explore the boundaries of the new freedom'. Even if they at first assumed that they were operating in accordance with the wishes of the party leaders (or perhaps of one faction of leaders), within a short time the spirit of free inquiry developed a momentum of its own, and the party found some of its most cherished dogmas under attack. It reacted with repressive measures: the editorial board of *Voprosy Istorii* was dismissed, and E. N. Burdzhalov, its editor, disappeared from view. In an earlier age this would have meant physical liquidation. But in December 1962 Burdzhalov re-appeared. At the all-union conference of historians, where he represented the Moscow State Pedagogical Institute, he denounced the continued publication of works that still bore traces of the 'cult of the individual' and called for the liberation of history from what he referred to politely as 'Stalinist "arrangements" (*ustanovki*)'.

Neither in 1957 nor at the present time has the party reacted to dissatisfaction among the historians by 'administrative measures' alone. Indeed, its whole policy in this sphere (and, some would say, in Soviet society generally) can be interpreted as an attempt to divert the forces of potential opposition and mobilize them in the service of the regime: to channel the enthusiasms aroused by destalinization along paths acceptable to the leadership. The party employs the historians on centrally approved and directed projects that absorb all their energies; it affords them a modest latitude (granting access to archives, publishing their work, etc.) which it hopes will satisfy their professional consciences; and in return it expects them to co-operate loyally in fulfilling the tasks allotted to them. As in Stalin's day the historian is seen as a soldier of the party: but now he is required to show much more 'spontaneous' zeal and enthusiasm. The re-emergence of the party under Khrushchev has led to a revival of Leninist ideology. Stalin's demands were relatively simple: he was satisfied with a formal compliance with orders from above, with the repetition of ritualistic formulas; he did not concern himself overmuch with men's inner motivations—which could in any case be fabricated for them, where necessary, by the police. Today the party requires not simple acquiescence, but fervent belief, translated into practical action. In a sense, therefore, the Soviet historian of the 1960s is *less* free than his predecessor under Stalin— although the western concept of freedom is not really very helpful when considering the Soviet intellectual milieu. The question one has to ask is not: 'how much freedom exists for the individual to express his personal opinions, as distinct from those of the party?', but rather: 'to what extent can he maintain a private sphere of thought and action, providing some relief from the powerful pressures brought to bear by the party?'

This brings us into a realm where no final answers are possible: the individual historian's psychological attitudes. There is no certain means of knowing how far men concur willingly in fulfilling the demands placed upon them by the authorities. The question may, however, be approached from another angle: for how long can myth and reality co-exist in the consciousness of the individual historian?

The contributors to this symposium starts from the assumption that Soviet historiography, like the Marxist-Leninist ideology that inspires it, contains a large element of myth. This is inherent in the partisan approach to history, which prevents the observer from recognizing the sanctity of objective facts, and requires him where necessary to deny the evidence of his senses: for there are occasions when he must subordinate his own personal concept of truth to that held by another individual or group of individuals—namely, the party. Now this is not the same thing as individual bias. As has often been observed, every historian selects facts, as an unavoidable step in the process of writing and interpreting history; and in so doing an element of bias is automatically involved. As Mr E. H. Carr has recently reminded us: 'The facts of history cannot be purely objective, since they become facts of history only in virtue of the significance attached to them by the historian.' The most the historian can do is to seek a limited objectivity by 'rising above the limited vision of his own situation in society and in history', and projecting his vision into the future, the better to assess the past. Yet however strongly the historian may be convinced of the truth of his vision, or the value judgements it implies, it remains essential that he should adhere to certain rules governing the selection and presentation of evidence or argument. In a pluralistic society the existence of different competing points of view, which may be freely expressed, acts as a corrective against undue bias. The situation is entirely different where the historian is required to accept the 'vision of the future' held by authority, and—what is still more important—to believe that that authority alone knows how that vision may be realized, and what progress is being made towards it.

Nothing could be more destructive of historical scholarship than the claim that the party is, in Mr Leonard Schapiro's phrase, 'the repository of supreme wisdom'; that it is the instrument chosen by History to accomplish its grand design. In the Soviet Union today historians, like everyone else, are required to believe that, by some mysterious process unfathomable to ordinary mortals, the party has been infallible: individual leaders may err, as Stalin erred, but the party has always retained its essential rectitude. This leads to the establishment of a 'closed sphere', within which facts may not be examined critically, lest they cast doubt upon the basic premiss. This sphere is extensive, since it includes everything said or done by the party during its long tenure of power in the USSR, the thoughts and deeds of the founders of Marxism-Leninism, and the history of the international working-class movement, in so far as it has been led by communists—in short, the most important subjects with which Soviet historians are expected to deal. Within the limits of this sphere what is written is not so much history, in the accepted sense of the term, as mythology: an effort to bolster the official view whereby the entire history of mankind reaches a glorious climax in the experience of Soviet communism. It involves the historian, not in a search for truths that can be verified, but in a campaign to present an image. This image need bear only a passing resemblance to actual reality.

The question now arises: what occurs when those who have believed in the myth—whether from conviction, or coercion, or a mixture of the two—are presented with new information that apparently contradicts their most cherished assumptions? This is the essence of the dilemma imposed upon Soviet historians by the dethronement of Stalin. Various rationalizations can be resorted to in an effort to reconcile the irreconcilable. But for how long can doubt be kept at bay?

Mr Leopold Labedz and some other contributors to this volume are inclined to take the pessimistic view that man's appetite for myth is inexhaustible, and that the dilemma can be resolved by adopting new myths in place of the old. The more optimistic observers believe that eventually the shock of continuous revelations, and the 're-writings of history' they entail, will produce a state of chronic psychological malaise, widespread disillusionment, and 'the end of ideology'. As Professor Ulam notes, an attitude of ideological agnosticism is already fairly widespread among Soviet intellectuals, particularly those who belong to the younger generation, for whom the official doctrine seems largely irrelevant to current needs. This apathy presents the party with the problem of justifying its role, which explains the renewed emphasis on Leninist teaching, subtly modified to give it fresh significance.

In the light of this situation one can understand why, at the 1962 all-union conference, Academician E. M. Zhukov should say that, as a result of the 'cult of the individual', historians were suffering from 'a psychological trauma', which they found immensely difficult to overcome. They had forgotten how to think for themselves, and had grown accustomed 'to repeating uncritically axiomatic formulas, although the facts, and life itself, often demand that essential corrections be made in these formulas'. Traces of this dogmatic approach still remained:

Some historians think that, if their research succeeds in illustrating some theoretical proposition of Marx or Lenin, this in itself indicates that their work is of sufficiently high theoretical quality. Frequently this approach forces the scholar on to the erroneous road of simply selecting factual data to support this or that theoretical conclusion already drawn at some earlier time by the classics of Marxism-Leninism.

The non-committed observer feels an urge to cheer: the problem could scarcely be put more clearly. But he may well query the subsequent assertion that, under the guidance of the party, everything necessary was being done to eliminate dogmatic assumptions and subjective views. The official line now is that in future scholarly work must be based 'not on quotations, but on the very essence of revolutionary Marxist-Leninist doctrine'—in other words, on the instructions of the party, as the sole authorized interpreter of that doctrine.

In this essential respect, therefore, nothing has really changed since Stalin. On the Soviet Olympus Clio sings to the tune of the CPSU—now a little abashed, perhaps, but still claiming the mantle of infallibility. The most important historical questions are not open to scholarly inquiry because the truth about them is already known. The task of the historian is to support and interpret the changing official image of the past, which is manipulated as the leadership thinks necessary to maintain its legitimacy and expand its power.

This is why the contributors to this symposium attach such importance to ideological control over Soviet historiography. There is, however, another side to the question. It is also possible that this ideological approach gives the Soviet historian certain advantages over his western confrères. Professor Aspaturian points out that a number of historical phenomena can be interpreted in such a way as to buttress the official myth and make it appear more plausible. Consider, for example, what may well come to be regarded as the most significant development of the 1950s: the break-up of the colonial empires in Asia and Africa. Most people in the West would maintain that this was brought about largely (if not wholly) by causes other than those specified by Marx or Lenin. But to what extent can Asian and African historians be expected to share this view? There is a possibility that the Soviet interpretation of history, which relates particular phenomena to a systematic theory of world evolution, may have its attractions for those who, for various reasons, may not feel impelled to inquire too closely into the theory's veracity in the light of observable facts. It is perhaps worth pointing out that the very concept of 'scientific history', as we know it today, is of relatively recent origin, and that its claims have not gone unchallenged even in western countries. In many parts of the world today men's vision of the past is shaped by traditional religious and political outlooks, according to which human actions obtain significance only in so far as they are related to a divinely-sanctioned natural world order. It is possible that they might find it easier to exchange this outlook for a secular pseudo-scientific ideology, with strong moral overtones, than for one governed by academic scepticism, moral neutrality, and the search for objective facts.

This issue could only be touched upon briefly at this conference; before useful conclusions can be drawn about the impact made, or likely to be made, by Leninist historiography in these areas, further investigations will need to be made. In particular, more needs to be known about the progress of Soviet Oriental studies which, as Mr Mancall points out in his essay, is a field still sadly neglected by western scholars.

Those who approach this problem from the standpoint of East-West rivalry may take comfort from the fact that large-scale Soviet interest in the contemporary East is relatively recent: the consequences of Stalin's rule were felt with particular severity in this field. Moreover, it appears that ideology can often be a hindrance rather than a help to understanding the Oriental milieu. Soviet historians are apt to fall into serious error by approaching the non-European world as Europeans: in Asia, after all, Leninism is a western doctrine. Since this conference was held the breach between the USSR and China has widened further, with major implications for Soviet historians as well as politicians. This gives the discussions here of their treatment of Sino-Soviet relations a special relevance.

Can any useful generalization be made at this stage about the future of Soviet historiography? It is perhaps stating the obvious to say that it will be determined by the same factors as will govern the evolution of Soviet society as such: the response to the efforts of the CPSU to shape the future of mankind according to its own precepts. More concretely: as progress is made towards the achievement of 'communism' as Mr Khrushchev envisages it, Soviet public opinion may well come to realize (if, indeed, it does not already realize) that this goal bears little relation to the Utopia predicted by Marx and Lenin: that it implies continued political coercion by the party, which is now expected to survive even after the state machine has 'withered away'; that it denies to the individual a reasonable degree of autonomy and privacy; and that social equality is still a mirage. The party will also find it difficult, to say the least, to make a reality of 'New Soviet Man'. This may well lead, if not to a modification in the nature of the Soviet regime (as some western optimists assert), at least to a questioning of doctrinal assumptions. Such tendencies will be reinforced by the necessity for the USSR to co-exist with non-communist powers (whatever the nature of their social and political systems). In such circumstances it is conceivable that Soviet historians may come to look upon the past in a less partisan and intolerant manner than they do today.

For this reason, and for others as well, most contributors to this symposium are inclined to follow Professor Fainsod in what he calls his 'qualified optimism'. At the present time, judged by western criteria, the state of historical scholarship in the USSR may appear rather bleak, but there are gleams of hope on the horizon. Until then independent historians will be glad to explore areas of agreement with their Soviet colleagues, and to encourage them, in so far as they can, to correct the distortions in the official mirror, and to obtain a clearer view of the realities it reflects.

I. Historiography and Change

MERLE FAINSOD

This essay undertakes an examination of Soviet historiography since the death of Stalin as a barometer of change in Soviet society. My approach to this problem can be briefly summarized. All Soviet historians to some degree, and historians of the recent past in particular, are expected to operate within the framework of Marxism-Leninism, as its requirements are currently interpreted by the party leadership or by those charged by the party leadership with the supervision of the historical sector of the cultural battle-front. These requirements shift with changes in the party line, so that Soviet historians face the occupational hazard that yesterday's heroes may become tomorrow's villains, and books which meet every canon of orthodoxy when they are written may become politically unacceptable shortly after they appear. This means, among other things, that scholars who wish to rise and prosper in the Soviet historical firmament must not only learn to serve the powers that be, but must also develop a keen sense of the direction of impending change and be able to gauge its limits as well as the potentialities which it unfolds. Periods of transition, such as the succession struggle after Stalin's death and the attendant confusion of the destalinization campaign, are periods of crisis for historians, too. When an uncertain trumpet blows, there will inevitably be some historians who fail to catch the tune. Once the confusion is dispelled and the new song sounds out loud and clear, a period of consolidation sets in, and historians again march in step.

But it would do less than justice to the Soviet historical guild to leave the impression that all of them are merely propagandists in uniform. Soviet historians, like their colleagues elsewhere, have their professional standards or at least their professional aspirations. Given the opportunity, they prefer to work in archives and with primary rather than secondary sources. A goodly number, who have concerned themselves with themes far removed from contemporary concerns, have made contributions of great distinction. Others have found refuge and a species of scholarly fulfilment in editing collections of valuable documents, which not infrequently lend themselves to interpretations at sharp variance with official requirements. Even among those whose major interest is recent history, where political demands are most compelling, there has been pressure in recent years for greater access to archival material, and a growing interest in foreign journals, publications, and international contacts. The appearance in 1956 in the pages of

Voprosy Istorii of a series of relatively objective and subsequently condemned articles in the highly sensitive area of party history may at least serve to remind us that there have been, and may still be, stirrings below the surface of orthodox Soviet historiography which register a greater devotion to historical truth than the current content of Soviet historical journals might lead one to think. If, since 1957, Soviet historians appear to have accommodated themselves thoroughly to the political commands which come from above, it should at least be noted that they now have access to the historical record to a degree which would have been unthinkable in the latter part of Stalin's reign.

This, then, constitutes one of the important differences between post-Stalinist and Stalinist historiography. Stalin was his own historian *par excellence*, and there was no room in his historical monolith for 'archive rats' who might come up with discoveries which challenged his own. The plight of the Soviet historian who concerned himself with party affairs under Stalin has been graphically portrayed in *Voprosy Istorii* (March 1956, No. 3):

The work of many researchers and teachers in the social sciences amounted to popularization of J. V. Stalin's ideas. This promoted the widespread dissemination of pedantry, dogmatism, and excessive use of quotations. There appeared in science second-rate people who had no initiative, who were unable or unwilling to think for themselves, who acted only within the limits of 'approved principles' and strove to camouflage their intellectual barrenness with someone else's authority . . . The significance of archive materials as historical sources was subjected to doubt, and the majority of these documents proved to be inaccessible to the research worker. There was no study of sources of party history. The discovery and criticism of new sources were considered unnecessary and even reprehensible. The overwhelming majority of dissertations were nothing more than compilations of quotations and miscellaneous facts, and to a considerable extent repeated each other.

After Stalin's death the thaw which set in in *belles lettres* did not immediately communicate itself to the historical field. Taught for years to follow directives and instructions, historians waited cautiously for a new line to emerge. Although there were a few early feelers which reflected the downgrading of the Stalin cult, the first substantial indication that fresh winds were blowing came at a conference of readers called by the editors of *Voprosy Istorii*, which met just before the twentieth party congress on January 25-28, 1956.[1] At the conference hitherto sacrosanct views were subjected to seemingly bold attack. Speakers were critical of the tendency to embellish the careers of traditional Russian national heroes and to conceal the fact that 'Tsarism was the deadly enemy of the Russian and the international revolutionary

[1] 'Konferentsiya chitatelei zhurnala "Voprosy Istorii" ' *Voprosy Istorii*, 1956, No. 2.

movement'. Tsarist policy towards the non-Russian nationalities was condemned as harsh and oppressive, and at least one of the speakers— A. M. Pikman—rose to the defence of Shamil who, despite the praise bestowed on him by Marx and Engels, had long been under a Stalinist ban. Exaggerated claims for Russian priorities in all fields of human endeavour were repudiated. A more respectful appraisal was made of the achievements of western bourgeois historiography, and some merit was even attributed to the work of earlier Soviet historians such as Pokrovsky, who had previously been totally disowned. The same issue of *Voprosy Istorii* which reported this conference and which went to press before the twentieth party congress met, provided an even more striking hint of what was to come. Buried in an unsigned review of some booklets on the congresses and conferences of the party was a suggestion that historians examine the speeches at the fifteenth and sixteenth party conferences of S. V. Kossior, P. P. Postyshev, A. V. Kosarev, V. A. Chubar, and other purged or disgraced party leaders whose names had been anathema for years.

But the main shock came at the twentieth party congress. First there was the speech by Mikoyan, with its denigration of Stalin, its restoration of party leaders such as Antonov-Ovseyenko and Kossior, who had 'wrongly' been pronounced enemies of the people, and its flat declaration that 'scholarly work in the history of our party and of Soviet society is perhaps the most backward sector of our ideological work'. Mikoyan enjoined the historians 'to make a genuine and profound study of the facts and events in the history of our party in the Soviet period— including those that the *Short Course* deals with', to 'delve properly into the archives and historical documents, and not only into the back issues of newspapers', to present 'without embellishment not only the façade but the whole many-sided life of the Soviet Fatherland'.[1] Mme Pankratova, dean of Stalinist historians, member of the central committee, editor of *Voprosy Istorii* (her own textbooks were examples of all that Mikoyan condemned), piously followed in Mikoyan's footsteps and rebuked her colleagues for prettifying historical reality and portraying the historical path of the party as a triumphal procession without difficulties. Quoting Lenin, she called on them to base their historical writing on 'exact and indisputable facts', and to put an end to the suppression of unpalatable material and the concealment of mistakes made by party organizations. And as if to give point to her remarks, Khrushchev in his secret speech at the close of the congress opened up the whole Pandora's box of Stalin's latter-day crimes and deficiencies.

The twentieth party congress pronouncements launched historians on an uncharted sea where the shoals and treacherous reefs ahead were still to be discovered. Some historians enthusiastically welcomed the party's changed attitude towards the writing of history and began immediately to probe the boundaries of the new freedom. Others were

---

[1] *XX Syezd Kommunisticheskoi Partii Sovetskovo Soyuza, Stenografischeskii Otchet*, 1956, Vol. 1, p. 325.

more conscious of the dangers and waited cautiously for events to prescribe limits on 'the forward march' of historiography.

Voprosy Istorii, led by its assistant editor, E. M. Burdzhalov, and with the somewhat reluctant co-operation of Mme Pankratova, the chief editor, became the rallying point of the revisionists. In the leading editorial (March 1956, No. 3) entitled 'The Twentieth Party Congress and Problems of Research in Party History', the magazine called for a new party history which would correct 'the far-fetched interpretations and outright falsifications' of the past. Addressing itself particularly to the role of the Mensheviks in the 1905 revolution, it advanced the thesis that 'the Bolsheviks were the most consistent but not the only force in the revolutionary-democratic camp'. While describing Menshevism as 'a trend hostile to Marxism in the workers' movement', it dismissed the view that Mensheviks were 'the accomplices of Tsarist autocracy' and called for a study of the joint committees of Bolsheviks and Mensheviks at the end of 1905. It went on to demand 'a truthful picture' of the situation within the party before Lenin's return to Russia in 1917, and insisted that proper due be given to the many heroes of October whose activity had previously been 'minimized or passed over in silence'. Calling for an end to distortion in historical writing, it proclaimed: 'The task of historians is to explain and not to hush up historical acts.'

During the next months *Voprosy Istorii* pressed the attack. In the March issue (No. 3), A. M. Pikman rose to the defence of Shamil. In the April issue (No. 4), E. N. Burdzhalov published a relatively objective article on 'The Tactics of the Bolsheviks in March and April 1917', in which he demonstrated that prior to Lenin's return and the adoption of the April theses, Stalin joined with Kamenev in defending the 'anti-Leninist' policy of Bolshevik conditional support for the provisional government, that Kamenev continued his opposition to Lenin at the April conference where Stalin switched sides, and that Zinoviev opposed Kamenev and upheld the Leninist line. These and other articles in the same vein, which called attention to distortions and omissions in the republication of memoirs of Old Bolsheviks and condemned 'the gilding of historical reality' involved in one-sided use of sources, began to arouse concern in high party circles, a concern which was no doubt reinforced by the spreading infection of revisionism in the international communist movement and by the ferment which Khrushchev's secret speech released within the Soviet party itself. The June 30, 1956 resolution of the party central committee represented a major effort to impose limits on the discussion which Khrushchev's secret speech had unleashed, and its reverberations were soon felt in historiography.

An article by E. Bugaev which appeared in the July 1956 issue (No. 14) of *Partiinaya Zhizn* (a companion piece appeared in *Kommunist*, No. 10) represented an early warning that *Voprosy Istorii* was embarked on a dangerous course. Its call for objectivity in appraising the work of bourgeois historians, Bugaev asserted, could only serve to 'confuse historians and students' and lead them to forget 'that peaceful co-existence of capitalism and socialism in the international arena does not at all mean an ideological reconciliation between socialist and bourgeois ideologies'. Its revaluation of party history, Bugaev continued, 'leaves the uninitiated reader with the impression that all works on party history published in the past fifteen or twenty years are junk'. Condemning such a 'nihilist attitude', he added that earlier party histories could not begin 'to compare favourably' with the *Short Course*, 'even though the latter contains many errors and inaccuracies'. He singled out Burdzhalov's article on 'The Tactics of the Bolsheviks in March and April 1917' for special censure for its allegedly biased presentation of the position of the central committee bureau at that time. '*Voprosy Istorii*,' Bugaev concluded, 'occupies an important place in historiography. This is all the more reason for the reader to expect thoughtful research from it. Only harm can come from clamour, cheap sensation, and haste . . . Judging by the fact that at present one-sided articles do get into the journal, it cannot be said that it is correctly orienting historians on all questions of historiography.'

It is a measure of the ideological confusion which still prevailed during this period that *Voprosy Istorii* did not accept this seemingly authoritative rebuke as ending the debate. While conceding that some of Bugaev's critical remarks were 'admittedly correct' and some theses advanced in the journal 'were not adequately substantiated', the editors vigorously defended a number of articles which Bugaev had attacked, including the article by Burdzhalov.[1] The editors took the view that they were correctly carrying out the injunctions of the twentieth party congress. 'Some comrades [and they made clear that they had Bugaev in mind] caution us against haste in re-organizing the work of historians and say that we must wait for special instructions and directives, as though the twentieth party congress had not given them. . . . We have people who are afraid of every new word and who do not wish to abandon their habitual views. E. Bugaev writes only about what should not be done; it is not necessary to re-examine everything, it is not necessary to go to extremes, to be one-sided, etc. . . . E. Bugaev's article in essence aims at leaving everything as it was. The author attacks opportunists who want to run with the tide. But is it possible to regard the struggle to carry out the decisions of the twentieth party congress as "running with the tide"? The twentieth party congress gave a clear programme for the fruitful development of Marxist-Leninist historiography. Soviet historians will consistently and undeviatingly carry out this programme.'

Meanwhile, the editors of *Voprosy Istorii* had been holding conferences with readers of the journal in Kiev and Leningrad. A report of the Leningrad conference which appeared in *Leningradskaya Pravda*, August 5, 1956, indicated that Burdzhalov, the assistant editor of *Voprosy Istorii*, spoke with more than the usual degree of frankness.

[1] *Voprosy Istorii*, 1956, No. 7, pp. 215-22.

Stating that 'we historians have no one to give us basic directives and instructions', he pointed out that *Voprosy Istorii* had lifted the ban on the treatment of many questions which had hitherto been dealt with incorrectly, and in appraising the state of Soviet historiography he developed a theory of gradations of truthfulness, according to which the historians of the twenties 'wrote more truthfully than the historians of the thirties, and the latter more truthfully than the historians of the 1950s'. He called for more young contributors to the journal, pointing out that while they might possess less factual knowledge, they were, on the other hand, freer from prejudices and the tendency to conform. He expressed the view that it was necessary to do justice to the 'revolutionary' spirit of Menshevism in the pre-revolutionary period and to give a more accurate portrayal of the activities of anti-Leninist groups and trends in the party. While his speech evoked enthusiastic support from some of the Leningrad historians, there were quick indications that Burdzhalov had gone too far. Taking his cue from the Bugaev article in *Partiinaya Zhizn* and its companion piece in *Kommunist*, A. Aleksandrov, who reported on the conference for *Leningradskaya Pravda*, launched a powerful attack on Burdzhalov's 'new and highly dubious formulations' and, in the name of the twentieth party congress, called for 'stronger ideological guidance, a strict safeguarding of the purity of Marxist theory, a vigorous struggle against remnants of bourgeois ideology, a stronger attack on the survivals of capitalism in the minds of the people, and exposure of those who harbour them'.[1]

Despite these clear warnings, Burdzhalov and his fellow editors of *Voprosy Istorii* persisted in their course. The August issue of *Voprosy Istorii* (1956, No. 8) contained a reply by Burdzhalov entitled 'More on the Tactics of the Bolsheviks in March and April 1917', as well as an article by M. A. Moskalev, on 'The Struggle to create a Marxist Workers' Party in the 1890s', which aroused the ire of the party orthodox because it argued that Lenin first developed the idea of an alliance of the working class and peasantry on the basis of the experience of the 1905-7 revolution, instead of as far back as the mid-nineties, as had previously been claimed. The next issue of *Voprosy Istorii* included the reminiscences of an old party member, F. I. Drabkina, on the March conference of 1917, the effect of which was to provide further corroboration for Burdzhalov's views.

The demand for a more sophisticated view of opponents of Lenin and Marx was also reflected in the columns of *Voprosy Istorii*. The October issue (1956, No. 10) carried a review by R. E. Yevzerov which criticized N. I. Krutikova's book, *From the History of V. I. Lenin's Struggle against Opportunism in the International Arena*, for its primitive treatment of Kautsky as a renegade and double-dealer and its failure to note Lenin's own tributes to Kautsky as an outstanding Marxist theorist in the pre-war years. In the same vein the editors pleaded for

[1] *Leningradskaya Pravda*, August 5, 1956.

more objective appraisals of such men as Lassalle and Bakunin, and the November issue (No. 11) carried a review by S. I. Kuznetsova and B. E. Stein on 'English and American Historiography of the October Revolution, Foreign Intervention, and Civil War in Russia', which was notably free of the abusive rhetoric ordinarily heaped on bourgeois historians who fail to fit into the 'progressive' mould.

Up to the 'Polish October' and the Hungarian revolt, Burdzhalov and his sympathizers were still able to fight a rearguard action, but now they found themselves faced with heavy artillery to which there was no reply. *Pravda* entered the fray on November 20th by publishing a letter to the editor from V. Smirnov, a Moscow University instructor in party history, which sharply attacked the Moskalev article and charged *Voprosy Istorii* with undertaking 'under the guise of criticizing consequences of the "cult of the individual", to revise . . . questions that have long been decided by the party and to cast doubt on indisputable truths'. *Partiinaya Zhizn*, in its December issue (No. 23), revealed that discussions of *Voprosy Istorii*'s attitude had been organized 'in the history department of Moscow State University and a number of other research and educational institutions', and that 'these discussions demonstrated that scholarly circles condemn the errors committed by *Voprosy Istorii*'. The editors of *Partiinaya Zhizn* expressed strong support for the position taken earlier by E. Bugaev and rebuked *Voprosy Istorii* for 'its negative evaluation of all the historical literature published during recent decades'. It implied that the journal had overstepped the bounds in its appreciation of bourgeois scholarship, and reminded the editors that 'the struggle against vulgarization must be conducted in such a way that no one receives the wrong impression that we are talking about "liberalizing" our ideology or about adopting a tolerant attitude towards the ideology of the bourgeoisie'. 'It is known', the editorial continued, 'that some of our scholars and scientists have failed to realize that peaceful co-existence of countries with differing social and political systems does not mean ideological disarmament—on the contrary . . . the ideological struggle between them will not weaken but grow stronger.' This time, not only Burdzhalov and Moskalev, but the chief editor, Mme Pankratova herself, was singled out for rebuke.

The last issue of *Voprosy Istorii* for the year 1956 made it clear that the warning had been understood. It contained an article by S. K. Bushuev on 'Caucasian Muridism' in which Pikman was censured for his favourable view of Shamil, and the progressive character of the incorporation of the Caucasian peoples in the Russian Empire was re-affirmed. All awkward problems of party history were avoided, though the issue did include an appeal by old party members 'for a truthful re-establishment of the events of the October Revolution and the civil war'. While Burdzhalov and company were now silenced and repudiated, they had still to be dislodged from their editorial posts.

The axe fell with a decree of the central committee 'On the Journal

Voprosy Istorii' dated March 7, 1957.[1] Its provisions offer a vivid insight into the ideological preoccupations of the party leadership at the time. The journal was accused of glossing over differences in principle between the Bolsheviks and Mensheviks on such basic issues as the question of the hegemony of the proletariat in the revolution, of embellishing the role of the Mensheviks while minimizing the leading role of the Bolsheviks in the 1905-7 revolution, and of failing to offer a principled Leninist criticism of the divisive and opportunistic tactics of the Mensheviks. It was also alleged that *Voprosy Istorii* ignored the fact that the Trotskyites and right opportunists transcended the framework of Soviet legality in their battle against the party. Burdzhalov's articles were specially censured for the 'objective' spirit in which they treated the activity of Zinoviev in 1917 and for seeking to demonstrate that the Bolsheviks occupied a semi-Menshevik position before Lenin's return in April 1917, and that there were powerful tendencies in the party pushing towards united action with the Mensheviks. *Voprosy Istorii* was also accused of conciliatory attitudes towards bourgeois historians and of failing to criticize revisionist and nationalistic pronouncements, particularly as they found expression in the Yugoslav press. The journal was directed to intensify its struggle against bourgeois ideology and revisionism, and to dedicate itself to the Leninist principle of *partiinost* in historical science. Burdzhalov was fired as assistant editor, but Mme Pankratova was permitted to remain at her post, though attention was called to the serious mistakes which as chief editor she had permitted.

The central committee decree was the signal for a full-throated assault on *Voprosy Istorii* which served merely to amplify and drive home the indictment. *Kommunist*, in its March 1957 issue (No. 4), reviewed the journal's errors and called for 'an uncompromising struggle both against bourgeois objectivism and revisionism and against dogmatism and the consequences of the cult of the individual'. *Partiinaya Zhizn* (1957, No. 6) was even more outspoken. It attacked what it called the 'bourgeois liberalism' of certain articles published in *Voprosy Istorii* and accused it of having blackened Soviet reality. Rising to the defence of Stalin, it declared that 'while criticizing Stalin's mistakes, the party at the same time defends him against the attacks of the revisionists and declares that it will not give up Stalin's name to [its] enemies'.

The March 1957 issue of *Voprosy Istorii* (No. 3) was not approved for the press until May 21st and did not appear until June. A new editorial board was listed on its masthead. Of the eleven previous editors, only three, Pankratova, N. A. Smirnov, and I. A. Khrenov remained, and Pankratova's death following 'a prolonged and serious illness' was announced on May 25th. The editorial which opened the issue reviewed and savagely attacked the 'errors' of the old editorial board and staked out a new militant line for the future. 'The Soviet

[1] For the text of this decree, see *Spravochnik partiinovo rabotnika*, 1957, pp. 381-2.

historian', pronounced the new editorial board, 'is not a sideline observer, a clerk, or a mechanical copyist of materials, a collector of information which may happen to come into his hands by chance.' Repudiating bourgeois objectivism, the journal called for 'genuinely scientific objectivity', which it identified with the principle of party allegiance in the evaluation of historical phenomena. It demanded a resolute struggle against revisionism, an emphasis on the fundamental differences between Menshevism and Bolshevism, and treatment of J. V. Stalin 'as an outstanding Marxist-Leninist who played a major role in exposing and routing the enemies of the party and in fighting for the triumph of the party's cause'. It summoned historians to under-line 'the progressive significance of the unification of a number of areas of the Transcaucasus, Central Asia, and the Far East with Russia', and to emphasize 'the need for constant and systematic treatment of the genuine patriotic traditions of the peoples of Russia and . . . of their historic achievements and their enormous contribution to the development of world scholarship'. It promised more attention to contemporary problems of Soviet and world history in order to disclose 'the world-historical significance of the Soviet Union', and 'the great advantages of the socialist over the capitalist system'.

This ideological manifesto, with its neo-Stalinist overtones, heralded a new period of consolidation in Soviet historiography. While the boundaries of permissible discussion were narrowed, they were at least set, and historians had their marching orders again. Since 1957 there has been no explosion remotely comparable to the *Voprosy Istorii* scandal. Burdzhalov has disappeared from view, at least so far as the historical journals are concerned, and it can be presumed that historians have drawn the appropriate conclusions from the treatment accorded him.

Yet it would be a mistake to dismiss present-day Soviet historiog-raphy as merely an atavistic throw-back to the Stalinist era, and to fail to recognize such improvements in the state of the art as have taken place. Soviet historians, to be sure, continue to operate within the confines of party directives, and in some fields, such as party history, the effect of recent changes has been largely to substitute new myths for old. But historians who are prepared to accept these limitations or who, indeed, may never even think of challenging them, have been given professional opportunities which were not available in Stalin's days.

In order to make this clear, it is necessary to review some recent trends in Soviet historiography. Perhaps the most important of these developments is the opening up of the archives on a greatly enlarged scale and the scope which this affords to Soviet scholars to acquaint themselves directly with documentary sources.[1] As a by-product of this lifting of the veil, the publication of documents both on the Soviet and

[1] See G. A. Belov, 'Utilization of the USSR State Archives in the Interests of Historical Science', *Voprosy Istorii*, 1960, No. 10.

the pre-Soviet period is by way of becoming a major Soviet historical industry. The energy which is being poured into this effort may suggest that it provides a relatively safe and congenial outlet for professional zeal. With archives open, venturesome scholars who write learned articles or monographs based on documentary sources are in a position to add a dimension of concreteness to their studies, in refreshing contrast to the pallid abstractions of earlier days. There are, of course, serious hazards which persist. Subjects and periods vary in their degree of sensitivity, and there are always difficult problems in deciding which documents to publish and which to omit, what evidence to cite and what had better be ignored. The task of the Soviet historian can never be an easy one. Even with his new-found resources, he must still know how to tack with the veering breeze.

A second important development is the breakdown in the isolation of the Soviet community of historians, the widening of international contacts, and the enlarged access which Soviet scholars now have to foreign 'bourgeois' as well as 'progressive' literature in their specialized fields. This expression of confidence on the part of the regime is not without its price. Soviet scholars are expected to demonstrate their loyalty to the cause they serve by unmasking 'bourgeois falsifiers of history' and by proving the superiority of the Marxist-Leninist world view. But things are not always as simple as they seem, and sometimes even the requirements of combat are honoured in the breach. The increasingly lengthy reviews of 'bourgeois' historical literature which appear in the Soviet learned journals are not precisely distinguished for their scholarly objectivity, but their authors sometimes communicate more than the authorities might wish, and their readers find in them more than the authors intend. There is reason to believe that some Soviet historians, at least, are not ungrateful for the stimulation derived from reading the works of the 'enemy', and that they eagerly welcome the trips abroad which enable them, not merely to tilt lances, but to clink glasses and even on occasion exchange ideas with their ideological foes.

Other developments which deserve to be noted are the expanding parameters of Soviet historiography and the proliferation of new journals which reflect these broadening concerns. In the aftermath of the *Voprosy Istorii* scandal, three new journals were founded: *Istoriya SSSR*, primarily devoted to domestic history, *Novaya i Noveishaya Istoriya*, focusing on foreign policy and international affairs, and *Voprosy Istorii KPSS*, which, as its name implies, is concerned with the party itself. These have been supplemented by others, too numerous to list, dealing with special periods, particular sectors of life such as the military, and with the history of the national republics.[1] The expansion of interest in Asia, Africa, and Latin America has been reflected in the establishment of new institutes, new journals, and the publication of a

[1] For a list, see the editorial, 'Soviet Historical Science at a New Stage of Development', *Voprosy Istorii*, 1960, No. 8.

wide variety of specialized monographs and general histories. Books
and articles on the history of the so-called people's democracies, as well
as of the capitalist countries, have multiplied greatly in number. Foreign
affairs have also been attracting increasing attention with the publication
of numerous collections of documents, and the scheduled appearance
of a new five-volume edition of *The History of Diplomacy*. Also projected
are an eleven-volume history of the USSR, a twelve-volume Soviet
historical encyclopedia, a history of Russian art, a history of Russian
culture, and a multi-volume party history. There are extensive plans
for the republication of the 'best' works of such pre-revolutionary
historians as Klyuchevsky, Solovyov, and Tatishchev. The impression
conveyed is of a rash of activity, of expanding opportunities for the
historical guild to engage in the practice of their craft.

It may be, as the editors of *Voprosy Istorii* have recently claimed, that
Soviet historical science is at a new stage of development.[1] Yet, as the
same editors note, 'Of course the scope and level of research on the
history of Soviet society are not yet up to the demands of the times or
to the growing requirements of the Soviet reader. We have few fundamental research works on the history of Soviet society. Scholars should
be bolder in tackling contemporary problems.' In March 1960 the
Division of Historical Science of the Academy of Sciences held a
conference on the historiography of socialist and communist construction in the USSR, at which similar sentiments were voiced. 'The
basic mass of our literature up to this time does not extend beyond the
boundaries of the Great October Revolution, the civil war, the revival
of the national economy (1921-5), and the first five-year plan. The
ensuing stages in the life of Soviet society are studied more weakly.'[2]
Soviet historians by their own admission are not yet in a position to
cast much light on recent changes in Soviet life.

At the same time they have begun to make substantial contributions
towards an understanding of some aspects of the revolutions of 1905
and 1917 and the earlier periods of Soviet rule. Perhaps the most
impressive progress has been evident in the publication of archival
material. One thinks in this connection of the huge collection of
documents on 1905 and 1917, of the republication of the protocols of
the party central committee meetings of 1917 and 1918, and the proceedings of the seventh party conference and sixth party congress of
1917, of the compilation which appeared in *Voprosy Istorii KPSS*
(1958, Nos. 2 and 3), with its great mass of detailed information on the
state of local party organization in 1917, of the *Correspondence of the
Secretariat of the Central Committee of the Russian Social-Democratic
Workers' Party (Bolsheviks) with Local Party Organizations*, of the
Decrees of the Soviet Regime, the collection on *Nationalization of
Industry in the USSR*, the documents on *The Agrarian Policy of the*

---

[1] Ibid.

[2] See 'Scientific Session on the Historiography of Socialist and Communist Construction', *Voprosy Istorii*, 1960, No. 8, p. 127.

Soviet Regime, the collection *From the History of the Cheka (1917-21)*, and many others.[1]

These documents, needless to say, have to be utilized with care. Even when, as in the case of the stenographic reports of party congresses, the texts have not been tampered with, the annotations frequently convey a completely distorted view of events. To read the biographical material on Trotsky, Zinoviev, Kamenev, and Bukharin which is appended to the protocols of the sixth party congress republished in 1958 is to sense the distance which Khrushchev's court historians have still to travel before they make contact with the truth. Documents, of course, can be and have been bowdlerized, and inconvenient ones are excluded from public view. But with all these caveats, we must remain grateful for such archival materials as Soviet historians have been permitted to release. Not the least of the reasons is that they occasionally tell a story that not even the most ingenious annotations can conceal.

Less useful than the documents, but still not without real value, is the increasing flow of articles and monographs based on archival research in the Soviet period. Some of them provide a wealth of factual data, to be sure carefully selected and winnowed, which nevertheless may serve to enlarge our understanding of developments during the early decades of Soviet rule. Within the limits of this essay, it is impossible to provide a comprehensive review of all of them, and a few samples will have to suffice. *Istoriya SSSR* (1958, No. 6), contains an article by V. K. Medvedev entitled 'The Liquidation of the Kulaks in the Lower Volga *Krai*'. Its general thesis is a familiar one. It was necessary to liquidate the kulaks as a class because they sabotaged the grain collection campaigns and stood in the way of collectivization. The decision to liquidate the kulaks enjoyed the overwhelming support of the poor and middle peasants, as well as the landless labourers. Once the kulaks had been eliminated, the kolkhoz movement was launched on a triumphant course. The value of the article, of course, does not lie in the reiteration of these well-worn and dubious propositions, but in the rich detail which it provides on the actual measures taken to rid the *krai* of its kulak element. It distinguishes at least two phases in the campaign against the kulaks: first, the measures taken against kulaks who opposed the grain collection campaign, and, second, the full-scale attack on the kulaks which followed Stalin's call at the beginning of 1930 to liquidate the kulaks as a class. In the first phase of the campaign, the severity of which has sometimes been overlooked, the author cites data in the archives indicating that 3,100 kulaks were exiled in one *okrug* alone, and that the organ of the GPU 'uncovered' and 'liquidated' 32 counter-revolutionary organizations and 191 kulak groups with about 3,000 participants in the *krai*. The second phase of the campaign is described in detail, including its organization, arrangements for

---

[1] For a more complete list, see G. A. Belov, 'Utilization of the USSR State Archives in the Interests of Historical Science', *Voprosy Istorii*, 1960, No. 10.

registering kulak property, and the classification of kulaks into four groups according to the degree of danger which they presented to the Soviet regime. The most dangerous were 'isolated' and dispatched to *kontslagers*; the harsh phrase 'concentration camp' is used without euphemism or softening. The second group was exiled 'to the northern *raions*, Siberia, and Kazakhstan'. The third category was divested of its land and transferred to less favourable parts of the *krai*, while the fourth group was permitted to remain in place. Again figures are cited for each category, though they are not complete. As if aware that all this might leave a bad taste, the author adds one touch to remind the reader that the Soviet Government was humane. It seems that all the wagons in which kulaks were sent into exile 'had heat'. The author even goes on to admit that there were 'excesses', that middle peasants were wrongly classified as kulaks because they opposed collectivization, but he also asserts that such actions were in no sense typical, and that most of the 'excesses' were corrected.

As one who has worked through similar material in the Smolensk archive, I think I can testify that there is much in this article which is recognizably authentic. But even more striking are its omissions and the way in which material has been arranged to fit a preconceived scheme. One looks in vain for references to the wealth of GPU reports which testify to the massive opposition which collectivization provoked, and one marvels at the capacity of the author to twist the facts which he does use to the purposes which he serves. There remains only the melancholy reflection that, having dipped into the archives, our author may not be unconscious of what he has left out.

Let me turn to a second example, an article by F. M. Vaganov on 'The Rout of the Right Deviation in the VKP (1928-1930)', which appeared in *Voprosy Istorii KPSS* (1960, No. 4). The article holds special interest because the activities of the right-wing opposition, in contrast to the left, have been poorly documented, and the author, as his citations reveal, has been able to draw on the central party archive. Again, as one might expect, the basic political line of the article follows a well-worn groove. The article begins and ends with citations from Khrushchev condemning the right-wingers and elaborating the usual indictment that they broke with Leninism, threatened the unity of the party, hindered industrialization, and sympathized with the kulaks. But scattered through the article are documentary citations which throw some fresh light on the party history of the period. There is an intriguing reference to the purge of *Pravda* in late 1928 which resulted in the expulsion of Bukharin and his chief supporters and their replacement by E. M. Yaroslavsky and M. A. Savelev as Stalin's representatives on the editorial board. There is an extended discussion of the struggle for the control of the Moscow party organization, where Uglanov, the first secretary, and a number of his *raikom* secretaries, threw in their lot with the right. The author goes out of his way to demonstrate, with quotations from speeches, that both Voroshilov and Kalinin, who, it has often been alleged, sympathized with the right-wingers, actually gave strong support to Stalin at the April 1929 plenum of the central committee and central control commission. Mr Vaganov's version is, of course, far from being the whole story, but the titbits which he throws out help to round off the tale. Similar articles could be cited by the dozen. What distinguishes them all is a basic orthodoxy of line combined with more richly elaborated detail and the appearance, at least, of a scholarly apparatus. Yet it should be pointed out that the impact of this research has yet to be felt at the textbook level. Even the most recent elementary histories of the Soviet period retain a schematic and stereotyped quality which rarely goes beyond summaries of statistics of progress and of the contents of important government and party decrees.

There are, however, occasional outcroppings in recent Soviet historiography which do not fit so easily into this perhaps too neat picture. The Shamil controversy furnishes one example. One would have thought that the issue had been settled in March 1957 when *Voprosy Istorii* was rebuked for its effort to rehabilitate Shamil. But since 1957 at least three works have appeared—*The Outline History of Dagestan* (1957), the second edition of Guseinov's *From the History of Social and Political Thought in Azerbaidzhan in the Nineteenth Century* (1958), and a volume of documents on *The Mountain Peoples' Movement of the North-east Caucasus in the Years 1820 to 1850* (1959)—which again present Shamil as a national hero and the leader of a just cause.[1] All these efforts, to be sure, originated in Dagestan and Baku. Yet the fact that they did not elicit a resounding rebuke provides at least food for thought. It is possible, but perhaps dangerous, to conclude that Moscow's tolerance of this anomaly reflects uncertainty on where the balance of advantage lies in the rival views.

There remains to consider how those charged by the party with responsibility for work on the historical front appraise the current state of Soviet historiography. One catches in the journals from time to time warnings that history must not be allowed to degenerate into 'factology', and that the propagation of Marxism-Leninism must take precedence over the professional preoccupation with fact-finding. The decree of the party central committee of January 9, 1960 'On the Tasks of Party Propaganda in Present-day Conditions' is even more explicit:

The party central committee, while noting the great importance and positive role of the social sciences and their personnel in working out and popularizing Marxist-Leninist theory and in the ideological education of Soviet people, at the same time considers that many shortcomings in the content of party propaganda are due to a certain

[1] For an excellent study of the Shamil controversy and the works cited above, see Lowell R. Tillett, 'Shamil and Muridism in Recent Soviet Historiography', *The American Slavic and East European Review*, April 1961.

lag of workers in the social sciences behind the practice of communist construction and the tasks of ideological work. Many economists, philosophers, historians, and other scholarly personnel have not overcome elements of dogmatism, do not have a bold and creative approach to life and to the experience of the masses' struggle, are poorly elaborating timely theoretical and practical questions and are often held in the toils of outdated and fruitless problems.[1]

Again, as so often before, historians are called upon to abandon their flight from the contemporary and to address themselves to present-day problems. The response has thus far been wary. Historians everywhere, by the nature of their profession, feel a primary obligation to illuminate the past, and in the Soviet Union in particular, the history of the Soviet period has always presented very special political hazards. Since Stalin's death, these hazards, in a sheer physical sense, have declined substantially, but, as the *Voprosy Istorii* scandal made only too clear, the re-interpretation of the recent past is strewn with hidden land mines, and the unwary and adventurous may easily fall foul of them. The large-scale opening of the archives since 1956 has made work in the Soviet period more attractive professionally, but one measure of the caution which such work inspires is the very considerable concentration of energy on the publication of documents. The monographs and articles which have appeared since 1956 make use of archival material on a much larger scale than previously, but the material itself is fitted into a political pattern dictated by the current needs of the party leadership.

What of the historians themselves as they strive to reconcile the line in history with facts which flatly contradict it? Are there still Burdzhalovs among them who feel deeply frustrated because they cannot write history as it happened rather than as it has to be tailored to meet orthodox demands? On this we can only speculate and perhaps raise a few questions. The capacity of the human mind to sustain contradictions and paradoxes must not be underestimated, all the more when living in a society which offers no alternative. Yet for those who believe that the desire to know and tell the truth is deeply imbedded in the human consciousness, there is comfort to be derived from what happened in *Voprosy Istorii* when the bonds were loosened. Since 1957 the Burdzhalovs and their like have been driven underground or have made their compromises with necessity. But one cannot help wondering whether they will not rise again from among the new generation of 'archive rats', the readers of foreign bourgeois history, or even those exposed to the pre-revolutionary Russian historians. Or have Soviet historians become so thoroughly conditioned by their time and place that they will henceforth find what they are taught to believe and no longer believe what they find?

---

[1] *Pravda*, January 10, 1960.

B

DISCUSSION

Explaining the background of this paper, Professor Fainsod said he had tried to look at Soviet historiography as a kind of barometer of the intellectual climate of Soviet society. He had been drawn irresistibly towards Burdzhalov—was he a hero, an oasis in the desert, or a mirage? Reading the articles he had produced before 1956, one would be tempted to conclude that he was a party hack like all the others. Why then the sudden change? He agreed with Mr Ulam that Burdzhalov and Madame Pankratova thought they were following the new line opened by gradual destalinization after 1953, as it appeared to emerge in Mikoyan's speech (of which Mme Pankratova's speech after the twentieth CPSU congress was an elaboration), and in Khrushchev's secret speech. There seemed to have been no opposition to them till Bugaev's article in *Partiinaya Zhizn* in July 1956. What had happened in the meantime? The ferment generated by the congress in the Soviet party, and particularly in the satellite parties, had begun to cause disquiet. At this point the divergence of views between the party hacks was manifest. The party directives themselves were sufficiently ambiguous to be interpreted in one way by Bugaev and in another by Burdzhalov, who could still feel that the fight was not lost. But after Poland and Hungary the line crystallized, and by December *Voprosy Istorii* responded to it, albeit reluctantly. Burdzhalov and his colleagues continued to fight a rearguard action, prepared to explore the boundaries of the new freedom. That Burdzhalov had considerable support among Soviet historians could be inferred from the reports of conferences which took place throughout the Soviet Union, and especially the conference of Leningrad historians. However, after the decree of the party central committee of March 7, 1957, the issue was foreclosed; Burdzhalov had to go and *Voprosy Istorii* shifted its ground.

Was there any residuum of the forward momentum represented by Burdzhalov? The changes one could detect represented a step backward from 1956, but in comparison with the state of Soviet historiography in the last years of Stalin's reign, the historian seemed to have more elbow-room from a purely professional point of view. He could consult and use the archives; he was permitted to have international contacts; he benefited from a broadening in the parameters of history, reflected in the multiplication of journals. He also had a new set of directives, which enjoined him to be a good soldier of communism, but also to write more convincing history than had been possible under Stalin. This meant writing with more concrete detail and with the appearance— not the actuality—of scholarship. An example of the new approach was the article on collectivization in the lower Volga region cited in Professor Fainsod's paper. It showed the extensive, though selective, use of archives; it was much more frank on the fate of the various classes of kulaks; some had been sent to concentration camps (the word was used), others exiled or forcibly transplanted. But despite this apparatus of scholarship, historians were conscious of the fact that they were still writing under a directive. Historians could not challenge Marxist, Leninist, or present Khrushchevist doctrine; they certainly could not challenge party infallibility—this was Burdzhalov's real crime, for by building up the Mensheviks in the past and dwelling on the mistakes made in preparing for the 1917 revolution, he explicitly or by implication raised the question of party infallibility. So long as the doctrine of party infallibility persisted, so long as it remained under the guardianship of a leader or a group of people responsible to him, Soviet historians would remain dependent upon its demands as interpreted by the current leadership. But the Burdzhalov affair and its reverberations showed a readiness on the part of historians to write in a more worth-while fashion if the opportunity were given them.

Dr Meijer agreed that most historians who were prepared to accept the limitations of *partiinost* were now enjoying professional opportunities which were not available in earlier days. But he was inclined to think that the whole process of change in Soviet historiography was partly conditioned by the fact that the historians were divided. In general one could distinguish between party historians and real historians, between those who were looking for confirmation of the party point of view and those who were trying to find out what happened. In the article cited on the liquidation of the kulaks, excesses had been described as 'in no sense typical'. What was considered 'typical' by Soviet historians? As in Soviet literature, 'typical' was what was representative, and what was representative was considered truer than what was not. In discussing the Shamil controversy, Professor Fainsod had written that Moscow's tolerance of some works favourable to Shamil might reflect 'uncertainty on where the balance of advantage lies in the rival views'. 'Advantage' was a term irrelevant to the pusuit of truth. Of course, the leaders were not concerned with the truth, but with educating and conditioning the Soviet people. Given this avowed purpose, could it be achieved, seeing that in the interval between the writing and publishing of a work the political line might well change?

It seemed to Dr Utechin that even in the worst days of Stalin's terror there had been historians who were trying to apply professional standards, and they seemed to have far better opportunities of doing so now than before Stalin's death. There were others who knew the techniques of the historian's craft but were prepared to put them at the disposal of the party leadership. This was the case with Burdzhalov before 1953. Destalinization was most relevant to this group who, if the opportunity arose, would try to interpret the official requirements in such a way as to allow them to stick as closely as possible to professional standards. Others were trying to present a somewhat more refined version of the official view of historical events. Finally there were the propagandists, for whom work on the historical front was in no way different from work elsewhere. Contrary to the situation in Stalin's day, the official line in regard to such people now was that they should not concern themselves with history.

What had been written since Stalin's death about the history of the Russian revolutionary movement was not a substitute for old myths, and did not necessarily have any particular bearing on the new requirements of the party leadership. It bore witness to a revival of genuine scholarship in a field which, at least since the publication of the *Short Course* in 1938, with its one sentence on the populists, had been altogether forbidden ground. Tvardovskaya's recent article on the organizational basis of *Narodnaya Volya* was in fact a very good account of that organization, with implications in respect of Lenin's views on party organization that could be very unwelcome to the party leadership.

Did this indicate genuine autonomy in historical research, or simply a change in the political requirements of the leadership? It seemed that the political needs of the moment dictated a show of liberality and that in the process of fostering this impression, the leaders were in fact allowing historians a certain autonomy. The effect was one of genuine liberalization, although the institutional situation might not have changed at all and the line might swing around tomorrow.

Professor Fainsod agreed that there were works by Soviet historians which represented a genuine contribution—there always were small loopholes within the totalitarian frame. But it would be a mistake to regard this as a characteristic feature of contemporary Soviet historiography in so far as it applied to the Soviet period itself. When he spoke of new myths replacing the old, he had in mind developments in the field of party history, the revaluation of Khrushchev's role in the civil war, and so on. The real test for the future was the sacred doctrine of party infallibility; in that respect he believed matters had changed very little. His reference to Medvedev's description of excesses during collectivization as 'in no way typical' was meant to illustrate one of the problems facing Soviet historians: they need not deny that mistakes had been committed, but they had to minimize them. Judging from the Smolensk archives on which he had worked, excesses had been very widespread indeed.

Professor Fainsod was genuinely puzzled about the fortunes of Shamil in Soviet historiography since 1957. The whole controversy seemed to reflect an attempt to find some kind of balance between Great Russian nationalism and the aspirations of the minority republics. Judging from Lowell Tillett's study, Moscow historians followed the 1957 line by presenting Shamil as the villain, whereas local historians were given more leeway and were allowed to suggest that he was at one time the leader of a just cause. This might be part of the greater flexibility of the current line.

In Dr Katkov's opinion, Burdzhalov had acted injudiciously; he did not seem to understand the techniques of controlled revisionism. He had attacked a universally established and accepted myth merely by adducing factual material to undermine it. This was not the way things should be done. To destroy an old myth, a new myth had first to be created and popularized; only then could the facts necessary to sustain it be adduced. F. I. Drabkina, for example, who had corroborated

Burdzhalov's views in *Voprosy Istorii*, had survived and was now publishing her most interesting memoirs in *Novyi Mir*. She had gone so far as to compare John Reed, author of *Ten Days That Shook the World*, to Alexandre Dumas; but she did this only after the revision of this period of Soviet history had been accepted, after the publication of Kazakevich's story in *Oktyabr*, in which Zinoviev was allowed to re-appear as a supporter of Lenin.

Mr Schapiro endorsed Professor Fainsod's moderate optimism and agreed with his estimate that the most encouraging recent development was the opening up of the archives on an enlarged scale. The stenographic reports of the early party congresses had been republished, and this provided something which had been conspicuously lacking in party history; a yardstick to compare the party as it existed today with the party as it was then. In the early years there had been a good deal of free debate. Against the background of stylized, organized discussion that has been the practice since about 1923-4, this must have had a marked impact. It would be interesting to see whether the series would be continued.

The form in which information was occasionally conveyed in the annotations to the published archives suggested the existence of clandestine scholarship in the Soviet Union; the re-publication of the minutes of the central committee discussions in 1917 and 1918 provided an interesting example. When these had been published earlier, some items on the agenda had been omitted. In the new edition they were still omitted, but the editors had inserted a note explaining the omissions on the ground that the debates had been occupied with interminable discussions connected with Kozlovsky and Ganetsky which were too confused to unravel. As these two were particularly associated with the accusations made against Lenin of receiving sums of money from the Germans, it was clear that the debates concerned the charge and the reply. The editors need not have put the note in; the old edition could simply have been reprinted. But the note was there, and was of considerable interest to the informed reader.

There seemed to be two levels at which party history was controlled: at one level was the writing of articles which had to conform to certain standards since the debacle of 1957; at the other was the publication of archive material, which often directly contradicted the official line. In her memoirs, Drabkina had confirmed Burdzhalov's contention that there was disorganization and uncertainty in the Bolshevik ranks, and Trotsky's minute of the same meeting published in his *Stalin School of Falsification* corroborated this. Yet Drabkina was never criticized. Again, two long and detailed articles with tables on the local party organizations in 1917, published in *Voprosy Istorii KPSS* long after the Burdzhalov affair, confirmed one of Burdzhalov's main points up to the hilt: that there was no striking contrast between Bolsheviks and Mensheviks in 1917, that in fact they remained united in many cases as late as September or even October.

Professor Ulam thought that in the circumstances in which they were written, Burdzhalov's articles revealed greater scrupulousness in using materials than his predecessors had shown, but certainly not independence of judgement. In the two years leading up to the twentieth congress an official attempt was made to contrast Leninism and Stalinism, to denigrate Stalin and extol Lenin. All that Burdzhalov did in the main article he wrote was to point out that until Lenin's arrival in Russia in 1917, nobody took the correct line and that Stalin as a matter of fact was close to Kamenev and others. This could hardly be taken as a sign of independence; it might just as well have been the action of an ambitious academic bureaucrat seizing what he thought a good chance to forge ahead. It would have been a better proof of independence of judgement if in that critical period of 1955-6 some historian had undertaken to defend Stalin's role in the revolution.

There were in Mr Wolfe's opinion good reasons for the special treatment accorded the *Narodnaya Volya*; it was really an extension of Bolshevism into the past. Lenin had even claimed this heritage in a well-known article. As to the Mensheviks, after Burdzhalov's unfortunate miscalculation (for that was all it was), they were as unhistorically treated today as under Stalin, albeit somewhat differently. He believed that the freedom of Soviet historians was sharply curbed not only for the Soviet period, but also in regard to the past. Anything written about any period, however remote from the Soviet era, showed concern not to call in question the institutional or sociological dogmas of Soviet Marxism. As an example he cited an article by a Mme Danilova in *Voprosy Istorii*, discussing the work of American medievalists, particularly their treatment of feudalism in old Russia. The article had all the paraphernalia of scholarship, including 164 bibliographical footnotes referring to American work. But all these writers without exception were either ignored or misrepresented in the text, and several of them had written nothing on the medieval period. He himself, who had never written a word on medieval history, found one of his works quoted as proof that Americans do read what Soviet historians write. Mme Danilova classified three American historians as good medievalists, William Z. Foster, Herbert Aptheker, and Marc Raeff. They had one thing in common: they had never written on medieval history. What was the motive behind this extraordinary exercise? It was a fact that American historians by and large tended to deny the existence of feudalism in old Russia, which was affirmed as an article of faith by Soviet historians, part of the general communist view of the march of history, according to which all countries go through the feudal era.

Professor Scheibert said much more was written nowadays on the Russian populist movement—it was part of a general tendency to restore the national historical heritage in so far as it did not conflict with party dogma. He thought it could be misleading to draw a sharp line between what we called sound academic scholarship and Marxist scholarship. Marxism and Leninism should not be used interchangeably.

There was a type of post-bourgeois historian coming to the fore throughout the Soviet orbit who could be called the 'open Marxist'. He could be found among the younger generation of Polish scholars, and among those who were coming over to Western Germany from the Soviet zone. Their approach to history was not just pragmatic; they tried not merely to analyse, but to interpret history in terms of a unified theory. In this respect Soviet scholarship was lagging behind that in Eastern Europe, where there had been interesting developments in historical methodology. The intelligent Marxian approach to history represented a challenge to western historians, who had a good part of Marx in their own historical heritage, whether they liked it or not.

Professor Fainsod agreed that Burdzhalov probably believed he was interpreting the mood of the party leadership, as reflected at the twentieth congress; but it was unfair to dismiss him simply as a man who toed the line of the moment. He had adhered to his views after it had become quite clear that they had been repudiated, i.e. after the June 30th resolution of the central committee and after the attack in *Partiinaya Zhizn.*

The whole affair reminded Dr Bolsover of the Varga controversy in 1947-8. Despite strong attacks, Varga held on to some of his positions, such as the need for reconsidering the inevitability of war, for quite a long time. One was left with the impression that he was able to hold out for so long because it was not a purely economic issue, but one that reflected differences among the leaders, some of whom must have supported him. Some light was shed on the question whether Soviet historians would, if permitted, switch from a Marxist to a 'bourgeois' line, by an article in *Kommunist*, in which Nechkina argued that it was an anomaly not to have re-published Pokrovsky at a time when they were re-issuing bourgeois historians like Klyuchevsky and Solovyov. She clearly thought it dangerous to expose the new generation of Soviet historians to the influences of these bourgeois historians without the counterweight of Marxist historians like Pokrovsky.

Dr Utechin had said that in wanting to create the impression of being liberal, the Soviet leaders did perhaps unwittingly contribute to actual liberalization. But in Mr Labedz's view, the test of this particular historical pudding was in the eating, and there was plenty of evidence that new myths were being fostered, admittedly by more sophisticated methods. But if sophistication meant sophisticated self-deception or more sophisticated deception of others, it was not necessarily a good thing. After all, it was more difficult to detect. An article by the eminent Polish philosopher and party ideologist Adam Schaff had been published in *Diogenes* in 1960 under the title 'Why is History Constantly Re-written?' Professor Schaff did not deal with the crude falsifications of Stalinist historiography, but based his argument on the rather sophisticated ground of historical relativity, referring to historians like Robinson Barnes, Charles Beard, Collingwood, Croce, etc. Mr Labedz thought the Soviet historians would soon catch up with the sophistication of the

Polish party ideologists—in fact, similar arguments to Schaff's had already been used in I. S. Kon's book *Philosophic Idealism and the Crisis of Bourgeois Historical Thought*.

Mr Nikolaevsky thought the Burdzhalov case important because it threw some light on the struggle that went on behind the scenes. The open conflict between *Voprosy Istorii* and *Partiinaya Zhizn* was one between two departments of the central committee secretariat: the department for Higher Education and Science, of which Pankratova was in charge until the twentieth congress, and the department for Cadres Administration under Aristov, who was at the same time Khrushchev's deputy for the RSFSR Moscow bureau. Bugaev himself was a small man; the important thing was that the attack on Pankratova and Burdzhalov was organized from the highest level. That the editors of *Voprosy Istorii* at first stuck to their guns showed that at this stage the department for Higher Education and Science was still behind Pankratova. The Burdzhalov case marked the first large-scale offensive by the Institute of Marxism-Leninism against the Academy of Sciences' Institute of History. The real issue was: who was going to direct the historical sciences?

For Dr Utechin the main criterion for judging the state of historical scholarship was: did the works produced add to our understanding of history? As far as his particular field went, he would answer with an unconditional affirmative. He had in mind not so much the formal characteristics of historical writing, but its genuineness. History was no longer populated by fictitious people, the practice started by Beria in his pamphlet on the history of the Bolshevik organizations in Transcaucasia. Even in the worst Stalin period historians could still produce work of real value on the Middle Ages; now the area had been considerably extended, encompassing several fields which were either completely fictitious or completely taboo before Stalin's death. For the period of transition from the pre-social-democratic phase in the revolutionary movement in Russia to the social-democratic phase, for example, there were a number of works which genuinely contributed to our understanding.

Mr Laqueur said that whoever decided who should be rehabilitated and who not, historians were not the only ones to carry out the operation. The most striking recent revision had appeared in a story by Kazakevich, published in *Oktyabr*, which amounted to at least a partial rehabilitation of Zinoviev and a wholesale rehabilitation of other members of the Leningrad group such as Lashevich and others. Obviously the writer would not have done this without some reassurance that it would be acceptable; unfortunately we did not know what exactly he was told and to what extent he was left to his own devices.

Professor Berlin said the discussion had centred on the question: was Burdzhalov a brave and obstinate man or did he speak in the name of a powerful protector? The two things were not necessarily incompatible—

he might have been a brave man and nevertheless received encouragement in his attitude. As we had no access to the individuals concerned, we could only discuss the question in the way one discussed problems in ancient history—in the light of general hypotheses. Perhaps the point made earlier by Dr Meijer was relevant here: that when people in the Soviet Union talked about an issue of principle, this meant that there was some connection between the point they raised and some important issue of current party politics. Like Burdzhalov, Varga had persisted in his views, while people like Tarle had caved in. In the Stalin period Tarle had been attacked for his history of the Crimean War and taken to task for saying that there had been a swift Russian rehabilitation after the crushing military defeat (Lenin had spoken of a collapse); and also for saying that the Russian people had been defeated, on the ground that this perhaps had been the case of the Russian government, but never of the Russian people. Tarle did not defend himself; he simply rewrote the history. The same thing occurred with Syromyatnikov's book on Peter the Great. Could one infer from this that Tarle and Syromyatnikov had given way, because the Crimean War and Peter the Great were not issues of burning importance in 1944-5, whereas Varga and Burdzhalov were raising questions of principle, i.e. issues which were current party issues as well and which therefore could not have been raised without the putative alliance of someone in the top leadership? Or were the differences in their reaction purely personal and psychological?

In reply Professor Fainsod said his own analysis had led him to the view that in the early phases of the controversy, Burdzhalov thought he was following the directive of the party congress. In the later stages the problem became more complicated. He may have still believed that he had protection, but in his speech in Leningrad he said specifically: 'We historians have no one to give us basic directives and instructions.' He obviously thought the situation fluid and ambiguous enough to persist; but it should not be overlooked that he stubbornly reiterated his views in the face of a specific rebuke in *Partiinaya Zhizn*, and after the central committee declaration of June 30th, which must have made him doubt the security of such protection as he enjoyed.

Some of the speakers had been pessimistic about the future of Soviet historiography, some had expressed pronounced optimism. Although there had been a tightening of the bonds since 1957, there were nevertheless channels open which had been closed before, through which new ideas were being expressed and propagated. The publication of archive material, which often contradicted the official party history, must at the very least raise a question in the minds of people. The fact that in a society where there was no alternative, people learned to live with incompatibilities and to make adjustments, did not make the dilemma any the less real. The interest of the Burdzhalov case was that it showed what happened when there was some kind of opportunity to transcend the accepted contradictions and incompatibilities.

B*

Finally, Mr Schapiro reminded the conference that the man who first opened the whole question of the writing of history by attacking the *Short Course* at the twentieth party congress was Mikoyan. Anybody would be pardoned for supposing that with Mikoyan's backing he could go fairly far, even if he were faced with an article by Bugaev in *Partiinaya Zhizn*. Instead of looking for protectors of Burdzhalov who lost out in the power struggle, it could be more reasonable to conclude that Mikoyan might simply have changed his mind after realizing the dangers of destalinization.

II. Party Histories from Lenin to Khrushchev

BERTRAM D. WOLFE

'Historians are dangerous people,' Nikita Khrushchev explained to a French delegation in 1956. 'They are capable of upsetting everything. They must be directed.' Archives are perilous places, too: dangerous for the 'archive rats' who rummage in them, dangerous for what may be fished up to reverse the supposedly irreversible flow down that drain which has come to be called the memory hole. 'The laws of history are irreversible', wrote Academician G. Aleksandrov re-assuringly in Stalin's last year.[1] But neither Stalin, nor his disciple and successor, is disposed to take any chances. Hence the archives have been for a long period, as the most touchy still are, in the scholarly care of the secret police; a fitting sumbol is the pen fastened down by ball and chain. Hence, too, the frequent reminders to historians that history must not be expounded in an objective spirit, for that would be a departure from the Leninist principle of *partiinost* in science.[2]

Out of this flow the admonitions that 'the sharp ideological struggle in the workers' movement is accompanied by no less ferocious battles in historiography';[3] the instructions for dealing with the future no less than the past ('It's a poor sort of memory that only works backwards', the Queen said to Alice in Wonderland); the proclamations that 'historical science has been and remains an arena of sharp ideological struggle, has been and remains a class, party science', that 'the struggle against bourgeois ideology has been and continues to be the foremost task of our historians', that 'the historian of the party is not a dispassionate recorder of the events of the past but a scholar-fighter', and that 'the science of the history of the party occupies an outstanding place in the ideological struggle of the communist party for the revolutionary transformation of society'.[4]

The same considerations dictate the stern commands of the central committee, the presidium, or the leader, to the practitioners of the historian's craft; the steady hail of precise formulations which must be 'verified' by history; the sudden changes in the editorial boards of the leading historical journals; and the emergence in due course of the single official history, besides which there shall be no other. It is the

[1] *Literaturnaya Gazeta*, January 1, 1952.
[2] *Pravda*, July 1960, No. 17.
[3] *Voprosy Istorii KPSS*, 1960, No. 5, p. 172.
[4] *Voprosy Istorii*, 1960, No. 5, p. 157; No. 8, editorial.

development of this sultry atmosphere in which historians must carry on their work, and the emergence amid storms and alarms of the single official history so suited to the single-party, dictatorial state, which forms the central theme of the present essay.

Each of the leaders of the communist party of the Soviet Union in turn, and each of the contenders for such leadership, has perforce been a historian of sorts. It was Lenin who set the example of harnessing Clio to his chariot every time he changed his tactics, got into a fight within his own movement, or in the Russian revolutionary movement as a whole, started another split, or celebrated the anniversary of one of those innumerable schisms in his life and that of his movement. Historicism, authoritarianism, pedantry, Marxist and historical learning or pseudo-learning, and *Rechthaberei* were all so strong in him, so charged was he with passion for theoretical battle, that he never tired of enlisting for each ideological fray, faction squabble, or tactical manoeuvre the entire panoply of the history of Marxism, the history of Russia, the history of its social movements, the history of his own faction and that of his opponents, and—not infrequently—the history of mankind.

To the socialist-revolutionaries, when he was telling them that they could never be 'socialists but merely revolutionary democrats', albeit 'devoted and honest revolutionary democrats', and graciously allowing that they had the right to a place in the Petersburg Soviet of 1905, since 'we are at this moment making precisely a democratic revolution', he explained that with their 'inconsistencies and vacillations we can easily get along, for history itself supports our views, at every step reality supports us'.[1]

Lenin felt he could not give battle to populism without setting down his own propositions concerning that movement's history, and the past, present, and inevitable future of Russia. He analysed the brighter pages of populism's history in such fashion that his own movement became the 'legitimate heir' of all that was admirable in it, leaving for latter-day populism only the dregs of 'vulgar, philistine radicalism'.[2] His volume on *The Development of Capitalism in Russia*, his 'What are the "Friends of the People"?', and 'What Heritage do we Reject?', are on varying levels typical of his use or abuse of history in his war with populism.

In the same fashion, his battles with the 'economists' prompted him to review the history of Marxism and social movements, while his war on the Kadets and zemstvo liberals called for similar excursions into the history of liberalism, socialism, and Russia. When *Iskra* fought the

---

[1] Lenin, X, p. 7. How literally Lenin took history's support is suggested by the style of this *obiter dictum*: for history itself supports our views, reality supports it at every step.

[2] The Russian reads 'poshlyi, meshchanskii radikalizm'. This analysis first occurs in Lenin, I, p. 246, but recurs again and again whenever Lenin returns to the subject.

other socialist movements and journals, and again when the Iskrists themselves split and Lenin joined battle with the other five *Iskra* editors, one of his main weapons was a thumb-nail history of Marxism, and of Russian and non-Russian social movements. Just as he had sought to outflank populism by claiming all he thought good in its heritage and identifying the residue with petit-bourgeois radicalism, so now he claimed to be the heir of Marxism and of all that was good in *Iskra* tradition, while he sought to identify the other editors with economism and with the Kadets. All this was done in the guise of historiography.

Nor did his technique vary essentially when his battle was with Bolshevik disciples who were deviating to left or right, or being 'conciliatory' at moments when he wanted a split, or holding to Lenin's earlier formulas and historiography against today's. The moment a fight began, he was ready with an *ad hoc* and *ad hominem* historical sketch of how his opponents got that way, of the various stages in their degeneration, of their 'essential identity' with some movement he and they had previously denounced, and of the inevitable path of their further decline.

One of the peculiarities of Soviet historiography is its obsession with 'periodization'. In part this can be traced to a vulgarization of Marx's famous 1859 listing of diverse stages in the history of society, which were stages according to some Marxists successive, and to others inevitable-progressive. With Marx the listing was ambivalently typological *and* 'progressive' or 'inevitable'. But when pressed he was ready to declare that the listing of ancient, feudal, capitalist, and socialist was typology rather than inevitable succession, and at most applicable to western Europe at a certain stage of its development. For Soviet historiography, however, every land has its unilateral path marked out for it: feudalism, capitalism, socialism, communism. For every society such periodization is obligatory. This is a marvellous device for ensuring feudalism where there is no trace of it, and socialism where there is neither capitalist industry nor a working class.

The author of the habit of 'periodization' in communist party history is Lenin. He is tireless in his use of it as a device for demonstrating the progressive rise and magnification of his own movement and the progressive decline of opposing movements. His periodization is rarely twice the same, but it always serves the same ends. In his conclusion to *What is to be Done?* the history of the socialist movement in Russia is divided into three periods, one of 'intra-uterine' existence without workers, a second of 'birth' as a political party looking to the working class but separated from its spontaneous movement, a third of decline and confusion (coinciding in time with the period when Lenin was in Siberia and unable to keep the movement on the right course), and a fourth triumphant age of true socialism fusing with the spontaneous movement of the working class and embodying itself in *Iskra*.

In a report prepared under Lenin's direction for the Amsterdam congress of the International (1904), there are four historical periods: pre-*Iskra*; *Iskra* period; second congress with its split; post-congress period with the triumphant development of Bolshevism into the true movement. New variants appear in his introduction to the collection *After Twelve Years* (1907); 'The Historical Meaning of Inner Party Struggles in Russia' (1910); 'On some Peculiarities in the Historical Development of Marxism in Russia' (1910); 'The Ideological Struggle in the Workers' Movement' (1914); and in his 'Result of Three Decades of Development of Social-Democracy in Russia', as given in *Socialism and War* (1917). When Lenin begins to lecture left communists in other parties of the Communist International in his *Infantile Sickness of Left Communism*, he gives a new periodization of the main stages in the history of Bolshevism. These periodizations may differ in periods (dating) and in summation (names and meanings assigned to the periods), and in this sense the periodization is *ad hoc* and history as flexible as a rubber band. But they all have one single, overall meaning, which may be summed up in Lenin's remark, already cited, to the SRs in the 1905 Soviet: 'History supports our views, at every step reality supports us'.

Soviet historians of the communist party have all made use of one or another of Lenin's formulations. Cut off now from the living, nutrient medium of contemporaneity, they are imbedded like fossils in every subsequent party history.

No one has yet compiled a collection of all Lenin's historical excursions, which would serve as a 'Guide to the Perplexed' for party historiography; but there is evidence that such a treatise is in preparation, to be called *Lenin as Historian of the Party*. In the meanwhile, the following quotations from *Voprosy Istorii KPSS* (1960, No. 5) can give us some notion of the general conclusions and approach to this theme:

1. Together with the rise of the Marxist party of the working class arose its historiography.
2. There is scarcely a single work of Lenin in which the history of the revolutionary movement is not illuminated from a Marxist standpoint.
3. The science of the history of the party occupies an outstanding place in the ideological struggle of the communist party for the revolutionary transformation of society. There exists a definite relationship between historical investigations and the political activity of the party, between historical problematics and the political tasks of the party.
4. The development of the science of party history can be understood only in its general connection with the entire ideological work of the party, in connection with that struggle which the party waged at its various stages against the multifarious enemies of Marxism.

Though every polemical work of Lenin was thus equipped with an 'offensive' history of the party and other historical weapons, Lenin himself was too busy to write a systematic textbook on the subject. This he left to faithful followers like Lyadov, whose *History of the Russian Social-Democratic Labour Party*, published in 1906, was republished three times under the Soviet regime. But in 1909 Lyadov fell into sin, or deviation from Lenin, and never brought his work up to date.[1] After the Bolshevik seizure of power everybody was too busy making history to write it. Lenin continued to clothe each polemic in the armour of history, his disciples echoing him as best they could. Minuscule works like Bubnov's *The Chief Moments in the Development of the Communist Party of Russia*, no bigger than a single long-winded talk, were of little interest then and are of less interest now.

The year 1923 marks a watershed in party historiography, for in that year Zinoviev delivered six lectures on 'The History of the Communist Party of Russia (Bolsheviks)' and Trotsky poured fat into a smouldering fire with his *Lessons of October 1917*. These two had turned their hand to history, not as a weapon of struggle against other parties but as a weapon of struggle for the succession in the communist party itself. From 1923 until the end of the 1930s, when Stalin ordered and edited the *Short Course*, intra-party warfare was the main function of party history. The lesser lights who engaged in the perilous craft, Bubnov, Nevsky, Kardashev, Volosevich, Yaroslavsky, Popov, Kerzhentsev, and Knorin (which last did not write but edited a history written by a 'collective' of the Red Professors' Institute of Party History), all had to weigh every line not merely as a justification of the Bolsheviks against the world, but, with still greater care, as a justification of the 'true' Bolsheviks against the deviator Bolsheviks, who in due course would turn out to be anti-Bolshevik enemies within the party.[2]

[1] There was also a *Sketch of the History of Social-Democracy in Russia*, by N. N. Baturin (N. N. Zamyatin), who in 1912 was a member of the editorial board of *Pravda*. Though it was reprinted eleven times after 1917, I have been unable to learn the date of original issue, or to secure a copy.

[2] *Voprosy Istorii KPSS*, in its editorial, 'Towards a New Upsurge of the Science of Party History', (1960, No. 5), recognizes the following as 'scientific works and systematized textbooks of party history' which in their time represented 'significant material . . but contained many methodological and theoretical errors': Lyadov and Baturin for the pre-1917 period; A. S. Bubnov, *Fundamental Problems of the History of the RKP*, 1924; V. I. Nevsky, *Outlines of the History of the Russian Communist Party*, Part I, 1923; N. N. Popov, *Outlines of the History of the All-Union Communist Party* (from 1925 to 1935—sixteen editions); V. I. Nevsky, *History of the RKP* (*b*), *Short Outline*, 1925 and 1926; Em. Yaroslavsky, *Short Outlines of the History of the VKP* (*b*), Part I, 1926; a collective work under the editorship of Yaroslavsky, *History of the All-Union Communist Party*, I, 1926, II-IV, 1929-30; P. M. Kerzhentsev, *Pages of the History of the RKP* (*b*), 1925; D. I. Kardashev, *Fundamental Historic Stages and Development of the VKP*, 1927; *History of the VKP* (*b*) *in Congresses*, ed. P. N. Lepeshinsky, 1927; A. S. Bubnov, *VKP* (*b*), in two volumes; Em. Yaroslavsky, *History of the VKP* (*b*), Parts I-II, 1933 (reissued until 1938); *Short History of the VKP* (*b*), ed. V. Knorin, 1934; *History of the VKP* (*b*), *Short Course*, under the editorship of a commission of the CC of the VKP (*b*), 1938 and a series of other editions. The rather chaotic chronological order is theirs. The fact that a historian starts a two-volume work and publishes only the first part, then starts a new

For the next decade, party historiography was in a steadily deepening crisis. Histories succeeded one another at a faster and faster rate, as if they were being consumed by a more and more irritable gigantic chain smoker who lit the first page of each new work with the last page of the old. Histories, and, a little later, historians, disappeared without trace. Nevsky published the first part of a two-part history of the party in 1923, but there was no second part. The published part was scrapped, and in 1925 he started over again. Yaroslavsky did the same. Indeed, Yaroslavsky kept writing histories which kept disappearing in favour of new histories by the same Yaroslavsky, so that by now no bibliographer can decipher how many Yaroslavsky histories there really were and what happened to them.[1] In 1926 he assembled a team, or *kollektiv*, of historians and issued a four-volume work (Vol. I, 1926; Vols. II-IV, 1929-30). But the fourth volume was obsolete within a year of its appearance. In 1933 he issued a new two-volume work which had a longer life, being re-issued at various times until 1938, when it disappeared. At that time Nevsky and Bubnov disappeared too, their histories having disappeared earlier.

To the outsider the bewildering thing is that each of these histories and cycles of histories had been entrusted to its respective authors by Stalin as weapons in his struggles with Trotsky, Zinoviev, Bukharin, and finally, with his own followers. Each was designed to belittle Stalin's opponents or annihilate them, and to glorify his name. But the heroes of one work became the dubious weaklings of the next and the villains and traitors of the third; persons of one work became unpersons in the next; the stature and single-handed achievements of Stalin became so much larger from one year to the next that each earlier version had to disappear, lest, rising from oblivion, it might bear witness against its successor.

In despair at the transitoriness of all these efforts of his faithful servitors, Stalin ordered a political lieutenant who was not even on speaking terms with Clio, V. Knorin, to assemble a *kollektiv* of pliable Red Professors to write the definitive party history. Knorin was an Old Bolshevik of Lettish origin, who had joined Lenin's party around 1912, perhaps a little earlier. He had been in the Comintern as Stalin's overseer of the German communist party in those fateful years when Stalin compelled it to 'direct its main fire' against the socialists and the Weimar Republic while Hitler rose to power. This seemed to be a

---

one, is a sign of the high mortality rate in these histories. There are other editions of works by Yaroslavsky and Bubnov which *Voprosy Istorii KPSS* has chosen to ignore, as they have such histories as Zinoviev's. The last work mentioned in the list is, of course, the one known as Stalin's *Short Course*.

[1] I have seen a number of Yaroslavsky efforts which are not mentioned in *Voprosy Istorii KPSS*'s bibliographical note. In *Kommunist* (1962, No. 4), Yaroslavsky is described as a 'renowned historian' whose errors had been criticized not by Stalin but by the now rehabilitated Pokrovsky.

suitable qualification for supervising a group of the Red Professors' Institute of Party History, with B. Ponomarev as group leader (*rukovoditel*). Published in 1935, Knorin's history proved to be as mortal as its predecessors. In 1937, its editor was arrested, accused of 'nationalist deviation', tortured, forced to confess that he had been a Tsarist agent first, then an agent of the Gestapo. He was shot within a year.[1]

This high mortality rate among Soviet party histories and historians has compelled western writers to resort to a kind of archaeological method, as if they were dealing with a long-buried institution in a long-buried civilization. They must dig through the mutually contradictory, successive layers of relative truth and calculated falsehood in an effort to determine which of the many layers represents the true Homeric Troy. It is possible to reconstruct the course of events by tracing the successive versions of some tender or touchy point—for example, why the Bolsheviks played no significant role in the 1905 Soviet, or in the February revolution of 1917; or what Trotsky's role was in the 1905 Soviet, in the 1917 seizure of power, in the Red Army and the civil war. Every tender spot, and these works abound in them, offers some hope that probing will establish the cause of the tenderness.

Or the historical detective may ask himself why a certain fact or a certain history has disappeared altogether. Thus we may well ask: Why is it that the most important party leader to engage in the direct writing of a party history (if we except Trotsky, who did most of his historical writing after he was no longer in a position to make history), namely Gregory Zinoviev, does not get into the canon of works which in their time represented 'significant contributions but contained methodological and theoretical errors'?

Zinoviev's history, which unfortunately stops at February 1917, was the reprint of a series of six carefully prepared and interminably long lectures, which he delivered early in 1923, when Lenin was already ill, but still able to dictate a few articles. His disciples were sizing each other up and manoeuvring for position, but the struggle for the succession had not yet flared up, nor were the disciples sure that the master might not recover enough strength to reprove them. Moreover, Zinoviev was closer to the past and more intimately acquainted with it than any of the later historians. We can therefore learn many things from Zinoviev's history that we cannot find in any subsequent account.

The Bolsheviks, we can see from his history, were in 1923 only beginning to get used to the one-party system. Hence the first of these six lectures is taken up with the question of what a party is and why the Bolshevik party is arrogating to itself a monopoly of power. Zinoviev grapples with various sociological definitions of a party; he tries to explain why a party is not a voluntary organization of like-minded individuals who agree upon a common programme; he rejects this view for the one that a party is the fighting organization of a class. He is troubled by the existence of a number of parties of the working class,

[1] See *Survey*, April-June 1960, pp. 112-3.

and the consequent implications that there may be 'classes' and a 'class struggle' inside the working class. He is troubled, too, by worker and peasant support for the SRs. We learn that the SRs claim to represent 'in the first instance the working class, in the second the peasantry, and in the third the working intelligentsia'. This, he insists, cannot be so; the 'true class party' can represent only one class. Thereby we are reminded that today the Soviet communist party claims to represent and be made up of the self-same three classes that the SRs once claimed.

The lecture on 'What is a Party?' is full of evasions. There are 'many parties of the working class' but 'only one party of the *proletariat*'. The bourgeoisie has many parties, liberal, conservative, etc., but they are really all 'factions of one bourgeois party'. Zinoviev realizes that this rule may also be applied to the many parties of the working class, making them really all factions of one party. His answer is that the other working-class parties must also be reckoned as 'only factions of the bourgeois party'.

We find names, and even currents of thought, that today are ignored. We learn that the Bund 'in the darkest night of Tsarist reaction was the first to rise in struggle'. We learn of the SRs that 'as long as it was a matter of victory over tsarism, these revolutionists had élan, energy, enthusiasm, and zeal . . . knew what they were fighting for . . . what they were sacrificing themselves for, and from their ranks came such great men as Gershuni'. There is praise for Plekhanov in really moving language. We are told that from Martov's 'instructive' *History of Russian Social-Democracy* we can learn much 'despite its errors'. We learn that Prince Obolensky was a member of the party at the beginning of the century and a contributor to *Iskra*. We will search in vain in all subsequent histories for such nuggets of information. But by using the archaeological method of ranging the various versions of an event side by side, and by probing for the tender spots, we can learn something from even the worst of them.

At last, after the blood purges had re-edited the age of Lenin by turning all his close associates into traitors, save only one, the survivor determined to fix the past himself.

Thus was born the first party history that lived long enough to grow up and circumnavigate the globe, 'the book that', according to *Pravda*, 'has sold more copies than any other in modern times, the work of a genius, *The Short History of the Communist Party of the Soviet Union*, by Joseph Stalin'.[1]

At this point party history was stabilized. No new history appeared for fifteen years. All works in the field, and in many other fields of political, economic, and philosophical writing, became glosses and

---

[1] The book was published in 1938. The *Pravda* quote was published twelve years later. Whether Stalin wrote it, or wrote only parts of it, it bears the unmistakable imprint of his unique temperament. It will hereafter be referred to as Stalin's *Short Course*.

exegeses derived in whole or part from the *Short Course*. There was even a secret Politburo decision that no one was to be permitted to publish anything new about Lenin, while countless already published memoirs were burned or pulped.[1]

Stalin's *Short Course*, though virtually unreadable, could be memorized by the faithful, and indeed, as a life insurance policy, had to be. It performed the function of ensuring that no communist 'need ever be at a loss for the official answer to every problem. No one understood better than Stalin that the true object of propaganda is neither to convince nor even to persuade, but to produce a uniform pattern of public utterance in which the first trace of unorthodox thought immediately reveals itself as a jarring dissonance'.[2] By 1953, fifteen years after its publication, it was still the definitive 'work of genius' and had been printed in editions of more than 50,000,000 copies in the Soviet Union, and in all the important languages of the world.

In March 1953 the author died. In July, some still duller writers calling themselves Agitprop issued 7,500 leaden words of 'Theses on Fifty Years of the Communist Party of the Soviet Union'. They were published in *Pravda* on July 26, 1953. Now the millions who had toiled to learn by heart every formulation in the *Short Course* realized that their 'insurance policy' had been cancelled. For, in the 'Theses', they perceived that Stalin, who until then had been up in front at the right hand of Lenin—the two of them alone re-making the world—was now no longer Leader, no longer co-founder of the party, nor master-mind of the seizure of power, nor creator of the Red Army, nor winner of the civil war.

Indeed, where was he? Lenin was mentioned 83 times in the 7,500 words, Stalin only four. Still worse, the 'Theses' gave no clue as to the current order of precedence. Apart from those of Lenin and Stalin, the only name mentioned was Plekhanov. All safely dead! To the initiated, this was a sign that a new time of uncertainty had begun and that no living name was mentioned because no successor had yet emerged. The only thing that was certain in this new time of uncertainty was that the *Short Course*, all 50,000,000 copies of it, had to be scrapped, and with it all the works of gloss and exegesis.

From the summer of 1953 to the summer of 1959, the much-chronicled Soviet communist party was without any approved history, except for the 7,500 words put out by the Department of Agitation and Propaganda.

Before a new history could be published, Stalin's ghost had to be wrestled with and its size at least tentatively determined. The dictatorship had to beget its new dictator; infallible doctrine its infallible expounder; authoritarianism its authority. The 'collective leadership', so unnatural in a dictatorial society where there are no checks on the

---

[1] The Politburo decision was adopted on August 5, 1938, but kept secret for twenty years. See *Spravochnik partiinovo rabotnika*, 1957, p. 364.

[2] Leonard Schapiro, *The Communist Party of the Soviet Union* (London and New York, 1960), pp. 471-2.

flow of power to the top, had to be disposed of, one by one or in batches, until one only should emerge as the embodiment of the party. Furthermore, the emergent authority had to have time to lay down the line on the problems, persons, and events likely to find their way into history. Only then could a new official history be written. For the present to be projected into the past, the present has to be authoritatively determined. So it was that on June 17, 1959, a new manuscript was given to the press, with instructions to print a first edition of 750,000 copies. This was the history according to Khrushchev.

Not that he claims personal authorship. Khrushchev is free from that pathological greed for credit that made Stalin claim credit for everything. The new history was prepared, like Knorin's in 1935, by an 'authors' collective'—eleven academicians, doctors or masters of 'the historical, economic, and philosophical sciences'.

Where so many histories have perished so swiftly, it was pleasant to find that the *rukovoditel* or leader for the Knorin history, B. N. Ponomarev, has survived the death of his earlier work, and appears as *rukovoditel* once more. And I. I. Mints, who has written so many legendary pages (*legend* is to be taken in its literal not its poetic sense) in histories of the civil war, is alive and present, too, though Stalin once denounced his work. If Ponomarev is once more *rukovoditel*, there is no longer a general editor to replace Knorin. Rather, there are signs on many pages that Khrushchev and his Agitprop secretary, Suslov, themselves took on the political overseer's task. For what we now have is quite manifestly intended to be the official history for the age of Khrushchev.

The history of Russia in the twentieth century has been a turbulent one: conspiracy, party strife, war, general strike and uprising in 1905, world war, fall of the Tsar, seizure of power by the Bolsheviks, civil war and intervention, Kronstadt and NEP, liquidation of the private peasant as a class, purge of all Lenin's closest lieutenants by one of them, Stalin-Hitler Pact, Second World War, struggle for the succession, emergence of Khrushchev. What material for the historian! But if the *Short Course* seemed dull and devoid of actual personages, motives, and events, it had at least a kind of fascination by virtue of the malevolence, the pathological boasting, the touch of the demonic on every page. Though in Khrushchev's *History*, as we shall now call it, whole pages are lifted from the *Short Course*, what was demonic in Stalin's history is only dogmatic in the latest work.

The Khrushchev *History* calls itself a 'concise account'. 'Concise' must be more extensive than 'short', for it is more than twice as long; nor is the additional flood of words altogether accounted for by the fact that an additional twenty years have had to be chronicled. Where formulas of boasting or denigration have not been copied verbatim, the new book is likely to use many more words to recount an episode than the old. Yet its pages seem strangely empty—empty of men, empty of events. In the place of men, there are the party, the government, the masses, and Lenin. In the place of events, there are theses and formulas.

No need to be surprised if the great Bolshevik hold-ups of 1905-1907 are missing; no party historian has spoken of them. But where are the Moscow Trials which formed the closing section of the *Short Course*, like the baleful hell-fire which lights up the last scene of Mozart's *Don Juan*? All of Lenin's close associates save one were tried, confessed, liquidated—surely a chapter in party history by almost any test. But not one word. Twice the party purges of the thirties, in which Nikita Khrushchev played a substantial role, are obscurely hinted at, obscurely justified, and as obscurely called in question. On page 463 we learn that the party was strengthened by purges but 'mistakes were made in the unfounded expulsion of so-called passive elements'. Yet, after the purges, 'two-faced and enemy elements remained in the party', and Kirov's murder 'showed that a party card may be used as the cover for abominable anti-Soviet acts'. Twenty-one pages later we learn that 'many honest communists and non-party people underwent repressions, being guilty of nothing'. But the villains now are Beria and Yezhov. Inexplicably, Yagoda, their predecessor as 'flaming sword of the revolution', is missing, both as the first great purger and as victim and confessed traitor. Just as inexplicably, for time is slippery in this history without a fixed chronological framework, Beria, whom Stalin appointed to call off the fury of the Yezhov purges, here precedes Yezhov.[1]

It is the disappearance of such large events and of so many persons which makes the pages of this thick history seem so interminable and so empty. A standard feature of earlier histories was a list of central committee members elected by each congress, a list of rapporteurs at each congress, and many other such accounts of persons and their posts or their proposals or their deeds. Too bureaucratic to be exciting, it yet peopled the pages of the text. But with each successive history the lists became shorter. More and more men were shifted to the anonymous 'and others'. Now many of those who still found a place in Stalin's *Short Course*, if only to be denounced, have dissolved in the acid of oblivion. Moreover, Khrushchev has names to eliminate from honorific lists whom Stalin delighted to honour as extensions of himself. The indestructible-seeming Molotov, the able and ruthless Kaganovich, who did what he could to forward Khrushchev's advancement, the rotund Malenkov, once Stalin's chief of cadres, a party secretary, a member of the supreme military council during the war, main rapporteur at the

---

[1] Even the delicate allusions and sporadic rehabilitations permitted during the 'thaw' are not to be found. As archives were published and memoirs, long suppressed, were re-published with excisions, footnotes were permitted. The climax of refinement came in the formula used in the brief biographical notes on twelve purged memorialists in Volume II of *Reminiscences of Lenin* (1957), of whom it was said: 'In 1937, he became a victim of enemy slander; later rehabilitated'. Only after the 22nd CPSU congress did rehabilitation become more public; but a large number of hapless souls still remain in limbo.

nineteenth congress, after Stalin's death both General Secretary and Premier—at least for nine days—have ended up without a past, rubbish for the 'anti-party' dustbin.

It is the now largely de-peopled and faceless party which is the protagonist, the party as the instrument of history, carrying out history's mandates and intentions. Its outstanding leader and master may in his last years have been grievously, even monstrously wrong, but the party which did not stay his hand was never wrong, never ceased to carry out history's will. In such a disembodied, uneventful, bureaucratic history, a party congress is an epoch-making event. At the nineteenth congress, shortly before Stalin's death, Molotov made the opening address, Malenkov delivered the main political report, Beria the report on the nationalities problem, Saburov on the fifth five-year plan, Khrushchev, Bulganin, and Mikoyan on the revision of the party statutes, and Kaganovich on the revision of its programme. Dealing now with the congress, the *History* mentions reports, but neither their contents nor the rapporteurs. Only N. S. Khrushchev remains as the sole rapporteur on the party statutes, from which a seven-line quotation rates inclusion in the pages of history.

Even those whom Stalin execrated have suffered further diminution. Stalin still had need of Trotsky as the Antagonist in the drama of good and evil. He had to paint Trotsky as saboteur of each of Trotsky's own chief actions, since one of the aims of the *Short Course* was to replace in men's minds that unity in duality, Lenin-Trotsky, by a new unity in duality, Lenin-Stalin. Thus Trotsky's name was still bound to large events, if only by a minus sign. Though Khrushchev's *History* copies some of these pages from the *Short Course*, he does not have the same need of Trotsky to play Antichrist to his Saviour; hence the baleful glare that lengthened his shadow throughout the *Short Course* is subdued here to a dingy light. The October Revolution takes place without the Chairman of the Petrograd Soviet and Military Revolutionary Committee, who directed the operations of the seizure of power and conceived its strategy. The civil war is fought and the Red Army built without him. The Kronstadt mutiny is gloriously crushed without either his or Tukhachevsky's intervention. Voroshilov has retroactively been appointed director of the attack on Kronstadt, while Marshal Tukhachevsky, who seemed on the way to rehabilitation until Zhukov fell, disappeared once more from history, to be yet again disinterred at the twenty-second congress.

If the climax of Stalin's *Short Course* was the 'Liquidation of the Remnants of the Bukharin-Trotsky Gang of Spies, Wreckers, and Traitors to the Country', which is the actual title of the closing section of its last chapter, the new Khrushchev *History* has no climax. It just stops, because when it was issued the twenty-first (extraordinary) congress was over and the twenty-second had not yet been convened. It was obvious that it would not last the fifteen years of its predecessor, for history would keep adding to its bureaucratic sum, and had already subtracted several of the leaders designated by the twenty-first congress, such as Belyaev and Kirichenko.

Further evidence that the 'Concise Account' is already becoming obsolete, and for really serious purposes unsatisfactory, is to be found in the plan for a new 'many-volumed' history of the party (actually six volumes, the first of which was reported at the end of 1960 as having already gone to press, and the rest as being prepared 'at high speed'). For these, both the archives and many of the earlier histories are being treated as 'useful material'. Most interesting is the partial rehabilitation of Stalin's *Short Course*, which Khrushchev had damned so thoroughly in his 1956 speech. After listing the other histories which enter into the canon of those which in their time 'contained a large amount of factual material . . . but [also] many methodological and theoretical errors', *Voprosy Istorii KPSS* (1960, No. 5), continues:

'From these errors the *Short Course of the History of the VKP* (*b*) was not free either, although it was also for its time a mighty stride forward in the development of party-history science. The fact that this book served for a long time as a peculiar standard for party-historical investigations significantly held back the further scientific working out of problems of the history of the party. Of course, this does not in any degree whatsoever justify the position of those historians who, incorrectly interpreting the decisions of the twentieth congress of the CPSU, tried, under the flag of a struggle against the cult of personality and its consequences, to re-examine some of the fundamental propositions of party theory and policy laid down in the *Short Course* . . . Characteristic of this insignificant number of historians was a nihilistic attitude towards the entire party-historical literature of the late thirties and the forties. They called loudly for a return to the textbooks of the twenties and thirties which contain innumerable theoretical and political errors.

The 'high speed' with which *Voprosy Istorii* promised that its Party History Section would produce the six-volume history, has since met with the usual traffic jam caused by conflicting red and green lights. In June 1962 a flurry of new directives descended on the heads of the historians. In *Pravda* (June 22 and 24) a long article appeared 'On the Forthcoming Many-Volumed History of the CPSU'. From it we learn that the six volumes are to consist of nine parts and to appear by 1967, in time for the fiftieth anniversary of the seizure of power.

The history must continue to reflect the 'irreconcilable struggle' of Lenin and Stalin against the Trotskyists, Left Communists, Democratic Centralists, Workers' Oppositionists, Right Capitulators, National Deviationists. Khrushchev's period is to be given enormously more space and importance:

'The entire content of the many-volumed history must be permeated with the spirit of Leninist ideas, base itself on the Marxist-Leninist

scientific method, the decisions of the party, especially of the twentieth
and twenty-second congresses, must be permeated with the spirit of the
new Programme of the CPSU, the Communist Manifesto of our time.'

In short, it is to be a Khrushchevist history. It is to contain formulas
resolving, at least bureaucratically, the new problems facing Khrushchev.
Thus:

'One of the most important tasks of the work is to reveal the role of
the CPSU in the world communist movement, the international significance
of the experience of the CPSU at all stages of its activity, the influence
of this experience on the successful construction of socialism in a number
of lands of Europe and Asia, on the development of the international
labour and communist movements, and also on the development of the
national-liberation struggles of the peoples of the oppressed lands. . . .
In it will be shown the continuous and consistent struggle of the CPSU
against splitters, revisionists, petit-bourgeois adventurers, dogmatists,
sectarians, for the unity of the international labour and communist
movement on the basis of Marxism-Leninism and proletarian solidarity.'

There is a new and greatly extended check-list of Stalin's errors to be
noted and developed, but once more the critique will be within the
familiar limits and his services, considerably diminished, are once more
to be noted. Once more, also, it must be shown that while these
grievous errors were being committed by the party under Stalin's
orders, the party remained sound and its actions correct. Thus the
authors will be called upon to perform an exercise in apologetic ingenuity unparalleled outside the field of church history and exegesis.
    The directives end, as was to be expected, with a glorification of the
congresses led by Khrushchev. The twentieth, for instance, 'laid the
foundations of a new epoch in the world communist movement' and
'showed that the party, its Leninist Central Committee with N. S.
Khrushchev at its head . . . revealed itself as the centre of the development of Marxist theoretical thought', and the twenty-first and twenty-
second congresses continue the wonders, accompanied by a spate of
rather banal quotations from none other than N. S. Khrushchev.
    Thus Khrushchev is still wrestling with the size of Stalin's ghost.
In a historiography in which everything is made to order according to
party needs, various sizes and patterns have been tried in an effort to
determine Stalin's place in history. To convince ourselves of that we
need only compare the Stalin of the secret speech at the twentieth
congress with the Stalin of the 1959 *History*, and with the grimly
enlarged but still far from complete list of Stalin's 'errors' in the directives on the projected many-volumed history as given in *Pravda*, June
22 and 24, 1962. At present the trend is towards Stalin's further diminution, but his legacy is zealously preserved and built upon. It is
instructive to close this examination with some consideration of the

'cult of personality', the formula which seems to have been the biggest event in party history since the publication and scrapping of the *Short Course*.

On the one hand, there was need to write Stalin smaller than in the *Short Course*, lest all his successors remain too dwarfed for any of them to succeed him. Moreover, his lieutenants, not without cause, so feared each other, and the party so feared the inevitable struggle among them, that it was necessary to give assurances 'that henceforth such occurrences should never again take place in the party and the country'. This was promised by a resolution of the twentieth congress and is repeated in the *History*. In so far as it implies the rejection of the pathological extremes of Stalin's vengeful reign, and seeks to put on him and his purged disciples all the burden of Khrushchev and company's co-responsibility, it may be taken seriously.

On the other hand, Stalin's successor could obscure but not destroy the link which puts him in the line of apostolic succession. For what else but the apostolic succession from Lenin, who seized power, to Stalin, who usurped it by taking over and perfecting Lenin's machine, has the present First Secretary? What other legitimacy and claim to rule over a great empire?

The inheritance includes many things for which the 1959 *History* gives Stalin great credit:

1. The annihilation of all rival parties, such as Mensheviks and Socialist-Revolutionaries and Kadets. (Hence the *History* repeats the absurdities of the frame-up trials of the Mensheviks, the Industrial party, the Toiling Peasant party.)

2. The annihilation of all anti-Stalinist communist groups (Trotskyists, Zinovievites, Bukharinites, for whose views there can be no rehabilitation).

3. Forced industrialization and the primacy of heavy industry over production for consumption.

4. The annihilation of millions of peasants and the forced collectivization of agriculture.

5. Party penetration and control of all organizations and the atomization of the individual. (This is a heritage from Lenin perfected by Stalin and is inseparable from totalitarianism.)

6. Stalin's conquests of the Baltic Republics, half of Poland, part of East Prussia, Finland, and Rumania, and Tannu Tuva.

7. The 'liberation' of the rest of Poland, of Hungary (two 'liberations'), of East Germany *and* Berlin, of the Balkan lands including Yugoslavia, of China, North Korea, and Vietnam.

8. The 'struggle for peace' and the enlargement of the 'peace camp' which permits of, nay requires, the 'liberation' of further parts of the non-communist world but not the 're-enslavement' of any part that has been liberated.

This is a large balance-sheet. In it Stalin's crimes against the Russian people, against the Russian peasants, against allies and neighbours and occupied countries, are all transformed into virtues listed on the credit side of the ledger. His crimes against other socialist and democratic parties and opposition communists are listed as virtues, too, with the sole reservation that he dealt too harshly with 'good communists' (which seems to mean Stalinists) when he liquidated them. Even then, when the guillotine falls on loyal Stalinists, the *History* does not cry 'Crime!' but mumbles 'Error' or 'Harmful consequences of the cult of personality'.

Its final verdict reads: 'Under the leadership of the Communist party and its Central Committee, in which J. V. Stalin played a leading role, the Soviet Union has achieved enormous, world-wide successes. J. V. Stalin did much that was beneficial to the Soviet Union, to the CPSU, and to the whole international workers' movement'.

Thus Khrushchev's tremendous indictment of Stalin's cruelty and paranoia in his secret speech dwindles into a bureaucratic formula for a little praise and much self-serving blame, now that Khrushchev himself is secure in the possession of his heritage.

What, then, is happening to the size of the 'personality' of Nikita Sergeyevich Khrushchev?

To get a perspective, we must bear in mind that this is not the final masterpiece of Khrushchev historiography but only a first attempt, analogous rather to the early efforts of a Yaroslavsky than to Stalin's *chef d'oeuvre*—the *Short Course*. Moreover, Khrushchev has difficulties that Stalin did not have. It is not possible for a man who joined the party only after it had won power to picture himself as one of the party's co-founders. Hence the book's only living hero (the dead heroes being Lenin and Stalin) does not enter into its 745 pages until page 314, then modestly enough as one of a list of Lenin's 'comrades-in-arms and disciples hardened in the civil war . . . on whose backs lay the burden of liquidating the consequences of the war and constructing a socialist society'. The list contains 23 names, in discreet alphabetical order, Stalinists all, and the impartial Russian alphabet puts Khrushchev in the twentieth place and Stalin himself in the eighteenth.

Not until page 608, with the nineteenth congress, does Khrushchev begin seriously to employ the technique of self-enlargement. Here, as we have seen, Molotov who delivered the opening address, Malenkov who delivered the main report, Beria, Kaganovich, and Saburov who reported too, all become unpersons, while Khrushchev holds the vast stage alone.

By the twentieth congress, Khrushchev had such a grip of the party machine that he did in fact hold the stage alone and make all the reports. The order of business was: opening address, Khrushchev; report of the Presidium and Central Committee (covering everything), Khrushchev; chairman of the committee to draw up a resolution on the report, Khrushchev; chairman of the new Bureau on Party Affairs of the Russian Republic, Khrushchev; secret report on the cult of personality,

Khrushchev. Only Bulganin was permitted a sub-report, a gloss on the First Secretary's remarks on the sixth five-year plan, and Bulganin has of course since disappeared from public view.

As for the twenty-first congress, which makes up the final chapter of this book, it had only one order of business: a report on the control figures for the seven-year plan, by Khrushchev. Such is the fitting bureaucratic climax, or anti-climax, to the strange transformation of so many clashes of arms and deeds of blood into bureaucratic formulas. Stalin's closing chapter ends with a quote from Stalin; Khrushchev's with a quote from Khrushchev. The First Secretary and former 'best disciple of Joseph Stalin' has learned his trade.

In each case the closing chapter is followed by a brief coda called 'Conclusion'. In the *Short Course*, Stalin jostles Lenin for first place. Whether it be good sense or greater need, in the conclusion to the new history Lenin and the party are given first place.[1] Yet even here Khrushchev is quoted four times. In the *Short Course* the last words are a quote from Stalin. In the new history Khrushchev bows out three pages before the end, while the last two sentences are eight words from Lenin on the party as 'the intelligence, honour, and conscience of our country' followed by twelve from Marx on communism's promise: 'From each according to his means, to each according to his needs'.

Such is the nature of the party history in which the two new features, lacking in the *Short Course*, are the 'liquidation of the harmful consequences of the cult of personality', and the recording of the substantial beginnings of a new cult.

Of the various learned societies which are beginning to send messages of admiration and appreciation to 'Nikita Sergeyevich personally', the most interesting to us is, of course, that of the historians. On October 20, 1960, the Section of Historical Sciences of the Academy of Sciences of the USSR held a general meeting to discuss the eleventh International Congress of Historical Sciences in Stockholm. The report on this discussion in *Voprosy Istorii* reaches its climactic end with these words, so obviously relevant to the order of business:

At the close of the General Meeting of the Section of Historical Sciences of the Academy, Academician N. M. Druzhinin read a letter addressed to the First Secretary of the Central Committee of the Communist Party of the Soviet Union, the Chairman of the Council of Ministers of the USSR, N. S. Khrushchev:
Dear Nikita Sergeyevich!
The General Meeting of the Section . . . warmly congratulates you, dear Nikita Sergeyevich, on the great and important successes achieved

[1] The final section of the directives for the six-volume history quotes only Khrushchev; Lenin gets in only when he appears in one of these Khrushchev quotations.

by you at the Fifteenth Session of the General Assembly of the UN [the session in which Khrushchev took his shoe off] . . . You displayed such many-sided and fruitful activity in the interests of the happiness and progressive development of the whole of humanity.

Your passionate and untiring struggle for peace . . . for general disarmament, for immediate liquidation of colonialism, has won for you the deepest gratitude of all honest people. Your amazing capacity for clearly and simply explaining the high humanist principles of our advanced Marxist-Leninist ideology exercises the most powerful influence on the widest masses of people on our planet.

We historians, specializing as we do in the study of the great events of the past, can easily distinguish in the contemporaneity of present events also those which have a transcendent historical significance.

We do not doubt that your activity at the Fifteenth Session of the General Assembly of the UN will go down in the annals of history as a most valuable contribution to the cause of the struggle for peace, as a bold and far-sighted act worthy of an outstanding statesman of the Leninist type. Proud of the fact that at the head of the Soviet Government stands a man who so well understands the basic needs and demands of our epoch, we, from the bottom of our hearts, wish you good health and the continuance for long years of your inexhaustible energy in the pursuit of the goals of the fastest resolution of the gigantic historical tasks placed on the order of the day—the freeing of mankind from wars and the evils connected with them, and disarmament.

The resolution was adopted unanimously by all who attended the meeting.[1]

After this conclusion to the discussion of the Stockholm congress, there could be no doubt that the *Concise History* issued in 1959 was already out of date, and that a drastic revision was needed, particularly of its closing sections. Small wonder that *Voprosy Istorii KPSS* (1960, No. 5), found editorially that the *History of the Communist Party of the Soviet Union*, issued in 1959, though it 'gives a Marxist-Leninist illumination of the basic stages of the historical road travelled by the CPSU up to our days, nevertheless is only a short textbook, in which, naturally, the many-sided activity of our party in its fullness and concreteness cannot be given'. And, indeed, in 1962 a new revised edition of the *History* was published, making the appropriate changes in the light of the 22nd congress of the CPSU. No sooner had it appeared than there were indications that it was already out of date and that further revisions were necessary to bring past history in line with the ever-changing present requirements.

What we can look forward to now is a six-volume work[2] with the

---

[1] *Voprosy Istorii*, 1960, No. 12, p. 113.

[2] *Pravda* (September 28, 1963) announced that all the 9 books of the 6-volume edition will appear between now and the 50th anniversary of the October revolution. By that time they will almost certainly be obsolete.

sixth volume devoted to the age of Khrushchev, and, at the same time, a new version of the 1962 history, or a succession of versions, in each of which the 'historians specializing in the study of the past' will also show that they 'can easily distinguish in the contemporaneity of events those which have a transcendent historical significance'. Can anyone doubt that what they are distinguishing now so clearly are the great deeds and thoughts, and the steadily expanding figure of Nikita Sergeyevich Khrushchev?

DISCUSSION

Introducing his paper, Mr Wolfe said Mussolini had offered the first definition of totalitarianism—all for the State, nothing against the State, nothing outside the State. Bolshevism had a different definition—all for the party, nothing against the party, nothing outside the party; the State was merely another transmission belt for the party. The subject to be discussed, party history, was therefore central to the Soviet regime.

The party was an infallible party, possessed of an infallible doctrine, blessed with an infallible leader and interpreter of that doctrine, who could stretch it to fit any conceivable situation without ever falling into heresy or revisionism. Its decisions concerning past, present, and future, its explanations of those decisions, and its actions determined what was meant by *partiinost* in the writing of party history. In other words, the history of the CPSU was Marxism-Leninism in action.

The writing of party history was a dangerous task. As *Pravda* reminded historians in 1960, they must always be aware that sharp ideological struggles in the workers' movement were accompanied by ferocious battles in historiography. *Voprosy Istorii* in the same year stated that the science of the history of the party occupied an outstanding place in the ideological struggle of the communist party for the revolutionary transformation of society. As such, party history had two main divisions: first, the history of the struggle with all other parties and with society as a whole; second, the history of the struggle of factions, cliques, policies, and individuals within the party itself.

The aim of the first branch was to destroy all rival parties, to remove the very traces of their views and activities in the past, to re-make Soviet man according to the image in a blueprint possessed by the party leaders in the Kremlin. The task of the second branch of party history was to create a single infallible body of doctrine and to re-make the party from an ordinary assemblage of disparate and differing human beings with some basic views in common into what Stalin so aptly called a monolith—a rather inhuman image suggesting a tombstone rather than a living party organization.

In the course of this second struggle, each contender for the leadership of the party had become either his own historian or the patron of historians obedient to his interests; at the same time he became the suppressor of historians who had favoured his opponents, and even of those who had expressed views which he no longer held.

The first historian who had provided the basic pattern of this process was Lenin himself. Lenin felt it necessary in every large or small struggle to write a thumb-nail history as part of his polemic. He also favoured two types of historian: the general Marxist historians like Pokrovsky, whose main task was to engage in controversy with the outside world, with other parties, and with society in general; and the comparatively unimportant Bolshevik faction historians, of whom Lyadov was a characteristic type.

The year 1923, when Lenin was near death, was a watershed in the writing of party history. In that year Zinoviev delivered his six lectures on the history of the Russian communist party, and Trotsky wrote the much more momentous *Lessons of October 1917*. These two books became the two poles of a new dispute concerning party history. They were aimed against each other with a view to the impending struggle for the succession. But the man who actually took over the succession, Stalin, began a new epoch in party history.

Although Stalin himself occasionally imitated Lenin with a trivial excursion into party history, he usually left the job to his adherents, of whom Yaroslavsky was typical. Although all these Stalinist historians were loyally writing books designed to enlarge the stature of Stalin, his doctrines, and his machine, the mortality rate among them was high. One book after another was in its time official, published by the Communist International, translated into many languages, reproduced in millions of copies, and then suddenly found inadequate and discarded. As a result of this endless succession of party histories, party historiography was affected by a profound crisis, and at last Stalin decided to supervise the writing of the definite party history—the famous *Short Course*. From 1938 to 1953 nothing substantial happened in the field of party history. 1953 put an end to fifteen years of stagnation and introduced a period of such confusion that no party history could be written. The *Short Course* was rejected, but nothing was put in its place. No new party history could appear so long as that makeshift device in a totalitarian system—collective leadership—filled the gap.

By 1959, however, a new party leader had emerged. He did not and might never occupy the place filled by the figure of Stalin, but he was the boss, who could declare his opponents not anti-Khrushchev but 'anti-party'. Once this point had been reached, a new party history was possible. It had not yet been explicitly approved by the central committee, or extolled as the *Short Course* had been. It was merely the first tentative essay in Khrushchevite party historiography, which would no doubt be superseded as circumstances changed. Although the 1959 history appeared to glorify the party and the central committee, it was really a glorification of Lenin and an attempt to link Khrushchev's name with his. One reason for the new party programme, attributed to Khrushchev, was to demonstrate that no one had been able to write a party programme since 1919. (Though the 1919 programme was largely written by Bukharin, it was now entirely attributed to Lenin.)

Mr Schapiro said that official party histories were not the work of historians but of politicians. He did not agree that the 1959 *History* was to be regarded as a transitional, tentative volume which would be amended when Khrushchev's position had been further strengthened. 1938, when the *Short Course* appeared, was a watershed, the end of the *Yezhovshchina*, the final consolidation of Stalin's position; the ripe moment for a re-statement of the whole position within the party. In some respects 1959 was a similar moment—a watershed after the process of destalinization and the struggle for the succession. Mr Schapiro doubted that the new party history would be re-written before Mr Khrushchev had gone and the succession had been settled.

Nevertheless, the new party history, like the *Short Course*, was primarily a political instrument; normal standards of historical assessment were inapplicable. Every government, but especially a revolutionary government, was concerned to establish its legitimacy. The legitimacy of the Russian communist party as a governing body from 1917 onwards rested on the fiction that its seizure of power was then and has ever since been supported by the proletarian masses; no party that intended to remain in power could allow this to be questioned. No history worth the name could be written with this incorrect assumption as its starting-point. Today, the legitimacy of the party's seizure of power was no longer an issue; the main problem was to uphold the legitimacy of the party supremacy in the State, i.e. the claim that the party had an inherent right to direct and control all public activities. Even to a Russian living in the Soviet Union it was not obvious that a factory director, who knew his job inside out, ought to be told by the party what to do; nor was it immediately obvious why a poet should be told how to write poetry by a party *apparatchik*. This right had to be constantly re-asserted—and now by methods more complex than Stalin's, who in his own inimitable way had relied simply on force. One of the vital points this kind of history tried to drive home was precisely the divine right of the party always to be superior in wisdom to the various State institutions that were subordinated to it. The party leadership was very much aware of the risks involved in the slightest challenge to party control. So long as party supremacy survived, it was unreasonable to expect official histories to be anything other than what they were. Fortunately, these official histories did not exhaust the entire writing on party history. There were works like Kozmin's history of the Russian section of the First International, or Tvardovskaya's study of *Narodnaya Volya*; these historians had been allowed to engage in real research within given limitations.

Professor Fainsod agreed that the question of what the function of party history is had to be answered largely in terms of a search for legitimacy. And because history could not stand still and change was inevitable, we were going to have more party histories, altered versions and changing myths in pursuance of this perpetual search.

In a certain sense, party history had never been more important and more difficult: important because with the abandonment of naked force and the necessity to seek consent, party history became an instrument of the search and so had to become more persuasive and more credible; difficult because the vocabulary of Agitprop was of little use in establishing a connection with the real problems of the daily life of new generations raised in changing circumstances. Moreover, there was a new challenge to party infallibility now from within the communist world itself, in the form of Chinese, Yugoslav, or Polish versions of party history. The problem was still one of *Gleichschaltung*, but in circumstances where co-ordination was much more difficult to attain. This imposed a new task on the party historian; in seeking to justify the power and the tactics of the ruling apparatus, he was inevitably forced on to a more rational plane. Professor Fainsod believed this process was bound to go on; Khrushchev could not rest on the party history of 1959.

Mr McLane doubted whether the writing of a suitable party history was of crucial importance to Khrushchev personally. Granted that Stalin did attach a great deal of significance to the *Short Course* (out of vanity and egocentricism as much as for political reasons), the same was not necessarily true of Khrushchev, who was a person of very different temperament and personality. Khrushchev had shown little more than casual interest in a new party history—it was indeed striking how little notice the book had received in Soviet journals.

It was easy to poke fun at the party histories, but it should be remembered that any strong autocracy with an ideology or religion would seek to articulate its past in a document that for the faithful was meant to be infallible. In the USSR this happened to be the party history. Whatever Khrushchev's personal interest in such a history, its appearance was entirely normal under a regime such as that of the Soviet Union. Like papal encyclicals, which in the past performed to some extent the same function in regard to the Roman Catholic Church, party histories were necessary and even serious testaments of the regimes and ideologies they recorded. To ridicule them seemed to Mr McLane a rather idle exercise.

Mr Labedz thought Mr Schapiro's and Mr Wolfe's differing views about the prospects of the new party history could be reconciled in the sense that the book would not be scrapped, but would go through several editions. Slight changes from the original could already be found in the English translation, and it was likely that this tendency would persist in future editions, especially in any new chapters on the twenty-second congress. He agreed with the previous speaker that the ritual of re-writing had come to be accepted as something quite natural. But unlike Mr McLane, he regarded both papal encyclicals and party histories as ideal targets for ridicule.

According to Mr Nikolaevsky, the real point about the writing of Soviet party history was that from the very start it had been linked with the struggle for the right to write freely on these issues. 'Free' was a relative and changing concept; nevertheless there had been constant attempts to widen the boundaries of the possible. In one sense Ponomarev's history was worse than Stalin's because it omitted more. For instance, in regard to the pre-revolutionary period, Stalin had touched on a far wider range of problems than Ponomarev. The policy of the present dictatorship was to say as little as possible about old issues.

Mr Nikolaevsky believed it was necessary to organize research in the West on the Soviet Union. There was a pressing need for the systematic collecting and editing of documents on Soviet history, because the mass of material supplied by thousands of Soviet volumes was one-sided and unrepresentative, and foreign authors who were obliged to rely on them could not fail to be misled in some measure by their tendentious and arbitrary selection. Two interesting books had recently been published in the Soviet Union: a collection of materials on the history of the Cheka, and an analysis of these documents; but the point was that a far richer and more balanced selection of such materials could be made from libraries and archives abroad. Even if the Soviet historian collected all the documents relating to his subject, he published only what was expedient from the point of view of current party policy. A historian concerned with the history of the Soviet Union should realize that there history was still politics projected into the past.

Mr Laqueur thought it would be interesting to establish to what degree the habit of re-writing history in the Soviet Union was unique; he doubted whether every totalitarian system had an immediate and urgent need for a history of its own. Though the Nazis had destroyed pre-1933 history books which presented facts unpalatable to them, and had partly withdrawn and partly re-cast the main Nazi guide after the 'night of the long knives' in 1934, neither Nazi Germany nor Fascist Italy had official party histories. It was at least possible to imagine that with the gradual erosion of ideology the Soviet Union might in the long run be able to do with less party history than it seemed to need just now.

Mr Laqueur noted that nowadays Soviet journals frequently reviewed foreign books and publications—a foreigner might even have a whole volume devoted to him. But this did not apply to party history. Although some years ago *Voprosy Istorii* had promised to review extensively Mr Carr's work, it had in fact not done so.[1] It was no accident that a long review of Mr Schapiro's book in the Soviet press had been written not by a Russian, but by a British communist. Histories of other communist parties were not reviewed at all; this was a curious omission at a time when Soviet writers were encouraged to extend their range.

Mr Kux noted that the *Short Course* had a special chapter on dialectical materialism, which after 1938 became dogma for Soviet ideology. The 1959 party history had no such ideological chapter, but there seemed to have been discussions on whether to include one: in the autumn of 1958 the East German journal *Einheit*, reporting a debate

[1] It was reviewed in *Istoriya SSSR*, 1963, No. 4.

C

between East German and Soviet party historians, published a draft of the new party history which included a final chapter on 'The Road from Socialism to Communism'; when the party history came out, the ideological chapter had been omitted, but it might well be included in future revised editions.

Mr Lasky returned to the question of the importance of a party history for the Soviet system. Mr Kux had suggested that all totalitarian systems had recourse to a similar type of party history, whereas Mr McLane thought it was pure accident what kind of book a society of this type produced as its central official text—a history of the Soviet Union, or a biography of Joseph Stalin might have served the purpose just as well as a party history. In Mr Lasky's opinion, the choice was determined by the structure of power within the society: in an absolute monarchy it would be sufficient to produce a brief biography insisting on the divine right of the monarch; in a national state like the Germany of the late nineteenth century, the search for legitimacy, or the problem of identity, would require a national history instead of a party history; in a totalitarian society of the type of Nazi Germany, *Mein Kampf* (which was not a history) symbolized the central image of power which, in complete contrast to the Soviet Union, was one of enthusiastic, personal, committed loyalty to the *Fuehrer*; given the structure of the Soviet Union, it seemed natural that the central document would not be a history of Russia or of the Soviet Union, nor a biography of any leader, however megalomaniac, but precisely a party history—for this was the essential basis of Bolshevik rule and authority.

Dr Utechin noted that Mr Wolfe's survey of Soviet party histories made no mention of the role of Beria's pamphlet on the history of Bolshevik organizations in Transcaucasia. It had been the prototype of Stalinist history, i.e. not just a slanted history, but a fictitious one. The fact that it was published in 1935 underlined the point made by Mr Nikolaevsky—that year was a watershed. He also agreed with Mr Nikolaevsky that on many points the 1959 party history contained even less information than the *Short Course*. It did not, for example, mention the Bolshevik faction split in 1904; true, the *Short Course* had suppressed the fact that Lenin had actually been expelled from the central committee early in 1905, but it did refer to the moves made by the central committee to restrain Lenin.

Mr Schram endorsed Mr Lasky's contention that every system seeks to establish its legitimacy in terms of its own inner logic. Looking through a German newspaper of 1934, he had come quite by chance upon a lecture by a party functionary to historians and teachers of history as to how history should be written: the whole emphasis was to be put on the *Fuehrerprinzip* and on the basic racial factors without which all civilizations went to pieces. Soviet leaders based their legitimacy on party history—history because they were the heirs of Marx, and party history because they were the heirs of Lenin.

Replying to the discussion, Mr Wolfe took up the question whether the Soviet re-writing of history was unique. It was true that at all times men had a tendency to put the best face on their deeds; it was equally true that earlier regimes had wielded sufficient centralized power to keep the historian on a string. But these analogies were false; we lived in an age with a new concept of history: with due regard to all our prejudices and foibles, we nevertheless aspired to the writing of honest history. This was an age of research, of reproduction of archives all over the world; we were using sound tests of scholarship, and because the Russians knew this, they tried to delude us by a sham apparatus of footnotes and documents. One should not be misled by false analogies which blurred essential differences.

Mr Wolfe agreed with Mr Schapiro that the history of the party was politics rather than history; he was less sure about the party being the hero of the 1959 history; in the long run, the party was only the hero when it was embodied in an infallible leader-interpreter. He believed that party historiography was once again moving in the direction of the personalization of party history. The 1959 volume introduced Khrushchev as soon as it decently could (he was obviously too young to figure in the early pages) and throughout the latter part his stature grew until in the last chapter there were actually more quotations from Khrushchev than there had been quotations from Stalin in the last chapter of the *Short Course*. It was another question whether Khrushchev would ever attain, or even desired to attain, as monumental a stature as Stalin's. The personalization of party history was not a question of personal vanity, but of the structure of the communist party, which required a single infallible interpreter, and that was the role now performed by Khrushchev.

The question of the search for legitimacy was especially difficult for the Bolshevik regime. A monarchical despotism based its legitimacy on hereditary succession; republican legitimacy was conferred by suffrage from below. But this was a regime that had proclaimed a permanent dictatorship, and had gradually drained the republican institutions of independent life. It could therefore never achieve legitimacy in the real sense and would always remain uneasy about it. Party history was one of its counterfeit weapons for legitimization.

Was it right to compare party histories in Russia, Germany, and Italy, and to use 'totalitarianism' as a common denominator for all these systems? Mr Wolfe thought that to discern similarities was not to overlook differences—because we recognized resemblances between anthropoid apes and man, we did not think of ourselves as monkeys. Modern totalitarianism was a new phenomenon, different from classic despotism: it aimed to be all-embracing, to decide the style of life in every field, and it had the technological means to enforce this ubiquitous control. There had been no party history in Hitler's Germany because Nazi ideology was much more sketchy and it was quite sufficient to have *Mein Kampf*, the history of the German *Volk*, the dogma of race, and the image of the infallibility of the *Fuehrer*. The important thing in

Germany and Italy had been the movement. The communist party was quite a different phenomenon with a different past, springing from an entirely different tradition, that of the socialist parties of the nineteenth century; the party history was thus inevitably the central document of the Soviet regime.

III. Continuity and Change in the new History of the CPSU

LEONARD SCHAPIRO

The new *History of the Communist Party of the Soviet Union*, which was published in book form in June 1959, naturally invited comparison with the famous *Short Course*, and commentators quite rightly pointed out that, from the point of view of standards of scholarship, the new history showed little advance on the old. However, as the appearance of the first official party history since the death of Stalin is an event of at least as much political as historiographical significance, analysis of its contents by itself tells one little. It is necessary first to take a glance both at the circumstances which preceded its publication and at the place which seems to have been assigned to it in propaganda and scholarship.

The assault on the rigid heritage of Stalin's era in the field of party history preceded the twentieth congress of the party, and was in full swing at all events by 1955. The attack was led by *Voprosy Istorii*, and particularly by its editor, Pankratova, and deputy editor, Burdzhalov. These two stalwart Stalinists—or so they had seemed while Stalin was alive—evidently took upon themselves the main burden of trying to shift the dead hand of the *Short Course*, which, so long as it remained authoritative, virtually stultified all serious research on party history by its rigid and usually completely inaccurate formulations. In 1955 *Voprosy Istorii* (No. 6) severely criticized a new course of lectures on party history, prepared by the department of Marxism-Leninism of Moscow University, for its failure to depart from the rigid framework of the *Short Course* and in general for its lack of relation to reality. *Voprosy Istorii* did not however succeed (no doubt, in the light of later events, because of opposition to Pankratova and Burdzhalov emanating from other members of the editorial board) in supplying the deficiency itself; the material it published before 1956 on party history was of little value. Both Pankratova and Burdzhalov were very outspoken in their criticism of this output of their own journal at a readers' conference held in January 1956. Burdzhalov, in particular, attacked authors who wrote about party history (he was referring in particular to works on the revolutionary year 1905) as if 'on the one side had stood the Tsar, the liberal bourgeoisie, the SRs and the Mensheviks, and on the other the Bolsheviks alone', and severely attacked the *Short Course*. He also reiterated a criticism, of which more was to be heard soon, that historians of the party were in fact writing without basing their work on original documents. It was a very heated debate, in which Burdzhalov was sharply reproved by Professor Kostomarov of Moscow University —who was, no doubt, rankling under the criticism directed against the course of lectures sponsored in his university.[1]

For the time being, however, Pankratova and Burdzhalov were able to hold their own. At the twentieth congress in February Mikoyan took up the attack against the backward state of party history, and Pankratova warmly supported him on lines which were by now familiar. With the full blessing of the party behind them, or so it must then have appeared, Pankratova and Burdzhalov now launched the attack in the pages of *Voprosy Istorii*. The leading article of the next issue (1956, No. 3) stressed several points: the need for better research and especially— here was obviously a sore point—the need to study the joint Bolshevik-Menshevik committees such as existed during 1917, instead of suppressing the very fact of their existence; and the need to deal more boldly with the fact that the party was in a general state of ideological disarray in 1917 before the arrival of Lenin in Petrograd. The article also complained about the valueless scholarship of the fourth edition of Lenin's works, as contrasted with that of the earlier editions; as well as the fact that stenographic accounts of party congresses had become 'bibliographical rarities'. Lastly, it was suggested that a special new journal should be created to deal with party history. Carrying precept into practice, the journal in its succeeding issues during 1956 printed a series of articles and notes, attacking such failings as the doctoring of source materials and memoirs, and providing a series of studies on the controversial issues of 1917, in particular, an article by Burdzhalov 'On the Tactics of the Bolsheviks in March and April 1917', which was soon to become famous.

Burdzhalov's article appeared in May. Attacks on it appeared very soon after,[2] but it required the events in Poland and Hungary to take their effect before the victory of Burdzhalov's enemies was complete. On March 9, 1957 a decree of the central committee[3] dismissed Burdzhalov, and severely reprimanded Pankratova. The board of *Voprosy Istorii* was now completely re-organized, although Pankratova was not removed from her post as chief editor (she died, however, soon after). Burdzhalov, who was, among other things, accused of 'violating the principles of collective leadership' on the editorial board, for some years vanished from the world of scholarship.[4] A further indirect attack on him by Bugaev, without however mentioning his name, appeared in *Kommunist* in 1962 (No. 6, p. 20). This included the ingenious suggestion that in denigrating Stalin for his wavering policy in

---

[1] *Voprosy Istorii*, 1956, No. 2.

[2] E.g. by Bugaev in *Partiinaya Zhizn*, 1956, No. 14.

[3] *Spravochnik partiinovo rabotnika*, 1957, p. 381.

[4] No articles by him are listed in the official bibliography of articles after 1956. He was next heard of in December 1962 (see above, p. 14).

1917, Burdzhalov had revealed his own Stalinism by exaggerating Stalin's importance. Several facts suggest that the original attack on Burdzhalov came primarily from the apparatus of the central committee, though it may be assumed, in Soviet conditions, that a number of academics could be found to support it. In the first place, the criticism of his article was launched by E. Bugaev, who then headed a section of Agitprop, and whose subsequent posts as chief editor of *Voprosy Istorii KPSS* and thereafter of *Partiinaya Zhizn* are a measure of his importance in the field of official ideological leadership. And secondly, when, following upon a central committee decree of January 12, 1957,[1] the new journal *Voprosy Istorii KPSS* came into existence in July 1957, its first editor was G. D. Obichkin, then the director of the Institute of Marxism-Leninism, and an official rather than an historian. Obichkin was a member of the editorial board of *Voprosy Istorii* as reorganized in 1953 after Stalin's death, and may be presumed to have been one of those who came into conflict with Pankratova and Burdzhalov. It soon became apparent that one of the intended functions of *Voprosy Istorii KPSS* was to provide official correction to the formulations as published in *Voprosy Istorii*, and thus to convey directives for the new history which was by then in course of preparation. Thus, the control of the new *History* was by 1957 taken over by the apparatus of the party and removed from the influence of the more genuine historians. It would seem that there must at some stage have been a change in the board of editors responsible for preparing the *History*, because Pankratova, who is known to have been a member of this board in 1956, no longer appears in the list of members of the board in the published volume. She was, of course, no longer alive at the date of publication, but in ordinary circumstances it is customary to list deceased members of editorial boards. The board is headed by an important member of the party apparatus, B. N. Ponomarev, and its members include I. I. Mints, who was one of the historians used to formulate the new directives on party history in the early issues of *Voprosy Istorii KPSS*, and I. M. Volkov, one of the members of the board of *Voprosy Istorii* dismissed after Stalin's death.

It was therefore a foregone conclusion that the new *History* when it appeared would be a statement of what the party considered to be the politically expedient view of its own past rather than an objective attempt to describe what actually happened. In this respect the *History* is similar to the *Short Course*, but a very different picture emerges when one considers the reception and influence of the two treatises. The *Short Course* was known to have been at the least edited and approved by the leader himself, and it was launched by an elaborate decree of the central committee on November 14, 1938. This made it abundantly clear that the new textbook was not only to be the basis of all political education, but was to become the only source of propaganda to the exclusion of all others, and in particular to the exclusion of primary

[1] *Spravochnik partiinovo rabotnika*, 1957, p. 372.

sources. The propagation of its virtues and authority continued unabated until Stalin's death. The treatment of the *History* has been very different. It has never been sponsored by the central committee. Indeed, after the laudatory reviews which followed its publication in the two leading party journals, it has received very little mention or publicity. Its dissemination abroad has, to say the least, been somewhat leisurely— the English translation, for example, appeared only in April 1961, nearly two years after the Russian edition. It is presumably still used for party training in official political courses, and in February 1962 it was officially stated that over five million copies of the new *History* had been distributed. But it is a curious fact that in several instances where it would have been natural to expect an official endorsement of the *History* no mention of it appears. For example, six months after its appearance a long decree of the central committee on the 'Tasks of party propaganda in present day conditions'[1] contained both criticism of the *Short Course* and injunctions on the importance of studying party history, yet made no reference in this context, as would have seemed natural, to the virtues of the new textbook. Or again, when in 1960 the section on party history of the department of social studies of the Ministry of Education prepared a new programme for the study of party history, it did not include the new *History* in its list of pre-scribed reading.[2]

More important, perhaps, is the difference in the effect of the two textbooks on subsequent academic work. The *Short Course*, as was plainly intended by Stalin, virtually put an end to all research on party history, and in particular, as was repeatedly stated by its critics after Stalin's death, caused the virtual disappearance of all source materials from the purview of scholars. Not so the *History*. Since its appearance, the publication of reasonably scholarly editions of the early party congresses and conferences has continued. Collections of documents of local party organizations have proliferated, and some of these at any rate have violated the accepted canons of scholarship as laid down in the *History* and in *Voprosy Istorii KPSS*[3] by actually including documents of Menshevik origin. Even *Voprosy Istorii KPSS* has published a few documentary studies based on archive material, though without any comment, which flatly contradict the new canon. For example, after the disgrace of Burdzhalov, the new journal was at great pains to correct his unlicensed disclosure (of what was indeed the fact) that there existed throughout 1917 at the lower levels of the party a strong trend towards Bolshevik-Menshevik unification, in spite of Lenin's policy in the matter. Yet two long analyses of party organizations in 1917 by V. V. Anikeyev, published by *Voprosy Istorii KPSS* in 1958 (Nos. 2 and 3) show quite clearly that no fewer than 351 party organiza-

---

[1] *Spravochnik sekretaria pervichnoi partiinoi organizatsii* (Moscow, 1960), pp. 417-42.

[2] *Voprosy Istorii KPSS*, 1960, No. 5.

[3] Ibid., 1958, No. 4, p. 8.

tions remained joint Bolshevik-Menshevik organizations, in many cases as late as September or October 1917. Nor is the *History* immune from criticism. For example, in the somewhat barren discussion of the 'periodization' of party history in progress in 1961 in connection with the projected multi-volume party history, the sub-division adopted by the *History* has been freely criticized.[1] Most important, perhaps, occasional works of real scholarship have not been inhibited. Outstanding among these is Yu. Z. Polevoy's study of the origins of Marxism in Russia between 1883 and 1894,[2] which in effect flatly contradicts the *History*, and for that matter Lenin too, by showing that a workers' movement of Marxist orientation was developing in Russia quite independently of Plekhanov's Liberation of Labour group. Polevoy's book was, it is true, violently attacked by *Pravda* (July 27, 1960) for its 'objectivist spirit' and for its 'departures from the Leninist principle of *partiinost*'. Yet the book remains on sale, and has apparently been rehabilitated, since a review in *Kommunist* in December 1960, though critical in some respects, squarely recognizes the value of the work as a contribution to scholarship. In short, if, as seems probable, the intention of the party apparatus was to create a final and authoritative canon of the correct interpretation of party history, it cannot be said to have entirely succeeded.

The row which exploded in the spring of 1957 and ended with the disgrace of Burdzhalov turned almost entirely on the treatment by the historians of the relationship between the Bolsheviks and the Mensheviks, although its repercussions probably included a general reminder to historians that they were not to presume to let the facts speak for themselves if the facts happened to conflict with the party line. The decree of the central committee of March 9, 1957, which reprimanded Pankratova and dismissed Burdzhalov, criticized the treatment of party history by *Voprosy Istorii*: in its leading article of No. 3 in 1956 and in Burdzhalov's article in the following issue the journal had 'blurred the differences of principle between the Bolsheviks and the Mensheviks on so fundamental a question as that of the hegemony of the proletariat in the revolution'; it had 'embellished' the part played by the Mensheviks and 'understated the role of the Bolsheviks in the revolution of 1905'; it had failed to offer 'Leninist criticism' of the splitting tactics of the Mensheviks, and of their opportunism; moreover, in dealing with the struggles of the party against the Trotskyists and the right opportunists, the journal had suppressed the fact that in their struggle against the party these oppositionists had 'overstepped the bounds of Soviet legality'.

To deal with the last accusation first: it was a reflection of the reaction which set in among the party leaders against over-hasty denigration of Stalin, of which the Hungarian uprising had been one result. Khrushchev's speech at the twentieth party congress had certainly gone far

---

[1] Ibid., 1960, No. 6; 1961, No. 2.

[2] Yu. Z. Polevoy, *Zarozhdenie marksizma v Rossii 1883-1894 gg.* (Moscow, 1959).

C*

enough to suggest that the purges and trials of the oppositionists were a frame-up, and that while their political activities were rightly condemned, the accusation that they were traitors was the product of Stalin's diseased imagination. By the spring of 1957 a more cautious attitude was considered necessary, and this would in due course be reflected in the *History*.

So far as the first group of accusations was concerned, it was true that a number of writers in *Voprosy Istorii*, including Burdzhalov, had discussed the role of the Mensheviks with greater regard for the facts than had been known in Soviet writing on party history since the early thirties. They had, in sum, committed the unpardonable sin of looking at the sources instead of repeating the absurdities of the *Short Course* on this question. And the result of looking at the sources was, of course, to produce such unpalatable conclusions as the fact that in 1905 the Mensheviks had been every bit as revolutionary as the Bolsheviks; or that the main blow against the Provisional Government in February 1917, the setting up of the Petrograd Soviet, had been the work of the Mensheviks and not the Bolsheviks; or that before the arrival of Lenin in Petrograd in 1917, and even after, there was considerable identity of views and indeed of organization between Bolsheviks and Mensheviks, and that the party picture of shining revolutionary truth on the one side and opportunist treachery on the other was a myth. It was, however, this myth which the party authorities were determined to force upon the historians. They did not confine themselves to the criticism contained in the decree of March 9th, or in the more detailed and expanded version of its accusations contained in the leading article of *Voprosy Istorii* (1957, No. 3) appropriately headed 'For Leninist *Partiinost* in Historical Science'. A series of articles was now put into preparation, which was clearly designed to undo the harm which Burdzhalov and his like had done by their un-Leninist objectivity, and these articles began to appear in the new journal, *Voprosy Istorii KPSS*, starting with its first issue, in July 1957. An examination of some of these articles reveals what was now to become the party line on the subject of the Mensheviks, to be reflected in due course in the *History*. The task of putting Burdzhalov right on 1917 was entrusted to Bugaev.[1] He had already crossed swords with Burdzhalov in 1956, but Burdzhalov, who knew the sources rather better than Bugaev, had then still been in a position to reply.[2] With Burdzhalov now conveniently kept out of the way with the help of the secular arm, Bugaev's arguments could at any rate enjoy the security of not being contradicted, even if they did not convince. The picture which Bugaev sought to present is one which shows the Petrograd Bolsheviks in 1917 as outright, consistent revolutionaries from the start, and the Mensheviks, to use his elegant phrase, as 'opportunist offal' (*shval*). The setting up

---

[1] E. I. Bugaev, 'K voprosu o taktike partii v marte—nachale aprelia 1917 goda', *Voprosy Istorii KPSS*, July 1957, No. 1.

[2] *Voprosy Istorii*, 1956, No. 8.

of the Petrograd Soviet by the Mensheviks is admitted, but explained by the fact that the Bolsheviks were too busy fighting in the streets to occupy themselves with work in committees. While there were some waverings and mistakes before the arrival of Lenin, including some hesitancy by Stalin which he himself later admitted, Burdzhalov's treatment of the indecision and dissensions in the party was slanderous. In spite of the persistence of some joint organizations of Bolsheviks and Mensheviks, this did not represent any movement for social-democratic unity on the part of the Bolsheviks, whose sole aim was to win the workers away from the opportunist Mensheviks by exposing them. It is of interest to note that Bugaev's reiterated attack on Burdzhalov for his 'Stalinism' printed in 1962 (which was referred to above) goes much further than Burdzhalov ever did in depicting wavering and indecision by many Bolsheviks other than Stalin before Lenin's arrival in Petrograd. But by 1962 this had become a convenient part of Bugaev's case against the historians whom he had helped to push into oblivion.

Two other articles must be mentioned, since they fall into this class of directives for the new history, then in course of preparation. One, by Professor I. I. Mints (of the editorial board of the *History*) entitled 'Throwing light on certain questions of the great October revolution',[1] was said to be based on his examination of no fewer than five hundred university dissertations submitted on the subject. Like Bugaev, Mints was mainly concerned to stress the revolutionary nature of the Bolsheviks, and, again like Bugaev, by careful selection of material and by omitting the evidence which does not suit his case, Mints has no difficulty in establishing his proposition. It is indeed beyond doubt that the rank and file of the party in 1917 were for the most part straining for action and highly revolutionary: but what Burdzhalov was dealing with was the party leadership, where the issues were not so clear-cut. Once again, Mints is mainly concerned to combat any idea that the Mensheviks might have been good revolutionaries too. For example, he strongly criticizes those dissertations which fail to show that it was in fact the Bolsheviks who were the leaders of the February revolution; and, while conceding that it is legitimate to point out that until the arrival of Lenin no one had reached the conclusion that the Soviets must take power, he stresses that it is wrong to forget, as Burdzhalov had done, 'the Leninist position of *partiinost*' and to portray the party before Lenin's arrival as almost semi-Menshevik and 'a prisoner of the illusion of unification'. With scant regard for the facts (which his readers could in any case soon discover for themselves by reading the two articles by Anikeyev mentioned earlier), Mints proceeds to establish that the joint Menshevik-Bolshevik organizations were not really joint at all, and in any case only survived after April 1917 in very few cases. Incidentally, it is Mints' article which contains the assertion, allegedly based on new evidence which is not however specified, that the Red Guard reached the figure of 200,000—an assertion which is duly re-

[1] *Voprosy Istorii KPSS*, 1957, No. 2.

produced in the *History*. The questionnaires filled in by the delegates to the Second All-Russian Congress of Soviets, he says, which suggest nothing like this total, underestimated the Red Guard in their districts, though no reason is offered to explain why they should all have made exactly the same mistake.[1] Lastly, mention must be made of an article published early in 1958 on the Petersburg Soviet of 1905, which is designed to put right the erroneous impression created by earlier articles, published by *Voprosy Istorii* in its unregenerate days, that Mensheviks as well as Bolsheviks were revolutionary.[2] Quoting the *Short Course* with approval, the authors of this article state that the Soviet failed in 1905 to carry the revolution to a successful conclusion because of its 'bad, Menshevik direction', and proceed to demonstrate that evidence which on the face of it suggests that the Mensheviks were also revolutionary is in fact misleading and unreliable.

These three articles, of which the main formulations all re-appear in the *History*, are sufficient to indicate how the vexed question of the Mensheviks was required to be treated by the party apparatus which took charge of the re-writing of history in 1957. It will be necessary to return to a discussion of the reasons for this party line on Mensheviks when the new image of party history is examined as a whole. Meanwhile, some comparison of the *History* and the *Short Course* is dictated by the strong family likeness between the two. The *History* is nearly twice as long, but then it covers nearly twice the number of years. The turgid, vulgar, aggressive Agitprop style has not changed very much in twenty years. Each chapter is followed by a summary of the main lessons to be deduced from the period covered, and the whole is crowned by a list of enumerated overall lessons. Neither can in any sense be regarded as an attempt to tell the story suggested by the facts, but must be viewed as a political manual in which the lesson for the future is of more importance than a true record of the past. Here we come to a contrast. The *Short Course* is a glorification of Stalin, but the *History* is a glorification of the party, not of Khrushchev. Khrushchev is, it is true, enumerated as one of the heroes of the civil war, which is mythology, but the main credit goes to him for defeating the anti-party group and for the policies of the last few years, which is deserved. The demotion of Stalin from the role of hero has necessitated certain changes in the earlier part of the history. For example, it raised the problem: who led the Bolshevik rising in 1917? The largely mythical 'Centre' invented for the *Short Course* (of which Stalin was a member and Trotsky was not) is no longer resorted to, but neither is Trotsky given any credit. And so a new invention has become necessary: the rising was led and directed by Lenin in accordance with a decision of the central

[1] On the Red Guard see my *The Communist Party of the Soviet Union*, (London, 1960), pp. 173-4.

[2] T. P. Bondarevskaya and A. Ya. Velikanova, 'Peterburgskii sovet rabochikh deputatov v 1905 godu', *Voprosy Istorii KPSS*, 1958, No. 1.

committee of October 3 (16), 1917.[1] In fact, of course, Lenin remained in hiding until the very eve of the rising, and the main practical direction of the rising was in Trotsky's hands—as all the evidence shows, and as was freely admitted until Trotsky fell into disgrace. Again, the collectivization of agriculture is no longer credited to Stalin as a revolution from above, but is said to have been carried out by the party (Chapter XII).

As one approaches more recent times, the treatment of Stalin is seen to be a great deal more reticent than at the twentieth congress, which reflects the desire not to overdo denigration. The purge trials of 1936-8 are not mentioned at all. Lenin's 'Testament' is referred to and quoted, but we are informed that Stalin was left at his post by the delegates to the thirteenth congress, to all of whom the 'Testament' was made available, on condition that he took Lenin's criticism into account. To have removed him from the secretariat would have been to play into the hands of the Trotskyists (p. 362). The only indication of the terror of 1936-8 is an admission that in 1937 Stalin had mistakenly put forward the thesis that even after the victory of socialism the class struggle must be intensified. As a result 'mass repressions' took place against ideological opponents of the party who were already politically routed. Owing to the faults of Beria and Yezhov the repressions also extended to 'many' innocent communists and non-party men. But in 1954-5 those 'who had suffered repressions for which there was no foundation' were fully rehabilitated (p. 484). The subject of Stalin is reverted to in connection with the twentieth congress and the resolution adopted on the 'cult of personality'. The subject is treated at considerable length: Stalin's services to the party and the country are recognized, but credit is also claimed for the party having had the courage, in the face of the risk that enemies of the Soviet Union would exploit 'open admission of mistakes', to take this course. Then follows a sentence in italics which seems significant: it explains that the campaign against the cult of personality was necessary so that 'henceforward such things could never happen again in the party and in the country' (p. 643). In the context, it reads very much like a solemn promise. One of the mistakes attributed to Stalin is his underestimation on the eve of the war of the possibility of a German attack (p. 519).

It is not, of course, possible, nor would it be very profitable, to enumerate all the distortions, falsifications, and suppressions contained in the *History*, which are in any case in most instances very similar to those already familiar from the *Short Course*. In addition to the suppression of Trotsky's part in the October rising and in the civil war, we now have the additional 'unpersoning' of Molotov and Malenkov in connection with the part they played during the war. (Zhukov, however, *is* listed among the commanders who distinguished themselves in the war—there are, it would seem, criteria for 'unpersoning' which are

[1] *Istoriya Kommunisticheskoi Partii Sovetskovo Soyuza*, (Moscow, 1959), pp. 234-5.

not clearly discernible.) The treatment of Trotsky is however in general different in character: in the *Short Course* he was still the sinister conspirator and traitor; the *History* tends on the whole to portray him as a ridiculous and rather discredited failure, who was always proved wrong by events. It is of more interest to consider the respects in which the *History* is either less truthful or more truthful than the *Short Course*. First, the less truthful formulations. It is a matter of controversy whence the real initiative came for the convening of the first congress of the party in 1898, though the evidence certainly suggests that the idea was current in more than one organization. Among those who played a big part in bringing the congress to fruition was beyond all doubt the Jewish Bund. The *Short Course* gives credit for the idea to several organizations, including the Bund. The *History* makes no mention of the initiative of the Bund, though it does mention its participation at the congress (p. 39). This reticence about the Jewish social-democrats seems to reflect a new fashion in party history, which decrees that the Jewish social-democratic movement (probably the most significant force in Russian social democracy until 1906) must if possible not be mentioned. Even Polevoy, in his generally scholarly work to which reference has already been made, uses all kinds of circumlocutions about 'national groups' and the like in order to avoid mentioning the Bund.

A novel form of untruthfulness adopted by the *History* is the occasional bold lie direct, but so formulated as to suggest to the reader that the statement made is based on incontrovertible documentary sources. One example is the statement that 240,757 (no more and no less) kulak families were re-settled between the beginning of 1930 and the autumn of 1932, and normal conditions of life created for them in their new places of work (p. 441). Another is a detailed statement that the British Government, while negotiating with the Soviet Union in 1939, was at the same time secretly negotiating with Hitler. Britain proposed to Hitler a division of spheres of influence: the Soviet Union and China were to be divided up, while Poland was to be handed over to Hitler entirely (p. 491). What is not explained is why Hitler did not accept this tempting offer. Now, the purpose of these outwardly circumstantial inventions seems clear enough. In each case something discreditable to the Soviet Union is involved—the excesses of collectivization and the deal with Hitler—and in each case detailed documentary evidence has been published outside the USSR, to which it is conceivable that Soviet readers might have access nowadays—the Smolensk party archives and the Nazi-Soviet negotiations documents. These two instances would therefore seem to be designed to supply an answer, perhaps for the benefit of foreign readers as much as Soviet, to awkward questions.

The main respect in which the *History* is much more truthful than the *Short Course* is in its treatment of certain aspects of Lenin's policy. For the *Short Course* Marx was still the Founding Father, with Lenin as his faithful disciple, and Stalin as the real executor of his will. The *History* lays much more emphasis on and devotes much more space to the development and practical application of Marxism, which was the work of Lenin. Again, the *Short Course* is in general very reticent about the tactics of the Bolsheviks against their political opponents before and in 1917, and leaves a general but not very clearly formulated picture of Bolshevik victory: the Bolsheviks were right and the Mensheviks were wrong, and the masses were behind the Bolsheviks. The *History* is a good deal franker in showing quite clearly, and of course historically much more truthfully, that Lenin pursued, at any rate after 1903, a calculated policy to destroy the Mensheviks politically—a determination in which he never wavered. Thus, the birth of the 'party of a new type' is now backdated to the second congress in 1903 (p. 63), which is a good deal nearer the truth than the hitherto traditional 1912, or some later date. Again, the *Short Course*, in dealing with the relations of the Bolsheviks and Mensheviks after their formal reunification in 1906 (in so far as it deals with the question at all), leaves the impression that the Bolsheviks did all they could to preserve unity, but that the Mensheviks simply made this impossible. The truth of the matter was that the Bolsheviks accepted the reunification as a 'shotgun marriage' (to use Zinoviev's phrase), secretly preserved their own separate organization, and never had any intention of making the unity work. This quite secret organization, or centre, as set up in 1906, is hardly referred to in party literature at all, even in memoirs, and it has required the detective work of historians in the West to unearth it. The *History* now states boldly that the Bolsheviks in 1906 continued to wage a war of principle against Menshevik opportunism and 'preserved their organizational independence and directing centre' (p. 109). (Something has gone wrong with the editing of the book, incidentally, since five pages later, when dealing with the fifth congress in 1907, the authors, having apparently forgotten what they said about 1906, state that the Bolsheviks 'created' their centre at this 1907 congress because they had no confidence in the newly elected joint central committee.) Even more interesting is the admission that when, in 1917, after the seizure of power by the Bolsheviks, discussions were initiated under pressure exerted by the railway union for the formation of a coalition government, Lenin's participation in the discussions was only intended by him as a tactical manoeuvre in order to gain time (p. 245). This is in fact true, as is evident from the minutes of the central committee meetings of the time, which were published in 1928. But it is a new departure in the writing of party history to admit it so frankly, where tradition demands that the pretence be kept up that it was only the intransigence of the socialist parties which prevented a coalition government being formed.

Indeed, the determination with which the socialists, but in particular the Mensheviks, are vilified and abused at every possible point in the history of the party, with complete indifference to fact, seems to be the most striking characteristic of the new *History*. It is carried to lengths which must appear absurd even to the Soviet reader, whose access to the

sources is more restricted than ours. For example, it will be recalled
that, so far as the victims of the 1936-8 show trials are concerned, the
History, in spite of the clear injunction of the central committee on
March 9, 1957, that they were to be treated as criminals and not only as
political oppositionists, nevertheless avoids doing so by not referring to
the trials at all. Yet the Menshevik trial of 1931, which was after all in
no way less of a frame-up than the later trials, is mentioned with
approval as fair and just (p. 435). It is at first sight difficult to see why
all this energy should have been expended in fighting enemies whose
chances of victory were never very strong and who have long ceased to
be of any practical importance in Soviet politics. It is, of course,
arguable that Menshevism, with its insistence on social-democratic
principles and on a self-reliant self-governing working class has only
now, with the emergence of a more educated working class in Russia,
become a serious alternative to communism. In other words, it could
be contended that while in 1917-21 dictatorial Bolshevism was the only
practical form of control, and Menshevik demands for greater freedom
utopian, today these demands begin to make more sense, are therefore
more likely to appeal to serious theorists, and have accordingly become
a more serious threat to communist legitimacy. To use the current
terminology, it could be said that the need to abuse Menshevism has
arisen as part of the struggle against revisionism, which has for some
years past occupied the centre of the stage in the ideological sphere.

My own view is that this aspect of the new *History*, if present in the
minds of the party apparatus which shaped its general outlines, is only
part of a broader pattern. The general picture conveyed by the *History*,
the image with which it is now sought to reaffirm the legitimacy of the
party and its right to rule, is one of historic, unshaken victorious
rectitude—the party was always right, and always certain of its course
at all stages of its history, from 1903 when Lenin split the second
congress until 1957 when Khrushchev routed the anti-party group. Not
only was the party always right, but the party *alone* was right, and none
other came anywhere near understanding the true course of history.
Individuals have erred—not only ridiculous individuals like Trotsky,
but serious Bolsheviks like Stalin—yet the wise, all-knowing, understanding party has always been able to set things right again. And so
it will be to the end of time, after the advent of heaven on earth in the
shape of communism, to which history is leading us—provided always
that the party remains in control. To listen to the blandishments of
revisionists in any form—Mensheviks in the past, Yugoslavs in the
present—is simply to court disaster, and to lose to the bourgeoisie all
the fruits of the long and hard struggle. Perhaps the creed was best
summed up in an article of which Bugaev was part author, in 1959:
'Only those can deny or belittle the leading role of the party in the
struggle for the dictatorship of the proletariat, for the building of
communism, for whom words about socialism are only a means to
deceive the workers and to subject them to the interests of the

bourgeoisie.'[1] Lenin himself could not have better expressed his own faith.

The *History*, however, is addressed not only to an inside audience, which can in any case be prevented from indulging in revisionist heresies by adequate disciplinary means, but also to the wide foreign audience who are cast for the role of helping the communist party to triumph outside the borders of the present communist bloc. That this is so becomes evident when one examines the conclusions or lessons at the end of the book, and compares them with the conclusions at the end of the *Short Course*. There are eleven such conclusions in the *History* as against six in the *Short Course*. Of the old six, five re-appear with little change in the new book: Victory is impossible without the party; there can be no victory without a Marxist-Leninist theory; the party must be self-critical; the party must wage a struggle against opportunists in its ranks; and the party must maintain close links with the masses. The sixth conclusion of the *Short Course* (it is actually the third in order) has no direct counterpart among the eleven new conclusions: the petit-bourgeois parties must be smashed. In place of this somewhat crude declaration of war against socialist parties everywhere, a rather more subtle ideology, better adapted for export and more attuned to the era of 'peaceful co-existence' and 'ideological struggle', is developed in six new conclusions: The transition from capitalism to socialism is possible only through the dictatorship of the proletariat; the unity of the working class is essential for victory; the party must have organization and iron discipline; the party is the truly patriotic party; proletarian internationalism is essential for victory; and finally, the *idée maîtresse*, history has demonstrated that the party has been proved right in its struggle against the parties of the Second International.

Will the new *History* prove more lasting than its many predecessors? At the time of writing (July 1962) there are several grounds for the view that its usefulness is already considered limited by the masters of propaganda. In the first place a much more concise, and therefore useful, document has been produced for external propaganda in the form of the Programme adopted by the twenty-second party congress in October 1961. Secondly, a new six-volume history of the party from 1883 until 1965 is projected for completion in 1967. The first volume is due to appear in 1963. Much discussion was devoted to this venture at two conferences held in the course of February 1962—a conference of heads of university departments of social sciences; and a conference of leading officials of the Institute of Marxism-Leninism and of party archivists. The substance of the discussions at the conferences is said to be contained in a long article by P. N. Pospelov published in 1962.[2]

In June 1962 two long unsigned articles in *Pravda* (22nd and 24th)

[1] From a review article by E. I. Bugaev and N. V. Ruban, *Voprosy Istorii KPSS*, 1959, No. 4, p. 25.

[2] P. N. Pospelov, 'O zadachakh nauchno-issledovatelskoi raboty po istorii partii v svete reshenii XXII syezda KPSS', *Vosprosy Istorii KPSS*, 1962, No. 2.

on the same theme set out for the general public the tasks of the historians engaged on this mammoth project. It is not possible to give even a summary of the many new aspects of interpretation of party history which these articles disclosed. But two anxieties on the part of the propagandists are apparent. The first is the need to provide an effective reply to works on party history published abroad (including the present writer's contribution), which are described as 'falsifications'. Evidently the new *History* is not yet considered an adequate answer to non-Soviet interpretations and accounts. The second is the need to demonstrate beyond doubt that, in spite of the official criticism visited on the period of the 'cult of personality' by the twenty-second congress, leadership by the party is an historical necessity; and that without this leadership none of the benefits of socialism or of imminent communism could be achieved. In this respect too, apparently, the new *History* is no longer regarded as adequate. Five years is a long time to look ahead in the present transitional stage of Soviet society. One may legitimately speculate not only on the possibility that the six-volume history may make the new *History* obsolete and unorthodox. One can also pertinently ask whether the first volume of the new work may not be consigned to the dustbin of history long before the sixth volume appears.

DISCUSSION

Introducing his paper, Mr Schapiro said that the main point he had tried to stress was that there existed a fundamental difference of objectives between the *Short Course* and the new party history. The *Short Course* was intended to silence history, to petrify it in this final, unpalatable form. It was launched with a stiff decree of the central committee and all further history was virtually suppressed. The fact that it was thought necessary to include a stern warning in the decree that there was to be no further discussion of the differences between Leninism and Marxism meant that there still were some bold spirits in 1938. At the same time there had been an unpublished decree of the central committee presidium stipulating that there were to be no more memoirs about Lenin—the *Short Course* was to be the last word on party history.

The relaxed and leisurely manner in which the new party history was launched, without any decree or any flourish in the press, suggested that it was really intended to serve a different purpose. The essential political difference between the two histories was the difference between the Russia of 1959 and the Russia of 1938. The contrast in the presentation of the two books could be discussed in terms of the different types of control in existence in the Soviet Union today and twenty years ago.

The basic similarity between the two versions was that neither was history in any real sense of the word: each was an attempt to project the present into the past, an attempt to establish legitimacy. Both were political instruments rather than narratives.

Strictly speaking, the history of the party should be the history of a political instrument of control. But the *Short Course* contained no analysis of the growth, development, or variations in the methods of control—it was more a history of the Soviet Union than a history of the party. From beginning to end it was a glorification of Stalin, whereas the new history was not really a glorification of Khrushchev, although it naturally reflected his rise to power. If anything was being glorified in the new history, it was the CPSU—not the party in terms of the individuals who commanded the levers of power, but the party as an abstraction, preserving through all vicissitudes its omniscience and wisdom. The party was glorified because the primary political purpose was to explain and justify why some *apparatchik* should have an authority which he enjoyed neither constitutionally nor legally.

The necessity for the rulers to justify their arbitrary power to replace the constitutional rights of the courts, of industrial managers, of government bodies, of soviets and professional organizations, was the crucial problem in the Soviet Union today. The Soviet system was irrational, illogical, and absurd. One set of people did the job and another set told them how to do it—this was party government since 1917. Mr Deutscher and others were right in thinking that by reason of the advance of education this problem became more and more irksome, but they were wrong in inferring that the party would therefore disappear or adapt itself. The party was fully alive to the precariousness of its claim to authority, but was nevertheless doing its best to preserve it. The new party history was one way of doing this. Dr Bolsover had asked how long the myth could survive once a certain amount of real history was let in. There was bound to be a conflict between reality and fiction, but the party evidently hoped to resolve the conflict; he himself did not think that myth and reality could co-exist for long—sooner or later one or the other would rule.

The new party history was more truthful in some respects than the old and less truthful in others. For instance, there was the striking admission that Lenin re-wrote Marx. In pre-Khrushchev days this would have been unthinkable, but now it was openly admitted and justified on the grounds that the strength of Marxism lay precisely in its ability to grow and develop. On the other side, there were instances of outright invention presented with full circumstantial detail; the sections on the Nazi-Soviet Pact, for example, or the period of collectivization, gave the appearance of having been written as a reply to what was being published on these questions in the West.

Another puzzling trait of the new history was the extraordinary concentration of attack on the Mensheviks. Every conceivable opportunity was seized to denigrate the Mensheviks, in particular to deny them any revolutionary role, to show them at all stages as opportunists playing into the hands of the bourgeoisie and secretly allied with it. Why all this emphasis on the Mensheviks, who, one would have thought, were not such a serious political problem in the Soviet

Union today? One possible explanation was that Menshevism had become relevant. The Mensheviks had believed in open discussion, workers' control of production, democracy in the party—all things disapproved by Lenin. It might be argued that in the chaotic years immediately after the revolution, these ideas of self-government and free discussion had little application. Today the workers were no longer backward and uneducated, and it might be that precisely because the tenets of Menshevism had now acquired relevance, it had become necessary to oppose them so vehemently. Another explanation was that the attitude to Menshevism was dictated by the fight against revisionism, designed to reinforce the moral that the party was always right and that the only right road to socialism and communism was the one mapped out by Moscow.

Mr Labedz thought that certain disagreements at the conference about the interpretation of the new party history were less a matter of principle than of degree of emphasis. It was hardly possible to say that there was a basic difference as well as a basic similarity between the *Short Course* and the new history—if there was a fundamental similarity between the two, then the difference was not basic, and *vice versa*. He agreed, however, with Mr Schapiro that there were differences in the way the two had been launched and the use made of them. Although the new textbook was not elevated to a sacred text, it was used as a basic handbook for the propagation of the new myth. On the other hand, Mr Wolfe had perhaps overstressed the similarity between the two. Both served the same function, that of myth-making. Although he agreed with Mr Wolfe that Khrushchev would probably gain in stature with subsequent re-writings, the degree of glorification in the last chapters of the new party history had been somewhat exaggerated.

On the co-existence of history and fiction in current Soviet publications, Mr Labedz cited the example of John Reed's *Ten Days that Shook the World*, published in the USSR with an introduction which was in complete contradiction to the text of the book. But to conclude from this that sooner or later either fact or fiction would win, was to apply a narrow kind of schematic rationalism to a complex problem. People had an infinite capacity for believing in two incompatible truths, on the institutional as well as the personal level. The co-existence of fact and fiction in Soviet publications could endure for a very long time indeed.

To Mr Schapiro's explanations for the concentrated attack on the Mensheviks in the new party history, Mr Labedz added another, based on the argument about legitimacy. The Moscow trials of 1936-8 were not mentioned in the new textbook because they concerned the intra-party struggle, whereas the 1931 trial of Mensheviks did not in any way affect Khrushchev's rise to power.

He believed that the glorification of the party was as characteristic of the *Short Course* as of the new party history—this was a constant that had not changed between 1923 and 1961. There was, however, a difference of emphasis; the two textbooks reflected very precisely the different position of the leader *vis-à-vis* the party in Stalin's time and in Khrushchev's. The glorification of the leader was in direct proportion to the authority of the leader; clearly Khrushchev did not have a comparable power position to that of Stalin and this fact was reflected in the new history.

The fact that the Chinese communist party had not until this moment produced an authoritative party history of its own threw some light, Mr Mancall thought, on the differences between China and the Soviet Union, and on the role that these party histories played in the USSR. The absence of a Chinese party textbook was all the more surprising because China had embarked upon a tremendous process of mass re-education, which exceeded anything ever undertaken in the Soviet Union. On the other hand, such a book was less necessary for China, where the succession problem had not yet arisen; the publication of a Chinese party history could not yet serve the purpose of justifying Mao's successor. Secondly, the break with tradition was far greater in the Soviet Union than in China. In establishing their legitimacy, the Chinese leaders could rely on many traditional institutions; even more, on their own past. They had come to power not through plotting, intrigue, or revolution, like the Bolsheviks, but on a territorial basis, as one of the many contending forces which were trying to seize power. Since Mao was still alive, nobody could re-interpret his works, as was being done in the Soviet Union with Lenin's; Mao's collected works, in their pristine form, without emendation and gloss, were still the essential frame of intellectual reference.

To Mr Schapiro's speculations on the reasons for the severity of the attack on Menshevism, Mr McLane added another suggestion: just as the *Short Course*, whose sole hero had been Stalin, needed a single villain or antagonist, conveniently provided by Trotsky, so in the new history, of which the party was the hero, the antagonist was also de-personalized from Trotsky to Menshevism. In this way cults of personality were avoided both amongst the orthodox and amongst the damned.

Mr Wolfe suggested that the difference between Mr Schapiro and himself on the role of the new party history was not so much one of substance, as of the criterion applied: Mr Schapiro considered the party history as a finished product, whereas Mr Wolfe had attempted to uncover the seeds of the next history. While the way in which the new history depicted the role of Khrushchev at the twentieth and twenty-first CPSU congresses was quite compatible with the facts, the actual part he had played at the nineteenth congress was already much inflated in its pages.

The Mensheviks had been fair game in all the earlier histories, and not only in the new party history. The difference was that in the *Short Course* Stalin was fighting his own people, his own party, even his own faction, rather than the opponents of Bolshevism outside. The Mensheviks were almost forgotten; but Khrushchev, who had inherited an atomized society, a collectivized peasantry, and a monolithic party, did not need to direct his fire internally, except to get rid of a few contenders for the leadership. For the rest, he could turn his attention to revisionism, polycentrism, the challenge of democracy, and all things for which, as Mr Schapiro had pointed out, Menshevism was a surrogate. In justifying Bolshevism's right to wrest power from the Mensheviks, he was justifying his present stand against all kinds of contenders from within and without.

On the possibility of the co-existence of myth and truth in Soviet party historiography, Dr Utechin cited the particular instance of the changed attitude towards the Russian revolutionary movement before the rise of the social democrats. Under Stalin the position had been that prior to social democracy the revolutionary struggle had been conducted by the populists; the subject had been given relatively little attention. But as soon as the thaw began on the historical front, several moves were made by historians interested in the subject to revise this view of the populists. Early writings on the subject, published before the middle thirties, were disinterred, and the whole treatment of populism and its relevance to social democracy and Bolshevism became at once more scholarly and more bold. To a certain extent the new party history reflected the results of these scholarly investigations. True, certain parts of the history quite clearly contradicted some of the findings of the scholars, especially those embodied in works published since the appearance of the party history. But he believed that the historians were aware of the problem and would in future try to assimilate the results of research as far as possible in the official histories, so as to avoid obvious contradictions. So long as the general political situation remained as it was now, there would be co-existence between scholarship and party history as a political tool, with scholars taking care to present the findings of their research in a way that could be taken as consistent with official requirements, and party history striving to give the appearance on the surface of being consistent with the results of scholarly research.

The current discussions on the periodization of party history in the columns of *Voprosy Istorii* were not, Dr Keep thought, without interest. What was at stake was the emphasis that should be given to various factors in drawing the dividing line between different periods in the history of the Soviet communist party. Emphasis on internal events as decisive assigned to the party its traditional leading role; emphasis on external events minimized that role. At present Soviet historians seemed to have struck some sort of balance: they talked of 1937 as a decisive turning-point, as it marked what they called the completion of the building of socialism and what we might term the culmination of the purges; on the other hand, they did not recognize the Second World War, which to any impartial outside observer seemed a great turning-point, as an important landmark.

He could see no clear distinction between the 'hacks', the official historians who were merely echoing party directives, and the so-called 'genuine historians'. Judging from the published results, it seemed that the party line was being put over more convincingly and effectively by mobilizing these professional historians; they had served to buttress the new Khrushchevian myth which had replaced the old Stalinist one in the party history. As to the work on the early history of the social-democratic party by Polevoy, bitterly criticized by *Pravda* but defended by *Kommunist*, it appeared to Dr Keep that the authorities must have decided that it was safe to allow a certain latitude in the discussion of early party history. The problems of the interpretation of the revolutionary movement in the 1880s or 1890s were after all not particularly relevant today; to the younger generation especially they seemed very remote. Whereas it was important to establish a definite line on the party's role in the revolutions of 1905 and 1917, because this was considered relevant to the situation in other countries, particularly in the under-developed ones, the question of the Russian underground was not really a live issue.

As to the influence of the current treatment of Soviet party history on less sophisticated historians in the West, it was not Leninism but the strength of the Soviet Union that impressed them. The critical historian should stress the difference between Marxism and Leninism. Marxism had a genuine appeal for historians by virtue of its emphasis on the social and economic aspects of the historical process, whereas Leninism as an ideology distinct from Marxism did not possess the same appeal; it was something independent of Marxism, a response to the specific conditions in Russia in the early part of the twentieth century, relevant perhaps to other under-developed countries, but wholly irrelevant to Western Europe and North America.

To Professor Ulam, the 1959 party history reflected a two-fold problem facing the Soviet leaders today: in so far as foreign communism was concerned, it was the problem of 'revisionism'; in so far as it touched upon the internal situation, it could be termed the problem of ideological agnosticism among party members, an agnosticism due to boredom, exhaustion, and disenchantment with ideology as such, and with the constant repetition of communist truisms and falsifications, seen to be irrelevant to the business of everyday living. All the discussions about communism and what it really meant reflected the uneasiness of the leaders. To some extent the 1959 party history mirrored the search for a way of making the party ideology and the image of the party itself alive and appealing to the younger generation, on whom in the long run everything depended. In regard to other members of the Soviet bloc, the party history aimed to show that socialism meant communism as practised in the Soviet Union, not to be confused with other brands.

Mr Schram thought that Mr Mancall had somewhat overstated the lack of importance of an official party history in Chinese communist society. Though there was no equivalent for the *Short Course*, there were several unofficial histories by collectives of authors; moreover, the core of an official party history was contained in the 1945 resolution on 'certain questions of party history', which laid down the framework within which all historians must operate. Though China was certainly very Chinese, it was also Leninist (even though it might be in the process of becoming Trotskyist), and therefore both the party and party histories played an important role.

Professor Aspaturian thought they should discriminate between those elements in Soviet totalitarianism that were indispensable and continued from one period to another, whether under Lenin, Stalin, or Khrushchev, and those that might be merely elements of style. The basic element of continuity in Leninism and Stalinism had been pointed out by Professor Fainsod: it was the infallibility of the party. This, however, should not be confused with the infallibility of party history. It had been Stalin's style to make party history a monument to party infallibility. Khrushchev, at least at this stage, did not deem this necessary, nor did it yet seem to be necessary in other communist states. Under Stalin there had been official textbooks in nearly all fields of study, and not only in party history. Their appearance was often accompanied by controversy at the highest level. When Aleksandrov's book on philosophy appeared, it was attacked by Zhdanov. Stalin's *Economic Problems of Socialism* was produced as a result of the controversy over another textbook on political economy. There were never two valid texts co-existing with one another—one superseded the other.

Soviet citizens had always been aware of the myth and the reality in their system. In fact, myth and reality co-existed in any society. In the United States the Declaration of Independence and the Fourteenth Amendment co-existed with segregation in the South. All American citizens knew them to be incompatible. Similarly, most Soviet citizens were aware of the incompatibilities in their own system. The question was whether they were in a position to do something about them. Awareness in itself was not sufficient to bring about change.

To Dr Katkov there was an essential difference between historians' studies of the phenomenon of the party and the political work of those who wrote textbooks like the *Short Course* and the 1959 *Concise History*. It was a difference in subject. The *Short Course* and the *Concise History* were not really studies of the CPSU; the *Short Course* was the history of Stalin's personality and of his role in the transformation of society. The party figured in it as the mother of the Messiah. It was more difficult to define the subject of the *Concise History*—it was certainly not yet Khrushchev and Khrushchev was not the party. In a sense it was the history of the ruling group, consisting of millions of people who had nothing in common with the revolutionary Bolshevik party except for a few survivors who were now members of this privileged social group. The party as an abstraction was a convention covering this group, and the party history was a justification for its existence and a promise that it would be maintained in its privileged position.

Commenting on the infallibility of party and leader and the relation between Marxism, Leninism, and Stalinism, Professor Berlin wondered to what extent people were right in thinking that Lenin betrayed Marx, Stalin betrayed Lenin, and so forth. The doctrine of infallibility was founded upon the proposition that the only way to get the right answer was by studying history, which yielded certain laws formulated by Marx; that these laws can only be discovered by certain people whose class position sharpens their awareness of things; that within this class there are the expert analysts of history who are scientists. If one really believed that Marxism is a science, then the Soviet system would appear not absurd, but perfectly coherent: for in that case it would be quite logical to have party experts to tell others what to do and to assume the role of spiritual directors. The belief that the whole art of government consists in being engineers of human souls could be deduced from the purest Marxist doctrine unadulterated by Stalinism.

As to the influence of ideas on Soviet practice, he wished to know whether the *Short Course* contained some specific ideological directive different from those embodied in the previous party histories written during the earlier years of the Soviet regime. Since ideas were officially of great importance, whatever the cynicism with which they were in fact treated, it would be interesting to know whether it was possible to write a kind of Soviet history of ideological progress. Were there various strands of dialectical materialism? Were some heresies denounced for purely ideological reasons? Professor Berlin was inclined to agree with Professor Ulam that at present in the Soviet Union the interest taken in ideology and ideas was extremely low; it could not be compared to the intense curiosity shown in Paris, Germany, or England. Had Stalin, for example, erred in theory? In 1956 Professor Berlin had been assured by a Russian communist that in the view of the party pundits Stalin had been entirely blameless in ideological matters and his doctrines perfectly orthodox, although he had committed many errors of practice and had infringed socialist legality. Was this still the official view?

Mr Labedz thought Marxism *had* been re-interpreted in Lenin's time, in Stalin's time, and in Khrushchev's time; to illustrate this process of ideological transformation in the Soviet Union, he took the concept of dialectical materialism; this in itself was a transformation of Marxist ideology—the term had never occurred in Marx's dialectics. Chapter IV of the *Short Course* mentioned three laws of dialectics, but during Stalin's time the so-called negation of the negation had been officially discredited. Questions such as whether non-antagonistic contradictions were possible in communist society seemed completely absurd to western philosophers; nevertheless they were the subject of fervent dispute in the Soviet Union. The reasons for these transformations in the ideology presumably had something to do with the character of social change and the dynamics of the revolution from above. The history of Soviet ideological changes could be written by tracing the development of certain concepts and the changes in their application, and by analysing the reasons for such transformations and their relevance in given historical situations.

Mr Wolfe said there was both continuity and change in Soviet ideology. Its fundamental continuity rested on Lenin's doctrine of organization; this had been developed, but not altered in its essentials: centralism, the infallibility of the leaders, the impossibility of challenging the party. This is why one had the impression that all the party histories were saying the same thing, which, in a sense, they were. But certain aspects of ideology had changed. For instance, the old socialist notion of equality had undergone considerable transformation: Stalin's contempt for *uravnilovka* continued in somewhat modified form under Khrushchev. Another tenet that had caused much ideological trouble was the withering away of the state. Nothing of the sort had happened. Stalin tried to solve the problem by saying that the state would have to grow stronger before it could wither away, and had applied himself to strengthening it. He had also said—rather carelessly, as it now seemed to Khrushchev—that the party would wither away. In tackling this tricky problem, Khrushchev was ready to concede that the state would wither away and offered various trivial examples to demonstrate that the process had already begun, but he firmly proclaimed that the party would grow stronger. As to the formula 'from each according to his ability, to each according to his need', which meant originally that goods would flow in such abundance that every individual would take whatever he needed, eagerly throwing into the stream whatever he could, this had now been replaced by Khrushchev's image of a new Soviet man so conditioned that he would need little and contribute much—in other words, one of the main ideological changes was the substitution of the completely conditioned man for the completely free man.

Professor Fainsod thought the proper subject of party history was not merely to record the power of the ruling group and its manipulations, but also to reflect some kind of response to the aspirations of an evolving society. The explosion of 1956 had revealed certain features of Soviet society: the protest against the privileges of the new class, the desire for equality, privacy, decency, and truth, and these had elicited certain responses from the rulers—not the responses one had hoped for, but nevertheless responses of a kind. The 1959 party history was very disappointing in not reflecting them sufficiently. Perhaps in future party historiography would narrow the gap between the aspirations of the people and the manipulations of the rulers.

Mr Schapiro agreed with Professor Fainsod that a new form of rule was being evolved in Soviet Russia. Once the use of violence and terror was precluded, the rulers had to devise other methods for achieving the same kind of control over the people. Khrushchev and the privileged group he represented appeared to hold the Utopian belief that a closed society could be re-created in which human beings would of their own accord follow the particular pattern considered historically correct. The new party history was partly designed to achieve this.

In regard to ideology, a great deal of confusion had been caused by the tendency to regard Soviet ideology as outlining an ideal course of conduct or an ideal scientific solution by which to guide action. Soviet ideology was organizational. It was more than anything else a tradition of practice, a traditional craft of government, the organizational technique of a privileged group. Controversies among philosophers about the negation of the negation no doubt had political implications, but what affected conduct was a general sense of the course of history moving in their direction, of the continuous advance of the form of rule they had created, of the extension of communism beyond the confines of the Soviet Union. This was not ideology, but faith or tradition, habit of mind or mythology.

Mr Schapiro dissented categorically from the suggestion put forward by Professor Berlin that Leninism differed little from Marxism. Marxist nineteenth-century Utopianism had nothing in common with Lenin's basic conception of organization fighting chaos, of organizational methods enabling a small group like the Bolsheviks to achieve full control. Because Marxism was not applicable to Russia in 1917, still less in 1890, there had always been Soviet inhibitions about it. Certain features of Marxism had to be repressed in writing party history because they did not fit the conditions.

IV. Western Post-War History in the Soviet Mirror

JOHN KEEP

Two world wars and the rise of totalitarian regimes have profoundly changed the climate in which the western historian surveys the past. Few are now bold enough to maintain an optimistic belief in the rationality of human conduct or the existence of a general upward trend towards enlightenment and progress. Determinism is at a discount, and some would deny that any readily discernible pattern or trend exists in the contemporary world. Sovietologists familiar with the rigidity of the Leninist mind and the realities of power in communist countries are perhaps more inclined than most to emphasize the essential 'planlessness' of human endeavours and the supreme importance of personality in politics.

Nevertheless, in considering the attitude of Soviet historians to the post-war western world[1] it may not be unhelpful to begin by setting down some of the more important historical trends characteristic of the area and period. The list that follows is intended merely as a practical working tool. No claim is made to completeness or originality; no attention has been paid to important divergences between individual countries; and it is not suggested that these trends are necessarily fundamental or exclusive to the West.

Subject to these limitations, most observers will probably agree that since the end of the war there has been:

(i) A general trend towards fairly rapid (if uneven) economic growth, based largely on the application to industry and agriculture of new scientific and technological discoveries.

(ii) Associated with this growth, and partly responsible for it, a trend towards the concentration of economic power in the hands of large private and public enterprises, managed bureaucratically, and aware of their social responsibilities as well as their narrow immediate interests. Similarly, as a countervailing force, the emergence of powerful centralized trade unions and other mass organizations.

(iii) In response to various pressures, a general tendency towards

---

[1] By 'western world' is here meant the industrialized states of Western Europe and North America. For reasons of space the illustrative material is mainly concerned with American and British history, but the conclusions may be regarded as applying to the western world as a whole.

rising incomes and living standards, the 'de-proletarianization of the masses' (a term coined by John Strachey), and a certain measure of social integration.

(iv) The preservation, despite the existence of strong contrary tendencies, of western-style political democracy, constitutional government, individual liberties, and the rule of law.

(v) In international relations, a tendency towards regional integration, both economic and political.

All these developments may be considered spontaneous—in so far as one can distinguish at all in any meaningful way between what is spontaneous and what is deliberately contrived in human affairs. If we were to suppose that, almost a hundred years after *Das Kapital*, a theorist with Karl Marx's penchant for universal categories were to attempt to establish the 'laws of evolution' of our epoch, we could expect these trends to feature in the picture that would emerge from his studies.

With Marx, of course, analysis of the facts was combined with a will to revolutionary change. He was not only a social scientist but also the founder of the world's greatest secular religion, who approached his scholarly activities with a Hegelian vision of the inevitable apocalypse. The dualism in Marx's thought between reason and faith, between empirical observation and uncompromising devotion to a predetermined messianic idea, was transmitted to all his disciples. With Lenin, and still more with Stalin, Marxism underwent a Russification that transformed its spirit, and suppressed the rational element in Marx. Lenin realized subconsciously that a socialist revolution would never come about spontaneously, through action from below by the dispossessed proletarian masses, since in capitalist society history was not proceeding in accordance with the Marxist predictions; he therefore determined to 'make' a revolution where the conditions were in fact ripe for one. This led to the effort in the USSR to construct socialism—artificially, as it were—from above.

As a result Marxism lost its original pretentions to be a social science and became instead an ideology, an official creed that served to legitimize the rule of the new revolutionary élite. Its inherent scholastic and dogmatic tendencies were intensified, creating in the end an intellectual climate in which there was an almost total breach between ideology and reality, between thought and life—a climate in which ideas were emptied of their content and turned into slogans sanctified by continual repetition. The Marxist dialectic, once a mighty weapon of critical analysis, was degraded into a crude propaganda instrument for advancing the cause of the communist party. In the social sciences (history included) objective study of the facts ceased to be possible: the test applied in evaluating any phenomenon was simply whether it existed on one side of the ideological barricade or the other. Thus the 'imperialist system' could be criticized for ancient social evils whether they existed in reality or not, while such evils continued to exist, often in the grossest form, but without acknowledgement, in the 'fatherland of socialism'. It became the function of the historian, and of his colleagues in related fields, to embroider and illustrate the hallowed formulas as interpreted by the supreme party leadership.

Contemporary history is a particularly sensitive subject, for it is intimately bound up with the current policies of the Soviet government. All free speculation is strictly taboo, and the official line is in practice laid down at periodical party congresses, when the First Secretary of the CPSU gives an authoritative analysis of the present stage in which imperialism finds itself as it hastens onwards to its inevitable doom.

It is important to bear this background in mind when considering Soviet works on contemporary history, for it may be said that they are distinguished from one another not by the conclusions reached, since these are largely determined in advance, but by the quantity and quality of the factual material adduced by the author in support of his argument. It is in this sense alone that we can speak of changes in the Soviet attitude during recent years. The post-Stalin leaders, concerned at the lack of realism in the treatment of history, have sought to overcome this defect in so far as this could be done without bringing into question the party's claim to be the ultimate repository of historical truth. Their aim has been to strengthen party control over the thoughts of all citizens (particularly the younger generation) by bringing scholarship 'closer to life'. No change has been made in the general approach to the subject, but the manner of presentation has been modified in an effort to enhance its popular appeal. Historians have been urged, notably at the twenty-first party congress in 1959, to devote more attention to the study of the contemporary non-Soviet world and to make more use of western sources in doing so. They are also now urged to make a point of refuting the erroneous views advanced by their bourgeois colleagues abroad.

In this field of historiography there has lately been a particularly marked expansion. Among general studies one may mention a two-volume history of the world since 1917, issued by the Higher Party School attached to the central committee of the CPSU.[1] Less authoritative, perhaps, but more stimulating in its choice of illustrative material, is the veteran E. Varga's second edition of his *Fundamental Questions of the Economics and Politics of Imperialism*.[2] Most works, as one would expect in the light of the official Soviet doctrine on national sovereignty, follow convention by treating the history of a single country in isolation. The USSR Academy of Sciences has published a two-volume history of the USA in modern times,[3] which in many ways bears traces of the brief thaw in Soviet-American relations during 1959. There are also a large

---

[1] *Noveishaya istoriya: uchebnoe posobie* (Moscow, 1958-9).

[2] *Osnovnye voprosy ekonomiki i politiki imperializma (posle II mirovoi voiny)*, (Moscow, 1957).

[3] *Ocherki novoi i noveishei istorii SShA*, (Moscow, 1959-60), referred to below as the *History of the USA*.

number of works dealing with various aspects of American economic conditions and foreign policy. The leading Soviet authority on the history of the United Kingdom, V. G. Trukhanovsky, is the author of a comprehensive volume on British history since 1918, as well as a shorter monograph on British foreign policy since 1945. The history of other western countries is not neglected, but it is the Anglo-Saxon powers that receive the lion's share of attention. Many of these works have a wealth of documentation hitherto unknown in Soviet historical literature. The *History of the USA*, for example, contains a bibliography listing some three hundred Western works, including the memoirs, diaries, etc., of many American statesmen.

In general the result has been to improve the scholarly appearance of Soviet works and to enable historians to put over their views more effectively than was possible in the Stalin era. Whether it signifies an advance towards objectivity, in the usual western sense of the term, is perhaps more questionable, since all works are of course required to manifest the proper 'party spirit'. The approach to statistical material is often distressingly casual, and quotation out of context all too frequent.

A certain element of risk is involved in this widening of access to knowledge that only a few years ago was still forbidden fruit, and one may legitimately ask whether it will not have repercussions unforeseen by the authorities. It is possible that the younger men, with no experience of the more ruthless measures of intimidation used against dissident intellectuals in Stalin's day, might be encouraged to experiment, although it has to be remembered that the pressures towards conformity are exceedingly powerful. Not only must historians show that they are well-grounded in Marxism-Leninism before they are permitted to engage in research, but most of them work on collective projects, which provides an additional insurance against individualistic tendencies. The mighty force of national sentiment can be effectively mobilized in the party's support. The very simplification required of the Soviet historian may have a certain attractiveness for him, in that use of the Leninist slide-rule enables him to reduce to manageable proportions the vastly complex pattern of contemporary history; he is free to disregard whatever cannot be made to fit his thesis. For these reasons, instances of concealed scepticism are likely to be fairly rare. For practical purposes we can assume that Soviet historians mean what they say—especially, perhaps, when dealing with the iniquities of 'modern imperialism'.

In considering the Soviet attitude to the trends in western post-war history mentioned earlier, it is possible to distinguish the element of rational argument from the dogmatically 'subjectivist' and propagandist shell in which it is generally encased.

The fact that industrial production and labour productivity have risen, and so made possible an improvement in living standards for the mass of consumers, presents the Leninist student of imperialism with an awkward problem. In Stalin's day it was simply side-stepped. In a work entitled *Questions of the General Crisis of Capitalism*, which appeared in 1953, no figures were given of US post-war industrial output, which was simply expressed as a percentage of output in the preceding year.[1] The new *History of the USA* is franker. It concedes that between 1918 and 1959 the average rate of industrial growth was 3·3 per cent per annum, and that over the eleven years 1947-58 output increased by 42 per cent.[2] But several arguments are advanced to weaken the effect of this figure. In the first place it is said that the rate of expansion has been disproportionately high in some sectors and low in others. This is not an objection that need be taken very seriously. Even rigorously planned economies often suffer from lack of balance (to use a polite euphemism), and one may well wonder whether truly proportionate development is ever possible in practice. Who, after all, is to decide which proportions are correct?

Then it is said that this expansion is only a temporary phenomenon, for a 'deepening of the crisis' is imminent. As every Soviet schoolboy knows, it is a fundamental contradiction of capitalist (and particularly American) society that 'productive forces' are continually tending to outrun 'production relations', i.e. that more goods are produced than the market can absorb. This, of course, does not inhibit Soviet critics from making the most of such shortages of consumer goods as may occur. Thus we are laconically informed that 'in 1944-6 the supply of TV sets and radio receivers, motor-cars, tractors, clothing, footwear, and furniture was in sharp disproportion to the increased demand for these goods[3]—the implication being that this was the fault of those in charge, rather than a natural consequence of reconversion to peacetime working. Belief in the imminence of serious crisis rests mainly on the evidence of fluctuations in the business cycle. It is not admitted that the state, despite its new role in the economy, can do anything to avert recessions or minimize their consequences. This is a fundamental article of faith. We are also told that there is evidence of crisis in the declining production in certain branches of industry, such as coal-mining or textiles. No hint is given that this may be linked with the transition to more economical forms of power or to the expanded production of artificial fibres—although both these developments are mentioned independently. In the same way the drop in railway goods traffic is not brought into association with the development of road haulage, although elsewhere figures are given for the rising output of commercial vehicles.

Such manipulation is necessary because the Soviet historian, clinging to the dogma that the world is split into antagonistic social systems,

[1] *Voprosy obshchevo krizisa kapitalizma*, p. 39.

[2] *Ocherki* . . . , pp. 668, 429. The report of the Congressional Joint Economic Committee, *Soviet economic growth: a comparison with the U.S.* (Washington, 1957), estimates the US growth rate at 3·6 per cent for 1928-55 and 4·4 per cent for 1950-5.

[3] *Ocherki* . . . , p. 329; for later years, cf. p. 391.

cannot afford to recognize the role played in economic development by scientific and technological discoveries, whatever the system. This brings them into conflict not only with common sense but also with Marx, who laid a good deal of stress on this point. It is true that Marx does not say to what extent he believes changes in the 'productive forces' are the result of technological developments, and to what extent the social environment has to be taken into account. (His critics have argued that the distinction is in any case unreal.) But Soviet writers confound the ambiguity still further by pretending that the division runs simply along what may be called 'socio-geographic' lines—i.e. that in the socialist countries the inventor's genius speeds economic progress and popular well-being, whereas in capitalist countries it merely swells private profits and brings nearer the day of reckoning. To state the problem thus is to reveal its crudity; in fact all countries undergoing a process of industrialization may be expected to make and apply the fruits of knowledge in a roughly comparable way; moreover, they will cross-fertilize each other. In actual fact there is no more justification for the theory of a 'general crisis of capitalism' than there is for one of a 'general crisis of socialism'. Both systems, if one may use the term, are going concerns, capable of growth, operating in accordance with their own principles, and meeting their own problems in their own way; comparisons between them can be meaningful and fruitful only in so far as they take into account the points in common as well as the differences. Actually Soviet theorists have undermined their own doctrine of two antagonistic camps further than they perhaps realize by proclaiming the feasibility of the Soviet Union overtaking the United States in *per capita* industrial output and other economic achievements: for how can one 'system' overtake another unless both are moving along the same road? This is perhaps a semantic point. But it remains a fact that Soviet historians are unable to grasp the nature of the struggle in which they conceive themselves to be engaged, which is not essentially one between rival economic systems.

The curious combination of realism and dogmatism in the Soviet approach to western history is most pronounced in writings on the distribution of economic power. Since the inherent tendency of the capitalist world towards monopoly was discussed at length both by Marx and Lenin, the high degree of concentration in industry and finance in most western countries today is frequently cited as proof that the official ideology is scientific and correct.

How are we to evaluate this claim? Certainly the element of reality is greater here than it is in the literature devoted to some other aspects of western economics. One feels tempted to say that the numerous works on this theme are among the more useful products of Soviet historiography, or at least would be if they were not vitiated by what may be called the demonological approach. The study of business practices, of the complex and ever-changing inter-relationship between

D

costs, prices, profits, dividends, wages, and productivity is a legitimate and necessary activity if the history of a modern industrialized society is to be written at all; certainly there is no need for western historians to surround these matters with unwritten taboos, which can only create an atmosphere of mystery and suspicion.

The passage dealing with this question in the official textbook is fairly typical:

'The furious chasing after maximum profits on the part of the monopolists creates almost unsurmountable obstacles to the development of productive forces in the countries of the capitalist camp. The most important feature of the post-war development of the capitalist world is the further strengthening of the role of the monopolies, in particular of state-monopoly capitalism. In the USA the 500 largest industrial companies produce half the country's entire industrial output . . . [there follow details for other western countries]. In this way control over the basic sectors of the capitalist economy is concentrated in the hands of the monopolies. Relying on their economic power, the monopolies subjugate the state apparatus and determine the policy of the capitalist countries. Endeavouring to enlarge the sphere of their capital investments and secure high profits, monopoly capital, with the aid of the state apparatus, effects the militarization of the economy and encourages a "cold war" policy and various military adventures.'[1]

This description is misleading in several ways. For example, it ignores the connection between concentration of ownership and increased output; nor is there any mention of high taxation cutting into distributed profits and providing an incentive to productive re-investment. From data cited in the *History of the USA* a simple arithmetical calculation shows that company profits after tax, expressed as a percentage of gross profits, were lower throughout the early 1950s than they were in 1950, although the impression given is one of a steady rise. No account is taken of depreciation in the value of the currency when calculating the increase in profits. In short, the treatment of the whole problem is crude in the extreme.

The main characteristic of 'state-monopoly capitalism', the survival of which it is the task of the Soviet historian to explain, is the greater part played by the state in the management of the economy. However, no Soviet writer dares to suggest that the centres of economic and political power are interdependent, since this would contravene the principle of the primacy of the economic factor. Instead it is asserted unambiguously that it is the monopolists who control and direct the state. This means that the nationalization of certain industries (in Britain and elsewhere) has to be presented as a move inspired not by reformist politicians, but by the monopolists themselves, seeking to consolidate their position by transferring to the taxpayer the burden of supporting

[1] *Noveishaya istoriya* . . . , pp. 273-74.

declining industries that had ceased to yield any significant profit. 'The right-wing labour leaders tried to convince the workers that nationalization was a socialist measure. In fact this nationalization was a state-capitalist measure, carried out within the framework of the bourgeois state and with the purpose of strengthening the capitalist system.'[1]

This demonological theory, attractively simple though it is, leaves some irritating loose ends, such as why, if nationalization is in the monopolists' interests, it should normally be opposed by business opinion? So keen is Trukhanovsky to minimize the political and social motives for nationalization in Britain that he explains criticism of the measure by American industrialists as due to their disappointment at having been thereby deprived of a potentially lucrative investment—although a moment before the reader had learned that these industries were unprofitable.

Marx's doctrine of the growing impoverishment of the masses under capitalism has long been something of an embarrassment to his orthodox followers. In Stalin's day unwelcome facts could simply be ignored, or concealed by vague generalizations. Thus the 1953 study already referred to merely states that real wages in the United States in 1952 were 30 per cent below the pre-war level, 'taking into account the 25 per cent increase in the intensification of the labour process' (a figure which is neither elaborated nor explained); the housing situation was then singled out as an indicator of increasing impoverishment, and we learn that 'in all the capitalist countries slums are an inevitable feature of large towns—masses of dark, damp, mostly underground dwellings in semi-derelict houses, where the popular masses take shelter, crawling in the filth and cursing their fate'.[2] Such crudities at least are now a thing of the past. The *History of the USA* still maintains that average wages bought less in 1950-3 than they did in 1939, but admits that they rose during these three years; an official American figure of 7·8 per cent rise in real wages for the years 1953-8 is reproduced later without comment.[3] The final conclusion is as follows (p. 671):

'During the epoch of the general crisis of capitalism the process of absolute and relative impoverishment of the American working class was intensified. The share of the labouring masses in social income became ever smaller. In bourgeois propaganda, as is well known, much publicity is given to the thesis of the rising living standards of American

[1] Trukhanovsky, *Noveishaya istoriya Anglii*, p. 457.

[2] *Voprosy obshchevo krizisa kapitalizma*, p. 21.

[3] *Ocherki* . . . , p. 407. The 'net spendable weekly earnings' of production workers in manufacturing industry actually rose from $39·76 in 1939 to $56·05 in 1952 and $61·44 in 1958, (US Dept of Labour: *American Workers' Fact Book*, 1960, p. 116). The data for the UK are also instructive. The 1953 study claimed a fall in real wages of 20 per cent since pre-war. *Ekonomika i politika Anglii* (p. 460) gives no figure for 1952 but asserts that the 1938 figure was exceeded for the first time (by 2 per cent) in 1956, the last date given.

workers, especially since the war. But an objective analysis . . . shows that American capitalism is unable to ensure normal living conditions to the whole working class. A relatively high standard of living has been achieved only by the most highly-paid categories of workers, those with the highest and partly with average skills. But such workers comprise only a part of the proletariat, although a significant one.'

The verbal acrobatics at the end of this passage suggest that the editorial collective found it difficult to produce an agreed formula. How significant is 'a significant part'? No one disputes, after all, that differentials exist: what has to be demonstrated, if the 'law' of absolute impoverishment is to be proved, is that the unskilled or under-privileged groups are increasing in numbers proportionately to other groups of the working class, and that their earnings are falling. But the figures show that the trend is precisely the reverse. Unskilled non-farm workers, who formed 6·6 per cent of the labour force in 1950, had fallen to 5·7 per cent in 1959, and their real earnings rose by 13 per cent between 1948 and 1958.[1] A similar picture is obtained by examining the statistics of families and unattached individuals earning less than $2,000 per annum (in 1950 dollars): these formed 6·1 per cent of the total number of such individuals and families in 1950, but only 3·7 per cent in 1957; those earning less than $4,000 per annum fell from 29·1 per cent in 1950 to 19·9 per cent in 1957.[2]

Another argument strongly pressed is that, whatever gains there may have been, real wages have lagged behind rising 'labour costs'. It is this criterion, based on the value of the social product created by labour, and not that of market prices, that Soviet writers use to determine minimum living costs, which are thus calculated to show that they are much in excess of the average wage. These figures are said to take account of the 'historical and moral elements' characteristic of the given society, i.e. they rise in accordance with changes in the pattern of consumption, although it is obvious that these changes are themselves the product of higher living standards. In this way living costs can always be kept a certain distance ahead of wages: as on the dog-track, the greyhound never catches the hare. The *History of the USA* (p. 407) complains that the cost of living has risen:

not only as a result of the rise in prices, but also because of the *increase in the general amount of new goods that have entered into the concept of the standard of living*. The mass production of passenger cars, TV sets, refrigerators, radio receivers of various types, heaters and other domestic appliances, has naturally raised the general level of living costs. But the rise in wages has not only lagged behind the cost of the labour force necessary for the reproduction and training of labour in contemporary

[1] *American Workers' Fact Book*, pp. 19, 116. This was less than the skilled and semi-skilled workers' gain (31 per cent), but it was not a decline.
[2] *Historical Statistics of the USA* (1957), p. 165.

conditions, but even further behind the rise in living costs calculated by the Bureau of Labour Statistics . . .

However, the calculations of the Washington Bureau are not given; instead the source quoted is a mysterious publication entitled *Facts on the Position of the Toilers in the USA*, not listed in the bibliography. (It is presumably a semi-official Soviet publication not generally distributed.)

Soviet discussions of the cost of living in capitalist countries take it for granted that there is only one breadwinner in the family. The practice of married women taking up paid employment, which for better or worse has become a typical feature of the social scene in the mid-twentieth century, is interpreted as evidence of increased exploitation. The same faintly neo-Victorian attitude is adopted towards hire purchase: figures of the debts incurred by hire-purchase customers are construed as evidence of their unfortunate dependence upon the power of monopoly capital. It is of course possible that some Soviet writers may be genuinely puzzled as to the true significance of hire purchase, for in none of these works is its operation explained. However, one suspects that the misconceptions are deliberate rather than accidental. For the same reason Soviet historians are almost completely indifferent to the remarkable changes that have taken place in social habits in the industrialized western countries over the past generation. The social problems that occupy the foreground of discussion in these countries at the present time (to take two random examples: the position of the family in a mass society, or the maintenance of incentives in conditions of full employment) lie almost wholly outside the pious Leninist's field of vision.

V. Lyubimova, writing in a collection of articles rebutting the 'revisionist' heresy, pleads that the concept of absolute impoverishment should not be interpreted in an over-simplified manner, since it is a complex process which makes itself felt in various ways in different places and at different times. Although temporary limited improvements may be possible here or there, she argues, the *general* tendency of capitalism is still towards militarism, inferior housing, urban unemployment and rural over-population, harder work on the job, competition from sweated labour, industrial injuries and sickness.[1] In other words, this flexible interpretation of the term produces a list of social evils allegedly typical of capitalism which is long and wide enough to yield a grievance to fit any situation anywhere, thus enabling the fiction of overall impoverishment to be kept alive. And if this catalogue should cease to be relevant, other evils could fairly easily be discovered.

[1] On the question of industrial injuries, Lyubimova gives an example of the carelessness with which Soviet scholars often treat statistical data. She claims that in the USA the industrial injury rate rose from 1·6 million cases in 1939 to 2 million in 1956. This takes no account of the growth of the labour force; in fact, measured against the number of man-hours worked, the number of disabling injuries fell from 14·9 to 12·0 per million in these years (*Hist. Statistics of the USA*, p. 100).

Thus even relative (let alone absolute) impoverishment can only be 'proved' by broadening the term to deprive it of all real meaning. About the methods of improving western societies there will always be vigorous debate. But if Soviet historians wish their arguments to be treated with respect in the West they will have to base them on some recognizable body of fact.

The demonological view of history is particularly attractive to students of political developments, who are required to believe that the bitterly hostile critique of democracy formulated by Lenin in 1917, as part of his campaign to discredit the liberal-moderate socialist regime in Russia, is applicable to all democratic states at all times. The basic assumption is that only revolution and the 'dictatorship of the proletariat' can bring about 'genuine' ('socialist') democracy, whereas 'bourgeois' democracy is simply a monstrous confidence trick devised by the omnipotent monopolist demons to delude the popular masses into believing that they have some control over their own affairs. In practice Soviet historians and social scientists are obliged to modify this extremist interpretation. They admit that some steps taken by bourgeois governments can 'objectively' benefit the people, although such admissions are invariably qualified by the face-saving claim that these measures are actually concessions wrested from them unwillingly by violence, or the threat of violence, on the part of the masses. The logical implication that, if popular pressure can be exercised under the supposedly bogus freedoms, and through the bogus institutions, of bourgeois democracy, these are of real benefit to the people, is ignored. (It should perhaps be added that official recognition in recent years of the admissibility of the 'parliamentary road to socialism' has changed nothing in this respect, since the parliamentary struggle is still seen simply as a prelude to a revolutionary transformation of society under the 'dictatorship of the proletariat'.) This dogma prevents Soviet historians from even comprehending a great deal of the recent political history of the western world. Whatever cannot be fitted into the concept of the class struggle must perforce be distorted beyond all recognition or omitted altogether. A further complication arises from the insistence, derived from Marx, on regarding one particular aspect of human affairs as in some way 'basic' or 'decisive'. Just as the Leninist cannot afford to recognize that technological changes can have a decisive effect upon *any* political-economic order, so too he is unable to acknowledge the existence of technical problems of government and administration that have to be solved, if a country is to be run efficiently, whatever the nature of the regime in power. The work of administrative bodies has to be supervised, laws have to be made and enforced—and, most important of all, the rights of the citizens have to be protected (unless, of course, they are to remain purely fictitious). The Bolsheviks' refusal to recognize the elementary principles of political science—indeed, their deliberate repudiation of centuries of accumulated constitutional wisdom—had unexpected and sombre results in the USSR. So far as Soviet literature on western countries is concerned, it leads to the neglect of the constitutional and administrative aspects of history, which are seen as derivative and thus relatively unimportant; the few works that exist on the subject suffer from grievous and fundamental errors. It is automatically assumed that in a bourgeois state the ruling class can have no genuine respect for its laws and institutions, and would disregard them all, and govern by brute force alone, were it not for its fear of the 'masses'—just as 'the party of the proletariat' has no inherent respect for them, and destroys them as soon as it seizes power. The view that men are motivated purely by class interest implies that they can have no higher loyalties.

But this, again, is too crude a theory to be applied in practice, since it is all too evident that the bourgeoisie does not in fact function as a single unit. One common-sense explanation of this phenomenon would be to regard the ruling class as split into supporters of various political parties, each seeking power in order to promote its interests and policies; there is of course a good deal of argument along these lines in the earlier Marxist writings. But for the Leninist this is unacceptable; he insists that political parties can only represent particular classes. To fill the gap he invents a mysterious and sinister-sounding entity, 'circles' (*krugi*); and the struggle between these circles for influence behind the scenes is regarded as the very stuff of history—along with the struggle in the streets. Both of these conflicts are seen as central, while the conflict of political parties and trends of opinion is regarded at best as marginal and at worst as a base effort to confuse the masses.

It is thus understandable that in the historical works under consideration little is said about parliamentary battles, even when communists may have played a large part in them. Electoral campaigns are presented as operations in mass deception, with the parties concerned stooping to the most cynical demagogy to attract votes, while the people look on in apathy. A tone of irony is often affected, or sometimes one of outraged moral virtue, more appropriate to a good Victorian liberal describing gerrymandering practices in the rotten boroughs before the passage of the Reform Bill. Much is made of the poor turnout of voters in comparison with 'genuinely democratic' polls in communist countries. During the British general election of 1955, we are told, 'in West Walthamstow, London, where Attlee was standing, only twenty people turned up at a meeting arranged to present the candidate to the voters. The organizers put them into cars and took them to another meeting where Attlee was to speak. But here only ten people were waiting for him'.[1]

This approach has the advantage that shifts of opinion to the right or left within the bourgeois parties can be ignored: indeed, both can be claimed as victories for the people, on the ground that the electorate saw through the hypocrisy of the concrete demands contained in the

[1] Trukhanovsky, op. cit., p. 556.

programmes, and really voted for the vague general phrases in the preambles to them, which promised them peace and progress. (This view has its parallel in the 'image' theory popular among some students of politics in the West: neither gives the voter much credit for rational judgement.) The *History of the USA* tells us that the Republicans owed their 1952 victory to the impression made on voters by General Eisenhower's promise to go to Korea and secure peace. But why should a Republican President be voted into office for a second term four years after his 'non-peace-loving' policy had been 'exposed'? No explanation is offered, and instead comfort is taken from the fact that 'many electors voted *against* the candidates of the Republican party because of their internal and external policies'.[1] The Conservative victory in the 1955 British election is attributed to successful manipulation of popular hopes for summit talks and an East-West *détente*. In the 1950 election they are said to have strengthened their position because the electorate had grown disillusioned with Labour's 'aggressive' foreign policy and the heavy economic burdens involved:

the external and internal policies of the Labour Government could not help but arouse the dissatisfaction of those who had voted Labour in 1945 . . . The strengthening of the Conservatives' position in Parliament was the direct result of the anti-popular policy of Labour.[2]

But why, if the voters were disgusted at Labour's record, did they move to the right instead of to the left? The communists, it is sorrowfully recorded, 'secured only an insignificant number of votes', although they were 'the only genuine workers' party'.[3] Three arguments are usually advanced to explain this apparently incomprehensible behaviour of the electorate. The first places the blame upon the communists themselves, who are said to have 'paid insufficient attention to the peace movement' and the trade unions, and to have wrongly condemned the Labour party *en bloc*, instead of distinguishing between the leaders (reactionary) and the rank-and-file (progressive). In the Higher Party School textbook all the western CPs are criticized for errors of one kind or another. Then there are complaints of repression—not only in the USA and Western Germany, where anti-communist legislation is in force, but even in such countries as Britain:

during the electoral campaign [of 1955] the communists were subjected to all manner of discrimination: it is enough to say that by decision of the stooges of the big monopolists in charge of the BBC, the CPGB was prevented from using such a powerful weapon as radio and television to popularize its ideas and positions.[4]

[1] *Ocherki* . . . , pp. 425, 463.
[2] Trukhanovsky, op. cit., p. 509.
[3] Ibid., p. 521.
[4] *Ekonomika i politika Anglii*, p. 556.

Lastly—an explanation advanced somewhat diffidently—there is the almost limitless credulity of the masses, who to judge by the evidence presented here have a most unwholesome appetite for bourgeois propaganda. In general 'the people' are treated in Soviet works on western history with polite condescension, as befits those who, though at heart potentially peace-loving and progressive, persistently allow themselves to be led astray. Occasionally a note of bitterness creeps in, and the confident phrases about the courageous and persistent struggle being waged by the western masses sound a trifle forced.

In addition, much can of course be done to conceal the true state of affairs by vastly magnifying the extent of popular support obtained by the extreme left. A case in point is the treatment of industrial unrest: what is in fact a more or less normal and accepted phenomenon in a free-enterprise economy is portrayed in Soviet historical writings as a challenge to the very existence of the system. Measured as a percentage of total working time, the hours lost through industrial disputes in the United States between 1946 and 1958 varied between a peak of 1·43 per cent in 1946 and a low of 0·17 per cent in 1957, the highest intermediate figure occurring in 1952 (0·57 per cent). The party textbook, after singling out a number of individual strikes for comment, sums up: 'all these facts indicate that in the USA sharp class conflicts are continuing to mature, that propaganda about "people's capitalism" has not had any serious success' (p. 494). The *History*, faced with the necessity of supplying annual figures, finds it difficult to give the required impression of steadily increasing discontent. 'Thus in 1953-9', we are told, 'the strike movement developed with unflagging force, although the most stubborn class struggles, as has been shown in the preceding chapter, took place in 1952.' A still more elegant way of conveying the notion of a decline occurs earlier in the same volume: 'However, the strike movement also continued to develop in 1947-8, but to a lesser extent than in the first post-war year.'[1] In the light of these remarks it is perhaps not surprising that this voluminous work contains no comprehensive tables of statistics (of strikes, wages, industrial output, etc.), and that the figures are given chapter by chapter; but this is admittedly a minor fault, and one must be grateful that the figures are given at all.

Judged as a whole, the picture formed by the Soviet student of the domestic situation in the USA after reading these works may well be a somewhat disturbing one, for the facts, even in the distorted manner in which they are presented, scarcely seem to justify their confident tone. Taking the evidence of these pages as a guide, the masses have for years been 'rallying behind their vanguard', waves of anti-imperialist protest have been 'mounting higher and higher', crises have been 'deepening even further', and so on—yet still the monopolist demons lord it over their vast domain. A sceptical reader might well wonder whether there is something wrong with the formula. For there is one explanation for the disappointing achievements of the communist parties in the western

[1] *Ocherki* . . . , pp. 348, 445.

D*

world that no Soviet historian could dare to mention: that communism may be irrelevant to an industrialized society. The original expectations of revolution in the West have not been fulfilled. It is now a common-place to western observers that the appeals of communism are greatest in the under-developed countries, where the 'revolution of rising expectations' has just begun. If Soviet historians were free to examine the contemporary world in a rational way, they would be obliged to recognize that there must be some 'fundamental' and 'objective' reason for the present state of affairs. But Leninist subjectivism requires them to believe that what they see is simply a mirage; that the pattern of events is really quite different; and that a handful of powerful demons have succeeded in holding up and diverting the course of history from its proper path.

Some years ago Professor F. C. Barghoorn singled out as a 'funda-mental characteristic of Soviet propaganda . . . the attribution to America and other free nations of the motives and tactics typical of Soviet communism'.[1] The Soviet image of the West has not been sub-stantially modified since then, nor has tireless repetition through all possible information media made the Soviet picture of the international scene any more convincing. The world is still asked to believe that the Soviet Union, which makes no secret of its desire to see its own political and social system triumph throughout the globe, at the same time stands for the maintenance of the international *status quo*, and for 'friendly equal relations between all states and non-intervention in their internal affairs'. The main threat to the established international order is said to come from the 'imperialist' countries, seeking to bring the whole world into subjection, while the USSR stands guard over the rights of peoples, defending their national sovereignty against attempts to force them into 'aggressive military blocs'. Thus words are used in a sense opposite to their normal meaning, and the Cold War continues on its wearisome course. The hostility of Soviet spokesmen towards the West is aroused, not so much by what it *does*, but by what it *is*: by their very existence the non-communist countries cast doubt on the merits of Soviet claims.

Fortunately for the prospects of world peace the two-camp doctrine is less crude than it may at first sight appear. For the argument is that while the socialist countries enjoy 'monolithic unity' the imperialist bloc is rent by inherent 'inner contradictions', which prevent them from realizing their aggressive potential and thus help to reduce the risk of war. Indeed, if the NATO countries were really as divided against them-selves as Soviet commentators sometimes claim they are, they could scarcely pose a threat to anyone.

The contradiction theory takes its origin from Lenin's interpretation of the First World War as a conflict between two rival blocs of imperialist powers. During the 1920s, and again after 1945, the principal

[1] *The Soviet Image of the United States: a Study in Distortion* (New York, 1950), pp. xi-xii.

contradictions—rather oddly, perhaps, at first sight—have been deemed to exist between the USA and Great Britain. The two Anglo-Saxon powers are seen as engaged in intense competition for markets, sources of raw materials and spheres of investment, as well as in conflicts over spheres of political influence and strategic bases in the under-developed countries.

In fact the rise in US exports to the Commonwealth countries has not been very significant. The level has been determined not so much by the relative economic potential of the two countries as by the difficulty experienced in making enough hard currency available. In a strictly Anglo-American context the dollar shortage is interpreted by Soviet writers as a device by which the United States keeps Britain (and other Western European countries) in economic subjection; and yet this same factor is recognized as having helped Britain to limit US competition and maintain her position in the Commonwealth, which it is allegedly the main purpose of the United States to undermine. This is indeed a contradiction, although not of the type envisaged by communist theorists. A. G. Mileikovsky draws up an elaborate list of the drawbacks and advantages possessed by Britain in her rivalry with the USA, during which he says that Britain's 'permanent excess of imports over exports, her chronic deficit on her trading balance, which is the cause of her unstable balance of payments, gives her *a certain advantage* in the competitive struggle; this dependence on imports is one of the main causes of the virility of the system of imperial preferences and the sterling area, those bastions of British imperialism . . .'[1] —bastions which by all the Leninist rules ought to have crumbled away long ago under American pressure. The Wall Street sappers do not seem to be very efficient.

American investments in the Commonwealth are another favourite target for the Soviet critics, who emphasize again and again that these have increased greatly since the war; they do not add that the total is still only a fraction of investments or reinvestments from Britain.[2] Since the sterling area accounted for less than 5 per cent of total US foreign investment, American investors would appear to have sufficient elbow-room elsewhere. From the recipient country's point of view the advantages and disadvantages of extensive foreign investment depend on many variables (the urgency of development projects, availability of capital elsewhere on better terms, amount of profits transferred out of the country, state of the dollar reserves, etc.). Each case has to be judged on its merits. To denounce all investment as 'imperialist' or prejudicial to national sovereignty is clearly doctrinaire.

Finally, the thesis that economic rivalry is the dominant factor in

---

[1] *Ekonomika i politika Anglii* . . . , p. 89.

[2] The figures for 1948-57 are: USA £725 million, UK £2,175 million. The USA total includes a certain amount of credit to India and other under-developed countries under Point 4. Cf. A. R. Conan, *Capital Imports into Sterling Countries* (London, 1960), p. 70.

Anglo-American relations loses much of its significance in the light of the current Soviet view that it is now the prime objective of 'us imperialism' to maintain the Commonwealth as a political barrier against revolutionary pressures in the under-developed countries.

The general impression conveyed by the literature on imperialist contradictions is a somewhat confusing one. Varga comes to the conclusion that although they are 'very deep' and could lead to 'open conflicts' (but not wars) from time to time, the countries concerned 'are bound together by their common purpose in maintaining the historically doomed capitalist system and their common enmity towards the socialist system'.[1] This vague formulation conveniently permits the theory to be invoked as correct whatever the actual state of the western alliance may be at any given moment.

Why does the Leninist historian find it necessary to 'demonize' the history of the modern western world? The question is more than one of commitment to a certain party line; it is rooted in the nature of Bolshevism itself. Lenin argued that the contradictions of capitalism were in the last instance due to unequal rates of economic growth, and that this led inevitably to rivalry between the stronger powers and those who tried to resist their dominion. Immediately after the Second World War there was indeed a crass disparity between the strength of the USA on one hand and the Western European countries on the other. But instead of the gap widening, it decreased. Aid under the ERP helped the weaker partners in the alliance to rehabilitate their economies and to resume their expansion. This put them in a position to compete for us markets, and evidence of this is eagerly seized on by Soviet historians to show that the contradictions still continue to exist, and indeed to grow more intense.[2] But this official optimism conceals a lurking fear that in fact contradictions of this superficial type may prove reconcilable, that the western countries may one day achieve financial stability and enter into a healthy economic relationship with the United States. The prospect of the political-military unity of the Atlantic Pact countries being reinforced by some effective form of international economic union, in which trade would flow freely and balance of payments problems would be a thing of the past, is nothing less than a nightmare to the Soviet ideologist. Of course, the historians and social scientists can be put to work to show that progress towards this aim has been slow and halting; but they cannot show convincingly that it is impossible. It is this unacknowledged realization that in the western world the 'objective laws of history' are not in fact working out as they should that compels the Soviet historian to resort to a crude subjectivist interpretation of

[1] *Ekonomika i politika imperializma*, p. 331.

[2] 'Historical experience shows that the diminution of the difference in the level of development of the capitalist countries, their levelling, is the basis for the intensification of the inequalities in the development of capitalism, for it is precisely because the less advanced countries are speeding their development . . . that the struggle sharpens for some countries to overtake others' (M. S. Dragilev, *Obshchii krizis kapitalizma* (Moscow, 1957), p. 261).

the pattern of events, just as Lenin himself once rejected the picture of the trends of his day that emerged from the Marxist analysis and sought instead to re-make the world in accordance with his own ideas.

DISCUSSION

Dr Keep said the subject of his paper was so vast that even after limiting it chronologically to 1945-61 and geographically to Western Europe and North America, he had been able to deal only summarily with a few selected phenomena that seemed interesting or important. A search through the dark cupboards of recent Soviet writing had not disclosed any independent thinking on contemporary international problems; if heretical views existed, they did not seem to have been judged worthy of comment or censure in the columns of *Pravda* or *Kommunist*. One was tempted to conclude that this was an area untouched by the thaw, because it was too sensitive and too intimately linked with the political interests of the Soviet leadership. No brave spirit had arisen to suggest, for instance, that the creation of NATO was to some extent a reaction to the line in foreign policy taken by Stalin and Molotov at the end of the war. There had of course been important changes in the spirit and orientation of Soviet foreign policy—the doctrine of the non-inevitability of war, the new attitude towards uncommitted countries, etc.—and these were reflected in Soviet writings on international affairs. Nevertheless the views of the present leaders were echoed as faithfully in current historical literature as were Stalin's while he was alive.

The most important developments in Soviet historiography in recent years had been the impressive increase in the number of works published, the improvement in the apparatus of scholarship, or pseudo-scholarship, with which they were equipped, and the greater relevance of the material to the expressed goals of the party leadership. The accent had been shifted to the study of contemporary problems, and although the result might appear deficient by western standards, it met with the approval of the authorities in the Soviet Union.

Soviet historiography since Stalin, particularly in relation to the non-communist world, was as militant and anti-objectivist as it had been under Stalin. However, the historians had been given the means to present the official view much more effectively and convincingly than they could do before, and it was likely that a high proportion of them were powerfully attracted by the content of the official doctrine, with its appeal to their sense of national pride, its promise of certainty and insurance against possible error, its demand that historians should commit themselves wholly to a fight against what was anyhow condemned by the inevitable march of history. In its present state Soviet historical science approximated closely to the official stereotype of the monolothic juggernaut; the sheer volume of output presented a formidable challenge. True, as the elephant charged towards us, we could detect an arrow sticking in its back, marked revisionism. But there was no evidence that the wound was proving fatal, or that it was likely to interrupt the elephant in its onward course.

The general conformity that existed among Soviet historians did not mean that their doctrine was a single, coherent whole. This was far from being the case, though there was perhaps room for disagreement as to the nature of its internal inconsistencies. In Dr Keep's view there was no such doctrine as Marxism-Leninism. Mr Wolfe had pointed out Lenin's emphasis upon the organizational factor, upon political power as an instrument for realizing the aims which Marx expected to be achieved as a result of the spontaneous unfolding of the historical process. Marx claimed to have stood Hegel on his head; it could be argued that Lenin performed exactly the same operation with Marx, shifting the emphasis from the class to the party, supposed to be the embodiment of the general will of the working class, and injecting into what had been essentially a European political theory certain concepts derived from the tradition of the Russian intelligentsia, brought up in the harsh climate of absolutism. In Soviet writings on contemporary western history, the Marxist heritage could be discerned when the historians sought to describe and understand the workings of spontaneous social and economic forces in a relatively detached and scholarly spirit. The Leninist heritage, on the other hand, could be seen in their inability to draw from their studies the appropriate political conclusions, because these were laid down in advance to suit the current official interpretation of a given epoch. This was not history, but 'demonology': the attribution to a handful of individuals of the power to hold up, through the exercise of their will, what was supposed to be the objective historical process, and the refusal to ask the obvious question which occurred to the impartial observer, i.e. whether this interruption of the historical process had not in itself some logical explanation, whether the founding fathers might not have been mistaken in their prognosis as to the likely course of future events. Instead, the old dogmas were mechanically invoked like magic formulas, regardless of the facts. For instance, figures which showed rising living standards in western countries were suppressed or manipulated in order to support the view that no real improvement had taken place.

The contradictions within the official dogma could also be seen in the context of the conflict between the commitment to international revolution and the more immediate aim of promoting Soviet Russian national interests, as seen in the treatment by Soviet historians of the relations between France and Algeria.

In each case it was necessary to distinguish between what bore at least some relation to reality and might even be a genuine contribution to scholarship, and what was simply official propaganda. Where the Soviet historian strove to weld factual evidence and dogmatic theory into a plausible and convincing whole, the duty of his western critics was to separate the wheat from the chaff.

Dr Gallagher commented on the image of the West projected in current Soviet histories of the war. He agreed that there had been no substantial change in the Soviet image of the West over the past ten years. In fact in the more recent histories there appeared to be a more consistent effort at blackening western motives and actions. For example, the Soviet theme of Anglo-American contradictions was developed with great ingenuity and thoroughness, especially in the interpretation of the different strategies advocated during the war by Churchill and the Americans. While Churchill's plan for an offensive in the Balkans was presented as designed to secure for England a dominant post-war position in Europe, the cross-Channel strategy of the Americans was interpreted as designed to weaken England's position on the Continent and to hasten the day when American forces could be shifted to the Pacific, where again the objective was said to be the displacement of British influence.

Side by side with this picture of the deep contradictions between the western allies, Soviet writers also presented a picture of the Anglo-American bloc united in common hostility to the Soviet Union and conspiring for common advantage at the latter's expense. In the current Soviet war histories the image of the hostile western bloc was emphasized more than the image of contradictions between the western allies. This might reflect both Russia's increasing preoccupation with America, and a growing awareness that their hopes for serious differences within the western world in this atomic age were not very realistic.

In connection with Dr Keep's statement that he had been unable to find a Burdzhalov among Soviet historians writing on the western world, Dr Bolsover suggested that perhaps there was no need for a Burdzhalov in this field in 1956, as Varga had played the part ten years earlier. The issues raised in Varga's book on the post-war world, published in 1946, provoked an intense ideological, political, and scholarly controversy; eventually, Varga was forced to give way on all points, although he held out on one until after the publication of Stalin's *Economic Problems of Socialism* in 1952. After Stalin's death, however, some of Varga's heretical views became the accepted doctrine. His contention that war between the capitalist and communist worlds was not inevitable was today accepted by Khrushchev. His emphasis on the significant change in the relationship between the metropolitan and colonial countries—he was concerned largely with India—has since Stalin's death been reflected in Soviet policy.

Dr Katkov thought the discussion would be vitiated if the conference concerned itself with establishing the degrees of veracity in the Soviet picture of the West, rather than its basic institutional mendacity. Professor Aspaturian had quoted the contradiction between the American Constitution and racial segregation as evidence that in the United States there existed the same difference between myth and reality as in the Soviet Union. The only condition on which he would be prepared to accept that remark as correct, would be if it were possible for a Soviet critic of the West to rise at a public meeting and to indict the contradictions of the Soviet system. Until this could happen, the difference between myth and reality in the Soviet Union could not be compared with anything existing in the United States.

Professor Aspaturian replied that he had invoked the American example merely to show that contradictions existed in all societies and that awareness of them was by itself insufficient to bring about a change. Dr Bolsover had been concerned not with the general co-existence of myth and reality in the Soviet system or any other system, but with the possibility of the official history of the party co-existing with views of certain episodes of party history which contradicted it. In this sense, his question bore directly on what Dr Katkov called institutional mendacity.

Mr Labedz suggested that the reason why Soviet history of the non-communist world was much more continuous than the historiography of developments inside the Soviet Union could be found in ideological developments and in the necessities of the revolution from above. By ideology he did not mean simply a body of ideas formulated to achieve certain purposes; he had in mind something more in line with the classical Marxist definition of ideology as false consciousness—ideology not as reflecting any view of the world, but more as a screen refracting reality in a certain direction.

One of the things for which Stalin had been condemned in Khrushchev's secret speech was his idea that internal contradictions grew sharper as socialism drew nearer. This important ideological premise had provided the basic justification for the purges of the thirties. Once it was discarded, Soviet historiography had to make another turn. But Khrushchev's explicit statement that peaceful co-existence means the sharpening of the ideological struggle was an exact parallel, on the external plane, of the Stalinist view of the sharpening of the class conflict. Like Stalin's ideological premise, it provided the starting-point for Soviet history of the non-communist world in Khrushchev's era. This explained why, as both Dr Keep and Dr Gallagher had noted, the view of the external world presented by Soviet historians had not become any more lenient. The problem that ideological agnosticism presented for the dynamics of the one-party system had been overcome after the revolution by direct patriotic appeals—this was the mechanism which Stalin used to strengthen his hold and maintain the momentum of the revolution from above. Now the same sort of ideological weakening could be overcome only by projecting the ideological struggle outside the borders of the Soviet Union—the dynamics of the revolution from above must find justification in the Manichean view of the world. This did not preclude at times a more rational approach to reality than the paranoiac views of the outside world propagated in Stalin's time. The basic contrast with the Stalin era was to be found in the attitude to the under-developed countries. But the admission that under-developed countries need not be classified exactly in the same way as western countries did not mean the abandonment of the aim of the seizure of power by a ruling élite. Those who believed in a necessary correlation between internal relaxation and the dynamics of foreign policy might find that relaxation at home could in some cases lead to the sharpening of Soviet foreign policy.

Professor Halle, distinguishing between myth and mendacity, referred to the situation before the American Civil War, when the Constitution of the United States guaranteed certain freedoms, while at the same time the institution of slavery was practised. That was an example of the co-existence of myth and reality. But if one denied the existence of the institution of slavery, that was an example of mendacity.

Mr Schapiro returned to the theme of the essential difference between Leninism and Marxism: whereas Marx had produced a certain social analysis, Lenin had adopted it and, long after it had ceased to correspond to facts, had turned it into institutionalized mendacity. Soviet ideologists were not out to analyse facts, but to present an image—for example, the image of the proletariat growing steadily poorer under capitalism. Having created the image, they used their organization to impose it. That is why Mr Wolfe was right in stressing that Leninism was an organizational ideology. Lenin was a Russian revolutionary who had found Marxism useful as a starting-point; but the creation and development of a revolutionary organization for the seizure of power, which was Lenin's unique and remarkable achievement, had nothing to do with Marxism.

Professor Rubinstein thought that what was legitimate in the Soviet image of the western world should not be ignored. In the sphere of foreign policy, the distinction between myth and reality was not nearly so sharp as in domestic affairs, where the contrast between the word and the deed was evident to the most defective vision. In regard to foreign relations there was enough evidence, at least viewed from the Soviet side, to warrant acceptance of many of Marx's predictions, such as his vision of the disintegration of capitalism in conditions of growing poverty. The capitalist world had disintegrated. Since 1945, the British, French, and Dutch empires had been dismantled, voluntarily or otherwise. The communist position in the world was much stronger than it had been twenty years before. Although standards of living in the United States, Great Britain, and Western Europe were rising, economic surveys continually emphasized the growing disparity between the rich and the poor nations. This would tend to reinforce certain ideological attitudes on the part of Soviet historians. It would be useful for the conference to attempt to isolate those elements of validity, or at least of partial validity, in the image of the outside world which might influence not only the writing of Soviet historians, but also the policy of the Soviet leaders. In this respect we might ask ourselves whether there was enough factual evidence to permit the Soviets to develop a plausible interpretation of the West as being in a progressive state of erosion, disarray, and disintegration.

Dr Keep's statement that 'unlike his western colleague for whom facts are facts, all potentially significant and needing evaluation, the Soviet historian is free to disregard whatever cannot be made to fit his thesis' should not, Mrs Degras thought, be allowed to stand without qualification. They could all think of books which showed that in the West too historians could be guilty of selecting facts which fitted their thesis and ignoring others. But the question went deeper than that. Facts were facts, and there were millions of them for every day of every week of every year—to collect them all was physically impossible. Besides, a collection of facts, however complete, was not history. No historian could really be more than a chronicler of events unless he approached his facts with some idea or purpose in mind. Adherence to methodological criteria alone did not produce history. Historians had to have theoretical criteria too, which gave their material a pattern and a shape and helped to reveal not only what happened, but why it happened.

On this point, Mr Labedz quoted John Dewey: 'This writer's reflection shows that the conceptual material employed in writing history is that of the period in which the history is written. There is no material available for living principles and hypotheses save that of the historic present. As culture changes, the conceptions that are dominant in a culture change. Of necessity new standpoints for viewing, appraising, and ordering data arise. History is then re-written.'

He wished to underline that the question was not really one of re-interpretation, but of a very special attitude to the facts—not merely of the Soviet historian's selection of the facts, but of the violence done to them.

Mr Wolfe made the distinction that, while we all approached history or any body of facts with tentative theories, in the West these theories sprang from the material itself, whereas in the Soviet Union they were dictated from above. Dewey was right in saying that we approached all facts in terms of the concepts of the present, but in a pluralistic society these concepts were multiple, whereas in a totalitarian society they were controlled and uniform—an essential distinction.

Mr Wolfe agreed with Professor Rubinstein that there were elements of truth in the Soviet view of the western world. But the examples he had selected were most unfortunate, for they were neither Marxism nor Leninism. Marx had spoken of the collapse of capitalism, not of its disintegration. On the contrary, he had expected capitalism to spread to the non-capitalist world and in his discussion of India he had shown how he thought this would be done. In the same sense, Lenin expected first, that England would fall the moment she lost her colonies, and second, that she would never release her colonies without a cataclysmic death struggle. Lenin had also expected that, once England lost her colonies, the working classes would immediately cease to be corrupted by the super-profits of imperialism, opportunism would disappear, and the English working class would show the way to the world in being revolutionary, Marxist, and Leninist.

Having spoken before of the plight of the Soviet historian writing on orders from above, Mr Wolfe now added that a great many people who worked in the intellectual field in the Soviet Union were capable of internalizing the commands given to them. Most of them had ceased to need to be commanded; they had accepted the formulas; they were used to selecting from the evidence only what supported their thesis and discarding what refuted it (which was sometimes done in our society too). The brave spirits that struggle for freedom were perhaps a minority in every country.

Professor Rubinstein said that in listing the factors that accounted for the way in which Soviet historians wrote history, there might be a tendency to ignore those interpretations of world events which, though differing from ours, were nevertheless legitimate. Political science in the United States was in danger of becoming scholastic in a way that might impair the ability to interpret the motives of Soviet behaviour. In raising the question of the Marxian image as seen by Soviet historians, he had wished to draw attention to what we tended to neglect: the dynamic quality in the Soviet view of a changing world. There were certainly imperfections and distortions in this view, but it was still a way of looking at the world. He was not interested in what Marx said, but in the way the Soviet interpretation of Marx affected their interpretation of events today.

Professor Scheibert agreed that the Soviet interpretation of foreign policy deserved attention for the elements of truth it might contain. The social and economic development of the western world was a crucial problem for Soviet historiography, perhaps more touchy than party history itself. For the evaluation of the development of the western world, which in many ways differed totally from the Marxist prognosis, provided the only point at which they could start the re-thinking and re-orientation of the Soviet social and economic system.

Professor Fainsod illustrated some of the points made in the discussion by an anecdote: in September 1956, when peaceful co-existence was in full swing, he had visited the Institute of Law of the Soviet Academy of Sciences. At a meeting with well-known Soviet professors, the inevitable subject, i.e. the position of the Negro in the United States, had come up. *Pravda* at that moment had been full of the Clinton riots and the burning of a desegregated school in Tennessee. Asked what he thought of this barbarous incident, Professor Fainsod said it was disgraceful, that many people in the United States thought likewise, and that he was glad that *Pravda* had drawn attention to it. However, when he followed this by remarking that he was puzzled not to have seen in *Pravda* any mention of the opening of integrated schools in Washington DC, Cincinnati, Saint Louis, and various other cities, there had been an embarrassed silence, until their spokesman had said: 'Well, these things may have happened, but that is not important. What is important is what happened in Clinton.' Professor Fainsod walked away from the meeting in company with a professor of administrative law, who turned to him and said: 'I know why these things weren't in *Pravda*, and I think that most of the people around the table also know. Good day.'

Professor Aspaturian thought that the question of whether or not Marxism, Leninism, Stalinism, and Khrushchevism were compatible with one another or with the truth was important if one studied the development of ideas, but it remained an intellectual exercise. It was only one dimension. Soviet ideology might not be *the* Marxism, but it was undeniably a variety of Marxism. These distinctions between Lenin and Marx taught us nothing about the effectiveness of Soviet ideology. It was not enough to establish the falsehoods or the occasional glimpses of truth in Soviet ideology. It was equally important to ask how effective it was as a theory of reality and to evaluate this effectiveness in terms of Soviet purposes, not in terms of ours. The way the Soviets related events might not correspond completely to reality, but there must be some correspondence that enabled them to act and explained their achievements, in terms of their own aims, during the past forty years.

v. Soviet Historiography after Stalin

S. V. UTECHIN

Few aspects of academic life in Russia since 1917 have been followed with such a sustained and intensive interest abroad as historical research and writing. As a result there was no backlog of ignorance and misconceptions to struggle with when dealing with the recent changes in the fortunes of our discipline in Russia, such as existed, for example, in the field of natural sciences before the first sputnik. The situation in the last years of Stalin's life was subjected to a particularly close scrutiny concerning the organization of historical studies, the official requirements, and the actual performance. One of the main reasons for this interest was undoubtedly the recognition that historical writing in Russia was a political tool in the hands of Stalin, and one that could be studied with comparative ease. The approach, therefore, to the study of Soviet historiography was often that of a political scientist rather than a professional historian. This approach has to a considerable extent persisted in the post-Stalin period and will certainly continue to be necessary so long as historical writing remains to a significant extent a political tool of the communist party. It is, indeed, largely applied in this paper; but precisely because of this I would like to stress here the limitations of this approach and the dangers inherent in an excessive addiction to it. There are two chief dangers: one may concentrate too much on the party directives, neglecting the historical writings themselves;[1] and one may attribute to the official standpoint what is in fact a scholar's conclusion from his research. Fortunately, it is usually not difficult for a specialist to assess the validity of a historian's argument.

It was, I think, due to the prevalence of the political scientist approach that developments immediately following Stalin's death have received hardly any attention—the political scientist was at the time fully occupied with evidence other than that provided by historical journals. Thus the appearance of the Soviet delegation at the tenth international historical congress in Rome in 1955 (after an interval of nearly twenty years) aroused considerable interest: how would they behave and what would they say in the changed conditions? After the congress there was a spate of articles, mainly by professional historians who had been shocked by the continued refusal, or in some cases apparent inability, on the part

[1] This seems to me to be the defect of the last part of Professor W. Philipp's paper 'Wandlungen der Sowjethistoriographie' in *Marxismus-Leninismus. Geschichte und Gestalt* (Berlin, 1961), pp. 82-88, dealing with post-1957 developments. The earlier parts of the paper, on the contrary, show what insights a professional historian's approach can yield.

of the Soviet historians to enter into a genuine intellectual encounter.[1] But this theme was soon swamped by the spectacle of the historians' participation in the general intellectual unrest in the Soviet Union in 1956-7 and the reaction after the events in Hungary. Views may differ as to the significance of what followed. The impressions of the 1960 congress at Stockholm, as far as one can gather, seem merely to confirm the general view of a return to Stalinist practices in Soviet historiography. I do not agree with this view (though I see how it can be held) and shall try in this essay to show why.

ORGANIZATION

One of the main features of the Stalin-Beria regime in historical studies was that access to sources was severely limited. The Chief Administration of Archives was transferred to the Ministry of Internal Affairs in the 1930s, and from then onwards the main consideration governing permission to work in the archives and to see specific sets of documents was to ensure that no document should come to the notice of historians which might contradict or be incompatible with propositions advanced by Stalin, Zhdanov, or Beria. Historians of the communist party and of the Soviet period of Russian history were obviously hardest hit by this, but those specializing in nineteenth- and early twentieth-century Russian history, and in the modern history of foreign countries, were also seriously affected. Publication of sources in these fields almost ceased, save for selections intended to illustrate some current campaign.

Complaints about this state of affairs began to be publicly voiced in 1954,[2] but the feeling must have been very widespread and strong, since the first measures to remedy the situation were taken immediately after Stalin's death. The Presidium of the Academy of Sciences, in its decision of March 20, 1953, on the reorganization of the Academy's Institute of History, provided for the setting up at the institute of a section for the publication of sources on the history of the USSR, and in April the then acting director of the institute—A. L. Sidorov—announced the forthcoming appearance of a new journal devoted to the publication of archival materials.[3] This last project must have encountered considerable obstacles, since it was not in fact started until 1955. Complaints about the inaccessibility of sources continued to mount until in February 1956, by a decision of the Council of Ministers, the rules governing the use of archives were greatly relaxed.[4] Scholarly work in archives has

---

[1] E.g. W. Hofer, 'Objektivität und Parteilichkeit', *Deutsche Rundschau*, 1956, No. 6; Karl Thieme, 'Möglichkeiten und Grenzen west-östlicher Historikerbegegnung', *Geschichte in Wissenschaft und Unterricht*, 1957, No. 10. Cf. S. V. Utechin, 'Soviet Historians and Historiography Today', *Occidente*, January-February 1956; *idem*, 'Soviet Historians in Rome', *Russian Review*, October 1956.

[2] *Voprosy Istorii*, 1954, No. 7, pp. 11, 180.

[3] Ibid., 1953, Nos. 5, 10; *Istoricheskii Arkhiv*, 1957, No. 2, pp. 217-19.

[4] The archives have not been thrown open, and the historians complain that the 'reconsideration' of what should be made available, which began in 1956, is proceeding too slowly (*Istoriya SSSR*, 1963, No. 2, p. 11).

also been facilitated by improved arrangements for assisting people to find their way about in them, and a number of leading archives have published guides to their materials. All this, together with the stress now laid on original research, has resulted in a constant increase in the number of scholars using the archives.[1]

Publication of documentary and other sources has also been greatly expanded. The Archeographic Commission of the Academy of Sciences, in existence from 1834 to 1922, and again from 1944 to 1948, was re-established once more in October 1956 and has since been doing excellent work. *Istoricheskii Arkhiv* (previously an occasional publication) was appearing as a bi-monthly journal from 1955 to 1962, reproducing for the most part documents on the Soviet period and on party history.[2] Apart from this, many collections of materials have been published, particularly numerous being those issued in connection with the fiftieth anniversary of the 1905 revolution and the fortieth anniversary of October 1917. An interesting special case is the publication of materials relating to Lenin. For two decades this was a monopoly of the Marx-Engels-Lenin Institute; the monopoly was abolished in 1956 and materials on Lenin were declared fair game for any publishing enterprise. This was followed by the appearance of several distorted versions of Lenin's writings, the result of incompetent editing, and in 1958 publication of Lenin's writings was again largely centralized.[3] Historians, particularly those working on economic and social history, can now also benefit from the systematic publication of official statistics, revived in 1956 and still expanding.

Another major complaint of the historians at the time of Stalin's death was that facilities for publishing their work were grossly inadequate.[4] In the whole country there were only three historical journals—*Istoricheskie Zapiski*, specializing in the medieval and modern history of Russia, *Vestnik Drevnei Istorii* for ancient history, and *Voprosy Istorii*, the leading historical organ. Here a radical change came in 1957, when six new journals were started: *Istoriya SSSR, Voprosy Istorii KPSS, Novaya i Noveishaya Istoriya, Vestnik Istorii Mirovoi Kultury, Voenno-istoricheskii Zhurnal*, and *Ukrainskyi Istorychnyi Zhurnal*. The expansion continued in the following years when a historical series began to be issued by the Moscow and Leningrad university *Vestniki*, and a history series was brought out as a separate journal within the framework of the new *Nauchnye Doklady Vysshei Shkoly*. All these new journals have had considerable success and show every sign of good

[1] In 1956-8 7,500 readers used the reading room of the Central Party Archive attached to the Institute of Marxism-Leninism, compared to about 2,500 in 1953-5; the reading-rooms of the state archives were used by 36,000 people in 1956-7 as against 23,000 in 1954-5 (*Istoricheskii Arkhiv*, 1959, No. 1, p. 4).

[2] Its publication was interrupted for six months in the first half of 1962 and ceased altogether after the end of that year.

[3] *Spravochnik partiinovo rabotnika* (Moscow, 1957), p. 364; ibid. (Moscow, 1959), p. 500.

[4] *Voprosy Istorii*, 1954, No. 7, pp. 177-82.

health.[1] In addition, a number of study groups and 'scientific councils' at the Academy of Sciences regularly publish collections of papers, and contributions on history have had at least a fair share in the rapidly growing number of occasional papers brought out by many higher educational establishments.

The publication of books on history has also increased substantially, although not steadily. There had been 819 titles in 1940, 688 in 1951, 556 in 1953; in 1955 the figure rose to 965 titles, and stood at 820 in 1956; it rose to 1,602 in 1957 but decreased to 1,381 in 1958 and to 1,367 in 1959; in 1960, it rose again to 1,656. Roughly speaking, books on the history of Russia made up about two-thirds of the total output in 1954-9, and just over one-half in 1960.[2]

There have been comparatively few changes in the organization of research. Historians, as before, are employed in three categories of institutions: research institutes of the Academies of Sciences, universities and other higher educational establishments, and the research and teaching bodies of the CPSU. The chief academic institution—the Institute of History of the USSR Academy of Sciences—was in trouble at the time of Stalin's death. The party authorities had found its work unsatisfactory in the light of Stalin's last theoretical pronouncement, the *Economic Problems of Socialism in the USSR*, and of the decisions of the nineteenth party congress. Academician B. D. Grekov was removed from the directorship of the institute (a fact that received surprisingly little attention abroad) and replaced by Sidorov, a former pupil of M. N. Pokrovsky, who had been prominent in attacking Grekov's policy. At the same time orders were given to close the Leningrad branch of the institute, which had concentrated on medieval Russian history and done much valuable work, as being useless (the decision was apparently not carried out). However, the process of destalinization set in almost immediately, and the people who had been appointed to carry out the incipient purge were now faced with the opposite task of 'normalization'. At the institute, at any rate, they have been reasonably successful in effecting this without the convulsions that *Voprosy Istorii* has had to undergo.

Two significant developments in the organization of research have taken place. One was the formation at the Institute of History of study groups for research in particular subjects. These groups are not administrative divisions of the institute, but relatively free and informal associations based on genuine scholarly interest. An ideological justification has been produced recently for this form of work; it is said to correspond to Khrushchev's idea of administrative functions being taken over by social organizations as a part of the 'withering away of

---

[1] Except the history series of the *Nauchnye Doklady*, which ceased publication at the end of 1961.

[2] These figures are taken from the relevant volumes of *Pechat SSSR v . . . godu* and *Voprosy Istorii*, 1959, No. 1, p. 17; 1961, No. 10, p. 5.

the state'.[1] While this arrangement has been beneficial, the other innovation is of a more doubtful character. A number of 'scientific councils' have been set up by the historical section of the Academy of Sciences to co-ordinate research throughout the USSR on a number of major problems of particular ideological or political significance.[2] It is too early to predict the effect of the activities of these councils, which were given wide powers under a decree of April 1961, but it may well prove detrimental, if only because the choice of subjects and methods of treatment may be restricted.

Another important novelty affecting research is the far easier access to earlier Russian and to foreign literature, even to works of Russian émigrés. (It is interesting to note in this connection that Lossky's and Zenkovsky's books on the history of Russian philosophy were published in Moscow in 1954 and 1956 respectively.) Personal contacts with foreign historians are also encouraged and a National Committee of Soviet Historians was formed in 1955 to organize and supervise them (headed at first by A. M. Pankratova and since her death by A. A. Guber). On the other hand, the party authorities have so far resisted the suggestions that a voluntary Society of Historians should be founded.

The main forms of party control of historical research and writing have remained on the whole the same as they were under Stalin, and need not be treated here in detail. Administrative or personnel changes, policy directives, and indication of official preferences: all these have been resorted to and the forms they have taken have also been the ones familiar in Stalin's time—party congresses and central committee decisions, pronouncements by party leaders, authoritative articles in the central party organs, official research plans, editorial policy of historical journals and publishing institutions, and ad hoc campaigns. One notices, however, that three methods used in Stalin's time are absent from this list: vilification, arrest, and liquidation.

Personnel changes are resorted to perhaps no less frequently than in Stalin's time, but with one exception they have been made rather quietly and without much loss of prestige to those removed. Thus Pankratova, who succeeded Grekov as secretary of the Historical Section of the Academy of Sciences, was replaced by M. N. Tikhomirov in 1953, and he in turn by E. M. Zhukov in 1957; Sidorov was replaced by V. M. Khvostov in 1959 as the director of the Academy's Institute of History. The editorial boards of the new historical journals have been very stable, but Voprosy Istorii has suffered no fewer than four major changes. The editorial board headed by P. N. Tretyakov that had incurred the displeasure of the party authorities at the time of Stalin's death was replaced by one headed by Pankratova and Burdzhalov. Having per-

[1] Voprosy Istorii, 1958, No. 3, pp. 203-4; 1960, No. 8, pp. 13-14; Vestnik AN SSSR, 1958, No. 4, pp. 90-5.
[2] Voprosy Istorii, 1960, No. 8, p. 13; Vestnik AN SSSR, 1958, No. 3, pp. 115-16; 1960, No. 5, p. 88.

petrated some of the worst revisionist heresies in 1956-7, including an open challenge to one of the party's central organs, it was 'reorganized' by a formal decision of the central committee[1] and the journal was entrusted to N. I. Matyushkin, a party official and pamphleteer. Relative normalcy returned when Professor S. F. Naida was appointed editor-in-chief at the end of 1958, but he was apparently unable to give the journal a new outlook, and was replaced in 1960 by V. G. Trukhanovsky, who again re-organized the journal's editorial board and apparatus in a way more in keeping with its function as the chief historical organ.

Official campaigns have been more often designed to stimulate than to castigate. Chief among them were those on the occasions of the 300th anniversary of the Ukraine's union with Muscovy, the fiftieth anniversary of the 1905 revolution, and the fortieth anniversary of the October revolution. The destalinization and anti-revisionist campaigns have been critical in character, but even at the height of the anti-revisionist tide the hysterical atmosphere characteristic of the campaigns against 'objectivism', 'cosmopolitanism', 'Marrism', and 'subjectivism' in 1948-52 was absent; at the worst, people were accused of 'grave errors'. Correspondingly, there has been none of the abject repentance on the part of the accused, and though editorial boards have promised to mend their ways, individual historians have not publicly renounced their views; Burdzhalov, the chief target of official attacks in 1956-7, maintained an ostentatious silence for five years (he is reported to have spoken 'sharply' at the all-Union conference of historians in December, 1962, about the need for a decisive fight against the remnants of the 'cult of personality').

The new campaign against ideological heterodoxy in the winter and spring, 1962-3, has left the historians virtually unaffected.

DIRECTIVES

At the time of Stalin's death the scene was dominated by a typical late-Stalinist campaign for eliminating 'subjectivism' and the 'remnants of Marrism' in history, and for the re-orientation of historical studies in the light of Stalin's *Marxism and Questions of Linguistics* and *Economic Problems of Socialism in the USSR*, and of the decisions of the nineteenth party congress. The campaign had been initiated by *Bolshevik*, and continued in *Voprosy Istorii*, which published a number of obviously inspired articles;[2] the decision, mentioned above, concerning the Academy's Institute of History, passed by the Academy's Presidium on March 20th, was a logical consequence of this campaign.

[1] *Spravochnik part. rab-ka*, 1957, p. 382.
[2] L. Maksimov, 'O zhurnale "Voprosy Istorii" ', *Bolshevik*, 1952, No. 13, and the leader in *Kommunist*, 1953, No. 2; I. B. Astakhov, 'Retsidivy marrovskoi "teorii" v razrabotke voprosov proiskhozhdeniya iskusstva', *Voprosy Istorii*, 1953, No. 1; E. N. Burdzhalov, 'Znachenie truda I. V. Stalina "Ekon. problemy . . ." dlya izucheniya istorii sov. sots. ob-va', ibid., No. 3; I. S. Galkin, 'Znachenie . . . dlya razrabotki voprosov noveishei istorii', ibid., No. 4; *idem*, 'K. Marks o klassovoi borbe v burzhuaznom ob-ve i diktature proletariata', ibid., No. 5.

With Stalin's death the campaign died away. Destalinization in the field of theory, publicly launched in *Pravda* on April 16, 1953, and in *Kommunist* (No. 8) on May 27th, was taken up by the new editors of *Voprosy Istorii* in its sixth issue, which appeared after a long delay. In a number of leading articles they repeated the main directives of the late-Stalinist period, but they also adopted the new official line on the role of individuals in history, stressed that 'dogmatism' and 'quotationism' were, in fact, the main defects of published works on recent history, abandoned the pretence that these practices were exceptions rather than the rule, and advocated 'businesslike, comradely' criticism. These themes were elaborated and amplified in statements by Sidorov in his capacity as head of the Institute of History at a meeting of its staff in January 1954, and by Academician M. N. Tikhomirov, head of the Academy's historical section.[1] Two new notes were also struck—concern over the lack of care for manuscript source materials, and encouragement for the writing of monographs, as opposed to excessive concentration on collective 'definitive' works.

A new series of leading articles in *Voprosy Istorii* in the second half of 1954 dealt *inter alia* with the lack of attention given to the history of socialist ideas, the peculiarly de-personalized character of accounts of the Soviet period of Russian history, the need to follow developments in foreign historiography and to take into account the views of historians in other communist states on the history of their respective countries, as well as the harm caused by excessive anxiety and by the tendency on the part of academic institutions and publishing houses to 're-insure' themselves. Stalin's stature was considerably reduced, though by implication rather than *expressis verbis*. Two warnings were uttered—against de-personalizing history in the process of overcoming the cult of the individual, and against the practice of 'overcoming quotationism' by simply removing the quotation marks and the name of the authority quoted. More important were the directives concerning the treatment of historical facts. Modernization of past events in the sense of distorting them to fit judgements of a later period and embellishment (*lakirovka*) of developments in Russia during the Soviet era—both common practices in Stalin's time—were condemned, as was also the equally common practice of presenting facts 'merely as illustrations of propositions stated beforehand'. 'These authors (wrote *Voprosy Istorii*, 1954, No. 7, p. 5) do not proceed from the material, from the facts to generalizations, but adjust facts to certain propositions, often treating them in a rather arbitrary manner.' And the editors went on to quote Lenin: '. . . it is necessary to take not individual facts but the *whole totality* of facts relating to the problem under consideration, *without a single* exception, since otherwise a suspicion will arise, and a fully legitimate suspicion, that the facts are selected or collected arbitrarily, that a "subjective" cooking is being presented instead of objective connection and mutual interdependence of historical events in their entirety.' This quotation has

[1] *Voprosy Istorii*, 1954, No. 2, pp. 177-80; No. 3, pp. 179-82.

since been repeated several times and historians exhorted to adhere to its prescription.

The leading articles of 1955 on the whole dwelt on the same themes, presenting them in greater detail and stressing that history must be neither 'improved' nor 'worsened', in other words, must not be falsified. A remarkably mild and conciliatory editorial article (1955, No. 8) greeted the forthcoming tenth international historical congress. It has since been noted by several people that the theme of the twentieth CPSU congress had been foreshadowed by historians in more than one respect. One of the most important pointers to the future (not recognized at the time by foreign scholars) was the omission from Sidorov's report to the historical congress in Rome in 1955 of any reference, not only to Beria's pamphlet on the history of Bolshevik organizations in Transcaucasia which had inaugurated the fictitious Stalino-centric historiography, but also to the *Short Course of the History of the CPSU* itself.[1]

It is hardly necessary to go again into the details of the tumultuous years 1956-7. As far as *Voprosy Istorii* is concerned, the editors largely refrained from outright directives—there were only two editorial articles in 1956 (Nos. 1 and 3), the latter being the chief programmatic statement of the editorial board. After this they used as the main forms of guidance the actual editorial policy and meetings of the journal's readers at which this policy was discussed.

The central committee in its decision of March 9, 1957 'Concerning the Journal *Voprosy Istorii*' imposed on the editorial board the obligation 'to guarantee consistent adherence to the Leninist principle of *partiinost* in historical science, decisive struggle against expressions of bourgeois ideology, and attempts to revise Marxism-Leninism'.[2] Following this decision the new editors, in their leading articles in 1957 (Nos. 3, 5, 7, 10) and 1958 (Nos. 1, 2, 4 and 12), gave vent to a lot of obscurantist sentiments, discovering a number of additional errors by their predecessors not mentioned in the party decision. This has greatly impressed observers abroad and is largely responsible for the view that Stalinism has re-established itself in Soviet historiography. Yet a closer examination shows that what was in fact demanded was adherence to Lenin's *evaluations* of historical events and figures. Only in a few cases (the most obvious being the thesis of the beneficial results to various non-Russian nationalities of their incorporation into Russia) was there a re-affirmation of late-Stalinist views. This is very far indeed from the late-Stalinist commands to create historical fictions, and does not even amount to a requirement to repeat such factual distortions as are found in Lenin's writings. The other main directive material of that time —the papers delivered at the all-union conference of heads of departments of social sciences in June 1957 and the recommendations of this

[1] A. L. Sidorov, *Soviet Historical Science, its Problems and Achievements: Brief Survey* (Moscow, 1955).
[2] *Spravochnik part. rab-ka*, 1957, p. 382.

conference—on the whole continued the destalinization line of 1953-6 rather than the new line.[1]

Thus the 1957 reaction was concerned almost exclusively with interpretation; the previous years' gains concerning choice of subject, access to sources, presentation of facts, were hardly affected at all. There has, however, been a renewed emphasis on collective works at the expense of monographs.[2]

The years 1958-60 brought to light a number of new instructions to the historians. They were to widen their field of study, to struggle against bourgeois and revisionist ideology, to contribute to the cult of Khrushchev, and to participate in exploring the approach to communism. Although these are by no means all welcome from the professional point of view, they do not necessarily have a seriously adverse effect on a historian's work. The struggle against bourgeois and revisionist ideology, though constantly held up as an absolute duty, is in fact interpreted almost exclusively as an obligation to 'unmask' alleged falsifications perpetrated by *foreign* historians. As far as Soviet historians themselves are concerned, the official stress has definitely been on achievements rather than deficiencies. This is, from the point of view of a Russian historian, a comparatively easy way out.

The widening of the field of study, extending it in particular to as many non-European countries as possible, in itself is welcome, provided it does not involve undue claims on the resources, particularly human resources. But the other aspect of this directive is far more serious. It consists in the claim, first advanced in connection with the 1960 international historical congress at Stockholm, that Marxist historiography is now in a position to exercise a decisive influence on the course of the further development of historical scholarship throughout the world.[3]

The cult of Khrushchev, apart from being a vulgar nuisance (it is almost necessary to refer to a saying of his in every preface to a historical work), has already reached the stage where his recent pronouncements on historical matters must be taken into account; in fact they come second only to Lenin's, ranking above those of Stalin and Marx. Fortunately, he has not made many such pronouncements and those on record are of a rather general nature.

The historians' participation in exploring the approach to communism was put forward as an urgent task in 1958 and elaborated at the twenty-first CPSU congress in 1959, and in the central committee decision of January 9, 1960, 'On the Tasks of Party Propaganda in Contemporary Conditions'.[4] The latter in particular made it incumbent

[1] *Materialy vsesoyuznovo soveshchaniya zaveduyushchikh kafedrami obshchestvennykh nauk* (Moscow, 1958).

[2] *Vestnik AN SSSR*, 1959, No. 5, p. 76; 1960, No. 5, p. 53; 1961, No. 4, p. 52. Opposition to this is again becoming apparent: cf. *Istoriya SSSR*, 1962, No. 3, p. 214.

[3] *Vestnik AN SSSR*, 1960, No. 5, p. 53; *Voprosy Istorii*, 1960, No. 12, pp. 28-9.

[4] *Vestnik AN SSSR*, 1958, No. 9, pp. 38-44; *Spravochnik sekretaria pervichnoi part. organizatsii* (Moscow, 1960), p. 440.

upon historians to carry out in the next few years, in co-operation with philosophers and economists, investigations into 'the most important, the most topical problems of the construction of communism in the USSR'. In this connection historians are urged to adopt some of the methods of sociological research. Again, in itself, especially in view of the absence in Russia of trained sociologists, participation in sociological field-work may even be beneficial, provided its results are not falsified.

The latest stage dates from the twenty-second CPSU congress at the end of 1961. The new party programme laid down the historians' tasks as follows: 'The investigation of the problems of world history and of the contemporary development of the world must uncover the regular process of the movement of mankind towards communism, the change in the relation of forces favourable to socialism, the sharpening of the general crisis of capitalism, the breakdown of the colonial system of imperialism and its consequences, and the upsurge of the national-liberation movement of the peoples. It is important to study the victorious historical experience, tested by life, of the communist party and the Soviet people, the regularities of the development of the world socialist system, the world communist and labour movement.[1]

The immediate reaction of *Voprosy Istorii* was very superficial. But the meeting of the historical section of the Academy of Sciences on November 17th and 18th clearly showed the liberating effect of the congress. Although Zhukov devoted his paper[2] largely to the task of containing the natural emotions of the historians, the second main speaker, M. P. Kim (chairman of the 'scientific council' on the history of 'socialist and communist construction'), gave a detailed analysis of the effects of the Stalinist regime on historiography.[3] The most important new point he made was that written sources of the Stalin period are to a large extent deliberate forgeries and require particularly careful scrutiny.[4] The editorial in *Voprosy Istorii* (No. 6, 1962) continued the destalinization line, especially by drawing attention to the terror in industry from the 1930s to 1953.

The last two decades have produced a whole crop of official meetings dealing with directives to historians; the all-Union conference on questions of of ideological work (December 1961); the all-Union conference of teachers in the departments of social sciences (October 1962); the all-Union conference of historians (December 1962); and a plenary session of the party's central committee (June 1963) devoted to ideological work. None of these meetings has brought much new material, the general tone being one of cautious and controlled destalinization. At the meeting of historians in December 1962, their main tasks at present

---

[1] Quoted in the editorial of *Istoriya SSSR*, 1962, No. 1, p. 3.

[2] 'XXII syezd KPSS i zadachi sov. istorikov', *Voprosy Istorii*, 1961, No. 12.

[3] Ibid., 1962, No. 1; cf. his article in ibid., 1962, No 2, and his speech at a conference in Kazan in April 1962, as reported in *Istoriya SSSR*, 1962, No. 4.

[4] It has also been stated now that archives had been 'processed' under Stalin and many valuable documents destroyed (*Istoriya SSSR*, 1963, No. 1. p. 224).

were stated (by Kim) to be: helping the party to develop creatively the theory and the practice of communist construction; actively participating in educating builders of communism; and actively fighting against the bourgeois ideology, unmasking the falsifiers of the history of the Soviet Union.[1]

All this shows that a complete normalization of conditions for historical research and writing is not yet in sight. Many Leninist fictions survive, notably the identification of scholarship and party spirit, and several new fictions have been created which historians must appear to accept. These are the new fictitious elements in Lenin's biography and several fictions relating to the present period, such as the fiction of the 'decisions of the twentieth congress', the fictions that the abolition of the cult of Stalin eliminated all obstacles to free research, that only now, after the twenty-second congress, historians realize the dimensions of the harm caused by Stalin, etc. But the difference between this state of affairs and that in the last years of Stalin's life is enormous.

PERFORMANCE

Organizational forms and party directives constitute the limits within which the historians can manoeuvre. How have they utilized the conditions prevailing since Stalin's death, and particularly during the years that have passed since the twentieth congress?[2] In attempting to answer this question I shall confine myself to two fields which were among the most unsatisfactory before Stalin's death—the social history of Russia during the Soviet period, and the history of Russian thought.

Serious work on the social history of the Soviet period was virtually stopped in 1937. After the war, despite frequent exhortations, practically nothing was done before 1953. Speaking of those years, V. P. Danilov, a leading specialist in this field, says that at that time the cult of Stalin 'became an obstacle to scholarly investigations into the history of Soviet society'.[3] But the opportunities presenting themselves after Stalin's death were seized upon, and a veritable flood of publications ensued and is still continuing. Since the late-Stalinist period had produced practically no work in this field, there is nothing with which to compare the new literature. Not that the present state of research can be considered satisfactory. There are still comparatively few publications of documents specifically devoted to social history, few monographs, and almost no general works on any of the major social classes, institutions, or processes. But the prospects are good. Lively and fruitful discussions on sources are proceeding and a useful though very incomplete bibliography of memoirs was published in 1958. The two official classes of Soviet society—workers and peasants—are receiving considerable

[1] *Istoriya SSSR*, 1963, No. 2, p. 217.

[2] Cf. *Sovetskaya istoricheskaya nauka ot XX k XXII syezdu KPSS*, ed. N. M. Druzhinin *et al.* (Moscow, 1962).

[3] *Voprosy Istorii*, 1960, No. 8, p. 43.

attention.[1] Some of the monographs (e.g. L. S. Rogachevskaya, *Iz istorii rab. klassa SSSR v pervye gody industrializatsii 1926-1927* (Moscow 1959), and Yu. V. Arutyunyan, *Mekhanizatory selskogo khozyaistva SSSR v 1929-1957 gg.* (Moscow, 1960) make use of much fresh material and raise many new problems. An increasing number of studies are devoted to the history of the Soviet intelligentsia, 'leading cadres', administrative apparatus, and the 'activists'. The pioneering work by I. Ya. Trifonov[2] has restored to the historical scene the post-1917 bourgeoisie. Of the social services, education[3] and the health service[4] have fared best, and their treatment is nearest to being satisfactory.

Considered as a whole, the recent literature on the social history of the Soviet period shows a definite shift from a kind of instrumental approach, when the life of a social group is treated almost exclusively as an object of measures by the party, to a more balanced view of various sides of its existence.

Turning to the history of Russian thought, we find a very different situation. Here the late-Stalinist period was one of very considerable activity and the changes since 1953 have been qualitative rather than quantitative. In 1949-53 work was largely concentrated on a few revolutionary and radical thinkers: Radishchev, the Decembrists, the Petrashevsky circle, Belinsky, Herzen and Ogarev, Chernyshevsky and Dobrolyubov, Pisarev. Outside this group, attention was given to Lomonosov, Ushinsky, Sechenov, Mendeleyev, Timiryazev and practically no one else. Their figures were progressively distorted and 'modernized'. The purpose of this operation was a double one—to demonstrate Russian priority (real or imaginary), and to represent renowned figures of the past as precursors of the Stalinist ideology. Destalinization here meant a return to the atmosphere of 1947-8.

The changes since 1953 have been manifold and almost wholly beneficial. First, the chronological limits were extended to include both the earlier times and the Soviet period, which had been almost completely 'de-populated' to make room for Stalin (Gorky, Makarenko, Pavlov, and Lysenko were almost the only exceptions). Secondly, as regards the most important period—the eighteenth to early twentieth centuries—the number of thinkers to whom attention has been paid has been increased and, more important, trends previously neglected

[1] Cf. articles by Baevsky, Matyugin, Danilov, in *Voprosy Istorii*, 1959, No. 12, 1960, No. 6, No. 8; by Astapovich *et al.*, in *Istoriya SSSR*, 1960, No. 3 and *Sovetskaya Istoricheskaya nauka ot XX k XXII s'ezdu KPSS*.

[2] I. Trifonov, *Ocherki istorii klassovoi borby v SSSR v gody NEP (1921-1937 [sic.])*, (*Moscow, 1960*).

[3] Collections of writings and speeches on education by V. I. Lenin, A. V. Lunacharsky, A. S. Bubnov, N. K. Krupskaya; D. S. Bershadskaya, *Ped. vzglyady i deyatelnost S. T. Shatskovo* (Moscow, 1960); F. F. Korolev, *Ocherki po istorii sov. shkoly i pedagogiki* (Moscow, 1958).

[4] *Ocherki istorii zdravookhraneniya SSSR (1917-1956)*, ed. by M. I. Barsukov (Moscow, 1957).

have been allowed to re-emerge.[1] As late as 1955 *Istoriya politicheskikh uchenii*, edited by S. F. Kechekyan, omitted any but revolutionary and socialist thinkers and writers in Russia from the mid-nineteenth century onwards. But already in 1956 N. A. Tsagolov[2] gave a very good presentation of various conservative and liberal trends, while the second volume of *Istoriya russkoi ekon. mysli*, edited by A. I. Pashkov and Tsagolov,[3] is excellent in its scholarly treatment of all the main trends in Russian economic and social thought in the second half of the nineteenth century. One could multiply such examples.[4]

A special theme which in a way belongs to both fields—the history of Soviet society and the history of Russian thought—is the development of Soviet historiography. It has been accorded a considerable amount of attention in recent years, and here again we find that the 'return to Stalinism' view is contrary to the facts. This will be especially obvious if one remembers that 'Stalinist historiography' in the common jargon of sovietologists means essentially Grekov's National Bolshevik school. This school, after it was raised to the official position in 1934-6, was twice in danger in Stalin's lifetime—for a brief period in 1948, when some of its prominent members were under attack for 'objectivism' and inclination to regard the Russian historical process as a 'single stream', instead of stressing its 'class contradictions', and again, this time more seriously, just before Stalin's death, for concentrating on earlier times and not paying enough attention to the Soviet period.

The years of ascendancy of Pankratova and Sidorov brought a partial rehabilitation of M. N. Pokrovsky, and this not only was not reversed after 1957 but has proceeded with increasing momentum. Pokrovsky again appears as a truly Marxist historian (with appropriate quotations from Lenin to this effect), while Grekov and Tarle are once more under suspicion as to the depth and genuineness of their Marxism.[5]

[1] E.g. D. S. Likhachev, *Chelovek v literature drevnei Rusi* (Moscow-Leningrad, 1958); I. U. Budovnits, *Obshch.-politich. mysl drevnei Rusi* (Moscow, 1960); I. S. Bak, *Antifeodalnye ekonomicheskie ucheniya v Rossii vtoroi poloviny XVIII veka* (Moscow, 1958); V. F. Malinovskii, *Izbrannye obshchestvenno-politicheskie sochineniya* (Moscow, 1958).

[2] N. A. Tsagolov, *Ocherki rus. ekon. mysli perioda padeniya krepostnogo prava* (Moscow, 1956).

[3] *Istoriya rus. ekon. mysli*, II, parts 1 and 2 (Moscow, 1959, 1960).

[4] A. Galaktionov and P. Nikandrov, *Istoriya russkoi filosofii* (Moscow, 1961) must be mentioned.

[5] In *Istoriya SSSR*, 1962, No. 3, p. 71, M. E. Naydenov writes that Pokrovsky 'played a prominent part in the development of historical science, as one of its talented initiators', but warns that restoration of his good name does not imply approval of his historical conception. See also M. V. Nechkina in *Kommunist*, 1961, No. 9 and *Voprosy Istorii*, 1962, No. 1, and O. D. Sokolov in *Kommunist*, 1962, No. 4.

E

VI. Soviet Historical Sources in the Post-Stalin Era

GEORGE KATKOV

The collection, preservation, and publication of historically relevant archive material is an important function of the Soviet Government. The government inherited a very considerable archive treasure from its Tsarist predecessor, and has added to it numerous nationalized archives taken over from private individuals and public institutions; it has also organized the systematic collection of documents relating to state administration during the Soviet period.

The system of archives in the USSR, their accessibility, and the terms on which research may be carried out on them, are all matters of great importance to historians of the Soviet period. Unfortunately—but not surprisingly—the Soviet authorities are not particularly forthcoming in supplying the necessary information. There is, of course, a 500-page volume of information on the USSR state archives (published in 1956). The information provided is, however, of a very general nature. There are also textbooks intended for the staff of the state archives and for the teaching staff and students of the Institute of Historical Archives. Legal texts relating to the archives were scheduled to appear in the course of 1960, under the title 'Archive Legislation in the USSR'; but the first issue was to deal only with legislation of the period 1917-41. Two further issues in this series were to bring the work up to date, but it is not known when they will appear. The Main Archive Administration (a department of the Ministry of Internal Affairs, to be referred to here as MAA) is also publishing a number of guides to the state archives for the benefit of scientific research workers. As far as the use of archives by research workers from abroad is concerned, no general policy seems to have been adopted. Every case is decided individually by the competent authorities, and there seems to be no way of legally protecting the interests of independent research from the arbitrariness of the state department concerned. This being so, the publication of Soviet archive material is of particular importance to the historian outside the Soviet Union. The questions arising in this connection are:

1. What material has been published, or is likely to be published in the course of the next few years, and when?

2. How has this material been selected? To what extent can it be regarded as a reliable cross-section of the archives?

3. What can be deduced from the material selected for publication

about those parts of the Soviet archives which have not been, and are not likely to be published in the foreseeable future?

4. How do recent publications of Soviet archive material affect our knowledge and appreciation of the historical events of which they treat?

The first question is not so easy to answer as might be expected. The bulk of the publication of archive material is planned by the MAA in conjunction with other institutions, such as the History and Economics Institutes of the Academy of Sciences, the Institute of Marxism-Leninism, the administration of the central and provincial party archives, the Commission for the Publication of Diplomatic Documents of the Ministry of Foreign Affairs, the Central State Archives of the October Revolution and Socialist Construction, the Institute of Oriental Studies of the Academy of Sciences, the Central State Archive of the Soviet Army and the Central State Archive of the Soviet Navy, and some others. The MAA publication plan for 1956-60 envisaged 326 publications of archive material, including those dealing with the pre-Soviet period. In fact, up to May 1, 1960, only 298 such publications had appeared, including some not envisaged in the plan. Of these, 181 dealt with the Soviet period, the overwhelming majority being publications commemorating the fortieth anniversary of the October revolution. It seems that in spite of the efforts of the MAA to co-ordinate and streamline the work of publishing archive material, some of this material appeared in print independently of it, particularly in the more remote areas of the Soviet Union where local authorities often took matters into their own hands. The head of the MAA, G. A. Belov, reports that 'Soviet archivists are incensed by the fact that nobody is co-ordinating and summing up on a national scale the experience gained in the publication of documentary sources. This leads, especially in collections of documents appearing in peripheral areas, to duplication of published material and to a lack of uniformity in the selection and archeographical presentation of documents' (*Voprosy Istorii*, 1960, No. 10, p. 15).

We should probably welcome the circumstances deplored by the archivists working under Belov; they suggest the possibility of checking the easily available publications of the MAA against those issued in outlying areas (although some, in particular the Georgian, Armenian, and Central Asian ones, appear in the local languages and are difficult of access). These publications are not ordinarily to be found in Soviet bookshops.

Most of the 181 volumes published between 1956 and 1960 containing archive material on the Soviet period deal with the history of the October revolution and the Civil War. Similar material appeared in most republics and provinces. We even have a small publication entitled *The First Revolutionary Committee of Chukotka 1919-20*, published by the Magadan archives in 1958.

Compared with the 1956-60 plan, the 1960-5 plan now in operation is a far more ambitious affair, envisaging the publication of 446 volumes of material on the Soviet period. They will include some volumes in series already started under the previous plan. Thus six out of ten volumes of a work on the October revolution were already out when the new plan was published: it includes the remaining four. The plan mentions the titles of the various volumes, the stage reached in their preparation, the date by which they will be ready for the press (though not the probable date of publication), the size of the collections, the institutions mainly responsible for their preparation, and those assisting in the work. It divides the projected publications into five main groups. The first deals with the October revolution. Apart from the four large volumes completing the ten-volume series begun in the previous period, there are fifteen further volumes, some of them apparently ready for publication; these deal with revolutionary events in Amur province, Uzbekistan, Adzhariya, Nakhichevan, and Armenia. (The latter is in the Armenian language, the only non-Russian publication envisaged in the plan.) Most of these works are prepared by local archive institutions, sometimes in collaboration with the local party archives; other, still smaller publications are produced with assistance from the most unexpected quarter; for instance, the collection entitled *The Struggle for Power of the Soviets in Semipalatinsk Province* is published by the state archives of Semipalatinsk and Pavlodar provinces in collaboration with the Semipalatinsk educational and zoological-veterinary institutes.

The second main group in the plan deals with the period of the Civil War and foreign military intervention. It should contain three 800-page volumes of basic documents on the period; one of these has already been delivered to the publishers while the others are in various stages of preparation. These will be supplemented by a number of more detailed publications, bringing the total for the second group of the plan to forty-four volumes. Most of these are not expected to be ready before 1962-5. They include two volumes (each of some 640 pages) on 'The Baltic Sailors in the Struggle for Power of the Soviets' (November 1917-December 1919), three volumes on the Civil War in the Ukraine, two volumes on the Civil War in Belorussia and a number of short popular publications such as 'N. A. Shchors' (by the Central State Archive of the Soviet Army in collaboration with the Shchors Museum), or 'Kalinin in Orenburg' (by the Archive Department of Orenburg province). Some of these publications are bound to contain interesting and historically valuable material.

By far the largest group of projected volumes is the third. It consists of material dealing with economic and cultural developments and embracing the whole Soviet period—311 volumes in all. These are subdivided into four periods. The first sub-division, 1917-20, contains 27 volumes, the second, 1921-5, 42 volumes, and the third, 1926-40, 128 volumes. The third sub-division falls into three parts: industrialization (44 volumes); the collectivization of agriculture (40 volumes); and the cultural scene in the USSR (45 volumes). The fourth sub-division deals with socialist and communist construction in the period 1941-60 and contains 113 volumes, divided into four parts: reconstruction and further development of industry in the USSR (16 volumes); aspects of the history of the USSR national economy (31 volumes); aspects of the history of USSR agriculture (7 volumes); and the cultural scene in the USSR (59 volumes).

The fourth main group of the plan covers the period of the Second World War (1941-5) (41 volumes); the fifth group deals with Soviet foreign policy and the 'international proletarian solidarity of the working people in the struggle for peace' (31 volumes). It includes volumes IV-XII of the *Documents on the Foreign Policy of the USSR* edited by the Commission of the Ministry of Foreign Affairs of the USSR for the Publication of Diplomatic Documents, and seven volumes dealing with Soviet-Polish relations between 1917 and 1960, to be published by the MAA in collaboration with the Slavonic Institute of the USSR Academy of Sciences, the Institute of Marxism-Leninism, the USSR Ministry of Foreign Affairs, and the Polish Academy of Sciences. The second subdivision of the fifth main group deals with the history of Soviet cultural and scientific contacts with foreign countries, and opens with a collection of documents and material on cultural relations between the Soviet Union and China in the decade 1949-59. It is to be published by the MAA and the Central State Archives of the October Revolution in collaboration with the Sino-Soviet Friendship Society. The other six volumes deal with Soviet cultural relations with Germany, Czechoslovakia, Rumania, India, France, and the countries of South-east Asia. The plan ends with the third sub-division of the fifth main group, seven volumes of some 560 pages, each dealing with what the plan describes as 'the international solidarity of the working people in the struggle against fascism and in the fight for peace in the post-war period'.

In order to answer the question: to what extent is the material selected for publication a reliable cross-section of the documents contained in the Soviet archives?, we have to consider both the general statements of policy made by persons responsible for publishing archive material, and the technical rules applied by those editing the various parts of the gigantic project. As far as general policy statements are concerned, they leave no doubt on the views of the leading authorities concerning the tasks and duties of Soviet archivists. 'Soviet archivists', writes the head of the MAA, G. A. Belov, 'who are an integral part of the workers on the historical front, are called upon to help our party and our people in a practical way to solve successfully the problems of communist construction; they are called upon to do everything possible in order to use the documentary material in the fund of the USSR state archives in the interests of the Soviet nation' (*Voprosy Istorii*, 1960, No. 10, p. 3). In an article on the study of the history of the October revolution in *Kommunist* (1960, No. 10), G. Golikov praises the work done during 1957-8 on the publication of documentary material on the October revolution. In 128 volumes of collected documents, more than 22,000 newly-published items have been 'brought into circulation among scholars for the first time'. This and the memorial literature helps Soviet historians to demonstrate 'the titanic activity of the Bolshevik party, of the working class and the toiling masses at all stages of their struggle for the victory of the socialist revolution'. Both Belov and Golikov refer to the resolution of the twenty-first congress of the CPSU 'On the Tasks of Party Propaganda in Present-Day Conditions' as constituting a basic directive for the work of archivists and historians. Both of them stress the necessity of strengthening the control of the central institutes over historical and archeographical research so as to facilitate the fulfilment of the political task entrusted by the party to Soviet historians. The introduction to the plan of publications issued by the MAA also quotes this resolution, and states that 'a wide and comprehensive use of the documentary fund of the USSR state archives in the interests of the building of communism has become an urgent task, to the solution of which all the other work of archive institutions should be subordinated. Soviet archivists have great opportunities to help our party and people in a practical way to fulfil the task of communist construction. The documentary material of the Soviet epoch is of especially great value in this respect . . . One of the main methods of using and popularizing documentary material is the publication of collections of documents on the history of Soviet society.'

The same concern with the political expediency of publishing archive material is expressed in the various collections of 'rules for the publication of historical documents' (referred to below as RPHD), which have appeared in recent years. There are two types of codified rules of this kind: one set is concerned with the publication of historical documents in general and is issued under the joint auspices of the Academy of Sciences, the MAA, and the Moscow State Institute of Historical and Archive Research; a second edition appeared in 1956. In 1960 the MAA issued a booklet specially designed for the publication of documents of the Soviet period (RPDSP). Both publications have appeared in a limited number of copies and are designed for the use of specialists.

Both sets of rules start with the choice of a theme for a volume of archive material. The theme should have a direct bearing on the political, economic, and cultural tasks undertaken in the course of communist construction. It should moreover demonstrate the active participation of the working people in communist construction, as well as the leading and organizing role played by the communist party. This general rule applies both to collections of documents having a purely scholarly aim, and to those pursuing an educational and 'popularizing' purpose, as well as to those intended for mass agitation. Educational and popularizing works are produced by methods very similar to those used in scholarly editions, although they may make more liberal use of material previously published, newspapers, etc. In publications of this kind the notes and indexes are, however, to be adapted to the interests of a wider circle of readers.

Publications intended for mass agitation are governed by somewhat different principles (RPDSP rule 7 b). The documents should be chosen with the widest circle of readers in view; no 'tendentious material emanating from the enemy camp' should be included, and 'the text should be presented in an amended form accessible to the reader'. Such books should be of restricted length, from 50 to 150 pages in all.

After the selection of a theme comes the study of the relevant literature and the compilation of a bibliography. Whatever the theme and purpose of the publication, the bibliography should include relevant resolutions and decrees of the communist party and Soviet Government, standard works of Marxism-Leninism, previous collections of documents on the same theme, and specialized studies and articles on it. The study of all this material should, according to RPDSP rule 12, lead to a critical and balanced approach, and be of help in working out a plan for research and eventually for bringing the documents to light and sifting them. Only at this stage should the operation of reproducing the relevant documents be entered upon. The production (*vyyavlenie*) of documents is the one operation for which the rules require the editors to exercise some degree of objectivity, and it should be as exhaustive as possible (rule 3 of RPHD). This injunction is repeated in rule 16 of RPDSP: 'In studying archive and printed sources an effort should be made to bring to light the maximum number of documents . . . so as to give the fullest and most objective presentation of the theme'. The lists of documents thus brought to light by Soviet editors should no doubt prove a fairly adequate guide to the contents of the archives drawn upon for any particular publication. I have seen no publication that lists *all* the documents assembled on a given theme; none the less, lists or surveys of this kind have been made, and perhaps occasionally even published. They may appear among the *addenda* to editions intended primarily for the use of specialists in historical research (rule 165 of the RPDSP). What we *are* allowed to see is the outcome of a further operation, namely the selection of material for publication. This is determined by a number of rules which leave no doubt as to the biased nature of the end-product.

When selecting material for publication, the editors should (according to rule 28 of RPDSP) take into account the historical circumstances in which the document first appeared, the manner in which it came into being, its authorship, and the question of whether or not it correctly reflects the policy of the communist party and Soviet Government. Here mention should be made of rule 8 of RPHD and rule 33 of RPDSP. The former states that 'the selection of documents must go hand in hand with a strictly scientific critical examination of the origin and contents of every document. In studying a document's origin we have to distinguish between cases where the authorship is collective, and pertains to an institution or organization (such as directives of the communist party and Soviet Government, decrees of the people's commissariats and ministries, minutes and resolutions of meetings, conferences and so on), and cases where the authorship is individual (such as a letter). In the first instance, the signatures on the document will not be decisive in regard to its publication; whereas in the latter instance the individual authorship will fundamentally affect the estimate of its contents and its suitability for publication.'

What this long-winded paragraph means to convey can be best illustrated by an example: private letters signed by Trotsky must on no account be published, but his orders of the day to the Red Army should be published in full, though, in accordance with the practice of the last thirty-odd years, with the omission of his name.

In order to make the principles of selection of documents perfectly clear, both sets of rules under review define precisely the conditions under which editors may publish material emanating from the enemy camp (i.e. documents produced under the Tsarist or Provisional governments, 'counter-revolutionary' temporary governments, White Guard or interventionist auspices). These conditions are: When the documents contain valuable factual material supplementing other parts of the publication; when they unmask the criminal policy of enemy classes and reveal the latter's true aims; and when they are published in conjunction with documents exposing their mendacity. This should make it obvious to the historian that the proscribed material which occasionally slips into Soviet publications may be extremely precious; but it should also warn him that no Soviet publication throws any objective light on the contents of the Soviet archives as far as non-Soviet or anti-Soviet material is concerned.

Side by side with restrictive rules of the kind mentioned, we have rules encouraging editors to include a considerable amount of material which might otherwise have been refined away in the process of selection. RPHD rule 10 says: 'In order to achieve a correct presentation of a given historical problem from the point of view of Marxist-Leninist theory, documents should be selected which reveal the part played by the popular masses in the development of society.' This explains the inclusion in some of the most recent publications of trivial and repetitive material such as resolutions adopted at mass meetings during the troubled days of 1917. These were all drafted on lines laid down by the propaganda department of the communist party, and far from illustrating 'the active role of the masses' merely reflect the party line at any particular stage of revolutionary history. They occupy hundreds of pages in editions containing documents on the October revolution.

Most of the rules in both the collections we are now considering deal with the uniform archeographic treatment and presentation of published archive material. They are either platitudinous or technical, but some points should be picked out as relevant to the overall policy of the editors. Rule 116 of RPDSP states that documents written in non-Russian languages should (at least in the case of scholarly editions) appear in the original, possibly accompanied by a Russian translation, whenever they have a bearing on the Soviet Union as a whole. RPDSP rule 117 lays down that publications sponsored by the union republics should for preference appear in two parallel versions, one in Russian and the other in the local language.

Of more significance are the rules dealing with the selective publication of documents (extracts or incomplete texts—rules 119-21 of RPDSP). Extracts may be made in the interests of brevity when the material omitted is irrelevant to the theme of the publication; or, though extensive, communicates facts of secondary importance only; or when it communicates facts already utilized in other publications. Rule 120 of RPDSP deals with omissions from the text of published documents; these should be mentioned in footnotes summarizing the contents of the omitted passage. The footnote reference mark should be appended to the word immediately preceding the omission. When the reasons for omitting several documents are the same, they should be stated in the preface to the edition.

Where documents are published in extract the signatures should be retained. As if this instruction were not sufficiently detailed, rule 121 of RPDSP insists that, with certain exceptions, all omissions should be indicated by several dots. Documents from which a section coming under a specific heading are omitted, should be marked to indicate that publication is selective, and a footnote should be added summarizing the contents of the omitted passage. The following is an example:

The heading of a document is given as: 'From the minutes of the meeting of the Moscow Soviet of Workers' Deputies'.[1] November 22, 1936.

These rules, as we shall see, have often been violated in the past, and whenever this happens there seems to be a special policy reason behind it.

Great importance is attached in the rules to the scholarly apparatus (commentaries, indexes, source references, and the like); this is particularly true of publications intended for research. The purpose of these elaborate rules would seem to be partly to introduce a uniform standard, partly to forestall arbitrary decisions by individual editors, but chiefly to provide guidance wherever the treatment of political subject-matter could give rise to embarrassment. Special stress is laid on the chronicle of events, which may appear as an appendix to the volume. A chronicle of this kind must contain a concise definition of the events listed and a learned and political appraisal of them (rule 146 of RPDSP)—for example: 'On December 15th there opened in the town of Nalchik the fifth District People's Congress, which mobilized the working people for the struggle against counter-revolutionary forces.' RPHD gives much more

---

[1] We omit points 4 and 6, dealing with questions concerning the green belt in the Krasnaya Presnya district of Moscow.

E*

detailed instructions on the method of compiling indexes. We should note in this connection rule 158, which lays down that the name index should contain not only the names of persons mentioned in the text of the published documents but also those occurring in the notes, commentaries, etc.

Finally, there is a singular omission in the rules which points to some decision on publication policy which remains unexplained. It had been the practice in many archive material publications to list the documents reproduced at the end of the volume. Thus, for instance, in the volume on the armed rising in Petrograd in 1917, issued in 1957, the list of the published documents is on pages 977-1040. Now the rules no longer require the publication of such lists, and accordingly the practice of publishing them has been discontinued even for the ten-volume series on the October revolution. The only stand-by in finding the documents is now the table of contents, which does not replace the list but groups the documents according to the Marxist-Leninist scheme evolved by the editor.

Even a preliminary analysis of the RPHD and RPDSP rules reveals two conflicting tendencies which the rules are trying to harmonize. In the first place, there is the definite instruction that the theme selected, the documents used to illustrate it, and the method of presenting the material, must all lend strong support to the official historiographical line, which is founded on the Marxist-Leninist view of the revolution and of the gradual transformation of the Soviet Union into a communist society. At the same time all publications of archive material except those avowedly intended for mass agitation purposes must conform to the most rigid standards of scholarship, lest the editors be criticized for taking liberties with their material on ideological or other grounds. We are therefore confronted with a situation typical of scholarly research in the Soviet Union. The rules try to impose on the scholar a dogmatic and intransigent approach to his subject-matter, thus undermining the very foundation of intellectual integrity; at the same time, fearing possible disastrous consequences, the rules try to make up for this by heaping a vast mass of meticulous and detailed regulations on the scholars.

The western historian making use of the Soviet material produced under these conditions thus has two lessons to learn. The first is never to regard the published material as exhaustive, or even as fully representative of what the archives contain. The second is to assume that, by and large, the documents reproduced are not forged or doctored. As regards the first, it is extremely difficult to determine to what degree the selection of the published material belies both the contents of the archive funds and the events of which they are tangible evidence. As a rule, of course, only direct access to the archives could allow us to assess the extent to which selectivity affects the reliability of the published material; but a close study of the historical sources published in the twenties does in some instances reveal the effects of this selectivity, and this in turn allows us to assess the methods of publication in general. We do have certain indirect means of ascertaining the principles of selection: for instance, we can compare the material published in the fifties with similar Soviet material from previous decades, or even with material from outside Russia.

Take, for instance, Volume 1 of the 10-volume series, *The Great October Socialist Revolution*—the volume covering the first few weeks of March 1917, after the abdication of the Tsar. Under No. 333 on page 429, is reproduced a letter (dated March 9, 1917) from the Minister of War, Guchkov, to the Acting Commander-in-Chief, General Alekseyev. This document is said to be filed in the Central State Military Historical Archives, to bear an identification mark, and to be an authenticated copy of the original. An editorial note points out that it is published for the first time. This is not so, for the document has been published in the appendix to Shlyapnikov's *1917*, and, in English translation, has appeared in the appendix to Chamberlin's *History of the Russian Revolution*. Shlyapnikov also published the highly relevant answer of Alekseyev to Guchkov, which explains what the exchange is about. The latest Soviet publication omits Alekseyev's letter completely, and replaces it by an inadequate footnote. This is how the rule advocating a cautious and sparing use of material from the 'enemy camp' works out in practice. Not only have Alekseyev and Guchkov been treated as belonging to the enemy camp; Shlyapnikov himself, who is, and will remain, one of the main sources on Bolshevik fighting tactics in 1917, has become a non-person, and his important work on 1917 is considered to be non-existent—so much so that documentary material appearing there can now officially be said to be published for the first time. This treatment of sources published in the twenties frequently extends also to other early publications on the events of 1917-18. References to the basic publications for the study of 1917 such as *Proletarskaya Revolyutsiya* or *Krasnaya Nov* are rare, although *Krasnyi Arkhiv* continues to be quoted.[1]

In the publication *The Baltic Sailors in the Revolution of 1917*, we have another instance of relevant material being wilfully suppressed in order to produce a biased picture of events. In this case the material has been so selected as to create the impression that the Bolsheviks had a completely free run in their propaganda work among the revolutionary masses of Kronstadt. None of the very illuminating proceedings of the Kronstadt Soviet of Soldiers', Sailors', and Workers' Deputies are reported, although there are copious quotations from the Bolshevik press. This in spite of the fact that the said proceedings were public,

---

[1] It is perhaps opportune to remind historians in the West that besides the three well-known volumes on 1917 by Shlyapnikov, there was published, in 1932, a fourth one, re-discovered recently in a West German library by Leonard Schapiro, which seems to have been more efficiently suppressed immediately after printing than the other three volumes.

and were reported in the daily *Izvestiya* of the Kronstadt Soviet, for some time edited by a Bolshevik, Lyubosh. But these proceedings in fact make it clear that the Kronstadt garrison and workers, although in a semi-mutinous state *vis-à-vis* the Provisional Government, were by no means completely dominated by the Bolsheviks. Indeed, the Kronstadt Bolshevik leaders Roshal and Raskolnikov were frequently rebuked by the Soviet and the Executive Committee for their demagogic activities among the sailors. Roshal was expelled from the Central Executive Committee of the Kronstadt Soviet for his behaviour during the April crisis, while Raskolnikov was advised to surrender to the Petrograd authorities after the July Days. Even in November, after the victory of the revolution, the Kronstadt *Izvestiya* pressed for a government of all socialist parties, and indeed adopted an attitude towards the Bolsheviks very similar to that of the railway workers' organization Vikzhel. None of this is even hinted at in the 1957 publication.

In a further volume in the series, *The October Armed Insurrection in Petrograd* (1957), a quantity of documents dealing with Kerensky's eleventh-hour attempt to recapture Petrograd after the October Days is printed under the heading 'The Crushing of the Counter-Revolutionary Mutiny of Kerensky-Krasnov'. (The choice of title conforms to the rules about 'documents from enemy sources'.) These documents contain some highly illuminating material in the form of recordings of conversations between various army headquarters and (principally) between General Headquarters and the HQ of the Northern Front. The text appears to be accurately edited, and there are references to the earlier partial publication of the same material in *Krasnyi Arkhiv*. But the editors ignore the texts of conversations published by émigrés in Berlin (e.g. in the *Arkhiv Russkoi Revolyutsii*, Vol. VII), where material supplementary to that published in 1957 may be found. These conversations relate to identical events and are perfectly genuine (during the troubled days of 1917 some of the tapes were sent to Kiev and subsequently taken abroad). One would expect a scholarly publication to have taken this material into account as it stands, since in order to form a complete picture of the extremely confused situation then prevailing at the various Russian Army HQs a historian of the period would need to compare *both* sets of telephone conversations. Notwithstanding this defect, however, the 1957 publication is of considerable interest. Incidentally it lends support to the theory that the responsibility for cancelling the order to switch front-line troops to Petrograd probably rested not with the Commander-in-Chief of the Northern Front, Cheremisov, but with Kerensky himself, who, succumbing to nervous exhaustion and despondency, intended to give up the struggle.

The total and doubtless intentional omission of all source material published by émigrés conforms to the practice established by Stalin in the early thirties. In the twenties, Soviet historians were allowed to use and quote émigré sources; indeed, a number of historical documents appearing in émigré publications were reprinted by various Soviet authors. Under Khrushchev, evidently, historical research has not yet caught up with the late twenties.

The application of the rules governing the publication of historical documents becomes somewhat erratic whenever an event is dealt with that is considered to be still a live political issue. We may consider as an example of the editors' nervous approach to such an event the otherwise meticulous edition of the minutes of the Bolshevik central committee in 1917-18. The minutes purport to be published in full, since there is no mention in the preface or introduction of any omissions, as would be required by the rules. On page 12, however, we find a note referring us to page 250, where we are told that certain passages in the minutes which deal with contentious matters involving Comrades Ganetsky, Kozlovsky, and others are omitted in the present edition, as they were in that of 1927. Disjointed, casual references to the affair, we are told, do not permit the reader to form an accurate idea of the subject. A check reveals that the affair was in fact discussed at central committee meetings no less than eight times, although in that relatively short period the committee must have had many more important things to do than discuss private squabbles. It is surprising that, having suppressed the material, the editors should have betrayed its real character by disclosing in a note the names of the persons involved. Both Ganetsky and Kozlovsky were prominent during the July Days, when they were alleged by the Provisional Government to be the main channels for the transmission to the Bolsheviks of German money. Lenin claimed at the time that Kozlovsky was not a party member, but came to Ganetsky's defence. (Contrary to the rules governing the compilation of indexes, neither name figures in the index to this publication.)

It is astonishing that in spite of all attempts to introduce a uniform policy for publishing archive materials, the work of the historians of the Soviet period should lack co-ordination to this degree. To pursue the topic of the passages omitted from the minutes of the central committee, it might be mentioned that the latest volume of the *Leninskii Sbornik* carries a letter by Lenin referring angrily to a central committee meeting held in his absence, which reversed the decision (successfully urged by him at a previous meeting) to appoint Ganetsky diplomatic representative in Sweden. The minutes omit the very passage to which Lenin's letter refers, making the whole affair most intriguing to any historian studying the complex problem of German financial support to the Bolsheviks in 1917-18. For on no point are Soviet historians, and some of their colleagues outside the Soviet Union, more touchy than on this, as I had opportunity to learn at the eleventh international historical congress in Stockholm.[1] It is therefore to some degree understandable that when this problem turns up editors should be tempted to tamper with the text, even in violation of the rules.

However, we find the same thing occurring even in matters of lesser

[1] See *Actes du Congrès*: XIᵉ Congrès International des Sciences Historiques, Stockholm, 21-28 août 1960, p. 224.

importance. Thus in 1958 there appeared a collection of documents on the history of the Cheka. It received approving mention in the article quoted above by the head of the MAA, Belov, who wrote: 'This collection of documents on the history of the Cheka (1917-21) tells us of the heroic struggle of the All-Russian Extraordinary Commission (Cheka) and its local organs against counter-revolution and sabotage, and of the consistent control of the Cheka's activity by the central committee of the RKP (b) and V. I. Lenin; it shows us that the entire work of the Cheka was founded on strict adherence to revolutionary legality.' The publication is, however, by no means as mendacious as this laudatory quotation might lead us to believe. It is, in fact, a rather formidable monument to the rule of arbitrary violence of which the Cheka under Dzerzhinsky, Latsis, and others was the main instrument. In their preface to the book the editors claim that it has been produced in accordance with the rules for the publication of historical documents. They do not specify to what category the book belongs, but from its general layout one can deduce that it is of the 'popularizing' type. The standards applied to it should therefore be approximately the same as those applied to scholarly publications. Yet neither notes nor preface reveal that some of the documents now appearing had already been brought out in the *Red Book of the VChK*, published in 1920 under the editorship of P. Makintsian; nor do they give any indication of the discrepancies between this (1958) and the earlier (1920) text. The *Red Book* suffered a curious fate. After a brief appearance on the market (it was still mentioned in some bibliographical works in 1924) the book vanished completely and no reference to it has appeared in the Soviet press for the last thirty years. It has moreover become almost unobtainable in the West (the Hoover Library of Stanford University possesses a typed version, made from a printed original specially loaned to the library).

It is particularly interesting to see how the treatment of identical documentary material differs in the *Red Book* and *Iz Istorii VChK*. The treatment of Dzerzhinsky's evidence on the assassination of Count Mirbach will serve as an example. In 1920 Mirbach's assassin, Blyumkin, was undergoing a process of rehabilitation and reinstatement to his official position in the security organs. The *Red Book* version of Dzerzhinsky's evidence was therefore expressly purged of all derogatory references to Blyumkin. But it gave a detailed account of his activities in the Cheka before the murder, and included a passage from Dzerzhinsky's deposition in which Blyumkin was alleged to be specially interested in the case of a certain Count Robert Mirbach, an Austrian namesake of the German envoy to Russia who had been arrested by the Cheka some three weeks before the assassination on the charge of spying for Germany. The detail is of some importance, since Blyumkin used the case of Robert Mirbach as a pretext for obtaining the interview with the German envoy that resulted in his assassination. For reasons not disclosed by the editors, the whole story of Robert Mirbach's arrest is left out of the 1958 publication. On the other hand all Dzerzhinsky's temperamental outbursts against Blyumkin's treachery, omitted in 1920, are restored to the text, as well as a lengthy report of a visit paid to Dzerzhinsky, some time before the assassination, by the People's Commissar for the Navy, Raskolnikov, and the poet Mandelshtam, who both denounced Blyumkin's irresponsible behaviour. The latter episode had so far been known only from the rather garbled version published in emigration by the poet Georgii Ivanov. None of these alterations of the text—whether omissions or inclusions—is marked in the 1958 publication, although the item containing the Dzerzhinsky deposition is entitled in the prescribed way 'from the evidence of Comrade Dzerzhinsky', indicating that the document is not published in full. But there is no note, as required by the rules, indicating where the omitted passages stand in the original, and what their contents are. A large portion of Dzerzhinsky's evidence, describing his arrest at the headquarters of the Left SR Central Committee by men of the Popov detachment, is likewise dropped without explanation. The work as a whole, in fact, is typical of present-day Soviet historiographical methods. True, some things hitherto concealed (such as the denunciation of Blyumkin by Mandelshtam and Raskolnikov) are now revealed; but other important issues (such as the Robert Mirbach affair) are suppressed. The historian cannot, therefore, afford to ignore such publications; at the same time he cannot treat them with the degree of confidence he would have in the documentary data published under normal guarantees of impartiality. What is most surprising about the whole business is that the passages dropped from the 1958 publication treat of events which are doubtless already familiar to the Soviet reader from recent publications, e.g. Sofinov's *Ocherki Istorii VChK* (1956). This mentions the Robert Mirbach case quite freely. The manufacture of history certainly seems to present almost insoluble problems; no wonder that Belov complains of the difficulties of securing a uniform, streamlined approach to the publication of archive material.

The activities of the MAA, the various institutes of the Academy of Sciences, and other subsidiary bodies have already resulted, and will continue to result, in a considerable output of historical documents on a period of Russian history which has scarcely begun to be investigated systematically in the West. The authenticity of these documents can hardly be questioned. The admitted political bias in the selection of material and the rules and regulations which the MAA and other central bodies attempt to impose on editors invalidate the claim to give a dispassionate and balanced account of what the archives contain. The rules and regulations are partly intended to restrain the editors from interfering too arbitrarily with their material; but by their very nature such rules cannot invariably succeed in this aim, and when considerations of political expediency begin to make themselves felt many of the constraints imposed by the regulations go by the board. The re-writing of history in the Soviet Union today neither requires nor permits of outright forgeries. The bias and falsification is introduced not through the historian's interpretation of his material, as happened in the twenties under Pokrovsky, but at the very root of historical research, in the process of revealing its primary sources, a process which is vitiated by preferential selection and tendentious presentation.

Certainly it is important that the western historian should expose these methods, not merely in a general way as has been done in this paper, but in detail, every time a new volume of archive material comes to the notice of a specialist competent to assess the degree to which it has suffered from tendentious editing. But it seems to me that we can do more. Over the years, a mass of documentary material has been collected in the West, and is now deposited in the United States and some European countries. In particular, for the period covered by the current MAA plan, we now have the Smolensk archives, of which Professor Fainsod has given us such a fascinating and tantalizing survey. The Smolensk archives presumably typify the kind of archives Soviet historians will draw upon for their documentation of collectivization and industrialization. These historians may even be dealing with the same areas, the same period, and the same personalities as appear in the Smolensk documents. Might I suggest that publication (at least in part) of the Smolensk archives, in an edition prepared with the maximum care in the original Russian and characterized by the strictest historical impartiality, would help us to gauge the significance of any future Soviet productions; and it might also dissuade our colleagues in the Soviet Union from interpreting too zealously the political directives issued to editors of archive material.

DISCUSSION

Dr Utechin said that one could look at Soviet historiography since Stalin in a number of ways. A political scientist interested in the nature of totalitarianism might try to discover how it was used by the political authority for its ends. A political psychologist could try to delineate the conflicting of motives in the mind of a historian working in such conditions. A historian would attempt to establish to what extent and in what way historical research in such conditions did nevertheless advance our knowledge and understanding of the past.

All these approaches were legitimate, useful, and necessary, provided one differentiated clearly between them. Only confusion could result if we substituted in our minds the official words for the actual performance of the historians. At the moment the historian was required to project the official policy of the party leadership into the past in a more sophisticated way than before, disguising it as genuine scholarship. But it would be a mistake to assume that the actual performance amounted to nothing more. If he could pretend to be engaged in historical scholarship, while in fact projecting party policy into the past, he could conversely pretend to project party policy in a more skilful manner while in fact trying to do genuine historical research.

In his paper Dr Utechin had tried to analyse the external conditions in which historians worked and the requirements of the political authorities, concentrating on a survey of the actual performance in a few chosen fields. It was right to condemn works detrimental to historical scholarship and to treat seriously and professionally those which did advance our knowledge and understanding of the past. There could be no greater gratification for a historian working in the conditions prevailing in the Soviet Union than the knowledge that his colleagues abroad treated him seriously as a professional historian.

The institutional framework of historical studies had not changed much since Stalin's time, nor did he believe that the changes which other academic institutions were now undergoing as a result of the recent decision to re-organize research would affect historical studies to any considerable extent. The only difference he could detect was the preferential treatment given to institutions engaged in the study of countries other than Russia, contrary to the policy in the thirties, when it had been the other way round. This could be seen from recent academic appointments.

What of performance? In the field of Russian history, to which Dr Utechin confined himself, the situation varied in different branches. For the earlier history of Russia, until roughly the middle of the nineteenth century, there existed a solid body of work and a solid corps of competent historians. Here we had not only older people such as Tikhomirov or Druzhinin, but also a whole generation of younger historians trained by Grekov, Bakhrushin, Bazilevich. These included Cherepnin, Zimin, Shmidt and others who were doing excellent work.

But it was the general climate of opinion in the country in relation to history, as much as the state of research institutions, that was relevant to the situation in this field. During the thirties and forties an increasing emphasis on the historical approach had been apparent in all fields, and historical studies had benefited from this, for example in secondary schools. It was here that the situation had changed radically. There was now a serious danger of a drift back into the position condemned in the thirties as a 'vulgar sociological approach to history'. The same approach now threatened to dominate the atmosphere in the secondary schools.

The situation was different in the field of the history of Russian thought, particularly political thought. In the last years of Stalin's life there had been a short period during which genuine scholarship in this area was virtually suppressed. The break was not long enough to have produced lasting effects, and now the history of Russian political thought had been taken up again with considerable vigour. He was thinking not so much of a fat textbook like Kechekyan's *History of Political Doctrines*, but of some recent monographs like Safronov's *M. M. Kovalevsky as a Sociologist*.

The history of the revolutionary movement in Russia, which occupied such an important place in historical studies in the Pokrovsky period, had suffered a long eclipse from 1935 to 1955. What was being done in this field now was to bring to light the earlier work, by publishing bibliographical guides and reprinting some of the earlier studies. In the last couple of years there had appeared a number of good monographs (some of them good by any standard, others only in view of present conditions in the Soviet Union such as Ovsyannikova's interesting study of the Blagoev's group, Kazakevich's study of the Tochisky fellowship, Polevoy's work and especially Tvardovskaya's study of the *Narodnaya Volya* in *Istoricheskie Zapiski*, which was far better than anything hitherto produced on the subject in Russia or abroad. He was not sure that he agreed with Dr Keep that historians could now treat the period of the 1880s and 1890s, the formative years of the communist party, more freely, because it was irrelevant from the point of view of the present leaders who were interested in the revolutions of 1905 and 1917.

Study of the history of Russian society during the Soviet period had been suppressed before it had had time to develop. It was almost a new branch of scholarship; here work was concentrated mainly on the survey of sources, on methods of the study and publication of source material, on the relative importance of different approaches to various topics, etc. Considering the inevitable lag in this branch of historical studies, Mr Utechin thought the results so far encouraging. Chernomorsky's articles on sources, for instance, were excellent. This author denounced the practice of doctoring memoirs and was trying to do as much as he could to remedy it. However, monographs of value were still few in this field.

Dr Katkov said the first part of his paper was a tentative examination of the plan of work of the Soviet Main Archive Administration, which suggested that a struggle was going on between the various institutions. It would seem that certain local party organizations and possibly some authorities of the union republics resented interference and dictation by the MAA and attempted independent publications—a practice deplored by the MAA as spelling anarchy and dispersal of effort.

The second part of his paper dealt with the political principles underlying publication of archive material. The first step was to locate the relevant documents and the second to select those that were to be published. The first operation was carried out without any control from the MAA. It was a pity that the lists of the documents found relevant to a theme were not published, for they would throw welcome light on the principles of selection. As to these, although he had not found it expressly stated in the Rules of Publication that nothing contrary to the party line could be published, his paper showed that in practice nothing appeared which did not serve the government's purposes. He doubted whether these rules were still absolutely obligatory. There appeared to be contradictions in the principles of selection which enabled some people to preserve a measure of independence.

In the third part of his paper he had attempted to evaluate the worth of these official publications; on the basis of some knowledge of the archive material, his examples were chosen from the 1917 period, of which he had some special knowledge, having worked in the Helsinki archives, where they had interesting material on the first days of the revolution, including the papers of the Governor-General of Helsinki at the time. It was significant that the material published by Shlyapnikov, which presented a fairly coherent picture of events, was completely ignored by the new publications. Publications after the 1930s were usually quoted, and even some earlier ones, such as the minutes of the Bolshevik conference in April 1917.

From these examples Dr Katkov concluded that the falsification of history in the Soviet Union had simply been transferred nearer to the source. If in the past people like Shlyapnikov or Semennikov, who worked on the 1917 period in the twenties, had shown bias, they showed it in their interpretation of documents which they reproduced (including documents published abroad by the White Russian emigration). The danger now was that the younger Soviet historian would regard the selectively treated material in archive publications as the real source.

Nevertheless, Dr Katkov thought that a great deal could be learnt even from false histories. Beria's book had helped him to understand why the whole Marr incident had taken place. Marr had written a pamphlet on events in Guria, *Guriiskie vpechatleniya*, which was incompatible with Stalin's treatment of the Guria republic in 1905—so Marr had to be discredited. Another example was the treatment of the connections of the Bolshevik party with the German Government in 1917. Dr Katkov was personally involved, as he had found and published in 1956 Kühlmann's letter certifying that money had been paid to the Bolsheviks by the Germans. Although he had been in the Soviet Union on the day the *Neue Zürcher Zeitung* published the document under his name, no one had asked him about it. Later they simply said that a certain Katkov had published the usual forgery on the subject. An indication of their attitude was to be found in the short essay by Kazakevich published in *Oktyabr*: in a description of what Lenin was thinking when he was in hiding in Finland it was stated that the one thing he could not stomach was the unspeakable accusation of having accepted German money. It was interesting to see the reflection of this attitude on the publication of the archives. Mr Schapiro had referred to the elimination from the text of the minutes of the central committee of the passages dealing with the so-called 'confusing cases of comrades Ganetsky and Kozlovsky'. The omission was particularly interesting because it violated the rules for the publication of historical documents, according to which the omission should have been mentioned in the preface, and not merely in a footnote. Moreover, Ganetsky's and Kozlovsky's names were missing from the index, whereas the rules expressly stated that all personal names which appeared in notes should be included in the index.

Dr Bolsover said that as far as he knew there were no copies in Great

Britain of guides to the Soviet archives. He had raised the matter with the head of the Soviet Main Archive Administration and had been told that the Russians could not provide photostatic or microfilm copies of documents in the Soviet archives unless they were given a fairly precise reference. This was a perfectly legitimate condition from an archivist's point of view, but it evaded the main point, namely, the impossibility of giving a precise reference if one had no guide to the archives. His attempts to enlist the help of Soviet historians in procuring a set of guides for the British Museum had not been very successful. The only one he had been able to obtain was a guide to the historical archives of the Leningrad branch of the Institute of History of the Academy of Sciences; this was extremely useful, but the archives of this branch were of course limited.

Complimenting Dr Utechin on his paper, Dr Gallagher said this must surely be the first account of Soviet historiography which managed to cover the year 1956 in one paragraph. He had concentrated on those developments which had a permanent significance for current Soviet history—easier access to the archives, increased publication facilities, etc. In this perspective, of course, 1956 was essentially irrelevant, since it was concerned not with improving the technical conditions of historical work, but with exploding myths. Burdzhalov had naturally been concerned with the tools of history, but his opponents were also champions of this kind of technical progress, advocating repeatedly the need for more journals and publication of documents. Nevertheless, Mr Gallagher thought that 1956 was the great dividing line. All the books mentioned by Dr Utechin as representing an advance over the Stalinist period were published in 1956 or later. He did not think that the qualitative change that took place around 1956 could be explained by technical developments alone or by a change in the character of the party directives. It was the anti-Stalin campaign which finally convinced people, from the Agitprop down to the institutes and editorial boards, that the party was in earnest when it asked for better history. Only then was there a move from simply talking about improvement to doing something about it.

The question of the purpose to which these archival materials were being put led Dr Raeff to some observations on the wider problem of the Soviet view of history and time. He wondered whether, in talking about history in the West and in the Soviet Union, we were not dealing with two very different conceptions (history being used here in the sense of discipline and of mental activity). The western conception had two main components: the first one was historicism, not in the sense the Soviets used the term, but in Meinecke's sense, which regarded historical events as unique and interesting because humanly meaningful in themselves; the second component was the desire to find a rational explanation for the sequence of events, their causes and consequences. Dr Raeff doubted that even the best among Soviet historians shared the western conception, which was the result of a long intellectual evolution. The difference was quite notable in the works of Soviet historians dealing with the pre-Soviet period, the Middle Ages, or the seventeenth and eighteenth centuries. The Soviet historian could not really approach his material with a genuine query, because the fundamental answer was already furnished by the ideological, philosophical, and mental framework in which he must operate. Therefore to him history was less an attempt at understanding, at finding causes and explanations, than an illustration 'on the basis of concrete factual material' (as they put it) of the accepted interpretation of the general scheme. In this sense Soviet historical writing was much closer to the histories written in Europe in the seventeenth century and before—it reminded Dr Raeff of Bossuet's *Discours sur l'Histoire Universelle* and his *Politique tirée de l'Histoire Sainte*, or even the Biblical chronicles, rather than history as we understood it today.

Perhaps this explained two characteristics of Soviet historical writing: in the first place it was rather unreadable, because disparate elements and facts were thrown together and forced into a common mould without apparent logical connection; secondly, the cavalier treatment of evidence and documents sprang from the function of Soviet history—it served to illustrate and not really to establish the truth. Moreover, it had a didactic purpose, as it had had in the West in the sixteenth century or earlier. Accuracy of presentation was not so important: historical events were meant to inspire men to accept a certain point of view. Hence the depersonalization, the lack of interest in human psychology, which helped to make Soviet historiography so difficult to digest, accept, or even discuss on the same level as western historiography. To Dr Raeff the major problem seemed one of communication—we did not speak the same language, and did not even pursue the same intellectual paths, as Soviet historians.

Expressing complete agreement with Dr Raeff, Professor Scheibert said he had pinpointed a crucial question. For the Soviet historian history was a scientific field of study with a definite goal; its attractiveness lay in its ability to yield the proofs that it was believed to contain. This approach seemed extremely dull to us, because of the complete predictability of the result—often it was only the footnotes in Soviet historical writing which were interesting. Most Soviet historians identified themselves completely with this approach to history. Therefore there was far less manipulation by party directives than we were inclined to assume. To understand what people in the Soviet Union really thought and wanted, it was not enough to search for evidence of the kind of thinking we were used to. We should recognize that our approach to history could be viewed as an impoverishment, for it meant that we had lost the link with an all-embracing philosophy. This was something which gave a good Soviet Marxist historian a feeling of superiority.

The possibility of access to the archives differed according to whether one was interested in the pre-revolutionary or post-revolutionary period. The typewritten doctoral dissertations in the Lenin Library and else-

where were full of interesting archive material published long before
1956 and even before 1953. A great deal depended on the sponsor of
the thesis. Eminent historians like Dmitriev and Druzhinin had been
independent and influential enough to allow their students to do really
excellent work. In fact, the spade-work for much that had appeared later
as a book or an article had been done in earlier years. One should not
conclude from the date of publication that a work was necessarily inspired by the directives issued at that time.

Prof. Lowenthal distinguished between the political factor pre-
determining the results achieved by Soviet historians and the ideological
factor which determined which questions they asked. Both Dr Raeff and
Dr Scheibert had stressed the importance of the latter factor; they believed
that there could be no communication between western and Soviet
historians because they worked with different categories and meant
something different by the writing of history. He did not agree with
Dr Scheibert that the stress on the element of uniqueness and the
interest in causal connections (which Dr Raeff thought characteristic of
western historical writing) led to an impoverishment of the concept of
history. Any interest in causal connections implied general concepts
and comparisons. It was true that a doctrinaire history, provided it
was not bound by the necessity to produce specific political results, but
was based on a general concept of laws, might be limited because it
only asked certain questions, those allowed by the doctrine; however, it
could also be extremely fruitful if it asked these questions genuinely
and within the sphere where they applied. By their Marxist approach
Soviet historians were limited to certain questions, but this did not
matter so long as they really asked them and were prepared to be surprised by the answer. What did matter was the political factor—
determined not by Marxism as a doctrine, but by the power structure
of the Soviet Union. This led to deliberately faked results, because
historians could not deviate from them and were therefore no longer
prepared to be surprised by the outcome of their enquiries.

Professor Aspaturian wondered whether the time might not come
when western historians would be completely at the mercy of the documentary publications issued by the Soviet Government, without being
aware that other documents had appeared and had since been suppressed. He also wondered why Stalin, who had been so intent on
distorting or changing history, did not have incriminating documents
simply burnt or destroyed.

Dr Katkov's interpretation of rule 28 of the Rules for the Publication
of Documents of the Soviet Period seemed somewhat narrower than the
facts warranted, at least in regard to the publication of Soviet foreign
policy documents. For instance, in Volume I of the *Soviet Documents
on Foreign Policy* Trotsky's name did appear under the relevant documents and his position as foreign commissar was given; the same applied
to Krestinsky, Raskolnikov, and a whole host of Soviet leaders and
diplomats who were later tried and executed or simply vanished. The

policy regarding the publication of foreign policy documents seemed to differ from that for other kinds of documents. This deviation could not be explained by the fact that these documents had already circulated in the West with the names in question, for in the Sabanin collections they had been reproduced without names. There appeared to be a new departure here. Similarly, the re-appearance of these people in the foreign policy documents was not accompanied by gratuitous annotations. In fact, Trotsky's name appeared next to Lenin's and Stalin's, which would seem to be almost sacrilegious.

Discussing the problems of Soviet scholarship with a small group of university students in Russia, Professor Aspaturian had found that although they knew that Trotsky had been the first People's Commissar for Foreign Affairs of the Soviet Republic, they did not know that he had also been the People's Commissar for War. Why did the Soviet authorities seem to mind Trotsky's association with the Red Army more than his connection with diplomacy?

On this question Mrs Degras said that in regard to Comintern documents, it seemed to be policy not to indicate names if these were embarrassing. For instance, references to the Comintern programme never mentioned that it was drafted by Bukharin. Similarly it was not stated that the manifestos issued by the first, second, fourth, and fifth Comintern congresses were written by Trotsky. A relevant article had appeared in *Partiinaya Zhizn*, 1956, No. 4: 'Publications of documents and research are often considerably impoverished because they do not include many official party and government documents which were the result of collective leadership and correctly express the policy of the party and the government, but are signed by people who were subsequently dismissed from leadership. Why should they not be published as a collective product without any signatures, but only with an indication of the organization from which they originated?' In respect to Comintern publications, this suggestion had been followed.

Mr Schram said it had been suggested that because of its Marxist and Leninist origins Soviet historical writing totally neglected the role of the individual and contingency in history. But even Marx, with his greater emphasis on determinism, did not wholly neglect this aspect of history, and Lenin did still less. While it was true that the individual was often absent from Soviet historical writing, with a consequent loss of readability, it still contained villains and heroes who were not presented merely as spokesmen for certain classes and groups, but were also treated as individuals.

He agreed with Mrs Degras that facts were not history until they were selected and interrelated. This implied that all history was to some extent distorted and partisan. He also agreed with Mr Wolfe and others that there was a qualitative difference between western and Soviet historiography—in the latter distortion was more frequent, crude, and systematic. But the difference should not be exaggerated. Though the framework within which history was written in the Soviet Union made the expression of unorthodox views far more difficult and dangerous than in the West, the psychological problems of western historians in their struggle between bias and objectivity could be compared to some extent to those of such Soviet historians as were not mere party hacks, but endeavoured to practise their craft more or less honestly.

At times Soviet and western historians arrived at the same conclusions out of opposite, or rather complementary bias. To illustrate this Mr Schram compared eastern and western accounts of the negotiations in Berlin between the Russians and the German leaders in March and April 1922, prior to the Genoa conference. In his book *Die Träger der Rapallo-Politik*, Helbig maintained that these negotiations were conducted exclusively between Maltzan and Chicherin, and that Wirth, who knew about them, preferred to remain aloof, while Rathenau would never have thought of soiling his hands by negotiating with the Soviets. In this case Helbig was not guilty of deliberate distortion of documents, but of affirming categorically things for which he had very inadequate documentation. In the German Foreign Office archives there was a minute which showed that Rathenau actually participated with Wirth and Maltzan in the negotiations with Chicherin and his colleagues. The purpose of Helbig's book being to show that nearly all Germans were good Europeans, Rathenau could not be allowed to bargain with the Soviets. In an East German account of Soviet-German relations in the early twenties, the author, who had no access to the West German archives, had accepted unquestioningly Helbig's statement that Rathenau had refused to negotiate with Chicherin for opposite reasons: for him the entire German bourgeoisie were villainous people incapable of understanding that Germany's real interest lay in coming to terms with the Soviets; only a man like Wirth had had the breadth of vision to realize that they should negotiate. Thus opposite bias could produce identical results. The conclusion that Mr Schram drew from this was that the differences of approach between western and Soviet historians were more complex than they seemed; it was not enough to say that Soviet historiography contained a monstrous amount of organized distortion.

Dr Katkov had agreed that at the present time Soviet falsification of history rarely took the form of deliberate fabrication of documents, but consisted rather in tendentious selection of materials. In this change Mr Schram saw some hope of western historians being able to derive more benefit from Soviet publications, mainly by comparison of successive versions. And with the passage of time some subjects might become less delicate than in the past and therefore more open to truthful treatment. The fact that Trotsky's name appeared (albeit once) in the first volume of the new series of *Soviet Documents on Foreign Policy*, but was never mentioned in connection with military affairs, suggested that some areas might be more sensitive than others. Thus one could expect somewhat more truthful documentary publications in the field of foreign policy than in party and military matters.

Taking up the point about sensitive areas, Mr Schapiro said there were some seven volumes of documents on the 1905 revolution publised for its half-centenary in 1955. The index contained neither the name of Trotsky, nor his pseudonym at the time, Yanovsky—so this appeared to be a sensitive sphere.

Like Prof. Lowenthal, Mr Schapiro found himself in considerable disagreement with Messrs Raeff and Scheibert. There was a fundamental difference between the selection of facts and their interpretation within the framework of certain theories and the faking and suppressing of facts. There were a number of exceedingly good Marxist historians—history would be considerably poorer without their contributions. In the Soviet Union itself the works of the members of the Red Professors' Institute and of the Communist Academy of the twenties stood up very well on their own merits, although their Marxist bias was perfectly plain. Similarly, the work of Marxist or determinist historians in the West might cause dissent because of its bent, but it was still valuable because of the scholarly treatment of the material. He could not accept Professor Scheibert's view that for Soviet historians history was something entirely different from what it was for their western counterparts. He believed Soviet historians knew perfectly well what history was, but a number of them of necessity became party hacks and did the faking required of them. In similar circumstances a number of us would do exactly the same. It did not follow that there was a basic difference of approach.

Professor Scheibert said the point he had tried to make was that one should not judge Soviet historiography only on the basis of its performance in regard to the post-1917 period, but in regard to history as a whole. He had personally come up against the different Soviet approach among students from East Germany, who were far more conscious of the philosophical impact of historical thinking than their western opposites.

Dr Raeff did not believe that it was the ideological framework which was responsible for the different Soviet conception of history. On the contrary, he often found Soviet historians only imperfectly aware of ideological, conceptual, philosophical problems.

In the controversy between Professors Raeff and Scheibert on the one hand and Mr Lowenthal, Dr Meijer, and Mr Schapiro on the other, Dr Utechin found himself on the side of the latter. He would only add that there were degrees to which historians who wanted to work properly could do so. For example, Safronov's book on Kovalevsky as a sociologist touched upon a whole sphere which had hitherto been totally neglected, such as the history of Russian thought on economic geography. There was also the possibility of a genuine bias. Mr Schapiro had said there were no Marxist historians left in the Soviet Union; but Dr Utechin did not agree. In Budovnits' recent book on the history of political ideas in early Russia he detected a strong Marxist and a nationalist bias, both refreshingly genuine. Some writers even went beyond Marxist dogma in their interpretation—in Lurye's recent book on ideological troubles in fifteenth- and sixteenth-century Russia, the author distinguished between ideas originating in class interests and those made use of for class interests.

Dr Utechin thought it a pity to concentrate in the discussion of Soviet historiography on those problems that loomed large from the point of view of Soviet historical propaganda. There was little point in harping again and again on Ivan the Terrible, Shamil, etc.—historical writing in the Soviet Union was not limited to them. Personally, he found what was omitted more interesting than what was emphasized. Particularly now, at a time when historical studies were being revived, omissions acquired a particular significance. Why, for instance, did none of the recent studies of the history of the revolutionary movement, nor the excellent bibliographical guide to this subject, mention the name and works of Teodorovich? In the early thirties he had produced an unconventional and original, though basically Marxist, conception of the history of the revolutionary movement in nineteenth-century Russia. He had been a right-winger and had disappeared in the purges, but his name seemed to have been rehabilitated and his wife was now honoured. It was all the more interesting that his works were not mentioned.

VII. The National Bourgeoisie

WALTER Z. LAQUEUR

This review of Soviet attitudes towards the national movements in Asia and Africa as revealed in Soviet writings is based on a fairly detailed study of the relevant literature published elsewhere[1] and summarized here only briefly. Its emphasis on publications of recent date does not reflect the personal predilections of the author but the simple fact that the volume of this literature has grown immensely in recent years. The Publishing House of Eastern Literature (*Izdatelstvo Vostochnoi Literatury*) of the Academy of Sciences now publishes a book on some Asian or African topic every second or third day all the year round. More books and articles on these topics are now being published in the Soviet Union *every month* than during the two decades between 1936-56.

'National bourgeoisie' is an awkward designation of doubtful origin; a strange mixture of political and economic (or social) concepts. It has been a cause of despair to politicians and orators—no audience has ever been stirred by a call for or against the national bourgeoisie, and it has been of little help to historians and economists; reputations have been damaged but none made as the result of extensive preoccupation with this *Hilfskonstruktion*. Nevertheless it is a very important problem that has beset Soviet historiography ever since 1917.[2] We all know about the close connection between historiography and current affairs —not only in Russia—but there is perhaps no other single issue in which the immediate impact of politics on scholarship has been so directly reflected. It has never been an academic topic, always *Zeitgeschichte*; the attitude towards national movements in Asia, Africa, and Latin America has been one of the cardinal questions in Soviet foreign policy, and the historical debates on the subject cannot therefore be traced without constant reference to world affairs. This problem has been discussed and disputed for decades under various headings—the 'colonial question', the 'problem of the national-revolutionary and the bourgeois-democratic movement in the colonies', 'national reformism', etc. Behind it, the issue at stake has always been whether, and to what

[1] W. Z. Laqueur, *The Soviet Union and the Middle East* (London, 1959).

[2] I have not been able to find the expression 'national bourgeoisie' in Marxist writings prior to 1917, though it may perhaps occasionally have been used in a different sense in the pre-1914 discussion on imperialism (Kautsky, O. Bauer, Hilferding, Rosa Luxemburg). The expression, in its present meaning, was apparently coined after 1917 and first appeared in the writings of Lenin, Radek, Safarov, Pavlovich-Veltman, and others.

degree, co-operation with the national movement in the East was possible and desirable. Various answers have been provided at different times to this question.

The communists had little ideological guidance to start with, because the problem had not existed in Marx's and Engels' day; the modern national movement in the colonies and dependent states came into being only around the turn of the century with the emergence of such groups as the Indian National Congress, Sun Yat-sen's movement, the Turkish 'Unity and Progress', and Mustafa Kemal's National party in Egypt. The development of capitalist, or quasi-capitalist, modes of production made unequal progress in the countries of the East, but even in India, where these developments had reached a far more advanced stage than in most other Asian states (not to mention Africa), the new middle class was as yet numerically weak; both its economic and its political importance was limited.

Marx and Engels had expected the European colonies to become independent one day, but not before the revolution had triumphed in Europe. They assumed that the European proletariat would have to take over the colonies temporarily and lead them as fast as possible towards independence. Engels regarded this prospect with mixed feelings, 'for we have enough to do at home'.[1] Engels even envisaged the possibility of the liberated countries of Asia and Africa turning against the revolutionary proletariat in the metropolis. By and large, however, Marx and Engels were preoccupied with Europe and North America, which they regarded as the key areas for the victory of socialism. Lenin, on the other hand, writing after the upheavals in China, Persia, and Turkey between 1906 and 1912, took account of the changes that were then taking place and noted that a new great storm-centre had come into being; on one occasion he even expressed the then novel idea that the ultimate fate of the world would ultimately be decided in the East, since the majority of mankind was concentrated in China, India, and Russia. The class-conscious workers of Europe, he predicted, now had the support of their Asian comrades, whose numbers were growing not daily but hourly.

Nevertheless, there was not a single orthodox Marxist thinker at the time who attributed decisive importance to developments in the colonial world, and for that reason one would look in vain for any systematic Marxist analysis of the leadership of this new revolutionary movement. Lenin thought Sun Yat-sen a Utopian socialist of the *narodnik* type, hardly worthy of serious discussion; there was no real confrontation between the revolutionary movement in Russia and in the other countries of the East before 1917. Such a confrontation did take place, however, at the second congress of the Comintern in July 1920. By that time the great expectations about revolutions in other European countries had come to naught, whereas the revolutionary ferment con-

[1] Engels to Kautsky, September 12, 1882; in Benedikt Kautsky (ed.), *Friedrich Engels Briefwechsel mit Karl Kautsky* (Vienna, 1955), p. 63.

tinued in Asia. In one passage of the final draft of Lenin's theses the new line was clearly expressed: 'The Communist International must be ready to establish temporary relationships, and even alliances, with the bourgeois democracy of the colonies and the backward countries. It must not, however, amalgamate with it. It must retain the independent character of the proletarian movement . . .' Lenin's chief antagonist on this occasion was the Indian M. N. Roy, who thought that the bourgeois-democratic movement in the colonies should not be supported because it strove for the establishment of a bourgeois order; communists should assist the mass struggle of the poor ignorant peasants and workers, and try to ensure that the leadership of the national movement would be from the very beginning in the hands of a revolutionary vanguard.[1]

The Comintern congress adopted both Lenin's theses and Roy's draft (in a somewhat watered-down version) and thus left the matter in abeyance. Neither was free of inconsistencies. Lenin favoured a temporary alliance on conditions which, if taken literally, would have made the alliance quite illusory; he opposed not only the social-democratic ('reformist') elements in the national movement, but also pan-Islamism, pan-Mongolism, and other such radical nationalist and 'pan-' movements, and he demanded as a precondition of co-operation that the bourgeois national movement should not oppose communist attempts to educate the masses in a revolutionary spirit, with the aim of eventually taking over the national movement. It is doubtful whether any bourgeois national movement in the East, however weak, would have been ready to co-operate on such suicidal conditions. Roy's proposals, on the other hand, even more extremist, would have condemned the Comintern to inactivity, for he realized that at first the Asian revolution would be neither proletarian nor agrarian; there would have been no opening for a communist movement insisting on its ideological purity in these circumstances.

This early discussion overshadowed Soviet and communist thinking on the subject for the next thirty-five years. Policy between 1920 and 1955 oscillated between conditional collaboration with the national movement in the colonies, and struggle against its leaders if it was not communist in character. Broadly speaking, 'liberal' views prevailed between 1920 and 1927. At the sixth congress of the Comintern—which followed the suppression of communism in China—a 'hard' line was adopted; with the beginning of the so-called 'third period', the leadership of the national movement was attacked as 'national-reformist'; and only in the middle thirties did Moscow revert to a more conciliatory approach. After Hitler's attack on the Soviet Union all 'class' considerations were subordinated to the struggle against fascism in which every ally was welcome. After the second world war, however, and in particular between 1948 and 1953, there was something of a revival of

[1] This debate has been described in considerable detail in Allen S. Whiting's *Soviet Policies in China, 1917-1924* (New York, 1954), pp. 42-58.

the 'third period' spirit; the national movement, with very few exceptions, again became an enemy of communism. This lasted until after Stalin's death when, as we know, the attitude towards the national movement was greatly modified.

These, in very broad outline, were the main landmarks in the history of the Soviet appraisal of the national movement in the East. Within each period there were certain changes in the communist attitude, occasional divergences of opinion, especially in the early years. The present essay, however, will deal only with the main trends of development.

Soviet historical writing on the national movement in the East (which term was often used to cover Africa and Latin America as well) was usually a faithful reflection of the party line at the time; the party line was the application of Leninist doctrine to the current world situation. Gandhi (or Nehru) thus was a reactionary and a traitor in 1931, the leader of a petit-bourgeois anti-imperialist movement in 1938, again a reactionary and obscurantist in 1948, and a positive historical figure after 1955, when Soviet historians were criticized for occupying themselves exclusively with Gandhi's philosophical views and ignoring altogether his objectively progressive role.[1]

The mere comparison of a textbook published in 1952 and another which appeared in 1959[2] shows radical differences not only in emphasis and overall appraisal, but even on facts. A few illustrations should suffice. Sun Yat-sen, according to the 1952 version, was born into a comparatively well-to-do peasant family. Now it is said that he was born into 'a peasant family' without qualification as to income bracket. According to the 1952 work, Sun Yat-sen 'did not yet appreciate the significance of the popular masses and did not appeal to the people'. Such derogatory comment is omitted in 1959. The 1952 *History* describes Tilak as a 'petit-bourgeois patriot', sharply criticizing his reactionary views and beliefs, and goes on to say that he 'was afraid of agrarian unrest and revolutionary movements'. In 1959 Tilak is introduced as an 'outstanding patriot, democrat, and savant'. His religious beliefs are

---

[1] A. Guber in *Mezhdunarodnaya Zhizn*, March 1956, p. 61. For earlier Soviet views on India see, for instance, *Noveishaya istoriya stran zarubezhnovo vostoka*, I, p. 188 (on Gandhi), or Balabushevich's expression of regret for having committed a 'liberalist' deviation, i.e. having described Nehru and Subhas Chandra Bose as progressive political figures (*Uchenie Zapiski Instituta Vostokovedeniya*, X, pp. 46-7); these 'pseudo-leftists', it was said in 1954, stood for the interests of the landowners and the bourgeoisie, helped to perpetuate feudal survivals, and actively opposed the class struggle of the workers and peasants.

[2] A number of important works of a general character have recently appeared, such as *Novaya istoriya stran zarubezhnoi Azii i Afriki* (Leningrad University, 1959), and the first volume of *Istoriya mezhdunarodnovo rabochevo i natsionalno-osvoboditelnovo dvizheniya* (Higher Party School, 1957). Both these books stop at 1917. The third and fourth volumes of the *Noveishaya istoriya stran zarubezhnovo vostoka* (published by Moscow University, 1954, 1955) bring events up to 1960. Since the first two volumes of this series came under heavy criticism for their 'hard line', it took considerable time to prepare (or to re-write) the later volumes.

mentioned in one sentence, but the emphasis is on the overriding 'progressive significance' of his movement. The national liberation movement in Egypt was covered in slightly more than one page in the earlier work, while the 1959 *History* allocates ten pages to the same topic. Mustafa Kemal, the leader of the pre-First World War nationalists, is described as a 'young journalist who was afraid of the activities of the popular masses', whereas in 1959 he has become 'the famous Egyptian patriot', the 'tribune of Egypt', and the social and political limitations of his movement are noted in much more cautious terms.

In a similar vein, the leaders of the AFPFL in Burma, including U Nu, were described in 1952 as a 'loyal opposition' to British imperialism and even as traitors,[1] the Naguib-Nasser regime was described as 'madly reactionary',[2] and the reforms introduced by Kemal Ataturk in the twenties were said to have been superficial and attuned to the interests of the Anatolian landowners and merchants.[3] Three years later both the Burmese government and the Egyptian junta had become progressive in character, and Kemal Ataturk had been restored to his status as a Turkish national hero.[4] This was the fourth radical re-writing in their lifetime for many Soviet historians. To complicate matters even more, Soviet historians not only had to take into consideration the general line, which could be found in many ideological pronouncements during each period; they had also to watch out for developments in the foreign political field. Soviet foreign policy was by no means always in accordance with Comintern prescriptions. If Soviet historians were prevented from publishing anti-Nazi studies between August 1939 and July 1941, the work of Soviet eastern experts was occasionally inhibited in a similar way by foreign political considerations of a purely 'tactical' character. But then the border-line between tactics and basic strategy was not always easy to discern.

Soviet writings on Kemalism may serve as an illustration in this context. When Mustafa Kemal came to power in Turkey in 1920, Soviet historians did not know what to think of him. Despite the support given by Moscow to Ankara, many of them at first stressed its temporary character. They complained that Kemal had introduced no radical social reforms, that he had suppressed the Turkish communist party, and had its leaders killed. Gradually, a more positive approach was taken: Kemalist Turkey was 'objectively progressive', particularly in its struggle against the entente. Kemal was supported even after the Turkish war of liberation was over, and after the 'class character' of his regime had emerged more clearly in communist eyes. He received such support partly for non-ideological reasons, as the only Soviet ally in the

[1] On Burma: A. N. Usyanov in *Zapiski*, etc., X, pp. 247, 268.

[2] On Egypt: *Imperialisticheskaya borba za Afriku i osvobozhditelnoe dvizhenie narodov* (Moscow, 1953), p. 126; see also *Narody Afriki* (Moscow, 1955), p. 213.

[3] On Kemalism: *Noveishaya istoriya*, etc., I, p. 312.

[4] I. Potekhin, the chief Soviet expert on Africa, wrote in 1950 that the 'petit-bourgeois nationalist organizations had been satisfied with purely formal independence' (*Sovetskaya Etnografiya*, 1950, II, p. 26).

East, partly because he was regarded as a 'lesser evil', to be assisted against his domestic foes; it was argued that even if one wing of the Turkish bourgeoisie had become pro-imperialist, Kemalism, and in particular its left wing, still had certain revolutionary potentialities. Comintern publications denounced the persecution of Turkish communists and on occasion even complained about the 'progressive fascization' of public life in Turkey. But on the whole the tone was sympathetic until the late thirties, when for reasons of foreign policy the Soviet attitude towards Turkey became much more hostile. The case of Kemalist Turkey shows the limitations of the impact of ideological considerations on Soviet historiography; on theoretical grounds, Kemalism should have been attacked by Soviet writers after 1923, or 1928 at the latest; in fact, a benevolent approach persisted for many more years.[1]

Comments on Israel in Soviet writings do not conform to any ideological pattern; between 1947 and 1949, at the height of the *Zhdanovshchina*, references to Israel were neutral or even friendly. They became extremely hostile precisely when the new liberalism was at its height, in 1955-8.[2] Israel was and is one of the few countries outside the communist bloc in which the bourgeoisie has been in political opposition almost from the beginning; power has been in the hands of the trade unions and the workers' parties. Nevertheless, the Soviet attitude towards absolutist monarchies like Yemen or Saudi Arabia has been much more favourable than towards Israel. The limitations of the impact of 'pure ideology' on Soviet *Zeitgeschichte* are obvious.

What is the character of the national bourgeoisie? For a variety of reasons it is not at all easy to provide an authoritative answer; in Soviet historical writings on the subject various definitions have been given at different times, while recent Soviet works of reference have an unfortunate tendency to refrain from publishing special entries on the subject; they carry detailed articles about the 'compradore bourgeoisie', but not about the subject of the present study. Our own, unauthoritative definition would be that 'national bourgeoisie' is the Soviet designation for the 'post-feudal' ruling stratum and the leadership of the national movement in colonies and other dependencies. According to

[1] See, *inter alia*, M. Pavlovich, *Revoliutsionnaya Turtsiya* (Moscow, 1921); M. Pavlovich and others, *Turtsiya v borbe za nezavisimost* (Moscow, 1925); G. Astakhov *Ot sultanata do demokraticheskoi Turtsii* (Moscow, 1926). One could also refer in the same context to the Soviet attitude towards Reza Khan in Persia and Amanullah in Afghanistan. If the approach to Reza Khan was somewhat more reserved, relations with Amanullah were for a while very friendly indeed. See the discussion in *Novy Vostok*, Nos. XII and XV; the latter issue of this Soviet periodical devoted almost 100 pages to a discussion of the question whether Reza Khan was progressive or not. Cf. *Afganistan i angliiskii ultimatum* (Moscow, 1924); I. M. Reisner, *Afganistan* (Moscow, 1924); A. Gurevich, *Afganistan* (Moscow, 1930); F. Raskolnikov, 'Rossiya i Afganistan' in *Novy Vostok*, 4, 1923.

[2] Typical of the present hostile Soviet appraisal of Israel is K. Ivanov, Z. Sheinis, *Gosudarstvo Izrail, yevo polozhenie i politika* (second edition, Moscow, 1959).

communist sources, the main difference between the bourgeoisie in the West and the middle classes in the colonies is the numerical, political, and economic weakness of the latter. Since the capitalist mode of production developed only much later in Asia and Africa than in Europe; since the metropolitan country, moreover, was not usually interested in developing industry in the colonies but often tried to hamper it, the bourgeoisie in these countries appeared much later on the scene and, with a few notable exceptions (Japan), never attained an influence comparable to that of the middle class in the West. Communist authors also stress the fact that the working class in the colonies developed earlier than the bourgeoisie because the first industrial enterprises were usually owned by foreign companies. According to the traditional Soviet view, the bourgeoisie in the dependent countries includes a minority, the compradores, who collaborate with foreign imperialism and serve as middlemen between foreign capital and the local market. On closer inspection it appears that the Soviet definition of the compradores is as vague and, on occasion, as self-contradictory as the definition of the national bourgeoisie. The *Politicheskii Slovar* of 1958 (p. 278) describes them as trying by every possible means to turn their respective countries into markets for the metropolitan country and into a source of raw materials for foreign capital. But the *Small Soviet Encyclopedia* (IV, p. 1106), gives a very different description: 'The compradores are the leading traders, bankers, and also some of the leading industrialists of a given country'. This, of course, contradicts the former definition, for it is difficult to imagine a leading industrialist trying to make his country a market for foreign competitors and a source of raw materials for them. such definitions should be approached with caution; they are always based on economic categories, but closer inspection often shows that these factors are not always decisive in the Soviet overall appraisal. Compradores are, in the last resort, all those who follow a conciliatory policy towards the West, whatever their class character or social basis. The national bourgeoisie, on the other hand, are all those who follow, at least temporarily, an anti-western policy. The communists and the national bourgeoisie have common interests in relation to the *ancien régime* (mostly, not always accurately, called feudal) and the colonial power. According to the communist version, a considerable section of the national bourgeoisie takes part in the general anti-imperialist struggle; in those countries where communism is not strong, the national bourgeoisie leads the national struggle. During the fight for independence it plays a progressive role—very much in contrast to the bourgeoisie in the industrialized countries of the West, where it has long since become reactionary. But once independence has been achieved, the national bourgeoisie loses its progressive character and its policy becomes 'double-faced' (I am following here the most recent exposition available —*Filosofskaya Entsiklopedia*, 1960, Vol. I, p. 202). After the common national aims have been achieved, other problems have to be solved; but 'because of its narrow class interests' the national bourgeoisie is

F

unable to carry out the social changes required, to tackle agrarian reform, promote industrialization, raise the standard of living of the population, etc. Such changes will be opposed by the national bourgeoisie; they can be carried out (to quote the standard formula) 'only with the active participation of the popular masses led by the working class and its party', meaning the communists.

If we accept these current views as retroactively valid, it follows that Moscow and the Soviet historians were mistaken in not supporting the national bourgeoisie all along in its anti-imperialist struggle. Today this is fairly generally realized; but since all major countries have by now attained independence, it is a reflection of purely historical interest. The other conclusion is of topical importance: when liberation from foreign rule has been achieved, the national bourgeoisie has fulfilled its historical function; communist parties (and communist states) have to oppose it.

We know that this has not happened. In 1948, when India achieved independence, it was communist policy to oppose Nehru and the Congress party; their new independence was regarded as a mere sham, and Professor Varga, it will be recalled, got into serious trouble for taking a more realistic view. Thirteen years later, on the other hand, relations between the Soviet Union and countries such as India, Burma, Indonesia, Ceylon, or the United Arab Republic, are closer than ever before, though the national bourgeoisie has (in theory) already had its day and should now be regarded as a reactionary force.

Historical materialism asserts that the superstructure usually lags behind the economic basis; but this can hardly be invoked as a mitigating circumstance for people who have long mastered the teachings of historical materialism. In justification of continued Soviet support for the national bourgeoisie, it might be argued that, though independence has been achieved by most countries throughout Asia and Africa, there are still many bones of contention between the former colonies and the West. Many newly independent countries are anti-western, or at any rate want to follow an independent line. In theory some division of labour should be possible by means of which local communist parties oppose the national bourgeoisie while the Soviet Union as a state continues to co-operate with the newly independent countries. In practice this is hardly feasible; Soviet professions of friendship towards India or the United Arab Republic would be invalidated if the local communist parties followed a radically different line. Where such a division of labour has been tried (the attacks on Nasser and Kassem in the communist press), it did not prevent the arrest of local communist leaders or the closure of their newspapers. It is also argued that circumstances beyond its control compel the national bourgeoisie to follow a progressive line in domestic policy; for instance, to strengthen the public sector in contrast to the private capitalist sector, that is, to introduce some form of state capitalism. State capitalism, for obvious reasons, is in communist thinking a progressive factor, at least for the

time being, very much in contrast to 'monopoly capitalism'.[1] Lastly, it
has been said by some Soviet historians that the class analysis as
practised in the past in regard to the under-developed countries has been
too crude, the lumping together of various groups and strata as
'national bourgeoisie' too sweeping. It has been suggested that a
re-examination and a re-definition are urgently needed.[2]

It is doubtful, even on communist premises, whether the 'national
bourgeoisie' as commonly defined is really the leading force in most of
the newly independent countries. The Indian Congress party, for instance,
is an alliance of social groups of a very heterogenous character, and the
economic policy followed by the Indian Government clearly shows
that the landowners, bankers, and industrialists often failed to get
their way. The ruling groups in Indonesia, Burma, Ceylon, and the
United Arab Republic are not exactly bourgeois in composition and
social origin; it would be difficult to argue that they act as agents of the
capitalist entrepreneurs, let alone of finance capital. As a result, new
designations have been introduced by Soviet historians and economists:
some talk about the preponderant influence of the 'lower national
bourgeoisie', others have drawn attention to the role of the lower
middle class,[3] and some have even formulated entirely new concepts,
such as the 'military intelligentsia'.

It has been argued that discussion has been bedevilled for too long
by certain shibboleths of the past—such as the resolutions of the
sixth Comintern congress in 1928, or Stalin's thesis of 1925 that the
Indian national bourgeoisie was irrevocably split between 'com-
promisers' and 'patriots'.[4] Some Soviet economists and historians
have suggested dropping the term national bourgeoisie altogether;
others, in a less revolutionary vein, have proposed differentiating in

[1] According to *Osnovy marksizma-leninizma*, 'in the countries of the East state
capitalism in its present form is not a tool of the imperialist monopolies; on the
contrary, it stimulates the anti-imperialist movement'.

[2] There have been three conferences on the national bourgeoisie in the Soviet
bloc in recent years. The discussion in 1955 was opened by V. A. Maslennikov, then
editor of *Sovetskoe Vostokovedenie* (see *S.V.*, IV, 1955, for a short report); another
conference in 1956, opened by V. V. Balabushevich, an expert on India, lasted longer
and went into greater detail (*S.V.*, I, 1957). The participants in these two Moscow
conferences were economists and historians, whereas the participants in the Leipzig
seminar on the national bourgeoisie and the national liberation movement (May
1959) were apparently exclusively party ideologists (see *World Marxist Review*,
August and September 1959). As far as can be judged from the published reports,
the two Moscow discussions were on a much higher level of sophistication.

[3] The lower middle class in the newly independent countries is not identical with
the lower national bourgeoisie in the Soviet definition. The members of the latter
exploit hired labour, thus absorbing part of the surplus value, whereas the former
are independent producers, mainly artisans or comparatively well-to-do peasants
who do not employ outside labour. They are believed to be both more progressive and
more reactionary than the latter. Though the element of exploitation is absent in the
lower middle class, it is often rooted in a pre-capitalist mode of production which
affects its ideology and political orientation.

[4] I. M. Reisner in the 1956 Moscow discussion; see *S.V.*, I, 1957, p. 179.

future between the upper, middle, and lower national bourgeoisie. The upper national bourgeoisie are/those most likely to become pro-imperialist, whereas the lower sections, the owners of medium and small enterprises, cottage industries, etc. are usually ready to follow an anti-feudal, anti-imperialist line and to co-operate with the communists in the national liberation movement. The middle sections are said to waver, sometimes supporting the progressive forces, sometimes turning against them. (There is not much to choose between this division and the Leninist definition of the bourgeoisie in the advanced countries of the West.) Some communists think that, *pace* Mao Tse-tung, the concept of the compradore bourgeoisie does not make sense in other parts of the world than China; can all those engaged in trade with foreigners, co-operating with investors from abroad, exporting raw materials, or engaged in industrial projects with foreign firms be regarded as compradores? As one Soviet historian put it, 'In reality it does not always happen that way.'[1] Finally (and here we face a real innovation), it has been maintained that any future analysis of the national bourgeoisie will have to be based not only (and perhaps not even mainly) on economic criteria.[2] With that we cross the border-line between the doctrinaire approach and a realistic analysis of the economic and political state of affairs in the *tiers monde*.

The Leninist and post-Leninist image of the national bourgeoisie as reflected in Soviet historical writing is a strange mixture of myth and reality. Communist theses and publications can frequently serve as a healthy corrective to certain schools of thought in the West, where until fairly recently far too little attention has been paid to the economic and social aspects of events in Asia and Africa; 'development' has become a magic slogan only during the last decade. Western observers have written and talked about the 'national movement' in these parts of the world in the most general terms, without any attempt at further analysing the important differences between countries or the differentia-tion within each country. Western historians have concentrated in their research on the traditional forces in eastern societies, ignoring or belittling the new forces that have emerged over the last decades. This refers not only to economic and social analysis, but also to the study of political movements. Even during the worst years of the 'third period', or between 1948 and 1953, Soviet and communist observers have not always been wrong; this is true in particular for their interest in the emerging radical forces. Since in many of these countries the radical forces were the 'wave of the future', they could not go far wrong.

The drawbacks and weaknesses of the Soviet approach have been equally obvious, and the only thing that can be said in mitigation is that a number of Soviet historians are now aware of some of the more blatant distortions and crudities. Soviet students of contemporary

[1] Kia Nouri in *World Marxist Review*, August 1959, p. 61.
[2] A. A. Guber in *S.V.*, I, 1957, p. 181.

history have been inclined to generalize about the national movement in Asia and Africa in a way that was often no less absurd than the generalizations of western writers about nationalism in the East. Ideological concepts were transplanted from one part of the world to another, often with disastrous consequences. This was sometimes due to 'ideological blinkers', on other occasions to wishful thinking, and frequently to ignorance. (It should be recalled that until recently Soviet experts had to follow events in Asia and Africa from afar and to base their analysis on second-hand sources.) The almost constant exaggeration of the political importance of the working class can be mentioned as illustrating 'ideological blinkers'. One Soviet Middle East specialist, writing as late as 1955, asserted that *only* the proletariat could lead the national liberation movement; the national bourgeoisie had tried at times to put itself at the head of the movement, but, wavering and inclined to compromise with imperialism, it had shown itself incapable of leadership. Less than two years later, the very same expert had to swallow her words: the active and widespread participation of the bourgeoisie in the national liberation struggle was a characteristic feature of the anti-imperialist battle in the Middle East, the national bourgeoisie had grown much stronger, whereas the proletariat (the leading force of 1955) was only *beginning* to play the role of vanguard.[1]

These and similar opinions were based on the prospects sketched out at the sixth Comintern congress in 1928, according to which the colonies would achieve political independence only after the working class (in alliance with the peasants and petit-bourgeois elements) had achieved the leadership of the national liberation movement. Since 1955 Soviet historians have freely admitted that political independence has been achieved under what they call national-bourgeois auspices. They were mistaken, but they find at least one mitigating circumstance: 'The new possibility arose mainly due to the growth of the socialist world and the rapid advance of the national liberation movement on a world scale.'[2]

The treatment of Africa in Soviet historical writings may serve as an illustration of error due rather to ignorance of the facts than to ideological prejudice. Soviet publications on Africa (admittedly very few until recently) have always operated freely with concepts such as 'proletariat', 'class struggle', 'national bourgeoisie'; first-hand observation on the spot would have convinced them within a week that these were flights of fantasy. It has only lately been admitted (for instance, with regard to Guinea) that a national bourgeoisie does not exist, that there is no 'feudal exploitation' in agriculture, and that one can hardly talk about the proletariat as a class in a country with no more than 90,000 wage-earners.

But the main weakness of the neo-Leninist concept has been its one-sided application of economic categories and the disregard of all other

[1] L. Vatolina in *S.V.*, II, 1955, p. 66; L. Vatolina in *Araby v borbe za nezavisimost* (Moscow, 1957), pp. 14, 18.
[2] Idris Cox in *World Marxist Review*, loc. cit., p. 66.

factors and motives. This often led Soviet and communist authors to misjudge a given situation; in other instances they had to perform tight-rope acts to square realities with the doctrine. The very social composition of the communist parties in Asia and Africa should have provided them with food for thought. It may be trivial to recall that neither Marx nor Engels nor Lenin was of proletarian origin, and that until fairly recently intellectuals played a leading role in the communist movement in the West. But the socialist, and later the communist movement in the West also had its Bebels and Thorez, Thaelmanns and Duclos, and sooner or later it also acquired a strong proletarian 'mass basis'. In most Asian and African countries, the leaders of the communist parties are all members of what Mao calls the 'lower intelligentsia' (many of whom are 'national-bourgeois' by origin); in many places the rank and file too, more often than not, belong to the same stratum rather than to the working class. Revolutionary nationalism in Asia and Africa is *par excellence* a movement of the intelligentsia. We would look in vain for a careful analysis of this phenomenon in Soviet historiography; for it is maintained to this day that the intelligentsia is not a class but a free-floating stratum and therefore of no great political consequence.

Soviet historians have frequently misjudged the real forces behind the national movement, just as they misjudged the class character of fascism in Europe. In communist theory (which in this point at least has not been basically modified to this very day) the rise of fascism and national-socialism was explained as the victory of monopoly capitalism—the essentially petit-bourgeois character of fascism was never openly admitted. Soviet writers have consistently misjudged the basically *political* character of anti-imperialism in Asia and Africa, and they therefore under-rated the revolutionary potential of this movement. The lawyers, students, teachers, and officers in such countries as Egypt and Iraq, Cuba and Indonesia, did not turn against western imperialism because their class interests compelled them to do so; anti-imperialism is a very complicated phenomenon in which national mystique and other political and psychological factors play a central role. Soviet historians for decades ignored the existence of an Asian and African nationalism that was by no means a monopoly of the bourgeoisie, but was felt more intensely by other groups and classes.

Communist theoreticians (as well as some writers in the West) have refused to admit so far that class interests do not play the decisive role in the policy of such leaders as Nasser, Kassem, or Castro; in a way they, like the stratum from which they hail, are 'free-floating'. Vested interests do not dictate their policy; they may opt for collaboration with the communists or against; the decision will always be largely political or psychological; only to a very limited extent will it be motivated by economic considerations. It is therefore quite misleading to define a leader (or a junta) of this type as the representative of certain class interests. Typical of this kind of practice is a quotation from a speech at an international conference in Leipzig called in 1959 to discuss once again the national bourgeoisie: '. . . it seems to me that the dominant role in Egypt is exercised by the national bourgeoisie, and that Nasser is a spokesman of the Misr monopoly group which has its grip on almost the whole of the Egyptian economy and is seeking to extend its domination over Syria's cotton trade, including the Central Bank of Syria.' This kind of analysis makes about as much sense as the representation of Hitler as a tool of Krupp and Thyssen, and of Mussolini as a puppet of Fiat or Pirelli.

If class analysis was of any value as a reliable guide to political action, the socialists should have been the party nearest to the communists in Asia and Africa as well as in Latin America. But in fact the communists have found it much easier to co-operate with the 'upper national bourgeoisie' than with the socialists—in India, Indonesia, the Arab world, and most Latin American countries. It might be contended that this argument is invalid, since the socialists are the communists' main political competitors, and that political considerations caused a distortion of economic motives. But, strangely enough, the same distortion is at work with regard to parties and movements that can on no account be regarded as direct competitors of the communists. The Muslim Brotherhood in Egypt has been more pronouncedly lower class in social origin than any other movement in Egyptian history. Most of its membership was petit-bourgeois, working class, and even peasant. Nevertheless, communist historians had no good word to say for this group, despite its very active participation in the anti-imperialist struggle. The same applies, incidentally, to similar groups in other Asian and African countries—such as the communalist parties in India and some right-wing groups in Persia; they are all predominantly lower class in composition; but their religious as well as nationalist fanaticism, and their generally 'non-progressive' character, led the communists, not unnaturally, to regard them as reactionary forces. In this they may be quite right, but it only shows that in communist practice—in policy as well as in historiography—the class character of a social or political movement is not always the decisive criterion in its overall appraisal.

Since the communist parties and the Soviet bloc have not been doing too badly in the countries of Asia, Africa, and Latin America during the last decade, it is legitimate to ask how they could have achieved such successes while basing themselves on a theory which, to put it mildly, often proved irrelevant and unhelpful. To the present writer it would appear that there are several explanations. The communists, to begin with, while rigid in their adherence to ideology, have by no means adopted the whole body of Marx's and Lenin's theories; they have whenever necessary disregarded that part of the theoretical heritage that was inapplicable or inconvenient. It should be recalled, moreover, that communists, as members of a revolutionary party, were natural favourites in countries facing a revolutionary situation; despite their mistaken analyses, the communists had a coherent conception of the way in which society should be transformed, which is more than can be said of most of their competitors.

There is no good reason to assume that 1955-6 saw the last major revision in the Soviet attitude to the national movement in Asia, Africa, and Latin America. On the contrary, it is virtually certain that the present leaders of the national movement in these parts will fare no better than Chiang Kai-shek (who in his own lifetime turned from a 'progressive patriot' into a 'reactionary running-dog of American imperialism')—unless, of course, they come to accept the communist blueprint for an 'independent national democracy' as a transitional stage towards full transformation into a communist society. The manifesto of the eighty-one communist parties in Moscow (November 1960) contained a reference to 'national democracy' as the higher phase of a national liberation movement in which the national bourgeoisie is compelled to share power with other forces (such as the communists); the internal structure of such countries may not be communist but they follow a revolutionary domestic and foreign policy.

The progressive role of the national bourgeoisie, like the progressive role of the bourgeoisie in the advanced industrialized countries, is only temporary; gradually this class turns reactionary and becomes an impediment to historical development as the communists envisage it. According to the Chinese, this has already happened; the Soviet attitude is that co-operation with the national bourgeoisie should still be continued.

Since the Sukarnos, Nehrus, and Nassers are committed to a policy of neutralism, of industrial development, and of state capitalism, in Soviet eyes they still fulfil a useful function in today's world. Under their regime, the argument runs, the prerequisites are created for the emergence of a mass party of the proletariat. It is quite intelligible that these assumptions should be subject to discussion and dissension among communists; for even if they are correct from a purely economic point of view (which is far from certain), it is doubtful whether the political climate in the 'guided democracies' of Asia and Africa is necessarily conducive to the development of strong communist parties.

Nevertheless, the appraisal of the national bourgeoisie since 1956 is perhaps clearer and more stable than ever before. If they use due caution and digest the lessons of the past, Soviet commentators will probably not be taken unawares when the line vis-à-vis a certain country or group of countries next changes. However, the element of surprise has not been eliminated once and for all. Communism in the sixties is polycentric, and it is quite possible that other centres will come into being in addition to those existing today. If the communist outlook has in the past been shaped mainly by a compromise between ideology and the realities of the world situation, these realities already include a new and important factor, perhaps even a new dimension, of which

little is as yet known: the whole complex of relations between the communist countries, and in particular between the main seats of power,
and the emergent national-communist regimes, which may not be
'transitional stages' on the road towards full communism but a new
political phenomenon. The whole problem has entered a new phase and
will no doubt soon find fresh forms of expression in Soviet historiography.

DISCUSSION

Mr Laqueur said that after listening to earlier discussions it had occurred
to him that it might be as well if those who specialized in one particular
aspect of Soviet historiography changed their field of study from
time to time in order to correct conclusions and generalizations drawn
from one field that might not automatically be right for another.

It was important not to get the wrong perspective: contemporary
history was only one aspect of Soviet historiography and, in terms of
sheer output, not an important one. At the Orientalists' congress in
Moscow, for instance, only about a dozen out of five or six hundred
papers dealt with contemporary affairs, and of these the majority were
written by non-Russians. Self-respecting historians in Russia tended to
shy away from contemporary history because there the controls were
so much narrower and stricter.

It was understandable that those who studied Soviet communist party
histories should take a rather pessimistic view of the changes that had
taken place since 1953; on the other hand an Indian, Indonesian, or
Arab who knew Russian and read some of the Soviet books published
in recent years would hardly reach the conclusion about their 'institutional mendacity' that Dr Katkov did. He might find them one-sided,
doctrinaire, or altogether wrong, but this he would put down to honest
error.

The immense output in recent years of the Publishing House of
Eastern Literature of the Soviet Academy of Sciences, which issued
historical publications on Asia, Africa, and of late also on Latin
America, indicated the great efforts now being made in this direction.
Apart from quantity, there had also been a change in contents and in
attitude. This went so far as to suggest that the old-fashioned class
analysis of historical materialism was of little use and should be replaced
by the introduction of political criteria and designations.

In studying Soviet attitudes towards nationalist movements in Asia,
Africa, and Latin America over the last forty years, Mr Laqueur had
found it difficult to draw a clear line between Soviet foreign policy and
Soviet historical writing. It could be said in general that whenever
Soviet policy was hard, historians found this line fairly easy to follow.
Difficulties arose whenever the Soviet Union adopted a softer approach,
and popular-front or national-front tactics, as was the case between 1935
and 1940, and again in recent years. At these times the attitudes of
Soviet writers were difficult to describe because there was much less

F*

uniformity. Some historians seemed far more opposed to national movements than others, and occasionally gave offence, which had at times embarrassed their government. For instance, the treatment of Gandhi in 1954 and 1955 was a subject of controversy between Indian public opinion and Moscow. Similarly, the Soviet treatment of Kemal Ataturk provoked much criticism in Turkey and was in fact modified in 1955 as a result of Turkish protests.

In the early twenties Soviet historians had been uneasy in their appraisal of developments in the East, for here, in contrast to the situation in Europe, they had no guidance. All the classics of Marxism and Leninism had dealt at great length with developments in Western Europe, even where they were unimportant, but had almost entirely neglected those in the East. Although there had been some hints in a couple of articles by Lenin in 1912-13, it was safe to say that nobody interested in the socialist movement had expected the revolution in the East to precede the revolution in the West.

Since 1918 Soviet historians, statesmen, economists, etc. had been confronted by all the problems of colonial or national revolution in Asia and Africa. There was much argument as to the character and the cost of the national revolution that was to take place; the dilemma was clearly stated in the exchanges at the second Comintern congress in 1920, between Lenin and Roy, the leading Indian communist at the time. It was also reflected in the writings of early Soviet authors on the subject, such as Safarov, Pavlovich-Veltman and Rothstein, as well as in the volumes of *Novyi Vostok* and other Soviet serial publications. Briefly, the problem was whether communists could and should collaborate with non-communist nationalists, and if so, on what terms and within what limits. Although this question was primarily one for diplomats, it had preoccupied Soviet writers from 1920 to the present day. There was general agreement that, in contrast to the bourgeoisie in the West which had outlived its function, the national bourgeoisie in the East continued to play a progressive role so long as colonial rule continued, for bourgeoisie and working class had a common economic and political interest in getting rid of the foreign ruler. But once independence was gained, this union would break up and each class would once again pursue its own ends. This theory, propagated in the twenties, thirties, and up to the late forties, was invalidated by the actual course of events.

Broadly speaking, Soviet writing, like Soviet policy on the East, could be divided into five periods. The first ran from 1922 to 1928, when no clear line had been set and both doctrinaire and more liberal views on the subject co-existed. In the period which followed, marked by the coining of slogans like 'social fascism' in the West and 'national reformism' in the East, collaboration with the national movement in the East became practically impossible, because even those closest to the communists within the national Left were branded as traitors and enemies of the working class. All this found its reflection in Soviet historical literature. In the middle thirties a more conciliatory approach was adopted. The popular-front policies of 1934-5 had their counterpart in Asia and Africa. (In Africa pro-communist forces were very few and far between at the time). After 1941, when the defeat of the Axis became the main objective, 'class' considerations were subordinated to the struggle against Hitler, in which every ally was welcome. After the end of the war, particularly between 1947 and 1954, there was a revival of the 'hard' line of 1928-34. At the height of Stalinism the national movements, which had meanwhile achieved independence in India, Burma, and Ceylon, were deeply mistrusted—an attitude clearly reflected in Soviet historical writing of the period. With the exception of writings on China, Soviet Oriental studies had ceased to exist by the middle thirties. Periodicals were suppressed, research workers arrested; between 1936-53 not more than a dozen books on Asian and African historical topics were published in the Soviet Union. In 1956-7 there was a great revival of Oriental studies, though the virtual disappearance of the old cadres created considerable problems.

In regard to his conclusion that the successes of the communists in Asia and Africa were not due to their basic theories, Mr Laqueur foresaw the objection that it was difficult to understand how communism could have possibly made such spectacular progress in Asia and Africa if it had based its case on an incorrect class analysis. But there was a simple answer to this: though communism might not have the correct interpretation of the eastern world, it had a revolutionary blueprint for its change; since the political emancipation of the under-developed world was in the nature of a revolution, it was hardly surprising that revolutionary theory should be attractive to people living there.

Professor Aspaturian thought that the most important factor in changing the Soviet attitude towards the 'national bourgeoisie' was the altered power position of the Soviet Union. It was now very different from what it was in the twenties. This explained the fundamental difference between the orthodox Leninist-Stalinist theory of revolution as applied to colonial and semi-colonial countries, and the Khrushchevian position. According to the orthodox version, the national bourgeoisie or the bourgeois-nationalist revolution or the national liberation movement (all different terms for the same idea) should be supported by communists because it was progressive at that particular juncture in history, being both anti-feudal and anti-imperialist. Bourgeois democracy or capitalist society was more progressive than feudal society or colonial dependence; once the bourgeoisie came to power, it would double-cross the revolution and try to stabilize the rule of the bourgeoisie—consequently the communist party must go into opposition and mobilize the masses for the overthrow of the bourgeoisie. This orthodox version was by and large still held by the Chinese— hence the conflict with present Soviet policies in the under-developed countries. (The Chinese had added their own peculiar twist by inventing the new technique of the so-called bourgeois-democratic revolution without the bourgeois democrats; this, being a bourgeois revolution led by the communist party, avoided the complications of having to stage a second revolution from below to get rid of the bourgeoisie. Having effected a bourgeois-democratic revolution, the communists could execute from above the final phase of the proletarian revolution.)

What was Khrushchev's distinctive emendation of this theory? Essentially, that because of the strengthened position of the Soviet Union in world affairs, it could now collaborate with the national bourgeoisie even after it came to power. As Mr Laqueur had pointed out, for a long time Soviet theory on under-developed countries was a theory in search of facts. The Soviets lacked empirical information on these areas; their theory was very general and did not apply everywhere. The concept of a feudal society was virtually inapplicable to Africa. It might be argued that it was no more applicable to Asia, but at least a somewhat more convincing case could be made out for Asia and Latin America. The theory clearly had to be modified. Khrushchev's particular contribution was based on the assumption that the national bourgeoisie, even after it comes to power, is still progressive in so far as it is anti-imperialist. Since the Soviet Union was also opposed to imperialism, it had a community of interest with the national bourgeoisie. Furthermore, the growing strength of the Soviet Union had established a new psychological dimension. The national bourgeoisie itself had been impressed by developments in the Soviet Union to the point of imitating certain Russian social or economic institutions. Thirdly, the Soviet Union was now in a position to use a variety of techniques in associating itself with the national bourgeoisie, one of which was economic assistance. Khrushchev had emphasized more than once that, in contrast to the 1920s and the 1930s, the Soviet Union today was able to extend direct tangible support to anti-colonial movements and thus to influence developments even where the national bourgeoisie was in power. Mao, and probably Molotov as well, had argued against this position from the orthodox standpoint that the national bourgeoisie was unstable, unreliable, and opportunist, that it would double-cross the revolution, and that consequently the international communist movement should build up a true communist following in these areas, which would be able to contend with the national bourgeoisie for power.

In a broader context, Professor Aspaturian emphasized that Lenin's pamphlet on imperialism and the entire Leninist-Stalinist theory of revolution in colonial and semi-colonial countries was the first systematically articulated theory of under-development. Ten years ago the notion of under-development as a theoretical concept hardly existed in the West; while in the 1920s and 1930s the Soviets had a theory but no facts, the West had all the facts but no theory. The situation was now reversed. The West still had all the facts, but it was in search of a theory and was trying to develop a framework for understanding and dealing with the under-developed countries. The Soviet Union, on the other hand, was now trying to assimilate empirical information and to adjust its general theory to hard facts. In some cases the very concept of the national bourgeoisie had been challenged. In the European sense of the word a bourgeoisie simply did not exist in many of the under-developed countries. What passed for a national bourgeoisie in Africa and a number of other under-developed countries was essentially a class of state employees, an educated élite, which was primarily political and social in character rather than economic. In many of the so-called national-bourgeois groups there were no local capitalists, no great landowners, no feudal magnates. A capitalist class was practically non-existent, because the function of capitalists was by and large pre-empted by foreign business. Structurally these local élites resembled in some ways the intelligentsia in the Soviet Union. However, the semantic problem should not obscure the fact that revolutionary élite groups existed, whether we called them the national bourgeoisie or not. The significance of these groups lay in their strong political aspirations.

The Soviet Union was favoured in its relationship to the under-developed countries, because owing to its theory it was ready for what Lenin and Stalin had called the disintegration of the colonial system. In fact they had been predicting this disintegration since 1917. The West, on the contrary, had been unprepared for the collapse of the colonial system. In the period before the war very few people in official positions foresaw its liquidation within the span of fifteen years. But it was primarily its power position which enabled the Soviet Union to take greater advantage of the situation, economically, psychologically, and otherwise.

A final important point was the emergence of the possibility of communist revolution from above in non-communist countries. Until two years ago this had been a purely hypothetical question. But the Cuban situation was a unique episode in that a local revolutionary élite had voluntarily declared the country socialist and aligned it with the Soviet Union. The possibility of this happening again should not be ignored, though it did not represent the general trend. Nasser and Kassem had moved in the other direction, despite the predictions of those who believed them to be on the verge of becoming communist. Nevertheless, the Soviets clearly thought that, as the balance of power shifted in their favour, the likelihood of national élites declaring their adherence to communism became greater. Perhaps this accounted for the reluctance of Moscow to stimulate communist movements from below.

Professor Rubinstein agreed that Soviet historians were now creating new categories within the general concept of the national bourgeoisie, in order to explain more adequately the complex developments taking place in under-developed countries. Since 1955 they had moved beyond the narrow confines of Stalinist categories. In particular they frequently manifested a greater interest in emerging radical forces than their western counterparts. Though the Soviets had made many grievous errors in interpretation and in policy in the past, circumstances had developed in a way that reduced the ill effects of these miscalculations; despite class analyses that bore little relation to reality, Soviet diplomacy had made impressive advances. How was this to be explained? The reason was that they had a coherent conception of the society they wanted to shape, whereas their competitors had not. It was vital to understand and seek an effective response to the attractive force of conviction and purpose which the communists claimed to have. The élite groups in under-developed countries had not gone through a period of disillusionment with Marxism and Leninism, as similar progressive groups had in the West. They were being greatly influenced, consciously or otherwise, by the Marxist-Leninist image of the world.

Mr Mancall fully endorsed Mr Laqueur's remark on the necessity to see the writings of Soviet historians as they appeared to the African or to the Asian. Having recently spent a year in Japan, he had been struck immediately by the fact that the scholarly world, particularly in the domain of history, was completely permeated by Marxism and in many areas even by Marxism-Leninism, a term widely used in Japan. Japanese scholars were doing remarkably good research. They were not bound by the restrictions imposed on historians in the Soviet Union. It was important for western scholars to make contact with the Japanese historians, who were doing more work on China than anybody else and were strongly influenced by Soviet scholarship. This required a better analysis of Soviet writing on the Far East than was available in the West at this moment.

In Mr Mancall's view everybody writing about the Far East, and under-developed countries in general, was faced with the problem that so little was known about these areas. For instance, it would be worth expanding on the historical background to the revival of the hard line from 1948 to 1953; what was happening in these areas at that time that caused the Soviet Union to embark on this policy? And what was happening in the USSR? Mr Mancall suggested that it would do a great deal of good all round if, in studying Soviet theory about the under-developed world, we were also to undertake the study of the background to the development of the theories in terms of the area in which they were worked out. He knew, for instance, of only one book which dealt seriously with the development of Marxist movements in South-east Asia. There were almost no books dealing with South-east Asian societies, and even fewer on Africa and Latin America.

Prof. Lowenthal thought that the concept of the national bourgeoisie was not a truly analytical but an operational concept. Just as in Soviet parlance a proletarian party was not a party which expressed the wishes of the proletariat, but one which did what the communists thought a proletarian party ought to do, i.e. a communist party, so in communist language a national bourgeoisie was the group which leads the first stage of the national revolution and has to be supported until it is supplanted.

In its origins and interpretation the concept of the national bourgeoisie was inseparable from the concept of the two-stage communist revolution in colonial and under-developed countries. When the term national bourgeoisie came into conflict with this operational meaning, the words were discarded. As an operational concept the national bourgeoisie had a built-in contradiction. The concept of the two-stage revolution itself had a serious inherent weakness. It was generally agreed among western analysts that the leaders of the national revolution in under-developed countries were the intelligentsia; in many cases it was an intelligentsia in uniform. The function of this intelligentsia, in turning itself into a bureaucratic dictatorship and into the skeleton of a new national state, was analogous to that exercised by the communists in their own countries, albeit with a different ideology.

All the countries in which the communists had come to power by revolution were under-developed countries; of all of them it could be said that they had not possessed the inherent dynamism of western societies. That being so, the striving for modernization could only be satisfied by political means. The role of the state, as distinct from society, had to be an infinitely more active and dynamic one. A national intelligentsia that set out to fulfil this function, by getting hold of the state machine and starting to modernize a backward society, would, if at all efficient, inevitably get into a very strong position. This made it difficult to proceed with the second phase projected in the communist picture of the two-stage revolution. This was what happened in China under Chiang Kai-shek for many years, and this was what went wrong with communist calculations in the Middle East. Hence the discussions in the Soviet camp on how to modify communist strategy in relation to the national bourgeoisie. The Maoist variant was based on the calculation that the communist party would carry out both stages and be the party not only of the proletariat but also of the petit-bourgeoisie, the peasantry, and everybody else. In other words, there might be two stages, but not two stages of power.

An alternative had been developed in recent years by the Yugoslavs. In their version, these countries would come to socialism without the communist party; the nationalist leaders who, as the Yugoslavs recognize, are not bourgeois may come to fulfil a socialist function. In this case, too, there were not two stages of power, but two stages of economic development under one power, though a non-communist one. Soviet strategy about the under-developed countries had been torn between these two alternatives, both of which were more realistic than the traditional communist concept of the two-stage revolution. The recent controversy with the Chinese could be understood in part in this light. The discussion centred on the question whether the Soviets were right in backing the nationalist phase or whether they should aid the communist bid for power. The Soviet policy of backing the nationalist dictators was partly due to the strength of the Soviet Union, which for the first time enabled it to have a world-wide policy as distinct from world-wide propaganda. But it was also due to the emergence of many new countries under non-communist regimes. Though the Soviets had been prepared in theory for the collapse of colonialism, they did not recognize it when it happened. There had been one period when the Soviets, in their attempt to keep the West divided, had actually tried to put the brake on colonial movements. Similarly the French communists were at first opposed to Algerian autonomy, and the Indonesian communists were among the moderates in the first years of the Indonesian revolution. In a word, the Soviets had not been well prepared for the emancipation of the colonial world, but they now recognized its importance, and were trying to find a way of denying additional spheres of interest to the West in these areas, rather than to communize them directly; the formula of backing the national bourgeoisie was in line with this outlook. In practice Moscow had lately inclined, not to the Yugoslav theory of recognizing these nationalist regimes as socialist, but to the Yugoslav practice of treating them as partners in the field of current foreign policy.

VIII. Soviet Historians and the Sino-Soviet Alliance

MARK MANCALL

The victory of the communists in the Chinese civil war in 1949 very likely took the Russians by surprise; they had not prepared for it, politically, economically, or, for that matter, historically. Russian activities in Manchuria in 1945-6 and the Soviet Union's continued relations with the Nationalist government point to this conclusion. After 1949 the USSR was obliged to create an ideological basis for the new Sino-Soviet alliance and to present it historically as due to something more than simply fortuitous circumstances. It was to be viewed as an integral part of the onward march of history; the communization of China may have come at an unexpected moment, but it was inevitable in the long run. China's history had to be fitted into the proper pattern of historiographical reference. The task appears to have been left primarily to the Chinese themselves. On the other hand, the demonstration that the Sino-Soviet alliance was inevitable was left to the Russians. Indeed, it is of no little interest that the Chinese appear to have shunned the field of Sino-Russian relations.

Since 1917 there has been a constant triangular strain between the actual interests of the USSR in Asia, the interests of the world communist movement, and the historical realities of the Orient itself, which has demanded a constant effort at some form of resolution. Before Stalin's failure in China in 1927,[1] the assumed identity of these three factors supplied guides to policy in an era when the Soviet Union was seeking allies in the Far East, and when in China, disillusioned with the West and in a state of turmoil, a communist victory did not seem impossible. Between 1927 and the end of the Second World War, China occupied a secondary place in Soviet foreign policy. After that, however, Soviet interest in China became dominant and the interests of the communist movement had to be subordinated to it. If Soviet national interests were to be an operative factor in China, the Chinese situation would have to be adjusted accordingly. Essentially, the basis of the alliance with China after 1949 had to be found in terms of this unity-in-subordination, as in fact it was.

The effort to build up a picture of China and of the alliance which would resolve these strains became especially evident between 1949 and 1951, particularly in defining the limits and principles of Oriental studies,

[1] For a detailed discussion of this period, see Conrad Brandt, *Stalin's Failure in China* (Cambridge, Mass., 1958).

and in assessing Russia's pre-revolutionary role in Asia. The effort was successful so long as China was in a subordinate, not an equal, position. But when China, in the post-Stalin period, graduated from subordination to equality and co-leadership, a new basis had to be found for the alliance—one which would satisfy the historical needs of the Soviet Union and China at a time when their ideological paths and their interests began to diverge. There has therefore been an attempt, particularly since the twentieth CPSU congress, to elucidate the precise historical bases from which the alliance sprang, to show that the alliance is a natural historical development not only, and not even necessarily, because of the unity provided by communism, but because there is a legacy of common experience, intercourse, and joint action.

The years immediately after the October revolution witnessed the beginning of the effort to assert the hegemony of Marxist ideology in the field of Russian Oriental studies. This presented considerable difficulties. The traditional Marxist analysis of European society provided a firm foundation for the treatment of European history, and by a simple process of extension involving some degree of exaggeration, this analysis could also be applied to Russia. The history of the Orient, however, with its widely different social, economic, and political institutions, created far graver problems for the Marxist historian than did Russian history. Had there existed a body of Marxist analysis of Oriental society, it could have been applied in detailed studies, but apart from vague references to a peculiar 'Asiatic mode of production', the body of pre-1917 Marxist theoretical literature was non-committal about Oriental problems, and by the end of the twenties, even the theory of the 'Asiatic mode of production' had been discredited in the disputes that marked the rise of Stalin to absolute power. Instead, it became the rule to apply the traditional Marxist socio-economic analysis, based on western experience, to Oriental societies. It was necessary to develop an approach to the study of traditional Asian societies which would show their development along accepted slave-owning—feudal—capitalist lines, and which would also involve a close analysis of imperialism in colonial areas. In a country like China, where feudalism had disappeared, essentially, by the second century BC, this created serious problems of periodization, and many ideological difficulties for the Oriental historian. One result was that many scholars shied away from problems which would involve them directly in the application of the Marxist analysis to the Orient.

Since, in the years between 1927 and 1949, there were few opportunities for positive Soviet action in China, this reform of Oriental studies remained an internal Soviet matter. The emergence of the Chinese People's Republic, however, created a new situation in which positive Soviet action in the Far East was not only possible but necessary, and this required some easing of the strain inherent in the relationship between the now powerful Soviet state and communist China, with their divergent interests. The Soviet response was on two levels: a new Soviet Marxist orthodoxy in Oriental studies was created, to provide the theoretical framework, and Russian pre-revolutionary orientology was rehabilitated to support the concept that Russia had played a 'progressive' role in Asia throughout its history. This construction, in turn, supported the role which the Soviet Union planned to play *vis-à-vis* China after 1949. The resolution of the tensions between these conflicting interests had become a matter of international concern.

The complete history of Russian orientology and sinology has yet to be written. The last work on this subject was published in 1925.[1] A series of studies appearing in recent years[2] is primarily biographical or bibliographical in approach, indicating that Soviet scholars are not prepared to evaluate the history of their subject until certain inherent and continuing contradictions are cleared away—between the Marxist and non-Marxist approach to the study of the Orient, and between Russian national interests and those of international communism; these must find some resolution before a comprehensive study is possible.

It is significant that it was not until April 1949 that there appeared the first statement in the post-war period on the problems of orientalists.[3] Until then, it appears, Oriental studies had escaped rigorous ideological control.

While the term 'orientology' had previously been dismissed as 'extremely relative and in fact non-scientific', as representing 'no particular discipline with defined subject-matter but merely an aggregation of sciences which are held together solely by a geographical indication',[4] it was now re-defined as 'a complex of various disciplines, among which an honoured place must be occupied by history'. The study of Asian history was said to be one of the most backward areas in the Soviet historical sciences,[5] in both quality and quantity. It did not meet the demands of the times. Only one Stalin prize had ever been given for an orientological work, and that in 1928 for a study of ancient Khorezm. The monographs and textbooks that had appeared all suffered from serious ideological and factual shortcomings; the study of Oriental history in the USSR was still subordinated to narrow philological interests. 'The country demands from Soviet historian-orientalists series of works on the history of Oriental countries, as well as monographic research on particular problems of the historical development of the peoples of the Orient in periods nearer to our times, which will aid the understanding of the historical events now taking place there.'

The same statement indicated clearly the approach to be taken in the

[1] B. Bartold, *Istoriya izucheniya vostoka v Yevrope i Rossii* (Leningrad, 1925).

[2] *Ocherki po istorii russkovo vostokovedeniya*, 5 vols. (Moscow, 1953-60).

[3] 'Neotlozhennye zadachi sovetskikh istorikov-vostokovedov', *Voprosy Istorii*, April 1949.

[4] V. Gurko-Kryazhin, 'Vostokovedenie', *Bolshaya Sovetskaya Entsiklopedia* (Moscow, 1929), XIII, pp. 289-93.

[5] 'Neotlozhennye zadachi . . .', loc. cit., p. 3.

study of Russian-Chinese relations. Soviet orientalists 'must show in their works the concrete reflection of the influence of the great October socialist revolution and the victory of socialism in the USSR on the development of the countries of the non-Soviet Orient'. Bolshevik *partiinost* demanded a decisive turn to contemporary themes in Oriental studies, the struggle against bourgeois ideology, and an active fight against the influence of foreign 'pseudo-scientific theories'. The Soviet historian-orientalist was to take part in the struggle of the Orient against imperialism and its servants, the bourgeois orientalists. 'Their direct duty is to help by their works to expose bourgeois pseudo-scientific theories and to oppose them on the basis of the great teachings of Lenin and Stalin.' Leninism-Stalinism was to be the chief weapon in this struggle, in the course of which particular attention was to be paid to peasant movements, the development of the working class, the formation of the nation and the conditions which retard this process.

During the summer of 1950 Oriental studies in the USSR were radically re-organized. What had been a fairly loose web of institutes in Moscow, Leningrad, Vladivostok, and the capitals of the union republics was now pulled tight and centralized. The various institutes in Moscow were amalgamated into an Institute of Orientology of the Academy of Sciences of the USSR. The central Institute of Orientology, which had formerly been in Leningrad, was moved, together with a sizeable portion of the library, to the new institute.

At the end of the year, *Voprosy Istorii* explained in an editorial (December 1950) that the aim of the re-organization was to raise the level of work and to liquidate the backwardness in Soviet orientology, which did 'not satisfy the requirements placed before it by life. On the newly reorganized institute of orientology . . . is laid the task of uniting the forces of Soviet orientologists in solving the most immediate problems in the area of the study of the countries of the contemporary Orient'. The new institute was to devote itself to the study of the history (contemporary history in particular), literatures, languages, and economies of the Orient. Above all, particular attention was to be paid to the study of the new Chinese People's Republic, the Chinese communist party, and the history of Soviet-Chinese friendship.

All this, of course, was an obvious response to the victory of the Chinese communist party; the new Sino-Soviet alliance required an ideological analysis of the historical past which would support it. It is surprising that thirty years after the revolution Soviet orientology had still not come completely under the control of the party; there had continued to flourish all through this period a generation of world-renowned orientalists, trained and active in the pre-revolutionary tradition, whose influence was so pervasive that nothing short of liquidation could remove them from the scene. The sinologist V. M. Alekseyev and the arabist I. Yu. Krachkovsky, both academicians, were cases in point. Both received their education before the revolution (Alekseyev had participated in one of Chavannes' expeditions to China) and maintained the traditions in which they had been brought up to their deaths in the fifties. Alekseyev throughout his life maintained his ties with scholarly organizations abroad, and even at the height of the anti-cosmopolitan campaign insisted that his students speak to him in English. Stalin, it is said, wanted to remove Krachkovsky from Leningrad University, but failed owing to mass opposition by the students.

The long and detailed article on orientology in the ninth volume of the *Large Soviet Encyclopedia*, issued in 1951, set forth the principles which were thenceforth to guide Soviet orientology. It defined orientology as 'the historically formed totality of the scientific disciplines which study the history, economy, literature, art, and monuments of the material and spiritual culture of the East'.

Although the attack on 'bourgeois' orientology was carried to a new extreme in this article, an entirely different line was taken on Russian pre-revolutionary orientology. Pre-revolutionary Russian orientology was, of course, part of 'bourgeois' orientology, and a resolution had to be found for this contradiction. It was found in terms of the 'age-old historical ties which had developed between the Russian and Oriental peoples', and, even more important in terms of future historiography, of the 'progressive role in relation to the Orient' played by Russia. This latter had scriptural sanction; for Engels had mentioned it in 1851.[1] The doctrine of Russia's 'progressive role in the Orient' has become, in the years since 1951, the key to much Soviet historical research on Russian-Chinese relations and on the Orient in general. It is said to have begun in the twelfth century; and later, when their western counterparts were serving the predatory purposes of imperialism, Russian travellers and scholars allegedly felt great sympathy for the masses and made important contributions to Oriental studies.

That enormous contributions to the field were made by Russian orientalists before the revolution is a fact which no one would deny. But this still did not solve the problem of giving these scholars a 'positive role', as opposed to the negative role of Western Europeans. This had to be done in such a way as to demonstrate Russia's progressive role in the Orient. It was done on the basis of what can perhaps be called the 'theory of salvation by association'—that is, the friends of a 'progressive' are apt to be progressive. Thus, 'Bichurin was an acquaintance of Pushkin and other progressive people in Russia in the first half of the nineteenth century and shared their ideas of liberation'.[2] This was the key to the rehabilitation of nineteenth-century Russian orientology which, in turn, was the foundation for the 'progressive role' theory. Russian orientology was said to have had a high degree of ideological consciousness; revolutionary-democratic ideas had decisively influenced the development of Russian orientalists. Belinsky, Chernyshevsky and Dobrolyubov all had an 'indefatigable' interest in the Orient, felt a deep sympathy with the enslaved peoples of the colonies

[1] Karl Marx and Friedrich Engels, *Sochineniya* (Moscow, 1928-47), XXI, p. 211.
[2] 'Vostokovedenie', *Bolshaya Sovetskaya Entsiklopediya*, IX, p. 195.

and semi-colonies, and made profound analyses of historical events in the area. They did not succumb to the fashion for *chinoiserie* which was a symbol in Europe of exploitation and idealization. Belinsky stated that 'China is a great phenomenon . . . India . . . occupies an honoured place in history.' Chernyshevsky studied Oriental languages, had relations with the great Russian arabist, G. S. Sablukov, and was deeply interested in the 'Oriental question', as well as in Arabic and Sanskrit studies. Dobrolyubov, who reviewed a book by Academician V. P. Vasiliev on Buddhism, 'first correctly noted the anti-popular and reactionary character of the policy of Shamil'.[1] While the Soviets admitted the limitations imposed by historical conditions, Russian nineteenth-century orientology was rescued by its association with the great Russian revolutionary democrats.

This saving grace is granted not only to scholars. While western travellers were servants of predatory imperialism, Russian explorers discovered and introduced into scientific circulation numerous important materials and contributed to Russia's 'progressive' role in Asia by honest reporting of actual social conditions in the areas through which they travelled. Thus the *Encyclopedia* resolves the contradiction between the fact that a bourgeois society must give rise to bourgeois ideology, and the theory that this was not necessarily so in the Russian case.

In 1956, in recognition of the greatly increased importance of China on the Soviet horizon, and possibly as a bow in the direction of Peking, the Chinese section of the institute in Moscow was split off and transformed into a separate Institute of Sinology, with its own centre and its own library. In 1958 there appeared four issues of a journal, *Sovetskoe Kitaevedenie* (Soviet Sinology), which was then discontinued. This was the organ of the new institute, and was followed by a new publication (still appearing), *Problemy Vostokovedeniya*, in which Chinese studies were united with all other Oriental studies. In 1960 the Institute of Sinology was itself closed down and its functions transferred back to the newly recreated Chinese section of the Institute of Orientology, which in turn was renamed the Institute of the Peoples of Asia. There is insufficient evidence to evaluate the significance of all these recent changes, except to point out that the rise and fall of the Institute of Sinology and its journal obviously reflected the course of the Sino-Soviet alliance, and in particular Moscow's insistence, after 1959, that it would not be dictated to by Peking.

The editorial introduction to the short-lived *Sovetskoe Kitaevedenie* dealt with Soviet Chinese studies after 1956. It re-affirmed the theories of the 'progressive role' and of 'salvation through association', noting that progressive pre-revolutionary Russian sinologists had been fettered by the study of ancient history and philology. It emphasized that it was the 1917 revolution which sparked off subsequent revolutionary activities in China. 'The struggle of the Chinese workers bears witness to the fact

[1] Ibid., pp. 195-6.

that under the influence of the October revolution there began a crisis of the colonial system pointing more clearly to the historical doom of the shameful colonial order.' The twentieth CPSU congress was given explicit consideration. It had rejected dogmatism, 'doctrinairism', revisionism, and enriched Marxism-Leninism; Soviet orientology had come under severe criticism at the congress. 'The cult of personality brought about stagnation in the analysis of the Chinese revolution. J. V. Stalin's view of the direction in which the main attack should be made at various stages in the Chinese revolution was mechanically transferred to Chinese soil.'

Nevertheless, it is obvious from the editorial that Moscow was not prepared to go so far as to denounce Stalin's role in the events in China of 1924-7. 'Under the flag of the struggle against dogmatism', sinologists were not to 'abandon the positions of scientific socialism, ignore the most important works of J. V. Stalin, in particular those which give a detailed criticism of the Trotskyite evaluation of the Chinese revolution of 1924-7'. Occupying an ill-defined position between Russia and China at the beginning of the ideological debate, the sinological fraternity was forced to step gingerly in evaluating Stalin's role in China, and they took their cue from Ch'en Po-ta,[1] a leading Chinese ideologist in the field of history.

In discussing future sinological research, the editorial listed eight areas which required basic work: (1) the periodization of Chinese history; (2) the genesis and peculiarities of the slave-owning period; (3) the genesis and peculiarities of the development of Chinese feudal society; (4) the development of capitalism; (5) the formation of the national state; (6) the development of ideology and culture; (7) the popular-democratic revolution; (8) the general course of socialist construction in China.

The dissolution of the Institute of Sinology and the suppression of its journal must not be taken as indicating reduced interest in sinological studies. On the contrary, study of China in all respects is increasing steadily. But in 1959 and 1960 the Soviet authorities must have been anxious lest such institutions become the focal point for spreading Chinese ideological influence among Soviet scholars. It is known, for instance, that the Sino-Polish Friendship Society in Warsaw was active in disseminating propaganda presenting the strictly Chinese position in the current debates. While the Sino-Soviet Friendship Society itself could not very well be liquidated, other institutions could be pushed into the background or done away with completely. But this did not diminish the continued and increasing importance of sinological studies in the USSR, particularly in the area of Sino-Russian relations. In the past decade a considerable effort has been made to develop an approach to the alliance from the historical point of view.

[1] Ch'en Po-ta, 'Stalin and the Chinese Revolution', *Current Background*, May 10, 1952, No. 2, p. 181, *passim*.

At first, the relationship between the two communist powers was seen by both partners as one of 'older brother' (the USSR) and 'younger brother' (China). Soviet sinologists developed this theme at great length before the twentieth congress. The process of destalinization after that congress, with its reverberations in Eastern Europe, the rise of China to a position of co-leadership in the bloc, and the development of serious divergences in Soviet and Chinese attitudes, created a new situation. Soviet specialists responded by seeking a pragmatic approach to the Sino-Soviet alliance which would be valid in spite of ideological and political differences, and which would create a solid basis for the study of the alliance. The change can best be studied in the columns of *Voprosy Istorii*. Purely orientological journals are too easily subject to specialized influences to serve this purpose. It is generally accepted that the short-lived *Sovetskoe Kitaevedenie* was closely controlled by Peking, while *Problemy Vostokovedeniya*, as the official journal of the Institute of the Peoples of Asia, is strictly orientological, and still markedly philological in approach.

The first article on China to appear in *Voprosy Istorii* was written by Kuo Mo-jo, the president of the Chinese Academy of Sciences (1945, No. 5-6). It was a short note on the study of Chinese history in China during the war. More than a year elapsed before the second article on China appeared (1947, No. 2), dealing with Uighur sources concerning the rebellion in Sinkiang in 1864. (This is, incidentally, a valuable piece of bibliographical research.) Two more articles appeared in quick succession—one a review of an American book on American-Russian relations in the Far East (1947, No. 4) and the other a discussion of the Japanese attack on Pearl Harbour (1947, No. 6).

The first substantial contribution on China *per se* appeared only in July 1947, and this, interestingly enough, was by G. Voitinsky, who had been in China in 1920 as an emissary of the Comintern. It is clear from this article that the Soviet Government was not expecting the communist victory in China. 'The Kuomintang at that time [1923] was the only serious national revolutionary group in China.' It was with the aid of the CCP that the KMT became a mass party, but it was the KMT itself which was the mass party. Voitinsky laid no stress on the role of Mao or on the influence of the October revolution, though he did deal with the role of the USSR in the formation of revolutionary forces. On the whole, the article was a remarkably fair account of events, given its author and place of publication.

By the end of 1948, a communist victory in China appeared not unlikely, and this was reflected in the next item on China to appear in *Voprosy Istorii* (1948, No. 12), a review of a book on the Sino-Russian Kyakhta treaty in the eighteenth century by a great Soviet student of Japan, the late A. Galperin. He wrote: 'It is difficult . . . to agree with one of the author's points in the very first chapter, when he writes that this treaty "embodied for the first time the principle of extra-territoriality for Russian subjects living in China" '; if, on the formal side, this point of view could to a certain extent be correct, in fact extra-territoriality in China was an outcome of the first unequal treaty between Britain and China in 1842-3. Russian treaties, up to 1859 at least, were completely equal treaties. 'The author should have given "priority" in the establishment of extra-territoriality in China not to Russia but to England.'

Three months later, in March 1949, an article appeared dealing with the period 1925-7 which emphasized Stalin's role in China and pointed to the hostility shown by Soviet workers in meetings all over the country to imperialist opposition to the Chinese revolution. This theme of sympathy was later to become very important. The article made hardly any mention of Soviet support and advisers in that period; the first work to deal with this in detail was the book rehabilitating Blyukher, published only in 1960.[1]

In the middle of 1949, with the communist victory in China approaching, a long article entitled 'The Successes of the Chinese People in the Struggle for Independence and Democracy', made several important statements.[2] Essentially, the article set forth the Stalinist line on China, with extensive citations from his works. It was probably intended to set the scholarly stage for the CCP victory and for a new attitude to China. The positive results of the Soviet victory in Manchuria over Japan (1945) were spelled out, and, in consideration of Chinese feelings about Soviet activities in this area, it was explained: 'With the liberation of North China, a great number of large enterprises, mines, railroads, ports, which were located in the northern industrial region and seized after their occupation by the Kuomintang forces . . . were transferred to the democratic forces.' China's future role in Asia, as an example for other Asian countries, was also discussed. However, it was clearly stated that the Soviet Union must lead this movement and victory could be attained only in close unity with it. American imperialism was identified as the great enemy, and 'even economically under-developed peoples can defeat imperialism if they unite and struggle together, relying on the aid of the entire democratic camp of peace, under the leadership of the working class and its vanguard, the communist party'. The article impresses the reader as a statement that China and the Soviet Union have common problems, but that they are primarily the problems of the Soviet Union.

Ten months later, a review article raised the question of Chinese studies.[3] It is not insignificant that the writer, Yefimov, was well known as a strict Stalinist. The study of China, he said, had now become particularly important: '. . . this gives special significance to the study of the history of the struggle of the Chinese people. The generalization of the experience of this struggle, its successes and failures, the history

[1] D. Lappo and A. Melchin, *Ot soldata do marshala* (Moscow, 1960).

[2] G. Astafev, 'Uspekhi kitaiskovo naroda v borbe za nezavisimost i demokratiyu', *Voprosy Istorii*, 1949, No. 5.

[3] G. Yefimov, ' "Uchenye Zapiski" Tikhookeanskovo Instituta. T. III. Kitaiskii sbornik', *Voprosy Istorii*, 1950, No. 3.

of the final victory of the Chinese people over foreign imperialism and internal reaction, is an honourable and responsible task for Soviet historians . . . Books about China are in great demand in our country. To satisfy the interest of the Soviet reader in events in China is an urgent task of Soviet orientological science.' 1917 had begun a new era in the history of the Chinese people, and with the May Fourth Movement the proletariat of China entered into political activity. (At this point, in 1950, these two events appeared to be regarded as parallel; later they were to assume a cause-effect relationship.) Yefimov also stressed the significance of Chinese communism for the rest of the Orient, and maintained that: 'The works of comrade Stalin on the questions of the Chinese revolution played an especially important role in the struggle and victory of the Chinese communist party.' (This statement contrasts interestingly with one made two years later by the Chinese historian Ch'en Po-ta: 'It was a great misfortune for our party that the opportunists, in the interests of disseminating their own erroneous concepts and proposals, either intentionally or unintentionally kept back Stalin's works on China.') The events of 1927, Yefimov believed, were not yet satisfactorily explained, and he took issue with one of the articles in the collection under review, which maintained that 1927 represented a temporary defeat of the revolution and the triumph of reaction. 1927 had seen the formation of the Red Army of China, and the creation of soviets. 'The communist party of China continued to fulfil its revolutionary duties with honour in conditions of temporary defeat of the revolution.'

The inability to provide a basic statement on Russian-Chinese relations which would do away with the causes of these historiographical disagreements and at the same time satisfy the needs of the moment was reflected in the editorial in the next issue of *Voprosy Istorii* (1950, No. 4). Quoting Mao in support of a statement that the study of the history of the friendship and aid which the Soviet Union had given to China was vital, it insisted that 'one of the most important tasks of Soviet historians is to show the historical growth of the friendly relations between the Soviet and Chinese peoples, the role in the world of the first country of socialism, and the role of comrade Stalin in the victory of the Chinese people'. This was more than just Stalinist sycophancy. It was a definite statement on Sino-Soviet relations. An article by Kovalev in the same issue stated that the decisive factors in China's development along the non-capitalist road to socialism would be the existence of the USSR with its experience, and the guidance provided by Marx, Engels, Lenin and Stalin.

The theory of Russia's 'progressive' role in Asia found expression in an article by Baranovsky in *Voprosy Istorii* in January 1952, shortly after the theory had been enunciated in the *Large Soviet Encyclopedia*. In 1860 Russia had helped China, while Britain and America were trying to destroy her. '. . . England strove for the complete capitulation of the Manchus, for their subservience to England, and the weakening of

Russia's influence in China.' Again: 'The Russian people have for a long time striven for the friendship of the Chinese people, have sympathized with the Chinese people's struggle against their oppressors. The progressive Russian people followed the course of the great peasant war in China with great attention. The leading Russian writer, I. A. Goncharov, who was in Shanghai at the time of the Taiping rebellion when the city was in the hands of the "Little Swords", sympathized with the rebels.' And again: 'The great Russian democrat N. G. Cherny-shevsky was happy that in distant China there was taking place a peasant revolution . . . In a short review of the book of the English consul T. Meadows, who was in Nanking, the capital of the Taipings, Chernyshevsky recommended Russians to read this book about "the current Chinese revolution" thoroughly . . . in his review Chernyshevsky spoke against the interference of foreign states in the internal affairs of China and against any such interference on the part of Russia. He believed in the victory of the Taipings . . . L. N. Tolstoy reproached the English for their activities in China.'

As an approach to the problem of Sino-Russian relations was worked out, the subject of the periodization of China's contemporary history also arose. It was discussed in April 1952 in the Chinese section of the Institute of Orientology,[1] where it emerged that periodization was to be based as far as possible on certain events in Soviet history. The discussion was opened by V. N. Nikiforov, who stated that 'The methodological basis for establishing a project on the periodization of China's contemporary history is the work of J. V. Stalin on questions of the Chinese revolution and also the statements of Comrade Mao Tse-tung relating to theoretical questions as well as to concrete questions of the history of China.' The year 1917 began the contemporary period for China as well as for the rest of mankind. The October revolution's direct reflection in China was the May Fourth Movement, which marked the beginning of the bourgeois-democratic revolution. But this was a new type of revolution since it was at the same time part of the world proletarian socialist revolution. Although 'November 7th must mark the beginning of the new period in China's history', for the periodization within this new period, the internal development of China was taken as the correct basis. Still: 'The periodization of internal history is bound to reflect the changes which took place in China's international position and in the whole international situation.' Consequently, the major events in China's modern history were the October revolution, the victory of socialism in the USSR, the Second World War, and especially the Soviet war against Japan. 'Japanese imperialism was destroyed above all by the united forces of the Soviet and Chinese peoples. That is why the end of the period of the national-liberation war of China against Japan (1937-45) coincides with the end of the Second World War.' The pattern was thus set: the major divisions were to be deter-

[1] 'Obsuzhdenie voprosov periodizatsii noveishei istorii Kitaya', *Voprosy Istorii*, 1952, No. 7.

mined by the participation of the USSR, while the sub-divisions were determined by events in China's own history.

The conclusion reached in the discussion was that the periodization should be as follows: (1) 1917-24 (period of preparation of the Chinese revolution); (2) 1924-7 (first revolutionary war); (3) August 1, 1927-July 7, 1937 (second revolutionary war); (4) 1937-45 (national-liberation war against Japanese aggression); (5) 1945-9 (popular-liberation war against American-KMT alliance); (6) post-1949. This was somewhat different from Nikiforov's original scheme (he saw 1919 as beginning a new period) and it emphasized the role of the USSR. It was agreed, however, that the naming of the separate periods and the chronological framework itself required further refinement.

1952 also saw the publication of a textbook, *The Modern History of the Countries of the Non-Soviet East*, published in April by Moscow University.[1] Reviewing it a year later (*Voprosy Istorii*, 1953, No. 6), Nikiforov and Romodin claimed that some matters were incorrectly or inadequately discussed. There were echoes here of the debate in the twenties on the Asiatic mode of production. The authors of the textbook had claimed that the 'backwardness of the Orient' resulted in part from certain 'peculiarities' of Oriental feudalism. The reviewers pointed out that this was incorrect. In the first place, it was wrong to oppose the West and the East, because there was no such thing as a 'single Orient' which runs from Gibraltar to Japan. In the second place, those elements which the textbook claimed were peculiar to Oriental feudalism (such as usury) were universal feudal phenomena. The explanation for the backwardness of the Orient under feudalism was not to be found in the peculiarities of Oriental feudalism, but rather in the strength of the feudal institutions themselves. 'The feudal lords of China, Korea, and Japan, by isolating their countries from the outside world, strove to reinforce the feudal structure. This reactionary measure, doubtless, was one of the basic factors increasing the backwardness of the feudal countries of the East.' Soviet scholars were not to introduce features into the structure which might lead to the conclusion that Chinese history did not follow the prescribed pattern.

A further link in the historical chain of Sino-Soviet friendship was forged at the end of 1953, in a *Voprosy Istorii* article (1953, No. 11), pointing out that both China and the Soviet Union were the objects of aggressive plans in the Far East by the same power. The Soviet army's heroic resistance to the Germans wrecked the Japanese plans to attack the USSR, and this had frustrated the reactionary plan for a 'Far Eastern Munich' which American imperialists had prepared against both the USSR and China. (The logic of the argument is particularly hard to follow.)

The Soviet role in China at the end of the Second World War was not restricted to military actions against Japan. An article published in

[1] I. M. Reisner and B. K. Rubtsov, eds., *Novaya istoriya stran zarubezhnovo Vostoka*, 2 vols. (Moscow, 1952).

October 1954 (*Voprosy Istorii*, 1954, No. 10), maintained that it was at the insistence of the Soviet Union that the Moscow meeting of foreign ministers in December 1945 adopted a resolution on the necessity to unify and democratize China and to end the civil war. It is interesting that the author makes no mention of Soviet aid to the Chinese communists; had there been material aid, it would probably have been mentioned in Soviet writings at this time.

Mongolia and its place in Sino-Soviet relations did not escape the attention of Soviet historians. The question of Chinese imperialism in Mongolia had to be avoided, but it had obviously become necessary to point out to China that the primary influence in the area was Russia's. It was admitted in a review of a study on Mongolia that the 'strongly regimented character of Mongol-Chinese trade in conditions which continued to strengthen the feudal parcellization of Mongolia' had hampered the growth of Mongolia's economy, but it was the West which was to blame.[1] 'With the penetration into China of foreign capital, the position of the Mongol peoples, as also of the other peoples of the Manchu empire, became especially difficult. In the epoch of imperialism, Mongolia became the object of a sharp struggle between the great powers, above all between Imperial Japan and Tsarist Russia. This work shows that as a result of the subjection of the country to the capitalist market, the feudal exploitation of the Mongol *aratstvo* increased.' Nowhere was it explicitly stated that it was Chinese and Russian capital which was responsible for this. On the contrary, the 'drawing together of the Mongol and the Russian peoples, the positive significance of the influence of Russian culture, progressive ideas, and the revolutionary movement of the masses of Russia on Mongolia is noted'. But the reviewer criticized the work as well, because 'too little material about the development of Mongolia and China is given'.

The twentieth CPSU congress in February 1956, the events proceeding from destalinization, which prompted the articles 'On the Historical Experience of the Dictatorship of the Proletariat' in the Peking *People's Daily*, and subsequent difficulties between China and the USSR, have all had their direct influence on Soviet historical scholarship in the field of Sino-Russian relations. Soviet writings in the years between 1949 and 1956 had emphasized the role Russia had played in Chinese history, both before and after the revolution, and had analysed Chinese history in terms consonant with it. The period since then has been marked by other tendencies, reflecting the new conditions in the Sino-Soviet alliance. As Soviet and Chinese views began to diverge, a new approach to the alliance was necessary. This was found in the area of shared historical experience. At the same time, as the divergence became more serious, a more wary attitude towards China was taken by Soviet orientalists, at times approaching almost open criticism.

The first article reflecting this new turn appeared in *Voprosy Istorii* in

[1] L. M. Gataullina, 'Istoriya Mongolskoi Narodnoi Respubliki', *Voprosy Istorii*, 1956, No. 2.

October 1956. It dealt with the joint activities of Russian and Chinese workers in the right-of-way of the Chinese Eastern Railway (CER), and showed that activities of Bolshevik organizations in the right-of-way of the CER helped to spread the influence of the Russian revolutionary movement in China. The Chinese hired to work with the Russians were subjected to especially severe exploitation. Some of them joined Bolshevik organizations, and at the time of the strike of November 29, 1905, the strike committee decided to aid the Chinese workers by keeping local traffic open, thus providing them with work and a livelihood for their families. The Bolsheviks emphasized the community of interests and the need for unity and co-operation between Russian and Chinese workers. At a meeting held in Harbin on January 9, 1907, to com-memorate the 1905 revolution, B. Shumyatsky called on the workers to strike. He spoke to the Chinese workers 'partly through an interpreter and partly with the aid of that Russian-Chinese jargon which received the right of citizenship in the Far East'. The Chinese workers constituted about one-fourth of all the workers in the yards, and they joined the strike shouting, 'Russian Tsar kill Russian workers, therefore we no work.' The Russians in turn helped the Chinese. During a printers' strike in the spring of 1907, the demands of the Russian printers' union in Harbin included the raising of wages and the improvement of labour conditions for the Chinese who worked in the Russian-owned print-shops. 'The Chinese workers in a friendly fashion supported their Russian comrades and thus helped the strike to victory.' The Bolshevik organizations of Harbin not only emphasized their ties with the Chinese workers but even tried to prepare them for the role of national-liberation vanguard in the struggle of the Chinese people against the Manchus. 'In their turn, the Chinese labourers rendered great aid to their Russian comrades. The Chinese helped the Russian Bolsheviks to spread revolu-tionary leaflets and proclamations . . .' In this way, the new approach was laid, based on a common experience which lay outside the realm of such matters as ideology, imperialism, or Russian influence on China. Although this new approach was covered by the common ideology, it was not as direct or as didactic as the approach before 1956.

Soviet historians were also called upon to re-emphasize Russia's right to certain areas which might in the future become the cause of dissension between the allies. A self-critical editorial said: 'We cannot approve the failure of the editors to elucidate in the pages of the journal the progressive significance of the unification with Russia of a series of areas in the Caucasus, Central Asia, and the Far East . . .'[1]

Criticism of Chinese historiography also began to appear in the pages of *Voprosy Istorii*. A long debate had been taking place in China on the nature of the beginnings of capitalism in that country. In June 1957 a review article on this debate appeared, deploring the fact that the Chinese often lacked sufficient data for the conclusions they reached and were not exact enough in their use of terminology. '. . . In our opinion,

[1] 'Za leninskuyu partiinost v istoricheskoi nauke', *Voprosy Istorii*, 1957, No. 3.

it is not necessary to operate with such terms as "sprouts" of capitalism, "factors" of capitalism, etc., inasmuch as in all cases one speaks about the origins of capitalism.' Capitalism must be viewed as a whole, as an historical process. The Chinese could not describe a certain period as capitalist simply because of isolated examples of the capitalist formation. With the relegation to the background of the theory of Russia's role in Chinese history, Soviet historians could take a more detached view of the periodization question and could demand a more rigorous exposition of the problem than would have been possible earlier.

The new approach to the alliance was carried a step further at the end of 1957 in an article published on the occasion of the fortieth anniversary of the October revolution (*Voprosy Istorii*, 1957, No. 10). It was a long article on the participation of Chinese volunteers in the Russian civil war. It is most interesting for the figures it quotes on the Chinese population in Russia in 1917. Exact data about the size of the Chinese population in Russia on the eve of 1917 were not available, 'but it may be supposed that it was about 300,000, a significant number of whom were immigrants'. A large group of Chinese workers joined the Moscow detachments of the Red Guard in November 1917. In 1918 Chinese labour organizations were created in various cities in Russia. At the end of 1918 the Union of Chinese Workers was formed in Petrograd and was recognized by the Soviet Government as having the right to represent Chinese interests in Russia. Chinese fought in the Red Army. To emphasize this approach, a similar article was published a month later on Korean participation in the civil war (*Voprosy Istorii*, 1957, No. 11).

The period of Tsarist imperialism now also required reconsideration. The occasion was a review of Narochnitsky's impressive volume, *The Colonial Policy of the Capitalist Powers in the Far East* (*Voprosy Istorii*, 1958, No. 1). The reviewer wrote that in the eighties the Tsarist Government feared that Korea might become a danger to Russia if it fell into the wrong hands. However, the economic backwardness of Tsarist Russia and its military weakness in the Far East prevented it from competing with the British, Japanese, and American bourgeoisie. (The spirit may have been willing, but the flesh was weak.) Up to 1884 the Tsarist Government felt that China's suzerainty over Korea was useful in preventing its subjugation by the Japanese and Americans. Consequently, it encouraged the Chinese Government not to abandon its claims. Russia started on the road of unequal treaties in Korea only *after* Japan, America, Britain, and Germany had done so. (Russia, it appears, was simply protecting herself *by means of a treaty* against the more advanced capitalist countries. Tsarism was not good, but it was better, owing to its weaknesses, than the western forms of imperialism.) This same approach was followed in the next issue in an article by G. V. Yefimov on the Treaty of St. Petersburg in 1896.

In April 1958 *Voprosy Istorii* returned to the theme of Sino-Russian co-operation during the civil war in an article by A. N. Kheifets. He discussed at some length the joint action which workers of both Russia and China took against the foreign interventionists, including the United States. By this time, the hate-America campaign in China had reached new heights, so that the article came at a most timely moment. The scene was again the CER, and now the underlying principle of the new approach to the study of the alliance was spelled out, albeit obliquely: 'In the events on the CER the indivisible unity and common interests of the Soviet and Chinese people appeared with special force. This was one of the many examples which show how deep and durable are the historical roots of that great and indivisible friendship which now unites the two great socialist states: the Union of Soviet Socialist Republics and the Chinese People's Republic.'

In May 1958, *Voprosy Istorii* published an article by a Chinese, 'From the History of the Spread of Marxism in China',[1] which is interesting in the light of earlier Russian articles dealing with the 1924-7 period. While briefly mentioning the 1924-7 period, Ch'iang completely ignored Stalin and even the fact of Soviet material aid to the Chinese revolution. This silence about the new tone in Soviet scholarship was recognized in a review article (1959, No. 2) entitled 'A New Book on the Struggle of the Chinese People against Imperialism', which concerned a Chinese book published in Shanghai in 1957. The review was critical of the Chinese work on at least two important counts. First, the Chinese author was criticized for not having dealt with the antipathetic position towards the Boxer rebellion taken by the bourgeois revolutionaries under the leadership of Sun Yat-sen. 'This shows that they did not understand the rebellion, that the Chinese bourgeoisie was by nature weak.' The second criticism was more serious: 'Finally, it seems to us that for the full evaluation of the significance of the Boxer Movement, the book must show the sympathy for the struggle of the Chinese people felt by the international labour movement.' In other words, it appears that no positive mention was made of Russia in the Chinese book.

In 1959 more articles were published in the pages of *Voprosy Istorii*, but they were studiously non-committal. By February 1960, however, the situation in the alliance had again obviously become worse. In an article dealing with a peasant rebellion in 1912-14, Liu Shao-ch'i was mentioned once, but there was not a single mention of Mao Tse-tung. Two months later, an article entitled 'Lenin and China' again contained not a single mention of Mao, though great emphasis was laid on Sun Yat-sen, and an obvious effort made to illustrate the ideological debt China owed to Russia and to Lenin.

DISCUSSION

In many ways the problems facing western historians of China were, in Mr Mancall's view, greater and more manifold than the problems confronting western historians of the Soviet Union. The latter now had

[1] Ch'iang Ch'ung-fang, 'Iz istorii rasprostraneniya marksizma v Kitae', *Voprosy Istorii*, 1958, No. 5.

limited access to Russia, while American scholars specializing on China were barred from that country.

First, there was the volume of documentation. He doubted whether any other civilization had amassed in the course of its history the amount of documentation which was available for the study of China, beginning from before 500 BC. Writing, particularly of historical literature, was a basic form of expression in China, with the result that there were countless libraries of source materials, including archives dating back twenty-five centuries. Moreover, not one but several languages had to be mastered in order to deal with these materials: modern colloquial Chinese for current research; several types of classical Chinese for materials published before 1917; some knowledge of Japanese, as Japanese scholars were doing so much research on China; and Russian too, which was rapidly becoming a *sine qua non* for sinological studies.

More important than all these was the problem of the orientation and the assumptions with which the study of Oriental history was approached. Modern research on China in the accepted sense of the word had really begun only in 1949. Before that the Chinese themselves had done very little work on Chinese history; the work done since 1949 in China and in Formosa was so tendentious—with the exception of voluminous publications of documents—that the western historian was left without any of the signposts which existed, for instance, for the intellectual history of Russia in the work of Russian historians in the nineteenth century. Consequently, we had to begin by stepping out of our skins to examine the basic assumptions on which we operated.

Our approach to western history was made within the context of unspoken assumptions, familiar to us because we ourselves were westerners, sharing common experiences. Our approach to the study of the history of non-western societies was inevitably parochial. The context was so different that the basic assumptions about history accepted in the West had to be closely re-examined. Croce's *History as the Story of Liberty* was one example of the basic assumption, the legacy of the nineteenth-century historical tradition, that England and America pointed the way to the kind of development we would like to see throughout the world. An extreme example of this attitude was Hegel's remark that because China was not developing historically in the same way as the West, it had no history. The western historian approaching the facts of modern Chinese history would tend instinctively to over-emphasize the significance of certain events and institutions at the expense of others—as shown, for instance, in the prevalence in western writings on China of studies of the Chinese middle class, of liberal ideas in China in the twenties, of Chinese constitutional and legal history. (Similarly, the tacit assumption underlying much western work on Russia seemed to be that if the communist party had not succeeded in 1917, Russia would have developed towards a liberal type of society; this was not necessarily so.)

In this respect we had a great deal to learn from Marxist historio-

G

graphy on the Far East. For instance, much work had been done in China on peasant revolutions of which we had never even heard. The communists were disinterring these lost data and showing their importance in the development of the Chinese social structure. Some of the questions being asked were important and required the attention of western historians dealing with Chinese history and trying to evaluate Russian research on China.

In terms of the study of the Far East, Russia was really part of the West. Russian intellectual traditions were largely a component of western intellectual development; Russian history might be an aberration in relation to the mainstream of European history, but *vis-à-vis* the Orient, Russia was the West. This meant that the Soviet historian dealing with the non-western world was faced essentially with the same problems as the western historian: the need for a conscious effort to comprehend the institutions, social movements, motivating forces within the society whose history he was trying to examine. This, with the language burden, created a certain bond of sympathy between the Soviet and the western historian, born of shared suffering. Though western orientalists had their serious differences with Soviet orientalists, they could only profit from the co-operation that was beginning to develop. Soviet sinologists, for instance, had no more access to certain crucial documents on Chinese communist history than western historians. Mr Mancall had heard a Soviet specialist declare at a public meeting that it was difficult to study the history of communist China in the Soviet Union because Chinese communist party documents could not be trusted.

Neither in Russia nor the United States were there studies dealing with traditional economic history or with traditional social institutions. Far more had been written on the last decade of Chinese history than on any previous period, at least in America. Questions of land tenure and water control, for example, remained to be studied. Soviet and western students of China were still faced with the problem of the undigested mass of documents now being published by Peking, where it had recently been announced that in the next few years four million documents would be issued!

Though possibly Marxism-Leninism did not provide a correct analysis of the societies of the Far East, the policies worked out on the basis of Marxist theoretical concepts had succeeded, and therefore, functionally, the application of Marxism-Leninism to the Far East had considerable validity. The success of the application of Marxism-Leninism to the Far East might serve to reinforce communist beliefs that the theory could be applied successfully also to the West. Although the application of western ideas about western society to the Far East had ended in failure, notably in 1949, nevertheless much of our previous research on the Far East had been based on our belief that western experience would be applicable. There were other areas beside the Far East where the Soviets could understandably see proof of the validity of their theories. The British empire might have died a peaceful death, but no one could suggest that the French empire in Indo-China or the Dutch empire in Indonesia had died peacefully. Western capitalism might not have disintegrated, but traditional societies in the Far East were disintegrating, so that the Soviet historian's approach to the outside world was reinforced by its success in one specific area. The standard of living of many of these countries was not rising, and the democratic regimes, or at least the regimes we called democratic and supported, had turned into instruments of oppression, which the peoples themselves—as in South Korea—were forced to overthrow. The role of monopoly capitalism, for instance, in Japan before the Second World War would tend to reinforce the Soviet historian's preconceived views, for, in Mr Mancall's opinion, the difference between myth and fact was far less in Soviet writings on the Far East than those on the West.

There had been a continuing struggle in the Soviet Union to impose the hegemony of Marxism on Oriental studies. Unfortunately, the whole field of the history of Soviet sinology and orientology was as yet unexplored, so that Mr Mancall's conclusions were purely tentative. The unexpected success of the revolution in China made the issue of Marxist hegemony in Soviet Oriental studies extremely pressing; in 1951 the *Large Soviet Encyclopedia* carried an article on orientology, which was the first admission for many years that there was such a field as Oriental studies; official policy until then had been to say that there really was no orientology, only historians, sociologists, economists, and anthropologists working on the Far East in their particular discipline. Oddly enough, American historians dealing with the Far East now tended to think that there was no discipline of orientology, and that they should be considered merely as historians. The trouble was that other historians did not accept them as such!

With the Sino-Soviet alliance the need for a historically grounded basis for the alliance became pressing, and as the alliance evolved from one in which the Soviet Union was dominant, to one of equality and then to one of open disagreement, it was necessary at every stage for Soviet historians to re-examine the assumptions behind their writings, and indeed their approach to Chinese history itself. In 1952 the conference on the periodization of Chinese history held in Moscow decreed that the divisions applicable to Russian history were to serve as the basic dividing lines for the periodization of Chinese history. This position had since been modified. The twentieth Soviet party congress was a watershed. As a consequence of destalinization, which had grave repercussions in China, a new intellectual basis was required for the Sino-Soviet alliance. This was provided by the concept of shared historical experience: the study of joint strikes in Manchuria, of the common threat from imperialism for both China and Russia in the Far East, became paramount in Soviet writings on Chinese history. In short, Soviet studies of Chinese history had been closely influenced by the state of the alliance. The study of Soviet historiography on China and on the Sino-Soviet alliance before 1949 could serve as a measure for assessing the nature of the alliance today as the Soviets saw it. It was an approach reflecting immediate needs regardless of ideological problems.

Mr McLane thought that it would soon be essential for students of Soviet historical writings to know what the Chinese were doing, and for students of Chinese historiography to follow what was being written in the USSR.

He was not wholly in agreement with Mr Mancall's claim that 'Voprosy Istorii represented the best available control-post for observing the development of Soviet historiographical attitudes towards China and the Sino-Soviet alliance'. This had placed in doubt the comforting assumption that the difference between Soviet journals was one of sophistication and not of reliability. To rely almost solely on Voprosy Istorii was to miss the larger perspective that might have been given through the Uchenye Zapiski Tikhookeanskovo Instituta, or through Problemy Vostokovedeniya, which in his opinion was a serious journal, and the numerous monographs on the subject.

Mr McLane also disagreed with Mr Mancall on the reasons why Moscow initially conceived the Sino-Soviet alliance as one of unity in subordination. It was not that the identification of world communism with Soviet national interests required such an attitude: it was that Stalin would tolerate no peers in the communist world. Immediately after his death the Sino-Soviet alliance had begun to undergo a gradual transformation, with new trade agreements, revisions favourable to China in the Sino-Soviet treaty, the visit of Khrushchev and Bulganin to Peking, etc., without there being any significant change in the imperatives of Soviet foreign policy, or any appreciable shift in the balance of power between the two. At the same time historiography, too, had begun to reflect this changed attitude towards the alliance.

Had the re-organization of the orientalists in 1950 been a response to the victory of the Chinese communists? Having studied Soviet documents and materials on the Far East, Mr McLane had been struck by the need in South-east Asia, and indeed throughout the colonial world, for a re-thinking of strategy in 1950. The last significant decision made by the Russians had been to encourage direct uprisings—a decision dating from late 1947 or early 1948 and often connected with the Calcutta youth congress of February 1948. By 1950 at least two of these enterprises had failed completely: in India and Indonesia. The issue was far from clear in four other areas: Indo-China, Burma, Malaya, and the Philippines. Meanwhile, a related effort in Korea had led to war. In short, it had become imperative to take a closer look at realities in Asia. This was precisely what orientalists had been asked to do. Obviously, China played a part in this; however, it was not just a study of China that was demanded in 1950, but a re-appraisal of the whole colonial question.

Mr Schram referred to Mr Mancall's suggestion that, with the growth of ideological divergences between Moscow and Peking, there had been a greater emphasis on the historical argument, i.e. the historic friendship between Russia and China, intended to replace the shaken ideological unity as an element of cohesion. Could this be due simply to the type of material used by Mr Mancall—might not historians produce historical arguments, just as ideologists used ideological arguments and economists economic ones?

Just as the shift of attention away from China in 1927 had been the result, not of a deliberate decision by the Soviet Union, but of Stalin's failure and a growing preoccupation with internal problems at that time, so, in his opinion, the new Soviet policy towards the national bourgeoisie was less a result of growing strength abroad, though this naturally played some part, than a result of internal consolidation, in regard to control over the Moslem minorities within the Soviet Union, which enabled them to appeal to Moslems outside Soviet Russia, and of economic consolidation after the Second World War, which allowed them for the first time to offer economic aid to under-developed countries. Here too the shift in policy was to some extent a reflection of Soviet internal developments.

Interesting conclusions could be drawn from a comparison of the 1951 and 1956 versions of the book edited by Zhukov on *International Relations in the Far East* from 1840-1949: it was obvious that between 1951 and 1956 the Soviets had either discovered the Chinese ideological and historical writings, or that now they thought fit to adopt Chinese terminology and to quote Chinese views instead of Stalin's. For instance, in the 1951 edition it was stated that the end of the first phase of the Chinese revolution in 1927 was marked by the glorious Canton commune; in the 1956 edition they very sensibly did not mention Canton at all, but instead put the emphasis on Mao's partisan activities. In general, there had been a marked shift from the Soviet to the Chinese line between 1951 and 1956.

Another instance of the changed attitude towards China was the treatment of the controversial question of the Chinese Eastern Railway. In both the 1951 and 1956 editions of Zhukov's book the Soviet position during the negotiations in the early twenties for the return to China of various Tsarist concessions was stated as being that the railway belonged to Russia, because it had been paid for by the money of the Tsarist Government. But by 1958, when the Soviets engaged in a polemic with American scholars on this subject, they obviously paid much more attention to Chinese susceptibilities and no longer talked of the Chinese Eastern Railway as theirs.

Mr Mancall defended his reliance on *Voprosy Istorii* on the grounds that in the middle 1950s many Soviet journals and authors had shown themselves susceptible to pressure from Peking. A case in point was the magazine *Sovetskoe Kitaevedenie*, of which eventually the Soviet orientalists themselves had enough, because, as they said, every article had been approved in Peking prior to publication, and they felt that this denied them the necessary freedom of expression.

There was enough circumstantial evidence from Chinese sources to show that Moscow was surprised by the victory of the Chinese communists, or at least that it was not until 1948 that the Russians began to believe in its possibility.

With regard to the 1950 reorganization of the structure of Oriental studies in the Soviet Union, Mr Mancall said that China was then and still remained the most important sector of the work. The central role played by China was reflected in the amount of research, the extent of publications, and the number of people employed. He believed that it was the situation in regard to Chinese studies which led to the reorganization of the Institute of Oriental Studies. The establishment in November 1956 of a special institute to deal with China alone again underlined the importance attached to this subject.

IX. Socialism in Current Soviet Historiography

ADAM B. ULAM

The Soviet historian, wrote *Voprosy Istorii* in March 1957 (p. 4), dare not be merely 'a by-stander, or a copyist of materials, [or] a collector of evidence which by chance has fallen into his hand.' He is an active participant in the work of socialist construction, an exponent of Marxism-Leninism, an interpreter of the past in the light of guidance laid down by his party and the state. An exasperated western observer may feel, after having absorbed a quota of contemporary Soviet historiography, that the art of writing modern history in the USSR has come to resemble that of an American writer on etiquette. The problem of what to do with the bride's divorced father who shows up at the wedding typifies the major methodological and classificatory dilemmas involved in assigning a 'correct' place in history to, say, Plekhanov. The father of Russian Marxism cannot be assigned the place of honour because of the transgressions of his later days, nor can he be pushed out of the church because of his organic connection with the proceedings. Exactly *where* to put him in the church and what degree of reverence and cordiality to observe towards him are the questions which confront a conscientious Soviet historian, and his answers, like those of Emily Post, have to be precise and in complete agreement with accepted theory and practice.

And yet it would be a mistake to allow this unfortunate aspect of Soviet historical writing to obscure its significance or to generate feelings of condescension towards the Soviet historian. He works under a variety of pressures and compulsions which can hardly be fully appreciated outside the USSR; nor has their relative absence in the West led to a great flowering of the social sciences or to freedom from fads and timidity. The permitted limits of historical criticism in Russia are never extended to the point where the writer can give full rein to his scholarly and critical propensities. It is precisely the periods of 'liberalization', the thaws, which confront him with the greatest danger. The *ukase* which ended the period of freer historical writing following the twentieth

The author is grateful to the Russian Research Center of Harvard University for its research facilities and assistance provided during the work on this essay.

CPSU congress was emphatic and characteristic in its philosophy: 'In the review by Yevzerov and in a number of other pronouncements the editorial board has called for an "objective" appraisal of even such figures as Lassalle and Bakunin. What was that if not a call for a revision of the appraisal already given by Marx, Engels, and Lenin?' (Ibid., p. 13). In a sense, the historian's dilemma reflects the general one of Soviet society: as social forces evolve they press upon the framework laid down by the dogma. The regime now seeks to reconcile dogma and life, but it resorts to repression whenever this liberalization encroaches upon a fundamental matter of belief. The historian's picture of the past, just as the writer's of the present, now has to be convincing as well as orthodox.

The problem of socialism is for the Soviet historian the central problem of modern history, just as it is the most delicate to deal with. The basic premiss of Stalin's successors has been that the diminution of physical repression would be compensated by a revival of ideology. Communism was no longer to be something to be learned by rote, but a vigorous and victorious creed not afraid to reveal its antecedents and expose its errors. Other branches of socialism were to be presented not necessarily as heresies, and their exponents not always as renegades. The task of the historian was to project this missionary and proselytizing picture of communism into the past, to rescue the creed from the Byzantine stiffness of Stalinism, and to endow it with a humanitarian and catholic gloss. While the Soviet leaders took to visiting Belgrade and Delhi, their academic subordinates were called upon to visit Plekhanov, Proudhon, and the young Marx.

The signal was given in an editorial in *Voprosy Istorii* for March 1955. It summoned Soviet historians to study the early history of socialism in Russia, to expand their studies of people like Belinsky and Herzen beyond the usual classificatory exposition of these early specimens of 'bourgeois-democratic' liberalism. The neglect in which socialist thought had dwelt in the fatherland of socialism was revealed in the statement that only two universities (Moscow and Odessa) had been offering full courses in the history of socialist thought. Utopian socialism, it was pointed out, was a proper field for research, as it had been a necessary prologue to the development of scientific socialism, and not just an obscurantist perversion.

The new era, which was to end abruptly in March 1957, was connected, of course, with the condemnation of the 'cult of personality'. But the change contemplated was to go beyond the removal of the litany to Stalin with which for a generation before 1954 every Russian historian, like every writer in the Soviet Union, had to open and conclude his work. Party history under Stalin ceased to be merely tendentious and propagandist and became ludicrous. If a revival of ideology was contemplated, and if communism was once again to make a major appeal to the non-communist Left, it could not do it well if the official histories of Marxism and socialism retained their palpable absurdities.

The reviewer of a book on the Moscow Soviet in 1905, sharing in the new wave of historical honesty, felt constrained to point out that the author's pre-1954 concept of party history had led him to plain falsehoods, and absurd ones at that.[1] Certainly it took some ingenuity on the part of the author to discover that the Moscow Soviet of 1905 was wrecked by the Trotskyites. Leading roles in the creation of the Soviets in that year were ascribed to, among others, Stalin, Molotov, and Kuibyshev. The reviewer points out that at the time Molotov was fifteen years old, while Stalin and Kuibyshev were (as anybody who read their biographies could find out) absent from the cities where they were allegedly leading the masses in the revolutionary struggle. The Stalinist school of history had not allowed for error or change of opinion by the infallible leaders, and so Kostomarov could write unblushingly that from the very beginning the soviet movement in 1905 had Lenin's enthusiastic support. Before 1955 Kostomarov's book would have been hailed as a valuable contribution, and when the new wave of historical criticism fell into disfavour in March 1957 it was the reviewer who was condemned for his alleged denigration of the role of the Bolsheviks in 1905, and not the author, who had written absurdities and lies.

The scholarly discussion of the nature and development of socialist thought came to an effective end in the early thirties, when Stalin reprimanded the then leading party historian, Yemelyan Yaroslavsky, for not realizing that the non-orthodox varieties of socialism and communism represented not merely deviations but a betrayal of the working class. From then on writings on the non-Leninist (and non-Stalinist) offshoots of socialism became simply a catalogue of epithets. The state of paralysis which gripped Soviet historical thought on the subject of socialism was reflected in a loss of interest in Marxism itself, and in the spread of ideological agnosticism and scepticism in the ranks of the party. The eventual danger to the regime was recognized by Stalin when, in his *Economic Problems of Socialism in the USSR*, he deplored the lack of ideological preparation: 'The point is that we as the leading core, are joined each year by thousands of new young cadres fired with the desire to help us, eager to prove themselves but lacking an adequate Marxist education and uninformed of many truths known to us, and thus obliged to wander in the dark. They are amazed by the colossal achievements of the Soviet regime, their heads are turned by the extraordinary successes of the Soviet system, and they begin to imagine that the Soviet system can do anything, that "everything is child's play" to it, that it can negate scientific laws and fashion new ones. What is to be done with these comrades? How are they to be brought up in the spirit of Marxism-Leninism?' The real answer of course could not be given by Stalin, because it would have required an end to Stalinism in history and ideology. His successors had to sanction and even to push for a reopening of historical discussion of some problems which simply could

[1] Z. M. Bograd, reviewing G. Kostomarov, 'Moskovskii Sovet v 1905 g.', in *Voprosy Istorii*, 1956, No. 3, pp. 158-163.

G*

not have been mentioned under the old tyrant. In that sense it was Khrushchev, Suslov, and Mikoyan who started what they later on branded as 'revisionism'. The experiment was initiated, perhaps with some realization of the possible danger to the party and the regime, in a freer discussion of the ideology; the alternative was considered to be more dangerous.

In order to discuss the official ideology and yet not to wander beyond the danger point one must resort to circumlocutions. The Soviet historian in 1955 was called upon to show the richness and variety of the Marxist tradition. But this higher criticism was not to encroach upon the essential infallibility of the doctrine of Marx and Engels, nor upon the uniqueness of its later interpretation by Lenin. An American writer who wants to criticize the prevailing system of mixed economy without lapsing into the currently unfashionable plea for straightforward socialism, may argue for increased spending in the public sector as opposed to the private one. Similarly, a communist historian whose researches might lead him to question the standard view of the Leninist interpretation of Marxism in 1902 or 1917 would find his opening in the variety of views, position, and hesitations current among Marxists *before* the infallible dictum had been laid down.

In appraising the work of the Soviet historians between the official encouragement to freer writing in 1955 and the condemnation of 'revisionism' in March 1957, it is unnecessary to accept the official verdict that the 'guilty' historians were engaged in a clandestine attack upon Leninism and Marxism, or were attempting to rehabilitate the Menshevik view of socialism as suitable to Russian conditions. It makes much more sense to assume that they were trying to squeeze as much as possible of historical truth into the framework of the official dogma. It would be silly to think that those people, some of them experienced academic bureaucrats, were motivated by any feeling of opposition to the regime or the ideology. And yet we must grant that there is an element of logic, even if perverse logic, in their subsequent condemnation. For in the historical sciences, as in other spheres of Soviet life, the thaw threatened to have, from the point of view of the rulers, undesirable results.

Central to the legitimacy of communist rule is the belief that the communist seizure of power in 1917 was in complete accordance with the Marxian canon. Indeed, the basis of the whole ideology rests upon two axioms: Marxism is the only true science of society, and the seizure of power by the Bolsheviks was the only correct application of Marxism in Russian conditions. To question Lenin's tactics in 1917-18, his rejection of parliamentarianism, suppression of the other revolutionary and socialist parties, confiscation of land and heavy industry, means not only to question the Marxist character of Leninism, but also, by indirection, to criticize some of the basic political and economic features of the Soviet state. Furthermore, under Stalinism the official interpretation of Lenin's tactics insisted upon their absolute and categorical character:

each major decision was the outcome not merely of a particular conjunction of events or pressures of one sort or another; it was the only proper and necessary application of Marxism. Those Bolsheviks who opposed Lenin at any crucial point were not exponents of different tactics or of a different brand of Marxism, but traitors and capitulators. The same was true of those foreign socialists who criticized as unMarxist one aspect or another of Bolshevik policy.

It is in this light that one can understand the reaction to a series of books and articles which, in the period under discussion, insisted that the historical reality of the years 1917-18 was rather more complicated than that presented in Stalin's *Short Course*. The most interesting among them, and the most innocent in what it said directly, but the one which was to provoke the most violent condemnation, was V. P. Nasyrin's 'Some Problems of Socialist Transformation of Industry in the USSR.'[1] He simply restated, what was very well known by everybody who had read the pre-1930 Soviet books on the subject, that the precipitate nationalization of heavy industry in the wake of the revolution was imposed upon the Bolshevik rulers, and that the previous Bolshevik programme had envisaged the gradual and cautious nationalization of the means of production. He referred to the resolution of the sixth party congress (which again could be found and read in Soviet libraries) calling for the immediate nationalization of banks and syndicates but *not* of heavy industrial enterprises. He recalled Lenin's misgivings about workers' control and about the attrition of technical specialists. Carried away by his discovery, the unfortunate seeker after historical truth quoted Marx's dictum about socialism ripening in the bosom of capitalism and Lenin's definition of socialism as 'state-capitalist monopoly turned to the benefit of the whole nation'.

There was nothing on the surface or in the substance of Nasyrin's article to justify a charge of heresy. The article did not challenge the revolution, nor did it detract from the picture of Lenin as a wise and far-seeing theorist and man of action. But the Soviet regime, even in its modified post-Stalin phase, encompasses the half-real, half-imaginary spheres of the 'hidden meaning' and 'where it all might lead to'; and by these criteria this unsensational piece of historical research opened up frightening possibilities: the Bolshevik party during the revolution evidently did not always act in perfect harmony with the masses. On the contrary, a spontaneous movement of the workers imposed upon Lenin and his colleagues a decision they were reluctant to take—the premature nationalization of heavy industry. Was the October revolution, then, a true Marxian revolution, or was it a Blanquist *coup d'état* (a view held by 'renegades' like Kautsky), with the Bolsheviks riding to power on a wave of anarchist disorders? To follow Nasyrin's line was not only to question the Marxist legitimacy of October, but to accept more than half-way the doctrine of evolutionary socialism and the necessity of complete industrialization before socialism can take over.

[1] *Voprosy Istorii*, 1956, No. 5, pp. 90-9.

And if so, to shift to concrete political problems, how can an ideological revival of communism in the USSR be encouraged if the dictum about socialism being merely a state-capitalist monopoly working for the benefit of the nation was allowed to pass? The new party history says laconically (p. 254): 'At the end of November 1917 the Soviet Government turned to the nationalization of heavy capitalist industry'.

Nasyrin's article was not the most celebrated deviation to emerge from the Pandora's box of freer historical criticism. A greater stir was created by Burdzhalov's articles on Bolshevik tactics following the February revolution. Burdzhalov's views are of little interest from the point of view of Soviet attitudes towards socialism, but they do point indirectly to the relative flexibility and eclectic character of Bolshevism before April 1917. Again, the notion that there was only one 'correct' line of Russian Marxism, which sprang ready-made from Lenin's head in 1902, assumed concrete tactical form in 1914, and was followed by all true Bolsheviks (i.e. except the outright traitors like Zinoviev, Kamenev, and Rykov), is confronted with the facts of history and found inexact. Unwittingly Burdzhalov suggests that Bolshevism had not completely overcome its social-democratic heritage before Lenin's return in April 1917, that parliamentary and coalition impulses were not lacking among the Bolsheviks after February, and that perhaps the true Marxist tradition is broader and more inclusive than Leninism-Stalinism.

That the Marxist tradition is purely revolutionary and that it rejects parliamentarianism *per se* is, of course, the foundation stone of Leninism. It was, therefore, something of a challenge to point out that in March and April 1917 Lenin's own party was not quite sure whether Marxism did not require it to join with the other socialist parties, and to support temporarily the bourgeois-democratic Provisional Government. The slogan that the only legitimate organ of the people's will was to be found in the Soviets, Burdzhalov points out, had come from the rank-and-file members. Their leaders vacillated on the subject of the Duma. In many places the Bolsheviks were renewing their collaboration with the Mensheviks, and there was talk about the possibility of re-uniting the two parties. Burdzhalov reminds his readers that the Petrograd Bolsheviks, led at the time by Stalin and Kamenev, were turning still further towards the right, and that the majority of the Petrograd committee agreed with Kamenev when on March 18th he said that to talk about taking over power was premature. The same note was sounded in the first reaction to Lenin's April theses, with the bureau of the central committee agreeing with Kamenev's and Stalin's view that 1917 was not analogous to 1871 (the Paris Commune) but represented a revolutionary situation on the 1789 or 1848 pattern. Thus the skein of events in 1917 was infinitely more involved than that traced by the *Short Course*: it was not a simple and edifying tale of heroism, wisdom, and correct Marxism on the one hand, and of betrayal and villainy on the other: it was, among other things, the period when some good Marxists still could not decide what was the proper Marxist solution for revolutionary Russia. The author leaves no doubt that it was Lenin who had the right formula, but he had said too much.

From one point of view, the thaw in historical criticism represented an effort to enlarge the legitimate sphere of Soviet historiography, and to make the writing of history meaningful. Ever since the condemnation of the Pokrovsky school by Stalin, the limits of historical discussion, which after all is what distinguishes history from mere chronology, had been steadily narrowed down. When it came to the history of political movements, the Soviet historian was reduced to being a copyist. Historical records, and writings contradicting the official line (including even some of Stalin's writings before 1930) were sequestrated. With relaxation the Soviet historian could begin (so it seemed between 1955 and 1957) to employ the tools of his trade. It became possible to enlarge the scope of historical study. While Burdzhalov, Nasyrin, and others pointed out the dissensions within the early Bolshevik ranks and thus suggested that even the Leninist version of Marxism was not, at first, monolithic but variegated, others could go back to the earlier periods of Marxism and again discover a multiplicity of tendencies and interpretations rather than a homogeneous science of revolution.

Even so, Soviet historians could not go so far as some western Marxists (and some in Poland too), who stressed the voluntaristic and evolutionary element in Marxism at the expense of strict determinism and the revolutionary message. But more emphasis was given to the connection of Marxism with other socialist and progressive trends and to the utterances of Marx indicating the possibility of a peaceful as distinguished from a violent revolution. Typical of that tendency is an article by B. A. Rozhkov: 'The Programme of the Chartist Convention of 1851' (*Voprosy Istorii*, 1957, No. 2, pp. 108-122), mentioning Marx's statement of 1871 that England was one country where a socialist revolution might come about peacefully and legally. The author concentrates on the relationship between Marxism and Chartism, and underlines Marx's opinion that the realization of the Charter in the England of the 1850s would have been equivalent to a revolution. Yet the Charter did not contain a single economic postulate, and the Chartist movement as a whole was very far from being socialist in any sense of the word. Here then was an attempt to anchor Marxism in the democratic and progressive tradition of the West, something, to be sure, in perfect accordance with the most orthodox view and yet suggestive of a new emphasis.

Did the trend of 1955-7 add up to revisionism in Soviet historiography? Two observations are relevant. In the first place, the word 'revisionism' itself obscures rather than clarifies what was going on. If by revisionism is meant the critique of Marxism associated with the name of Eduard Bernstein, a definite political philosophy and a view of history, then of course the historians had very little to do with it. They were writing in the spirit of what they conceived to be the new orthodoxy. If by revisionism is meant the phenomenon which occurs in the Marxist and communist world whenever blinkers are removed, revealing that there are several Marxes and not just one, and that there are several roads to socialism and not just the one traversed by the Bolsheviks, then of course the Soviet historians, together with the rest of Soviet society, were participants in the revisionist movement led and abetted by Khrushchev and the presidium of the Soviet communist party.

Soviet communism finds itself in a profound ideological impasse. That impasse, to be sure, is masked by the successes of the Soviet state and of the communist movement in the world at large, but it can be seen in the struggle waged by the party against the half-phantom and half-reality of revisionism. Its appearance was the consequence of the decision to disestablish the worst features of Stalinism, a decision reflecting the conviction that communism was now a strong and vigorous ideology which no longer needed terror and rigid dogmatism as a shield, but could be counted upon to advance in the world because of its inherent superiority. The condemnation of the 'cult of personality' was the first and decisive step in this *official* revisionism, and it was accompanied by denunciation of 'sectarianism' and 'dogmatism'. By admitting the legitimacy of Yugoslav communism, by allowing a degree of autonomy to their smaller communist neighbours, the Soviet leaders sanctioned a multiplicity of roads to socialism, and admitted that the road they had travelled in constructing socialism was not necessarily the only correct one. But implicit in these concessions was the assumption that they would bring immediate and substantial gains to the regime. Yugoslavia would be drawn once again into the orbit of the Soviet Union; the other communist regimes would now be bound to the USSR not only by force but also by gratitude and stronger ideological ties. And, most important, internally the reforms would be followed by a revitalization of the ideology and a greater and more genuine rallying of all the social forces around the party and the regime.

For all the gains in popularity and in efficiency gathered by the regime, the ideological premises of communism, as practised in the Soviet Union, were called in question. It would be foolish to believe that the discussions among historians or the literary thaw threatened the actual foundations of the regime. But a free-ranging debate about the sources of Marxism and Leninism, taken in conjunction with the events in Hungary and Poland, suggested that a new generation of intellectual rebels might arise in post-Stalin Russia, and firm action was taken to check the undesirable tendencies. What probably prevented an earlier and sharper denunciation of revisionism was the continuing split in the highest party councils which lasted until the summer of 1957. Even before the question of leadership was definitely settled, steps were taken in February-March 1957 to curtail historical criticism of the views on ideology and party history accepted up to 1955, to narrow down the scope of historical discussion, and deprive the historians of most of the gains of the past few years. The change required a re-definition of the historian's task which in its frankness and its clear directive to subordinate history-writing to the needs of propaganda went beyond Stalinist strictures. In so far as socialism was concerned, the task assigned to Soviet historians was to expose revisionism, to show the organic connection between every departure from the line advocated by the CPSU and the views advocated sixty years earlier by Bernstein and his followers. This has been done. A veritable flood of books and articles has made of revisionism an *omnium gatherum* of every type of criticism of the Soviet Union, any theory of non-revolutionary Marxism, and any plea against the monopoly of power. In the ranks of revisionism have been found persons as diverse as Harold Laski, John Gates, Léon Blum, and Marshal Tito. It still remains for an ingenious Soviet historian to close the circle of deviationism by asserting that 'sectarianism' itself is in essence a species of revisionism, and to discover that Malenkov, Molotov, and Kaganovich were really revisionists masquerading as Stalinists.

It would be a mistake to think that the new trend is merely a reversion to the pre-1953 days. One concrete gain has been preserved, and that is the possibility of describing views and subjects which in Stalin's days were simply not fit for discussion. In condemning various perversions of Marxism, the historian still has the opportunity to display the richness and variety of the socialist tradition. His treatment, though biased, can no longer stop at mere vilification. History, like other branches of intellectual activity in Khrushchev's Russia, is expected to conform but at a more intelligent level than under Stalin.

The difficulty in meeting the new requirements is well illustrated in a survey of some recent western literature on Marxism.[1] The title suggests the style of polemic, taking one's mind back to such classics of the Reformation as the *First Blast of the Trumpet Against the Monstrous Regiment of Women*, but the writing and the reasoning are, unfortunately, inferior to John Knox's. The author has taken to task a rather motley assembly of authors (including Boris Nikolaevsky, Maximilien Rubel, and Harold Laski) for suggesting an evolutionary view of Marx's philosophy after 1849. The main target is the thesis, going back to Bernstein, that after the *Communist Manifesto* Marx began to eschew purely revolutionary tactics. This view, which contrasts the brief revolutionary period of 1847-9 with Marx's mainly humanitarian socialism previously and evolutionary socialism subsequently, has become something of a fad among western socialists. It has also found echoes in the writings of Leszek Kolakowski and some other Polish communists.

It is indisputable that the weakest part of the attempt to democratize Marx is to call as witness his pre-1847 writings, when he was just groping for a philosophy of history. But our author cannot forgo the argument that Nikolaevsky's views are false simply because he is anti-

[1] E. P. Kandel, 'Iskazhenie istorii borby Marksa i Engelsa za proletarskuyu partiyu v rabotakh nekotorykh pravykh sotsialistov', *Voprosy Istorii*, 1958, No. 5, pp. 120-130.

communist. Nor can he refrain from protesting too much, as in his assertion that the communist historian exhibits exemplary scholarship precisely because of his devotion to the party. What is striking is that, rather than dismissing the argument of 'humanitarian Marxism' as resting on evidence pre-dating the formation of Marxism as a coherent system, the reviewer feels constrained to deny the evidence. Marx could not be as hostile to Blanqui as Nikolaevsky claims, because Blanqui in 1848 defended the interests of the French proletariat. Here and there he strikes a more reasonable note. Of what weight, indeed, are the early scribblings of Marx in appraising his whole system as compared with the *Anti-Dühring*?

If a relatively weak interpretation of Marxism, in its own way as one-sided as the Leninist, is contested so clumsily and on an *ad hominem* level, what argument will meet a more serious assault upon orthodoxy? One can dig very deep in Marx, the alleged revisionists point out, and still not find a plea for a one-party dictatorship. On the other hand, Marx's approval of the Paris Commune would imply that even the dictatorship of the proletariat did not preclude a multi-party system. This point is ignored by the reviewer in his treatment of Harold Laski's 1948 introduction to the *Communist Manifesto*. Why the late Mr Laski is taken as an exponent of contemporary revisionism, and why a more representative work of his is not selected for discussion, can be a mystery only to those who do not understand that in a work of this kind a sort of national symmetry has to be preserved, and the main western powers have all to be represented. Thus Laski is arraigned alongside the representative of French revisionism, Rubel, and the German and American sufferers from the same disease, Landshut and Nikolaevsky. Laski's argument is disposed of by a rhetorical question: Why does the Labour party refuse to let the British communists affiliate to it?

Why this compulsion to register the most diverse forms of activity— political, literary, and philosophical—and the most diverse types of personalities—a former Menshevik, a Labourite, and people who have never been Marxists and consequently have nothing to 'revise'—under the common rubric of revisionism? It is difficult to answer, except on the supposition that whenever history becomes a part of propaganda its task is to over-simplify, to obscure vital differences, and to paint in the garish colours of socialist realism. During the period of relaxation many Soviet historians began to say that certain elements of the doctrine and history of the socialist movement were more complicated than had hitherto been believed. Now a historian begins his account of real revisionism as follows: 'Analysis of the revisionism which arose in the nineties of the nineteenth century shows vividly its identity, both in theory and in practice, with the views of contemporary revisionism. The latter represents, in essence, the newest type of Bernsteinism, revived and adjusted according to the new historical conditions.'[1] It is

[1] B. A. Chagin, *Borba marksizma-leninizma protiv filosofskovo revizionizma v kontse 19-vo—nachale 20-vo vv.* (Leningrad, 1959), p. 5.

a formula as clear-cut and suitable for the catechism of a party instructor as the answer to the question 'What is Leninism?'—'Leninism is the Marxism of the era of imperialism.'

Another reason for dragging in Bernstein to dispose of Marshal Tito, western socialists, and the Polish would-be reformers of Marxism, lies in the doctrinal and scholastic character of the official Soviet creed. Bernstein's views were condemned by Lenin and officially rejected by the German social-democratic party. Hence new revisionism was rejected in advance as having no scriptural authority. The burden of discussion is very seldom placed on the nature of the old or new deviation, but is borne by a string of citations from the authorities: Marx, Engels, and Lenin. A sample of the argument will convey its flavour: 'As early as 1893 Bernstein and Kautsky capitulated to international opportunism. For instance, they removed from a work of Eleanor Aveling, *The Elections in Great Britain*, the correct characterization of the Fabians as opportunists. Engels most resolutely protested, pointing to Bernstein's sympathies for the English opportunists. He opposed Kautsky's attempt to entrust to Bernstein the writing of an article about the socialist movement in England. Engels did not trust Bernstein, and his revolutionary common sense did not deceive him.'[1] It is clear that the author projects the atmosphere and phraseology of Soviet communism into the life of the international socialist movement of the 1890s. It is 1893, but the 'opportunists' and 'capitulators' are being tracked down by socialist vigilance; by people like Engels, Lenin, and Plekhanov. There is no attempt to present *in extenso* the arguments of Bernstein and his followers or to discuss their substance. The technique employed is to sketch the bare outlines of revisionism, to note the sympathetic reactions to it of liberal and bourgeois circles in Germany, and to spear it with a quotation from Rosa Luxemburg, Liebknecht, or Lenin. It is hard to classify Chagin's treatment of revisionism as historical; it is rather a projection of Soviet politics into the German social-democratic scene at the turn of the century. Since Kautsky was to attack the October revolution, it cannot be stated that in the period under discussion Kautsky, the leading interpreter of Marxism, was on Lenin's side. Even the strongest opponents of revisionism, like Rosa Luxemburg, are criticized for their toleration of Bernstein and the failure to eject him from the party. That, for all their revolutionary interpretation of Marxism and militancy, Rosa Luxemburg, Liebknecht, and others like them simply did not possess the mentality suitable to purges, recantations, and *ex cathedra* pronouncements, is a matter of regret and a reflection on *their* Marxism.

The attack on revisionism, in its rigidity and perversion, reflects another aspect of contemporary Soviet politics. Original revisionism was not a diabolical invention of Bernstein or Vollmar but a response to the facts of political and economic life which made many theorems and conclusions of Marx, based on the study of England in the 1840s

[1] Ibid., p. 27.

and 1850s, simply inapplicable to Germany of the end of the century. And, in a sense, the USSR of the fifties and sixties of this century has undergone a similar development. The message of Marxism-Leninism had been found convincing in the revolution. The logic of Marxism had provided the impetus behind the drive towards industrialization and modernization which occupied most of the Stalin era. But what is the message of Marxism now? The very incoherence with which the communist leaders try to spell out the meaning of the transition to communism which the USSR is said to be now undertaking, itself bears witness to the irrelevance of the old doctrine to the conditions of an industrialized society.

In this broad sense revisionism is a recurrent phenomenon, and not only in Marxism. It recurs whenever the ruling doctrine no longer offers clear goals for the future, when it has either to be liberalized and alternatives allowed, or to be frozen into a dogma preserved by repression and indoctrination. The German social democrats, in condemning their revisionism, destroyed any possibility of collaboration with the liberal elements which might have transformed Germany into a parliamentary democracy, while the non-revolutionary temper of the German worker made it impossible for him to follow the revolutionary programme. The Soviet leaders arrested the process of liberalization at the point where they judged it threatened the communist dogma, and, in the long run, their totalitarian system. But in doing so they have not restored their doctrine, nor given it new vigour and meaning. It would be hard to see in the comrades' courts, or the projected abolition of the state committee on sports, the first tokens of the 'withering away' of the state and the first symptoms of communist society. The recent measures against some marginal survivals of private property are no more than a feeble swing of the pendulum in the never-ending alternation between the policies of incentives and egalitarianism; a decisive turn towards the latter is simply unthinkable in a modern industrial state.

But if, internally, Marxism-Leninism has little to offer, in the world at large it is still an ideology and a technique of both revolution and industrialization with tremendous powers of attraction. To that extent foreign successes have obscured, on the domestic scene, the relative uselessness of the doctrine and its sole remaining function as a rationale for one-party dictatorship.

The struggle against revisionism is, then, a struggle on a world scale, and one of its most important aspects is the fight against 'excessive' claims for autonomy by other communist parties. This is one aspect of modern revisionism which has very little to do with the original version. Eduard Bernstein, an advocate of democratic socialism and of internationalism, would consider it an insult to be regarded as the patron saint of Yugoslav communism. Revisionism has also become a euphemism for any tendency on the part of a communist party to claim a degree of *ideological* as well as political independence from Moscow.

Ideological consolidation was the more necessary as the purely administrative and police methods of controlling the Soviet empire were abandoned after Stalin's death. Moreover, as new states emerged, most of them not industrialized and therefore ideal areas for the spread of radical philosophies and movements, it became important that no other brand of radicalism but the one stamped 'approved' by Moscow be allowed to claim the heritage of Marxism. When the attempt to re-integrate Yugoslavia into the communist camp was followed by disorders in Poland and revolt in Hungary, Titoism again had to be cast out. The programme of the Communist League of Yugoslavia, which the Soviets condemned as revisionist in 1958, contained nothing which was not implicit in Titoism in 1955 and 1956, when Moscow acknowledged it as a legitimate form of communism.

The Soviet historian's task then became to re-appraise those elements in the history of radical thought which could suggest a variety of permissible approaches to socialism or hinted at a greater latitude in Marxism than that currently allowed by Soviet communism. There has been, for instance, a general downgrading of all socialist thinkers in the West who cannot be associated with an unqualified approval of the October revolution and of the Soviet state. Kautsky appears now not merely as a renegade from socialism after his reaction to the October revolution, but as a man who from the first was inclined toward revisionism.[1] Readers of a recent work on German socialism during the First World War will discover only with the greatest difficulty that Bernstein and Kautsky occupied during the war an anti-militarist position.[2] Even the Spartakists are severely reprimanded for their democratic scruples, for their failure to organize a purely revolutionary party apart from the Independent Socialists, as well as for their occasional pacifist scruples. In other words, even the most radical socialist movement is judged by the yardstick of the behaviour of the Bolshevik party in 1917, or rather what the official party histories after the 1930s began to represent as the behaviour and ideology of the Bolsheviks in 1917. It is made a matter of reproach to the Spartakists that after February 1917 they had so little faith that they believed a socialist revolution in Russia could survive only if supported by successful workers' revolutions elsewhere!

The same claim for the uniqueness of the Bolshevik formula is inherent in the Soviet historian's approach to the non-Marxist socialist movements. The traditional Marxian view has held 'non-scientific' socialism to be a preliminary if misconceived step in the achievement of class consciousness by the proletariat, a product of the very conditions which later on would turn the workers to Marxism. It was in this spirit that Marx and Engels hailed the left-wing Chartists, or for that matter various radical and even nationalist movements on the Continent. For

[1] A. Mileikovsky (ed.), *Reformizm, revizionizm i problemy sovremennovo kapitalizma* (Moscow, 1959), p. 9.

[2] Z. K. Eggert, *Klassovaya borba v Germanii vo vremya pervoi mirovoi voiny* (Moscow, 1957).

all its polemical tone, classical Marxism was not anachronistic; it saw the stages of economic development reflected in corresponding periods of social thought. The decision to destalinize history called among other things for wider research into the precursors of Marxism and Leninism, for an end to the obscurantism which would apply to historiography the formula of politics: 'He who is not with us is against us.' But the more recent period has brought back the tendency to lump together all forms of non-Marxian socialism as being in effect anti-Marxian and anti-Soviet (a label sometimes by implication attached to writings published before there was a Soviet state).

The sum total of the Soviet appraisal of modern socialism is thus vitiated by the tendency to find the enemy, revisionism, in the most unlikely places and in the most unrelated theories and phenomena; the nature and the causes of what might with some justification be called genuine modern revisionism are obscured rather than clarified. This kind of revisionism is to be found not so much in Yugoslavia, where alleged revisionism is really a euphemism for Tito's unwillingness to subordinate his foreign policy to that of the Soviet Union, but rather among some Polish and Italian communists and left-wing socialists. It was they whom the shock of the disclosures about Stalinism led to undertake a theoretical re-appraisal of Leninism, and even of Marxism. In Poland this re-appraisal never went beyond a vague assertion of the humanitarian rather than deterministic essence of Marxism. In Italy, however, a greater variety of theoretical divergences infiltrated the discussion, and it is Italy, where for a time the highest communist functionaries appeared willing to accept the new views, that is of the greatest interest to the student of modern revisionism.

The essence of Bernstein's views consisted in his assault on the doctrine of the gradual worsening of the lot of the working class under capitalism and on the general Marxian notion that the exploiting essence of capitalism is unchangeable; and it was from this position that Bernstein developed his critique of the classical Marxian views of the state, the class war, etc. This is the feature which marks genuine revisionism and distinguishes it from criticisms of the Soviet Union's foreign policy, the details of organization of the communist state, etc., all of which have been lumped together by the Soviet writers.

In dealing with the aberrant Italian communists, a recent Soviet publication obscures the theoretical element of their protest, reducing it to a breach of party discipline and opposition to the Soviet Union's leading role in the socialist camp. The source of Italian revisionism, the author helpfully explains, lies in the 'maximalist' tradition of Italian Marxism (i.e. in the very opposite of democratic socialism). Superficially, maximalism indicates an uncompromising revolutionary posture, but in fact it leads to the loosening of party discipline and to a policy of waiting for a spontaneous revolution by the masses. From there the road leads straight to deviations such as those of A. Giolitti, a former communist, now a Nenni socialist. He has abandoned the true Marxist position that the state is but an instrument of monopoly capitalism, and holds that the bourgeois state may challenge the monopolies. He has disputed the impoverishment canon and in general has fallen under the influence of bourgeois critics of Marxism.[1] The criticism of Nenni's socialists is extensive but subdued. For all the luxuriant growth of heresies among them, they remain allied with the communists. But the range of their deviations is truly amazing: they stretch from Nenni's emphasis on individual freedom to Lelio Basso's proposal to renounce Leninism as the basis of revolutionary socialism.

What is characteristic in such discussions of modern socialism is the attrition of their intellectual content. After all, original revisionism found worthy opponents and scholarly counter-arguments in Rosa Luxemburg, Kautsky, and Hilferding. Their successors today, if they do not simply resort to epithets, dismiss the revisionist or pseudo-revisionist argument with a simple fiat from Lenin or (much more seldom) Marx or Engels. The hunt for unorthodoxy, while not so primitive as in Stalin's time, is equally inclusive. A scholar of undoubted Marxist orthodoxy and high standing, such as Jürgen Kuczynski, is assailed for stating the simple historic fact that the 'masses' in Germany at the beginning of the First World War were pervaded by patriotic rather than revolutionary sentiments, and that the social-democrats, in voting for the war credits, were responding to popular pressure.[2] What there is of genuine intellectual argument is on an appallingly low level. In dealing with John Strachey's and Benedict Kautsky's case against the impoverishment theory, the Soviet reviewer flatly denies that Marx and Engels postulated an *absolute* decline of the workers' standard of living,[3] but is unable to suggest a coherent alternative interpretation.

The student of Soviet historiography must ask the question which faces every analyst of any sphere of Soviet life: how much change has there been in the last decade, and has it been real or illusory? It is much too simple to see the developments as following the cycle: repression, liberalization following Stalin's death, and then a retrogression beginning in 1957 which has brought the situation back to where it was in 1953. The Soviet historian now is certainly not free to arrive at any conclusions to which his researches might lead him. If a student of Russia's beginnings still feels constrained to see in the 'Norman' theory an invention of western reactionaries designed to suggest that the Slavs are incapable of ruling themselves, then it is unreasonable to expect an objective study of Bernstein, the Russian populists, or guild socialism.

Nevertheless, there has been a change. The historian is not only supposed to re-state and repeat; he now engages in active argument, both with his confrères in the West and, in so far as our subject is

[1] Mileikovsky, op. cit., pp. 343-5.
[2] M. G. Kabin, *Voprosy Istorii*, 1959, No. 3, p. 144.
[3] Mileikovsky, op. cit., p. 102.

concerned, with the non-communist socialists of the past. This creates greater opportunities for the Soviet historian, and greater ideological dangers for the Soviet rulers. The future meaning of communism in the Soviet Union and its relation to the views and policies of the Chinese and other communists raise perplexing and perhaps dangerous problems for the future, and these are reflected not only in official speeches and declarations, but also in the day-to-day work of the Soviet historian and philosopher. Superficially, it might appear that Bernstein could be safely relegated to the *curiosa* of intellectual history, and that a catalogue of Rosa Luxemburg's merits need not always be accompanied by an enumeration of her errors. But while neither revisionism nor Luxemburgism threatens to sweep the Soviet Union, they do raise questions concerning the role of the Soviet Union in the international communist movement and the role of the totalitarian party in a communist society. The struggle against revisionism is not so much a struggle against an actual ideology as a prophylactic campaign designed to prevent the erection of ideological shelters for present and future political discontents.

How far is the present state of Soviet historiography the result of genuine indoctrination, and how far is it the product of opportunity? The testimony of 1955-7 is fairly instructive. When it appeared safe to write a more professional type of history, even on subjects as perilous as that of the history of the communist party and of international socialism, there was no shortage of historians who both in their conclusions and in their use of materials demonstrated their ability and willingness to be genuine historians. To be sure, they were fulfilling what they assumed to be a new directive, but their example shows how imperfectly even the most efficient dictatorship can stamp out the scholarly state of mind.

DISCUSSION

Introducing his paper on 'Socialism in Current Soviet Historiography', Prof. Ulam said that the nature of his task had obliged him for the first time to read systematically a great deal of Soviet historical writing. His main objection was not so much to the falsifications as to the frightful dullness of much of the work on the history of ideas—a field in which one was entitled to expect some speculative capacity.

Almost by definition, the subject was one which precluded objectivity. In any kind of Marxian society, there would be doctrinal assumptions and a conditioned way of approaching other political ideologies and political systems. Marxism itself was temperamentally and intellectually intolerant. In view of the extreme importance of the definition of socialism and its relation to the political system, there was bound to be an official point of view which could not be easily contradicted by a writer.

The directive to historians in *Voprosy Istorii* in 1955, which urged a more detailed study and freer historical discussion of other socialist creeds, did not disprove the main point about control from the centre. The new ways of dealing with, say, Plekhanov or the western precursors of Marxism during the relatively freer period of 1955-7 were hardly more interesting intellectually, or freer from the frightful semantics and classification mania of the Soviet historians, than were their previous or subsequent efforts.

The party's profound concern at the growing ideological agnosticism in the Soviet Union can be traced back to Stalin's last years. Sheer ignorance of the history of socialism was encouraged by the fact that to discuss Marxism scientifically was taken as a reflection on the official party line. The safe way of relying uncritically on the most primitive textbook treatment of the subject was not likely to gain enthusiastic adherents for the ideology. Another reason for this ideological agnosticism, even more pronounced in recent years than in 1950-3, was the general transformation of Soviet society; many of the issues which excited interest, or were at least relevant to contemporary life, in the twenties or even at the height of the purges in the thirties, now seem somewhat divorced from the realities of Soviet life.

The leaders of the communist party had a built-in awareness of ideological dangers, a sense that ideological differences, if unchecked, could eventually threaten the political structure. The attempt to liberalize Soviet historiography, in fact the whole destalinization campaign in 1955-6, could be interpreted as a reflection of fears among the leaders of possible dilution and erosion of the ideology. The broadening of the legitimate sphere of criticism in such allied fields as the history of the party and the history of socialist movements was officially sponsored and encouraged, but from the intellectual point of view the fruits of this relaxation were not particularly exciting. It was difficult for Soviet historians to shake off the paralysing effect of the Stalinist style of writing; they found it well-nigh impossible to rid themselves of the mania for classification, which to a certain extent derived from the traditions of Marxism proper, but had been carried *ad absurdum* under Stalin. In dealing with any personality in history, the main concern was to place him in a neat category, to label him as progressive, socialist, renegade, heretic, etc., before entering into any discussion about him. The period from 1955 to 1957 had been too short to allow Soviet historians to recover from the crippling diseases contracted during the previous decades. But like all species that lose one faculty, they had developed compensating organs. So long as the subject was safe, they indulged in a welter of statistics, footnotes, and data. Prof. Ulam found it difficult to see in articles like those by Burdzhalov or Nasyrin, who tried to inject some realism into the question of Lenin's position on nationalization after the revolution, examples of genuine historical criticism; it was simply that certain subjects seemed in 1956 and early 1957 to have become safe, so that historians could indulge in righteous indignation at the suppression of evidence. But even those very modest shoots of criticism, in conjunction with certain social developments, provoked the reaction of 1957. This was the hour of the more prudent historians, who had been quiet during the years of ferment, and now had their day against the iconoclasts of 1955-7.

The period of the historical thaw was one of experimentation, of finding out how far it was safe to go. The limits of experimentation were set by the events of 1956 in Russia and abroad. Historical writing was measured against certain political and social effects. The result was the campaign against revisionism, in history as in other fields.

The treatment of revisionism illustrated the fatal fascination that Soviet historical writing exercised on western scholars whose job it was to deal with it. They had adopted Soviet terms, or rather their confusion of terms, lumping together most diverse phenomena under the same heading. The term 'revisionism' itself was most inaccurate and certainly inapplicable to Yugoslav communism and some other theories. In the same way Stalin had grouped together most diverse forms of political opposition and established some fictitious connection between them. It was typical of Soviet historical writing on the subject of revisionism to lump together people like Marshal Tito, Harold Laski, or G. D. H. Cole under the same heading, and to trace their aberrations back to the common fount of 'Bernsteinism'.

In a way the ideological tightening after 1957 represented a setback even compared to the Stalinist period. For whereas beforehand the Soviet historian had been largely called upon to give bare facts, however incorrect or one-sided, now he was expected to engage more actively in ideological criticism and so add a warped ideological background. Thus one got the strange phenomenon of a book on German social-democracy during the First World War accusing Rosa Luxemburg of not acting in 1915 the way Lenin acted in October 1917.

There was today a more vociferous and self-conscious propagation of the ideology of communism, at home and abroad. Its domestic dimension was expressed in the endless and largely meaningless discussion of the shape of communism in Soviet conditions. The impossibility of spelling the problem out in genuinely Marxist terms was quite obvious, but at the same time the regime felt the need to fill in the ideological vacuum. The international dimension was more interesting, for so-called revisionism concealed a variety of ways in which communists in countries outside the Soviet Union—in Poland, Yugoslavia, Italy—tried to preserve Marxism and at the same time to detach Marx from his fruits in Russia, if indeed they were his fruits. In these countries Marxism was still much more relevant; it genuinely engaged the interest of many people, whereas in Russia the growing volume of propaganda barely disguised the general boredom with all ideological categories —Marxism, Leninism, and so on. Prof. Ulam admitted a preference for the Soviet interpretation of Marx to certain attempts outside the Soviet Union to turn him into a humanist and non-determinist. His sympathy did not extend to the Soviet way of criticizing these new interpretations by calling their adherents tools of imperialism, etc. In face of the potential intellectual danger of 'revisionism', it was the task of Soviet historians of ideas to try to preserve the orthodoxy and to provide formulas justifying the changed political posture of the Soviet regime.

Turning to the prospects for the future, Prof. Ulam reverted to the question of the co-existence of historical truth and active falsification. Such co-existence seemed to him easier in the field of the history of political thought than of the history of the party, for the historian of the party had access to documents and books that proved conclusively how party history had been falsified. But the historian of ideas dealt with something less tangible and so it was easier for him to justify the kind of pragmatism à la Stalin, who once said: 'May the devil take all formulas. The important thing is the victorious progress of the Soviet Union.' This led Prof. Ulam to a melancholy conclusion: as political ideologies and ideas found their justification in the facts and general tendencies of history, and not so much in the neat scholarly footnote or the observance of internationally accepted standards of scholarship, the Soviet historian of socialism and of political ideas had little incentive to doubt the general correctness of his mutilated and bowdlerized tradition of historical writing.

Professor Scheibert expressed complete agreement with Dr Ulam's paper. He wondered what had prompted Stalin to stop research into the history of socialist thought prior to social-democracy, and suggested that it would be useful to correlate the different stages in Soviet historiography and in the corresponding political situation.

The reason for discouraging the study of utopian socialist movements, which was in vogue in the late twenties and early thirties, was easier to guess. To point out how much Chernyshevsky, for example, owed to Fourier and Saint-Simon, was thought to diminish the stature of the Russian.

Prof. Lowenthal agreed with Prof. Scheibert that a great deal of what was being labelled revisionism was not just the attempt to revise Marxism à la Bernstein, but to revise Leninism in order to go back to Marx. This was the core of the problem. The accusations of revisionism lumped together people who really worried the Soviets ideologically with the Bernsteins, the Laskis, the Coles, etc., to conceal their real origin. The sources of their revisionism were two classical documents: one was the speech by Marx in 1872 (mentioned by Professor Ulam) about the possibility of different roads to socialism, including a peaceful road; the other was Rosa Luxemburg's critique of the Russian revolution.

A revisionist was somebody who came from the communist movement and who began to doubt that a party dictatorship was either necessary everywhere or necessary at all. That was what had happened in a number of countries as a result of destalinization. In this sense there was a community between the Yugoslavs, the Poles, and the Italians. The Yugoslavs had been putting forward for years the thesis that a Leninist dictatorship was necessary for some countries, but not for all.

And they delighted in quoting Marx's 1872 speech. In Poland, too, after the Polish October, prominent revisionists advanced the idea that reformism might be as effective in some countries as revolution in others. The same ideas also appeared in the writings of many Italian socialists. It was the proliferation of that kind of doubt within the communist ranks about the universal necessity or desirability of a party dictatorship for achieving socialism which had caused the wave of attacks on revisionism.

In the USSR today there was a marked tendency to reproduce the roots of such revision. To see that, one had to go back to the differences between Marx and Lenin. One of the great revisions of Marxism that Lenin had perpetrated was to stress the voluntarist element, whereas in the Marxian concept the basic idea had really been the inevitability of the victory of the socialist revolution. Lenin instead emphasized that success was impossible unless the vanguard of the proletariat, i.e. the communist party, got complete power. This twist was needed to justify the dictatorship as a permanent necessity. But out of the present situation of the Soviet Union, its industrial strength, its weight on the international plane, and the revolutionary situation in the developing countries, there had arisen a new confidence that the wave of history was favouring the communists. This new confidence, shown in the exuberance of Khrushchev's speeches, was at variance with the need always to insist on the indispensable power of the party. There was an increasing stress on spontaneity, on the thought that history was working the Soviet way. In many of the things that Khrushchev said there was a kind of unconscious Marxist revisionism of Lenin. He did not intend this. He wanted to keep the power of the party supreme and to go on justifying it, but at the same time his over-confidence tended to undermine his intentions and to push him towards revisionist tendencies.

Mr Wolfe said that the condition of socialism in our time was a rather contradictory one. On the one hand the socialist element in the economy of western society continued steadily to grow. On the other, socialism as a total crusading ideology was in decline. Writings about it had become banal and dull, and had lost the excitement they had had in the nineteenth century. This was true even of socialism in France and Italy with their powerful communist parties. It applied to West Germany, where the main opposition party aspiring to power was the social-democrats, as much as to East Germany, where the only party was the socialist-communist SED. It was evident also in the decline of ideological fervour within the British labour movement.

Along with this there had been a growth of sheer ignorance. Lenin and Bukharin had obviously read their Marx and read him with excitement. Mr Wolfe was convinced from the evidence of Stalin's works that Stalin knew only insignificant fragments of Marx's writings. As for Khrushchev, there was little evidence that he had read the basic works at all. There was nothing in the fifties and sixties published in Russia or within the Marxist current abroad, which could rival in interest the articles in *Pod Znamenem Marksizma* in the twenties. The publications now were dull because the interesting questions could no longer be asked. The intellectual excitement generated in Poland and Hungary during the thaw was largely due to the fact that Poles and Hungarians were beginning to ask these questions again.

In the writing of the history of socialism there was a similar decline. So long as Ryazanov had been alive and active, Moscow could still be considered the centre of Marxist studies. But after the disappearance of Adoratsky from the scene, the real centres of Marxist studies were to be found in the un-Marxist West. The work of the International Institute for Social History in Amsterdam, or of men like Maximilien Rubel in France or G. D. H. Cole in Britain was superior to anything produced in the USSR.

Mr Labedz recalled that when Khrushchev went to America, a famous American commentator prepared for his TV discussion with the Russian leader by reading *Capital* the previous day. It had been a case of the blind leading the blind, for neither of them was capable of understanding the sacred text.

The writing of the history of socialism was as important as the writing of the history of the party itself, for its function was really to preserve the central myth which legitimized the system. This explained also the gradual progress in dullness, for what we were witnessing was the progress of ritual. The same thing could be seen in other ideological evolutions—the formulas became less and less intellectually exciting, more and more formalized and ritualistic. What Mr Wolfe had referred to as dull questions with dull answers built into them was precisely the definition of a ritual.

The central myth which this ritual was designed to preserve and legitimize consisted of a certain body of ideas which was a theory and a doctrine at the same time. The doctrine could not stand up to reality, because it neither described the reality adequately nor foretold developments correctly; nor could it adjust itself to the reality on the basis of the old formulas. The same had happened with other ideological movements: early Christianity was not the same thing as the Christianity of the Middle Ages, for example. Mr Labedz then referred to Professor Ulam's criticism of the way Soviet historians lumped together all sorts of divergent standpoints under the single label of revisionism. Professor Scheibert had touched a very real issue in stressing that 'revisionism' was not just a historical phenomenon linked to the Bernstein episode, but had a sociological meaning as well: for the ideology needed to be continually readjusted to bring the doctrine closer to reality. In this sense revisionism, as Prof. Lowenthal had also emphasized, was a necessary corollary of the doctrine itself, just as heresy was a necessary corollary of religious doctrine. Thus the two first revisionists in the history of socialism had of course been Marx and Engels. One could illustrate this by referring to Marx's doubts about the general applicability of his scheme when he started to study more closely the history of revolutionary movements in Russia. The same applied to Engels' doubts about and revisions of certain elements in Marx's statements after the death of Marx. The process had continued, and in this sense all the writers on Marxism and all writers in the Marxist tradition were revisionists. Of course, if one took the historical definition of revisionism with Bernstein as its starting-point, then one was justified in refusing to apply the label to the revisionists in Poland and Hungary after 1955. If, however, one took as one's starting-point the sociological definition of revisionism as a necessary corollary of ideological development in systems where the doctrine played the part it did in Russia, then it was clearly legitimate to apply the concept to people who had very little to do with Bernstein. We were not the masters of language; we could not dictate how concepts should be used; we were ourselves largely conditioned by the general use of the language. Therefore it would be over-fastidious to refuse to apply the term revisionism to people actually engaged in the revision of certain Marxian statements and tenets, simply because they had no historic links with the Bernstein episode in the history of socialism.

Professor Berlin asked to what degree Soviet historians today, or at least in the recent past, could be said to write as socialists—that is to say, to apply socialist categories (or Marxist, Leninist, Khrushchevist categories for that matter) in their writing of history. He did not mean artificial categories imposed from above and used reluctantly, nor the kind of double-think whereby a certain awareness of the truth is accommodated to opportunistic statements dictated by temperament or circumstance; he meant the genuine use of concepts and categories different from those used by most bourgeois historians in the West— whether because they had been subconsciously imbibed through education or because they corresponded to honestly held convictions. This touched on the earlier discussion of the problem to what degree Soviet concepts generally differed from ours. For instance, if a western socialist were to write history, would he in any way be closer to Soviet historians than liberal or conservative historians? In other words, to what extent could Soviet historians be called in some sense socialist, irrespective of the quality of their writing.

Professor Ulam thought that vulgarized categories of Marxism had entered very firmly into Soviet historiography. He believed that even if the leash were to be completely removed, those general crude categories would still remain. Only the passage of time would lead to a more sophisticated type of Marxism, not to speak of the willingness to discuss other points of view.

For example, when Soviet historians were urged in 1955 to discuss the Utopian socialists more sympathetically, they must have been told not merely to classify them as Utopian socialists and be done with it, but to try a more practical approach. But the average Soviet historian would be quite at a loss to understand somebody like Proudhon. Even if he were at liberty to do so, he would not be capable of displaying a much wider range of speculation. Professor Ulam limited this observation to Soviet historians of political thought—he did not know whether it would apply to other fields of Soviet historiography.

x. Trends in Soviet Historiography of the Second World War

MATTHEW GALLAGHER

No event cut more deeply across the fabric of Soviet history, or left larger gaps for the official historians to repair, than the Second World War. In a dozen different ways it was an embarrassment for the Soviet Union. The pact with Hitler in August 1939, the failure to anticipate and prepare for the German invasion, the forced retreats, the loss of huge territories and populations—all would have defied ready explanation by any government, let alone a regime with pretensions to foresight and infallibility. For Stalin, the remedy was simple: research into the history of the war was forbidden, and the official account was compressed into the formulas of Stalin's war-time speeches.[1]

For the present regime no such simple expedient is available. The anti-Stalin campaign resolved some difficulties, but created new ones; and while the passage of time has salved some wounds, others remain unhealed. From the ideological standpoint alone, no fact could be more awkward than the anti-Hitler coalition itself—the incongruous alliance of the world's first socialist state with the citadels of world capitalism.

It is not surprising, therefore, that Soviet historians have approached the war with caution, mindful of the need to manipulate the official record to fit the present leadership's image of itself and the world around it. What is notable is that some progress has been made towards providing an account of what really happened.

This progress has been confined for the most part to the purely military aspects of the war, and has been counterbalanced by an increasingly elaborate political propaganda justifying the party and its policies. From this interplay of conflicting tendencies has emerged a history of the war significantly different from anything the Soviet Union produced during the first ten post-war years.

The new history combines changes and adjustments which have

[1] Reports in *Istoricheskii Zhurnal* and *Voprosy Istorii* during 1945-46 reveal that plans which the historians had laid for extensive research into the history of the war were abruptly cancelled in 1946. *Voprosy Istorii* carried only one article on the history of the war during the first five post-war years. The military journals fared a little better, and a thin smattering of books and pamphlets appeared, particularly towards the end of Stalin's life. Stalin's war-time writings and speeches collected in the volume *The Great Patriotic War of the Soviet Union*, and his electoral speech of February 9, 1946, were the most important sources from which general historical interpretations were drawn.

accumulated as by-products of the regime's long efforts first to shed, and then to strike a balance with, its Stalinist traditions. In this process three periods stand out as particularly relevant. The first was the 1955 revision in Soviet military thinking which resulted in the repudiation of certain tenets of Stalinist military doctrine, and the re-casting of the official version of the war which embodied them. The second was the twentieth Party congress and the sweeping re-assessment of Stalin's historical role which it stimulated. The third was the reaction in the Soviet official mood after the 1956 events in Hungary, which had as one consequence the re-assertion of party prerogatives in the interpretation of history, and a heavier ideological emphasis in their exercise. The effect was cumulative, each stage adding to, amending, or qualifying— but not supplanting—the earlier contributions. It is a noteworthy feature of this process that the professional military interests which imparted the initial impetus to the movement continued throughout to exert a strong influence.

The revisions of 1955 centred on the question of the significance of surprise attack in war—a question of some importance for history since it bore on the interpretation of the early period of the war. In both Stalinist military doctrine and the Stalinist version of the war, the significance of surprise attack was depreciated. Surprise was listed among the 'temporary' factors of war which lost significance as soon as the 'permanently operating' factors could be brought into play; and the German failure to turn initial successes into victory was ascribed to excessive reliance on surprise alone.[1] Thus when Soviet military planners began to adjust their thinking to the importance of surprise attack in nuclear war, they found it necessary to revise not only current military doctrine but also the historical texts in which it was expressed. The revision of the official history of the early period of the war which followed was limited but fundamental; in emphasizing the importance of surprise attack, the Soviet military planners were implicitly under-lining the disastrous consequences which had flowed from an under-estimation of this factor in the past.

The 1955 revisions were essentially a clearing operation, aimed at removing ideological dead wood which impeded a fresh assessment of the realities and implications of the first period of the war. Criticism centred on the doctrine of 'active defence', the old official claim that the operations of the first period of the war had been conceived in advance and skilfully applied to bring about the defeat of the enemy.[2] It was now

[1] Doctrine on this question derived from Stalin's Order of the Day of February 23, 1942, which forecast a Soviet victory on the strength of the 'permanently operating' factors which decide the outcome of war.

[2] During the war the term 'active defence' was used to convey the notion that Soviet defensive tactics were designed to keep up the morale of the troops, to 'temper their regiments' for subsequent offensive action. This meaning derived from Stalin's Order of the Day No. 308, of September 18, 1941, which created the first guards units. In post-war propaganda it began to take on the broader strategic overtones described above; the cue was given in Stalin's electoral speech of February 9, 1946.

asserted that there had been no such plan. 'What the position was in fact we all well remember. Our experiences in that period so desperate for our country are sufficiently fresh in our memories', ran an editorial in *Military Thought*.[1] It pointed out that the official interpretations had 'entered into the programmes of instruction of our military-pedagogical institutes', and had hampered the creation of a truly professional atmosphere in military thinking. The enthusiasm generated by this editorial threatened here and there to undermine the whole edifice of historical interpretation which had been erected around the war,[2] but the main pillars remained intact. The traditional image of Stalin as war-time leader and military chief was not seriously disturbed; the derogatory assessment of Allied motives and performance was retained. The main contribution of 1955 to the history of the war was to remove the veneer which Stalin had applied to the catastrophic failures of the early days.[3]

The twentieth party congress imparted a vigorous forward thrust to this movement by setting in motion new critical currents which broadened and deepened the channels cut by the military historians of 1955. Khrushchev's secret speech, which portrayed Stalin as a military ignoramus reponsible for the initial unpreparedness of the Soviet Union as well as for subsequent defeats, set the co-ordinates of the new offensive. As before, the critical barrage was directed at the initial period of the war, but now the early defeats were ascribed not only to the surprise of the German attack but to the negligence of the Soviet Government in failing to prepare the country adequately for war, and to take the precautions which elementary prudence and ample intelligence warnings had indicated were necessary. Konstantin Simonov, with his characteristic ability to catch the mood of the moment, summed up the spirit of much of this criticism in a bitter essay published later in the year. Recalling the post-war criticism of Fadeyev's *The Young Guard*, he parodied the mealy-mouthed formulas of the critics which he now presented as typical of the whole post-war distortion of the history of

[1] *Voennaya Mysl*, 1955, No. 3, pp. 7-8. This was the first major statement of the new line.

[2] For example, Colonel-General P. Kurochkin, writing in issue No. 5, 1955, of the same journal, criticized the way the so-called 'ten Stalinist crushing blows' of 1944 had been presented in official histories. Only a few of these operations, he said, were carried out according to plan. Some took longer than expected, others developed into operations larger than had been foreseen.

[3] The first fruits of revision, a collective work edited by P. A. Zhilin entitled *Vazhneishie operatsii Velikoi Otechestvennoi voiny 1941-1945 gg.* (Moscow, 1956), showed distinct improvements over past histories both in the candour of its treatment of the initial period and in the quantity of data presented. The more highly publicized *Essays on the History of the Great Patriotic War, 1941-1945*, which was prepared earlier, is for long stretches little more than a collection of tributes to the feats of heroism performed by Soviet soldiers and workers—a chorus of those 'oh's and ah's' which the poet Tvardovsky once said it was the function of war-time writers to utter. The Zhilin book was published by the Ministry of Defence, the *Essays* by the Academy of Sciences.

the war. 'Not everything went smoothly,' he mocked. 'How can one use such words of a war in which, by 1942, the fascists had occupied a territory with a population of almost seventy million?' Again mimicking the official formula, he wrote: 'Various unforeseen circumstances arose'. 'What sort of language is this? One can use such words about a train being late, or about early frosts, but not about the war, whose whole course from the very outset was, to our great misfortune, an unforeseen circumstance.'[1]

Some of the additions made by the writers of 1956 to the officially approved revisions have since disappeared from Soviet writings on the war. *Voennyi Vestnik*'s bold hint that more attention should be paid to the 'casualties and losses of material in various battles and operations'[2] has been forgotten, and the call for a more appreciative evaluation of the contributions of 'our partners in the anti-Hitler coalition',[3] found no response. But the main content of the 1956 revision, the principal substantive points of Khrushchev's indictment of Stalin's war-time role, have remained a part of the Soviet history of the war, although in softened form.

Signs of a retreat in official attitudes began to appear early in 1957. The military chiefs, apparently stung by the critical current they had helped to loose, were in the forefront of this reaction. Marshal Malinovsky, in the major Armed Forces' Day article of 1957, took a stand directly across its path. 'It must be said outright,' he wrote, 'that this [the German invasion] was not unexpected by the Soviet supreme military command.'[4] More important were the actions of the party, which from about mid-1957 began to wield a stronger hand. The decision of the central committee in September to sponsor a new multi-volume history of the war, and the creation of a special section in the Institute of Marxism-Leninism to prepare it, marked a major turning-point. This was followed by the dismissal of Marshal Zhukov in October—an act which dramatized the supremacy of the party over the military command. The party was at pains to emphasize—both in the resolution itself and in subsequent comments—the implications for the history of the war. Henceforth, the role of the party in the war was to be shown in a light suitable to its newly re-asserted pre-eminence.

By the end of 1957 the official attitude towards the history of the war had been relatively stabilized. Having eliminated or tamed the internal forces which might impede the adjustment it was seeking, the regime was now in a position to reach a settlement with its Stalinist past. The settlement was a compromise reflecting the conflicting needs of the regime, for while seeking to re-harness history to the requirements of the party, it did not wish to shackle the progress that was being made in military thought—progress closely connected with, and partly depen-

---

[1] *Novyi Mir*, 1956, No. 12, p. 246.
[2] *Voennyi Vestnik*, 1956, No. 4.
[3] *Voprosy Istorii*, 1956, No. 5, p. 150.
[4] *Pravda*, February 23, 1957.

H

dent upon, the historical revisions of the past few years. Thus the new line combined a concern to retain and develop the gains made in 1955 and 1956 with the desire to bolster and refurbish the party's historical reputation and ideological credentials. In its main tendencies this line has since been steadily pursued.

A comparison of current with past interpretations of certain major issues throws light on the practical effects of these developments. In making these comparisons it will be useful to consider the military and political aspects of the war separately.

The question of the military preparedness of the Soviet Union on the eve of the war was first raised by Khrushchev in his secret speech. He said that because of Stalin's negligence Soviet industry had not been properly geared to defence needs in the immediate pre-war years, so that when the attack came the army found itself critically short of all kinds of weapons and equipment. This charge obviously struck exposed political nerves in the military department, and the public statements on this issue over the next year provide a singular case of virtually open debate between the party and the military over the interpretation of history.

Ironically, in view of subsequent developments, it was a military organ, *Voennyi Vestnik*, which first made the charge in public. That this was only the initial reaction of the military propagandists to Khrushchev's speech, and not the considered view of the military chiefs, was indicated by *Krasnaya Zvezda* in its Victory Day editorial two months later. It was 'surprised and grieved', it said, by the incorrect and harmful opinions expressed in *Voennyi Vestnik*, and it described as 'strange and unconvincing' the assertion that the defeats of the early period were due to the unpreparedness of the armed forces. In July, *Krasnaya Zvezda* in its turn was rebuked by *Kommunist*, and the charge that there had been 'serious omissions in the planned development of military industry in the pre-war years' was reiterated.

On July 19th, two days after this issue of *Kommunist* was passed for the press, *Krasnaya Zvezda* announced its capitulation. But the capitulation was neither abject nor unqualified, for the paper took the opportunity to reiterate its defence of the military chiefs. It pointed out (as had the central committee's June 30th resolution) that the negative consequences of Stalin's personality cult had been mitigated by the independent actions of other leaders, 'including outstanding Soviet military commanders'. And it took pains to point out that among the factors that had been distorted in Stalinist histories of the war was 'such an important factor as the role of the generals of the Soviet Army'. The sense of corporate identity and pride reflected in these statements was expressed even more directly seven months later in Marshal Malinovsky's Armed Forces' Day assertion that 'the Soviet supreme military command' had not been caught unawares by the German invasion.

The key to the army's discomfiture was the role played by Zhukov.

As Chief of the General Staff in the immediate pre-war period, Zhukov obviously shared responsibility for the state of the country's defences at that time, and was bound to share the blame in any charge of mismanagement. Marshal Konev drew particular attention to this point in his broad-ranging attack on Zhukov's military reputation when the latter was expelled from the central committee in 1957, and it was aired once again by Major-General E. A. Boltin the following year in an authoritative article on the history of the war.[1] Surprisingly, the charge was not followed up in subsequent histories until quite recently, although Zhukov presented the classic qualifications for a scapegoat on this issue.

The first volume of the new official history of the war, published in 1960, asserts that 'leading workers of the People's Commissariat of Defence' did not appreciate the urgency of the moment, and were 'impermissibly' slow in evaluating the designs of new weapons and equipment and in getting prototypes into production. However, blame is laid only on individuals of secondary importance: Deputy Commissars G. I. Kulik, L. Z. Mekhlis, and E. A. Shchadenko.[2] By contrast, the second volume of the same history, published in 1961, includes the names not only of Marshal Zhukov but of Marshal Timoshenko in the indictment.[3] But even in this account the charges against Zhukov, as well as against Timoshenko, are presented with regret rather than recrimination. This forbearance towards Zhukov did not completely disappear from Soviet accounts until well after the twenty-second party congress, when for the first time echoes of the harsh tones of Konev's original attack re-emerged.[4]

The general charge that the Soviet Government was negligent in failing to prepare the military establishment for war has been retained in the current histories and greatly developed. The newer accounts reveal the scale of disorganization in Soviet military industry on the eve of the war. Only 17 per cent of the aircraft in active status were of modern design; the serial production of Yak-1's and Mig-3's (the first

[1] V pomoshch politicheskomu samoobrazovaniyu, 1958, No. 7, p. 19.

[2] Istoriya Velikoi Otechestvennoi voiny Sovetskovo Soyuza, I, pp. 415-16. G. I. Kulik was named Deputy Commissar of Defence in 1939, and promoted to Marshal of the Soviet Union in 1940. His biography is not listed in the Large Soviet Encyclopedia. L. Z. Mekhlis (1889-1953) was chief of the Main Political Administration of the Red Army from 1937 to 1940. He was named Commissar of State Control in September 1940, and at the outset of the war was assigned to work in the Soviet Army, according to the Encyclopedia. E. A. Shchadenko (1885-1951) held a number of posts mainly in the political apparatus of the army before the war. During the first years of the war, according to the Encylopedia, he occupied 'responsible offices in the central apparatus of the Commissariat of Defence'.

[3] Ibid., II, p. 10. Whatever political reasons may have prompted the inclusion of Marshal Timoshenko in this indictment, his vulnerability to historical criticism was beyond question. He had been successively Commissar of Defence, acting Commander-in-Chief of the Armed Forces, and Commander-in-Chief of the Western Direction during the period in question.

[4] Cf. article by Matsulenko, Krasnaya Zvezda, February 20, 1962. In it Zhukov is described as a 'politically insolvent figure' who sought to glorify his own person, and who 'crudely' violated the party line on training and educating military cadres.

modern types) began only in 1941; the rate of production of automatic weapons and machine-guns actually fell during 1940 and the first half of 1941;[1] the *first* anti-tank guns began to come out only in October 1941.[2] And the list could be extended. These facts might be taken to mitigate the discredit of the military defeats of the early period, but the Soviet accounts do not present them in this way, nor does this appear to be the purpose of the revelations.

The accounts of the initial German attack are also remarkably revealing and equally well furnished with factual credentials. The picture of Soviet military unpreparedness drawn in German accounts of the war are now fully confirmed in the current Soviet histories. It is now conceded—and corroborated with a wealth of detail—that border fortifications were not completed, troops had not been placed on a war footing, many divisions of the border screen were at reduced strength, and others composed of untrained contingents newly called up on the eve of the war, etc. These failures of military leadership, it is said, were compounded by political mistakes. To avoid giving the Germans any pretext for hostilities, most divisions of the border screen were ordered to keep only one of their regiments on the border, while the main forces were held in camps or military towns well behind the frontier.[3]

While always extolling the 'staunchness' of Soviet resistance to the German invasion, these accounts provide many details which bring out the scale of the initial catastrophe. One gives exact figures on the extent and tempo of the German advance, and freely acknowledges the ineffectiveness of Soviet resistance at particular junctures. For example: 'Neither in the border area, nor on the line of the western Dvina, nor at the Pskov and Ostrovsky fortified regions could the troops of the North-western Front hold back the adversary'. Or again: 'The Command of the South-western Front was unable to organize the leadership of the military operations of the encircled troops. Direction of the troops was lost, and the withdrawal took place in an extremely disorganized manner, by separate groups and units'.[4]

One of the most time-honoured of Soviet interpretative devices applied to the early period of the war—the doctrine of the 'counter-offensive'—appears to have fallen by the wayside in current historiography. No other concept loomed larger in the Stalinist histories of the war, and although it was closely allied to the 'active defence' concept it did not suffer the fate of the latter during 1955 and 1956. According to the doctrine—originally developed by Major General Talensky[5] but appro-

[1] *Voenno-istoricheskii zhurnal*, 1960, No. 3, pp. 21-23.

[2] A. M. Samsonov, *Stalingradskaya bitva ot oborony i otstuplenii k velikoi pobede na Volge* (Moscow, 1960), p. 66.

[3] Cf. S. P. Platonov, ed., *Vtoraya mirovaya voina 1939-1945 gg.: voenno-istoricheskii ocherk* (Moscow, 1958), pp. 176-9, and *Istoriya Velikoi Otechestvennoi voiny Sovetskovo Soyuza*, I, pp. 473-9.

[4] S. P. Platonov, op. cit., pp. 186, 219.

[5] *Voennaya Mysl*, 1946, No. 6.

priated by Stalin in 1947—the defensive operations of 1941 before
Moscow (as well as of 1942 and 1943 before Stalingrad and Kursk
respectively) were parts of a grand strategic design aimed at creating the
conditions for a successful counter-offensive. The idea was developed
extravagantly over the next few years, both directly in encomiums on
Stalin's military genius and indirectly in historical revaluations of
Kutuzov's strategy of 1812, which Stalin had presented as a prototype
of the 'counter-offensive'. The new official history, however, reveals
that the concept of the counter-offensive had not even been raised in
Soviet military theory before the war, thus clearly implying that it could
not have affected the planning and conduct of operations during the
early period. It also states that defensive strategy as a whole was badly
under-developed in Soviet military doctrine before the war. Soviet
strategy recognized defensive action as 'possible and necessary' on
individual sectors, 'but not on a whole strategic front'.[1]

These and other changes have affected the presentation of a number of
other military operations. The withdrawal operations of 1942 leading up
to the battle of Stalingrad, for example, were formerly presented as a
skilful manoeuvre designed as a prelude to a counter-offensive. The first
direct criticism of this concept appeared in *Voennyi Vestnik* in its
editorial of April 1956. From the accounts of this battle sponsored by
official propaganda, the writer observed sarcastically, the conclusion
seemed justified that 'it was fitting and even proper that Soviet troops
should have retreated to Stalingrad, since this caused the enemy to
"expose" his flanks'.

The latest book on this period gives a clear picture of the forced
character of the Soviet retreats during the summer of 1942. 'The enemy,'
it says, 'having a considerable superiority of forces, held the initiative
completely, while the Soviet units withdrew ever further southward.'
It cites the German author Hans Doerr: 'In those days the Soviet Union
underwent a severe crisis . . . To all appearances the Russians, even
though they had executed a planned withdrawal to the Don, were
forced under pressure from the German units to retreat to the Volga
and the Caucasus earlier than planned; in several sectors their retreat
turned into flight'. The Soviet writer disputes Doerr's view that there
had been a 'crisis' and that the Soviet retreat was geared to a time-table,
but he does not take issue with the assertion that the retreat turned into
flight in places, and explicitly admits that the military situation had
'sharply deteriorated'.

The same source provides a vivid account of the disorganization
which prevailed in the Soviet retreat towards the Caucasus before the
southern thrust of the two-pronged German offensive of 1942:

'There were no prepared defensive field-works on the left bank of the
Don and our troops, hurriedly assuming the defensive, were forced to
repel the attacks of the enemy from unprepared positions. The artillery

[1] *Istoriya Velikoi Otechestvennoi voiny Sovetskovo Soyuza*, I, p. 441.

fell behind at the crossing of the Don and the defending troops were virtually deprived of artillery support. Because of shortages of aircraft the troops at the front received no air cover. The situation in the rear and the material-technical supply of the troops was bad. Shortages of munitions, gasoline, and food were badly felt because the rear installations and bases were cut off and regular supplies to the troops interrupted. The roads were torn up by vehicles, carts, and herds of cattle which created jams and slowed down movement.'[1]

The claim that the German strategic objective in the summer of 1942 was neither Stalingrad nor Transcaucasia, but Moscow, and that Stalingrad was simply a way-station in a vast enveloping manoeuvre aimed at the Soviet capital, has also been discarded in current Soviet writing. The first direct attack on this interpretation was launched by Marshal Yeremenko in a commemorative article on the fifteenth anniversary of the battle in *Kommunist*, 1958, No. 1: 'Our former interpretation of the German command's plans for the summer of 1942 . . .', he said, 'was unjustified.' The true intention, he asserted, was to seize the rich material resources of Transcaucasia, and the operations against Stalingrad developed out of the military needs of this strategy. While this correct interpretation now appears to have been accepted, the older view dies hard. Recent accounts adduce writings by Field-Marshal Von Paulus (prepared after the war) which give support —as they were undoubtedly intended to do—to the original Soviet interpretation. According to Von Paulus, the ultimate objective of German strategy in the summer of 1942 was indeed the envelopment of Moscow, and he explains the absence of any reference to it in the German operational directives of 1942 by the phased nature of the alleged strategy: as events developed in 1942 it became clear that the ultimate objective could not be undertaken until 1943. In first presenting this account, *Voenno-istoricheskii Zhurnal* introduced it with the non-committal statement: 'In the interests of collating different points of view relative to the plans of the German command in 1942 it is not without interest . . .'[2] Elsewhere it was given in a footnote without comment, while the text provided an accurate account of the German documents bearing on the question.[3]

In addition to these major revaluations, there are other signs that military historians are taking a fresh look at the whole history of the Second World War. Subjects never broached before—evaluations of actual command decisions, and the actions of high military personnel and individual officers—have now apparently been opened. In the

[1] A. M. Samsonov, op. cit., pp. 127-8, 305. The latter passage is quoted from A. S. Zavyalov, T. E. Kalyadin, *Bitva za Kavkaz 1942-1943 gg.* (Moscow, 1957), one of a number of books on individual operations which have appeared over the last few years.

[2] *Voenno-istoricheskii Zhurnal*, 1960, No. 2, p. 82.

[3] A. M. Samsonov, op. cit., p. 106.

article referred to above, for example, Yeremenko criticized a General
Headquarters decision in connection with the Stalingrad battle, as did
General Tyulenev, in an article in *Voenno-istoricheskii Zhurnal*, 1960,
No. 3 (which incidentally provides unusual insights into command
disorganization during the early days), complaining that a General
Headquarters decision had prevented the timely withdrawal of his
troops at a critical juncture of the war.

In another departure from past practice, Tyulenev recounted a war-
time episode which reflected unfavourably on a fellow-general, and a
similar though less personally derogatory reference was contained in an
article by Marshal Grechko in another issue.[1] Even officers now enjoying
high honours have had to swallow a mild dose of criticism.

The most dramatic example was a critique of Marshal Yeremenko's
memoir-history of the Stalingrad battle carried in *Voenno-istoricheskii
Zhurnal*, 1962, No. 1. The review, by Colonel-General S. P. Ivanov, an
officer whose career appears to link him to the General Staff, disputes
Yeremenko's claim that he and Khrushchev, his political opposite-
number in the wartime Military Council of the Stalingrad and South-
eastern Fronts, were chiefly responsible for initiating the plans for the
Soviet counter-offensive leading to the ultimate victory at Stalingrad.
Khrushchev is not specifically named in the criticism, but the pages in
Yeremenko's book cited in the review include those which recount
Khrushchev's alleged collaboration in working out the Stalingrad
strategy. The language of the review would be harsh even if its target
were merely an ordinary historian rather than a state figure of great
prestige and political influence. The marshal is charged with trying to
'exaggerate' the role of the Stalingrad Front and to 'minimize' the role
of General Headquarters in the events which he describes. The reviewer
'doubts' whether Yeremenko had in fact—as he claims—begun to plan
for the Stalingrad counter-offensive some three and a half months before
the event. Here, says the review, the author 'clearly sins [against truth]',
confusing the wish with the deed in an effort to credit himself with the
honour of having first conceived the idea of the counter-offensive. The
attack is the more surprising in that it appears to reverse what had
seemed to be a well-established official attitude towards the marshal's
work. *Pravda* had given the book a flattering review on June 24, 1961,
and had drawn approving attention to the generous assessment which
Yeremenko had given to Khrushchev's role at Stalingrad. The willingness of the *Voenno-istoricheskii Zhurnal* to underwrite such a vigorous
intervention in a politically sensitive matter casts a revealing light on the
self-assurance now enjoyed by military historians.

At the same time, this case highlights one of the negative aspects of
recent Soviet historiography—the build-up of Khrushchev's reputation
as a wartime hero. Yeremenko's book is one outstanding example.
Another is the new account of the Kiev battle of 1941 given in the
second volume of the new official history of the war, published in the

[1] *Voenno-istoricheskii Zhurnal*, 1960, No. 2, pp. 28, 108.

spring of 1961.[1] This battle had long been a sensitive area because of the scale of the disaster suffered there—German accounts claim that over half a million Soviet troops were trapped there—and of Khrushchev's involvement in the disaster by virtue of his positions as first secretary of the Ukrainian party and member of the Military Council of the South-western Direction (the responsible command echelon). Past histories did not refer to Khrushchev in connection with this event, although some of them did imply that responsibility for the defeat lay with the local command. The new account removes these shadows from Khrushchev's reputation by shifting the blame to General Headquarters. It asserts that the responsible military and political officers on the spot during the Kiev operation—Budenny and Khrushchev—had foreseen the impending defeat and had requested permission to withdraw a week before the decision was finally taken. This new version of history was widely publicized in connection with the twentieth anniversary of the Nazi invasion, and it has become a staple of current propaganda on war-time themes.

Finally—to return to the positive features of current military historiography—military historians have shown signs of professional impatience with the way those concerned with propaganda have handled the history of the war. Professor Telpukhovsky's recent book, *The Great Patriotic War of the Soviet Union 1941-1945*, for example, was given a highly critical review. Among the 'multiplicity of facts and figures' provided by Telpukhovsky, complained the reviewer, 'the main thing is submerged—the military actions of the Soviet troops and their results . . . Instead of instructive conclusions and generalizations we get only a collection of phrases and wordy discussion.'[2] A similar tone of professional impatience coupled with what appears to be an overtone of soldierly resentment at the civilian rear—is reflected in a review of Kiryaev's *The CPSU—Inspirer and Organizer of the Victory of the Soviet People in the Great Patriotic War*. The main complaint is that the book underestimates the events at the front. Conceding that the examples of labour heroism with which the book abounds are authentic, the reviewer nevertheless points out that these examples are isolated from the surrounding circumstances—circumstances 'which, strictly speaking, were created by the heroic feats of the soldiers'.[3]

The trend in military writing towards recognition of the utility of truth (or at least the liabilities of falsehood) cannot be understood in isolation from the re-affirmation in political writings that history must ultimately serve the objectives of the regime, and that it can do this best by reinforcing the regime's image of itself and of the world context in which it operates. Accordingly, since late 1957 Soviet historians have

[1] *Istoriya Velikoi Otechestvennoi voiny Sovetskovo Soyuza*, II, pp. 107-9.
[2] *Voenno-istoricheskii Zhurnal*, 1960, No. 5, pp. 105, 107.
[3] Ibid., 1960, No. 8, p. 91.

been engaged in drafting interpretations designed to fit the history of the war more firmly into this political framework.

The initial and central question for Soviet history was to define the character of the war. In this, as in so many other areas of the history of the war, the problem had been created by Stalin. In his electoral speech of 1946 he had declared that the war had assumed 'from the very outset' the character of a war of liberation and that the entry of the Soviet Union had merely 'strengthened' this character. The formula contained some pitfalls, however, which became obvious as the post-war campaign of denunciation of the West brought with it a complete revaluation of Allied motives and pre-war policies. A more fundamental difficulty was that the formula provided no respectable explanation for the role of the Soviet Union during the first two years of the war, or for the activities of the communist parties of Western Europe, which had opposed the war until the Soviet Union entered it.

These questions were largely evaded during the Stalin period by treating the Soviet-German war as a distinct historical entity, somehow separate from the war as a whole. During the first years after Stalin's death, historians resorted to the traditional Soviet propaganda distinction between the 'governments' and 'peoples' of the western states—a device which permitted recognition of the western contribution to victory while leaving basically intact the hostile assessment of 'imperialist' policies. This solution was presented in the major historical work of that period, the *Essays on the History of the Great Patriotic War*, published in 1955. The struggle against fascism had been justified, it explained, because the fascists aimed at world domination and the subjugation of other peoples. 'This is why the Second World War, despite the fact that it arose out of the struggle of two hostile imperialist groups, had a liberating character from the very beginning for the peoples of those countries which had been attacked by the fascist aggressors or were threatened by such attack. The liberating, anti-fascist character of the war became still more marked when the Soviet Union later entered it.'[1]

The formula came up for review along with the rest of the Stalinist history of the war in 1956. In his biting criticism of the *Essays*, Major-General Boltin rebuked the historians for failing to acknowledge the positive contributions of the Allies in the war, observing that as a result the 'thesis on the strengthening of the liberating, anti-fascist character of the Second World War is left hanging in the air'.[2]

In preparation for the new multi-volume history of the war decreed by the party in September 1957, a meeting was organized by the editorial board of *Kommunist* and produced what the journal later described as 'heated disputes on the character of the Second World War'. According to *Kommunist*, the new section on the history of the war in the Institute

[1] B. S. Telpukhovsky (ed.), *Ocherki istorii Velikoi Otechestvennoi voiny Sovetskovo Soyuza 1941-1945 gg.* (Moscow, 1955), p. 25.

[2] *Voprosy Istorii*, 1956, No. 5, p. 150.

H*

of Marxism-Leninism had undertaken a serious study of the problem, and a lively discussion had begun among the historians.

The outcome of these deliberations was an elaborate general theory of the character of the war which was first presented in an article in *Kommunist* early in 1958.[1] The new theory, distinguished from the earlier formulas mainly by greater elasticity and comprehensiveness, has held up well. Its essential points, drawn from this and two subsequent articles,[2] may be summarized as follows:

Before the war the policies of the western states were affected by two basic 'contradictions' in the world balance of forces, the first stemming from the expansionist pressures of Germany, Italy, and Japan against the Versailles settlement, the second from the rise of the Soviet Union heralding the birth of a new socio-economic order. While the latter tended to deepen and exacerbate all the old conflicts within the capitalist system, it served also to unite the reactionary forces. Hoping to use Germany as a striking force against communism, the western states helped to build up German military power, and directed their whole pre-war policy to instigating a war between Germany and the Soviet Union. But Hitler, not wishing to be used as a pawn, launched war first against his imperialist competitors. The response of the western states to Hitler's attack on Poland was prompted by a desire to defend their imperialist positions. Hence the war began as an imperialist war on both sides.

However, unlike the First World War, fought for a re-division of markets and spheres of influence, the second involved the very existence of states and the further spread of fascist tyranny. Thus opposition to Hitler took on the character of a liberating mission. The western states did not share this mission during the first part of the war; instead of resisting Hitler they settled down to a 'phoney' war, persisting in efforts to arrange a deal with him and plotting attacks on the Soviet Union from Finland and from the south.

The 'people', however, recognized the true nature of Hitlerism and began to struggle against it. 'In the course of time,' wrote *Kommunist*, 'the gradual accumulation of elements of struggle for liberation could not but influence, and did in fact influence, the character of the war. Thanks to the active anti-fascist struggle of the popular masses of countries occupied by Germany and Italy . . . the war, which international imperialism had envisaged as a means of dividing up the world, began, through the efforts of the popular masses, to turn into an anti-fascist, liberating, just war.' This changing character of the war justified the change in the attitude of the western communist parties. Having correctly assessed the war as imperialist on its outbreak, the communist

[1] P. Derevyanko, D. Proektor, 'K voprosu o kharaktere vtoroi mirovoi voiny', *Kommunist*, 1958, No. 5.

[2] E. Boltin, G. Deborin, 'The Character of the Second World War', *World Marxist Review*, 1959, No. 9; introduction to *Istoriya Velikoi Otechestvennoi voiny Sovetskovo Soyuza 1941-1945*, I, xv-xxiii.

parties opposed it. However, when the situation changed, the communists 'came out for a decisive prosecution of the war, for the unification of all forces able to rebuff the onslaught of the Hitlerites'.

For individual countries the character of the war changed at different times. In Poland the struggle was from the outset one for justice and liberation. In Britain the change occurred (in May-June 1940, according to the first two accounts) when the government, 'forced' by the pressure of public opinion, and itself recognizing the peril of the moment, began to fight for the independence of the country. In France the change came with the rise of the Resistance movement. The war had already become one for liberation when the United States came in, and hence its contribution began to share the character of the general enterprise. However, the nature of the bourgeois governments, the class character of their policies, did not change. Although the 'objective consequences' of their opposition to Hitlerism were progressive, their aims and motives remained imperialist throughout.

The policy of the Soviet Union was based upon a correct assessment of the anti-Soviet intentions of the imperialist states. In their conversations with the Soviet Union in 1939, the western states were merely attempting to conceal their concurrent efforts to arrange an alliance with Germany. The threat of a single imperialist bloc against the Soviet Union was averted by the acceptance of the German proposal for a non-aggression pact. By this 'outstanding' diplomatic victory the Soviet Union struck a blow at imperialism, strengthened the position of socialism and democracy throughout the world, and won valuable time to prepare for war.

This in general outline is the political framework in which the current Soviet interpretation of the war is set. Its effect has been to reinforce the traditional interpretations, and to give a darker shade to the colours in which the history of the Allied part in the war is presented.

The case against the United States, particularly, has been drawn tighter. In 1958 an account of the Munich negotiations presented the Americans as merely sympathetic bystanders, sharing the objectives of Chamberlain and Daladier, but unable to take a direct hand in the affair. The most recent official history by contrast concludes its account with the words: 'That was how the governments of the United States, Britain, and France staged the abominable farce.'[1]

Finally, the newer accounts carry a heavier embroidery of facts—evidence that Soviet history is beginning to recognize the need for a more plausible presentation of its interpretations than it has given in the past. The treatment of the Nazi-Soviet pact in the first volume of the new official history is illustrative. First, the amount of space devoted to the episode—four and a half pages of concentrated text—is in sharp contrast to the past practice of skipping lightly over this event. In three recent general histories covering the period, for example, the pact receives two and a half pages in the longest account and three sentences

[1] *Istoriya Velikoi Otechestvennoi voiny Sovetskovo Soyuza*, I, p. 152.

in the shortest.[1] More important, the new account is closely tied to a set of facts. For the first time in Soviet history, to the author's knowledge, the Astakhov-Weizsäcker exchanges are acknowledged. The first contact is placed in May, and the intiative is attributed to Germany. The course of the negotiations is presented as a drama of ardent pursuit on the part of the Germans and virtuous rejection on the part of the Soviet Union, with the latter defending its innocence to the last. But despite the sanctimonious tone, some impression of the course of the negotiations is conveyed. And in quoting Astakhov's report in mid-August that, in his opinion, the Germans were prepared to make declarations and gestures which 'a half-year back' would have appeared unthinkable, there is even a hint of the murkier background of exchanges which preceded the acknowledged ones. The novelty of the presentation is one of form, not of substance; the familiar rationalizations and justifications are offered. The Soviet action is presented as a *pis aller* necessitated by the nature of the last German offer. If it had been refused, war with Germany would have become unavoidable. Its acceptance, however, brought many favourable consequences, and to a large extent 'predetermined' the ultimate victory.

DISCUSSION

Dr Gallagher opened the discussion by explaining the approach he had taken to his subject: he examined Soviet historiography as an expression of the political purposes of the Soviet state, using it as a tool to aid our understanding of the Soviet Union as a political phenomenon. Describing developments which had taken place in the field of the history of the Second World War in the past few years, his paper sought to relate them to political decisions reflecting party and state interests.

The debate on Stalinist military history, which was initiated in the General Staff journal *Voennaya Mysl* and gathered momentum in 1955, reflected more than the desire of the party to discredit Stalin's doctrine on surprise attack. The spirit of root-and-branch revision informing the discussion pointed to the regime's intention to encourage the military to develop a more imaginative and self-reliant approach to their professional problems, in accordance with the new needs of the Soviet Union as a great power in the nuclear world.

The revision of military doctrine inevitably affected military history, since the doctrine was encased in the existing Soviet accounts of the war, and also because in the Soviet Union military theory and military history have always been closely related. The movement for more imaginative thinking in the military sphere, though primarily sponsored by military interests, had as its corollary greater professional initiative in this field of historical writing. The rejection of the former interpretation of German strategy in 1942 was an example of Soviet accounts being

---

[1] G. A. Deborin, *Vtoraya mirovaya voina* (Moscow, 1958); *Istoriya Kommunisticheskoi Partii Sovetskovo Soyuza* (Moscow, 1959); *Istoriya SSSR: epokha sotsializma* (Moscow, 1958).

brought into line with the facts, simply because the facts were inescapable and there was no compelling reason to suppress them.

Dr Gallagher stressed the particular interest of the history of the Soviet-German war—an embarrassing episode in the history of the party—as a tool for gauging Soviet political attitudes. To argue that the party had succeeded in disengaging itself from responsibility for the wartime errors by shifting the blame on to Stalin would be to underestimate the party's need to prove its historical legitimacy: the past can never be openly disowned, it has to be disguised or re-written. The resentment against the government and the party for the disasters which befell the country may have cooled but the bitterness voiced by some writers in 1956 and 1957 concerning the war suggested that this was still a delicate subject for the regime. He had devoted little attention to the political history of the war, because he thought the presentation of this had not changed substantially in the past ten years.

As regards method, the paper was concerned primarily with developments in the writing of history, rather than with the relationship of these developments to the facts. The judgement that the general trend in the domain of military history was towards a fuller and more accurate account of what really happened was founded on an analysis of the treatment of some of the major distortions propagated in the Stalinist period.

The doctrine of the counter-offensive provided an illuminating example. This doctrine, one of the major props upon which Stalin's reputation as a military genius rested, became one of the most prominent elements of the Stalinist interpretation of the early period of the war. Even serious military historians in the West had been persuaded by Soviet propaganda to assume that the counter-offensive was a genuine element of Soviet military thought during the war, whereas it actually became a part of official military theory only during the post-war period. The projection of this doctrine into the past entailed historical revaluations of Kutuzov's strategy in 1812: thus Tarle was attacked in 1951 and forced to revise his book *Napoleon's Invasion of Russia* in the light of the contemporary myth of a well-prepared counter-offensive. In his reply in *Voprosy Istorii*, Tarle promised that he would attempt to present to the Soviet reader the history of the war of 1812 'on the basis of the existing methodological instructions proceeding from that strategy which in the sight of our own generation led the army of the Soviet Union to the greatest victory in world history'. From the internal evolution of these concepts one could judge the general direction of Soviet history in this field: in relative terms, an improvement was noticeable both in the rejection of past fabrications, and in the greater amount of detail, citation of sources (now including foreign literature), and archive material made available.

Finally, Dr Gallagher drew attention to the materials published on the twentieth anniversary of the German attack. The new account of the Kiev battle in 1941 (given in Yeremenko's and Platonov's reviews of the new volume of the official history) represented an important revision, designed to absolve Khrushchev, who was the top political officer on the spot at the time, from responsibility for one of the greatest Soviet disasters of the war, in which the Germans claimed over half a million prisoners. Another important innovation revealed by the anniversary materials was the implication of Timoshenko in responsibility for the initial unpreparedness of the Soviet Union. Could this be linked with his removal a year before from the command of the Belorussian military district, and taken as a sign of the marshal's impending disgrace? It was unlikely that the revelation was prompted merely by regard for truth.

In conclusion, Dr Gallagher wondered whether the developments towards greater accuracy outlined in his paper could be explained by the fact that military history was in a somewhat different category from ordinary history, in that it engaged the interest of a special group at the highest political level with objectives and requirements which were distinct from those of the party.

Mr Schram commented on the Soviet treatment of the diplomatic origins of the war as illustrated in the first volume of the History of the War. A striking instance of destalinization was the paragraph on the eighteenth party congress and its decisions, in which the name of Stalin was not mentioned once, although it was Stalin's speech at this congress which initiated the new and ambiguous line in Soviet foreign policy. Three further points of detail illustrated the general problem of how changes in the international diplomatic situation might affect the way in which Soviet historians treated a particular period. The first concerned the appeal of Rakovsky, as President of the Soviet Government of the Ukraine, dated February 7, 1919, to Clemenceau, stating the Ukraine's claim to Bessarabia. The document as originally published included a paragraph which attacked the pogroms in Rumania and eloquently argued that under these conditions it was impossible to abandon Bessarabia to the Rumanians. This paragraph disappeared from the series of documents published in 1945, because at that moment it was in the interest of the Soviet Government to humour the Rumanian bourgeois Government of the day. It had now been restored in the new series of documents on foreign policy, obviously because the Soviets were no longer motivated by the same concern.

Another example was the incident of the La Croix telegram. Georges Bonnet published in his memoirs the text of a telegram he received from La Croix, French Minister in Prague, dated September 20, 1938, at a time when England and France were trying to persuade the Czech leaders to accept the terms agreed in conference between the Western Powers and Germany. According to Bonnet's evidence at the French parliamentary commission of inquiry after the war (cf. *Les événements survenus en France de 1933 à 1945*. Rapport au nom de la commission d'enquête parlementaire, II, Paris, 1951), La Croix said in his telegram that an emissary of Beneš had come to tell him that the Czech leaders were ready to yield, but wanted to be covered with regard to their own public opinion and requested that pressure be put on them so that they could show their hand had been forced. La Croix flatly denied this, accusing Bonnet of distorting his telegram by suppressing the first paragraph. The new Soviet History of the War cites the report of the French parliamentary commission of inquiry without any indication whatsoever that the evidence is contradictory, and opts unhesitatingly for the version which puts the blame squarely on Beneš and the Czechs. Mr Schram did not know whether this had something to do with the Soviet hatred for social-democrats, and their concern to bolster the position of the Czech communists by denigrating the bourgeois leaders of Czechoslovakia, or with the desire not to antagonize France too much at the present moment; but the point deserved attention.

Comparisons between the way the same events were treated in relatively scholarly writing (like the History discussed by Dr Gallagher) and in popular writing could lead to interesting conclusions. In this connection Mr Schram referred to a book by Borisov on Franco-Soviet relations and security in Europe, first published in 1955 and issued in an enlarged edition in 1960. Borisov again repeats the legend that in 1938 Stalin charged Gottwald to tell Beneš that the Soviet Union was ready to come to Czechoslovakia's defence, even if France did not march. This legend was already invalidated by the documents published in 1958 in Moscow and Prague on the twentieth anniversary of Munich, and it is not mentioned at all in the new History of the War, yet it continues to be propagated in a popular book like Borisov's. With regard to the negotiations leading to the Nazi-Soviet Pact and the recent Soviet admission that there were contacts as early as May, and not merely in August, as hitherto asserted by Soviet historians, Mr Schram agreed with Dr Gallagher that even though the new version bore little relation to the true sequence of events as set out in the German documents, it might help to erode falsehoods and myths and to sow doubts in the mind of the reader of a book such as that by Borisov. In any case, the new approach might yield some useful information to the western historian, as in the case of the Munich documents, which enabled us to refute the legend about Stalin's promise to Gottwald.

Dr Keep thought Dr Gallagher's paper prompted reflections about the methodology of western Sovietologists; because they tended to be preoccupied with the structure and nature of totalitarianism, they were led to follow the Soviet historian's own general emphasis on matters ideological and political, perhaps neglecting other avenues of approach. In deciding where to draw the line in various periods of Soviet history, it was important to strike the right balance between objective factors, i.e. external events, and internal events in the life of the party. Ninety-nine out of a hundred Soviet citizens over the age of thirty would say on the basis of their own experience that the beginning and end of the war were the most crucial dividing lines in the history of the Soviet Union—not only because of the vast destruction and suffering, but also because the war unleashed tremendous forces in Soviet society itself, weakening and undermining the controls exercised by the party. Soviet historians refused to recognize the existence of this phenomenon. Instead they emphasized the party's role to an extent quite out of proportion to reality.

It was curious to find that Soviet military historians were so much more realistic and factual than the party historians. In the West, military historians tended to be preoccupied more with detail and were, on the whole, more conservative in their approach than historians who had been influenced by the growth of interest in economics, sociology, etc. Dr Gallagher's paper revealed a very definite correlation between historiography and politics, in that, according to some observers, the military seemed to have attained a position of increased importance in the Soviet Union over the last three or four years as a result of the nuclear situation. (Although Zhukov's fall in 1957 was rightly interpreted as a stage in the assertion of the party's supremacy vis-à-vis the army, the importance of this one incident should not be overestimated.) Perhaps Dr Gallagher had even been a little conservative in evaluating the possibilities of the existence of a more or less autonomous school of military historiography.

Dr Katkov asked what historians were saying now about the Soviet pre-war thesis that the war was going to be fought on the enemy's territory. Was the argument being repeated that the Soviet defence had been neglected because the military were preparing for an offensive war? Khrushchev's 1956 revelations about Stalin's collapse during the battle of Moscow were partly borne out by the Soviet press and radio at the time, which in November-December 1941 mentioned Stalin's name less and less, while giving full credit to the defender of Moscow, Zhukov, and the generals who supported him, including Vlasov. Was this press material of the period being used by military historians and was the temporary collapse of Stalin noted? After the Moscow battle, Stalin seemed to have again taken an active part in preparing certain counter-offensive measures, such as the ill-fated operation of the Second Shock Army on the Volkhov river in April 1942, where Vlasov was taken prisoner, and the even more disastrous Kharkov operation. How were these events treated nowadays? On the political side, did the military historians show awareness of the sensation of elation, of liberation, which broke out in Russia in 1941 despite the invasion, as we knew from the statements of displaced persons after the war, as well as from Soviet literature during the thaw? A remarkable instance of the divergent views presented to the public was Nekrasov's book on Stalingrad, widely debated in 1955-6 as the most truthful representation of what the war was really like. Nekrasov took up the same theme again in 1958, in a travelogue of his journey through western Europe: in the form of an evocation of the big panorama of the battle which has now been built in Stalingrad, he voiced his thoughts on the falsifications of military history. In general, it was worth checking the literature inspired by the war with the specifically military sources.

Mr Schapiro asked whether Dr Gallagher could give the source of the circumstantial story which appeared in the new History of the CPSU about the secret negotiations which the British were supposed to have conducted with Hitler, while at the same time negotiating with Russia. Second, was there a deliberate and sustained build-up in the military history not only of Khrushchev, who in Mr Schapiro's view had been a very able political commissar at Stalingrad, but also of other people associated with him in that command? It seemed that Khrushchev was steadily promoting his own Stalingrad friends, as well as his personal military reputation.

Dr Gallagher wound up the discussion by answering some of the points raised. The spirit of liberation in Russia during the period of the initial German advances was a phenomenon reflected not only in Soviet literature after the thaw. It was indicated in the war-time speeches of Stalin, who fulminated against disorganizers of the rear, weak-willed people, etc., and in a number of literary accounts up to 1948, describing the defeatism of the population and their willingness to collaborate with the Germans. But in the official military histories there was no mention of it.

The first account of the defeat on the river Volkhov in April 1942, which seemed reasonably well related to the facts, appeared in the official military history, *The Second World War*, published in 1948 by the Ministry of Defence by a collective of authors and edited by Platonov. It did not go into detail and was by no means a complete record, but it admitted that there had been a defeat and ascribed this to the treachery of Vlasov. There was nothing in the Soviet accounts about the weakness of the Soviet defences in the initial stage of the war being due to expectations that the war would be an offensive war. The question of Stalin's failure of will at the time of the battle of Moscow was, of course, brought out very vividly in Khrushchev's secret speech. One could see confirmation of this in Stalin's request to the British, in September 1941, to send an expeditionary force to Russia—a very singular thing for him to have done. For when military help was offered later on, at the time of Stalingrad, this was interpreted by the Russians as an attempt on the part of the Anglo-Saxon powers to occupy Russia and was rejected on those grounds.

Concerning the alleged negotiations between the British and the Germans during the spring and early summer of 1939, the account in the History of the CPSU seemed to be a reference to conversations which took place in London at that time between Wohltat, the commissioner of the German four-year plan, Wilson, a close confidant of Chamberlain, and Hudson, of the Board of Trade. The Russians alleged that these were concerned with spheres of influence, etc. They had first been mentioned in Soviet accounts around 1948.

As to the rise in the fortunes of the military group associated with Khrushchev during the war, Dr Garthoff, an expert in this field, had suggested that a distinction should be drawn between the so-called southern group (Chuikov, Yeremenko, etc.) and the headquarters group (Zhukov, Vasilevsky) in Moscow. It did seem that as the generals of the southern group had prospered in the train of Khrushchev, their reputations were rising too, although it should not be forgotten that a man like Chuikov had always enjoyed a high reputation as the hero of Stalingrad.

On the question of the independent role of the military Dr Gallagher preferred to be cautious. He thought that if the military enjoyed a certain degree of independence, this would be more likely to show up in internal policy than in foreign policy. For instance, at the time of Khrushchev's rise in 1954-5, when there was a dispute over the priority of heavy or light industry, the military joined forces with Khrushchev, because they were opposed to Malenkov's consumer goods policy and in particular to his plan of drawing on the strategic reserves. There was an ingrained institutional interest of the military in maintaining investments in heavy industry, because this sector of the economy was the source of armaments. It was conceivable therefore that Khrushchev's recent shift of emphasis in this field would be resisted by the military. However, it was doubtful that they could impose their will effectively.

XI. Diplomacy in the Mirror of Soviet Scholarship

VERNON V. ASPATURIAN

During the Stalinist era international politics and diplomacy were matters reserved exclusively for the Politburo. A regime of fabrication and stultification descended upon Soviet scholarship and all journals and books dealing with foreign policy. Works on diplomacy implicitly bore the imprimatur, not merely of official tolerance, but of quasi-official inspiration. For each subject, an official textbook was the rule, which was invariably superseded by another work, usually a symposium, in accordance with changes in policy. General texts on international relations, Soviet foreign policy, and international organization were virtually non-existent. Specialized monographs on international legal subjects and official textbooks on international law pre-empted the field.

The two general reference works on diplomacy, the *Diplomatic Dictionary* in two volumes, and the three-volume *History of Diplomacy*, edited in both cases by active or retired officials of the Soviet Foreign Ministry, constituted the *summa theologica* of Stalinist scholarship on diplomacy.[1] By way of documentation, there was a collection of treaties published annually and a handy series of compilations of Soviet foreign policy documents, which ceased publication around 1950. Since the writing of a textbook on Soviet foreign policy was only slightly less hazardous than writing a history of the party, not a single scholar could be found to undertake the task, and no comprehensive account of Soviet foreign policy was in fact published. The only book on the United Nations was an innocuously descriptive volume by S. B. Krylov, published in 1946.[2] As surrogates for scholarship there was a profusion of tendentious propaganda booklets paying tribute to Stalin's genius as a statesman.

The special risks involved were dramatized by the fate of one of the chief editors of Volume I of the *Diplomatic Dictionary* (published in 1948), S. A. Lozovsky, an old Comintern functionary and a former Deputy Commissar of Foreign Affairs, who vanished just before the appearance of the second volume in 1950, in which he was not even

[1] *Diplomaticheskii slovar*, I, edited by A. Y. Vyshinsky and S. A. Lozovsky (Moscow, 1948); II, edited by A. Y. Vyshinsky (Moscow, 1950). *Istoriya diplomatii*, 3 vols., edited by V. P. Potemkin (Moscow, 1945).

[2] S. B. Krylov, *Materialy k istorii Organizatsii Obedinennykh Natsii* (Moscow, 1946).

given an entry. His dismal end was officially recorded in the second edition of the *Large Soviet Encyclopedia* (Vol. 51, p. 180).

Things started to change soon after Stalin's death. In 1954 the Soviet journal *Mezhdunarodnaya Zhizn* was revived, and while its contents did not materially deviate from the Stalinist tradition, its appearance alone was a welcome innovation. (A journal with the same title was published in the twenties as an organ of Narkomindel.) It was the twentieth party congress, however, which relieved Soviet scholarship of the Stalinist incubus. Characteristically, the party leaders blamed the intellectuals for the deficiencies and stagnation of Soviet scholarship and rebuked them for not taking a more imaginative and active role in discussing international relations and contemporary history, and for failing to demonstrate more courage in resisting the fabrications of the Stalinist era.[1] The depressing state of affairs was revealed in a series of letters to the editors of *Mezhdunarodnaya Zhizn* in 1956-7,[2] which read like a carefully rehearsed five-year plan in which scholars, publishers, and propagandists exchanged mutual recriminations and confessions of negligence in a mood of inspired self-criticism.

The first letter was submitted by four distinguished scholars, headed by the veteran jurist Yevgeny Korovin, in which the publishing house Gospolitizdat was censured for publishing only propaganda to the exclusion of serious works of scholarship on foreign policy, and the journal itself reprimanded for not demanding higher standards from its contributors:

We are of the opinion that the necessary stimulation of research work on the study of current world affairs is proceeding too slowly. Evidence of this is to be found above all in the fact that new and original scholarly works of research into the most important current international problems are not being published . . . We find that popular booklets on general themes occupy the dominant position . . . Actually no monographs on the basic problems in world affairs are available . . . Furthermore, books on general political subjects, history, economics and, law are reviewed very irregularly in our periodicals. So far there has not been a single work of any importance . . . generalizing and offering a scientific evaluation of the activities of the UN and its agencies. The present paucity of reference works on international economic and political problems is impermissible. Why, for example, have we no works of biographical reference containing information on the political figures of various countries, no scientifically edited and systematically published editions of documents of foreign powers, no reference books dealing with political parties and government bodies, no year-books of world events, such as are very widespread abroad, etc?[3]

[1] Cf. the speeches by A. I. Mikoyan and Madame A. Pankratova.

[2] *International Affairs*, 1956, No. 12, pp. 98-9; 1957, No. 1, pp. 159-68; No. 2, pp. 133-6.

[3] *International Affairs*, 1956, No. 12, pp. 98-9. The letter was also signed by Academician A. Guber and Professors N. Lyubimov and A. Manfred.

The four scholars went on to urge that 'the teaching of the history of international relations and international law in higher educational institutions . . . be radically improved'. Existing courses, they noted, 'devote too little attention to questions of the history of diplomacy'.

The letter elicited two responses in the next issue, one from S. Mayorov, the head of the Department of Literature on International Problems of Gospolitizdat, and another from I. Ivashin, head of the faculty of International Relations of the Higher Party School, whose sacred cows had been attacked by Korovin and company. Mayorov, recognizing true inspiration, responded with reluctant but equally inspired agreement. The charge was accurate but the target was a case of mistaken identity. The real culprits were the scholars themselves, who refused to produce suitable manuscripts.

We applied to all the appropriate research institutes . . . and the higher educational establishments with departments of international relations and general history, requesting that they inform us of their plans for research . . . The result was a great disappointment, for very little of the material offered could be included in our publication plan.

The scholars, it seemed, under the spell of some strange malady or subject to equally strange idiosyncrasies, were eminently uninterested in current problems of international relations and organizations, but were enamoured of 'topics dealing with the past'. The deficiencies in the area of Soviet foreign policy were truly monumental and just short of scandalous. 'The most serious shortcoming,' Mayorov asserted, 'in the work of research institutes and university departments studying international affairs . . . is the absolutely unsatisfactory state of the study of Soviet foreign policy, its history, and relations between the USSR and other countries.' Not a single scholar in the Institute of History of the Academy of Sciences—the *sanctum sanctorum* of Soviet scholarship— was engaged in the study of Soviet foreign policy, and its 'research programmes for 1955 and 1956 did not contain a single Soviet foreign policy topic and not a single such topic was studied'. Even more reprehensible, 'the institute does not train any experts in this field. Not a single post-graduate submitted or even prepared a thesis on Soviet foreign policy.'

Comrade Ivashin's reply was less humble and in some respects positively aggressive. Whereas Korovin and company were disturbed by the rate at which scholars and scholarship were being displaced by hacks and propaganda tracts 'on peaceful co-existence', Ivashin castigated the scholars for producing works that were worthless for the propagandist. 'They indiscriminately censure all booklets on the peaceful co-existence of the two systems,' he complained, and in turn exacted his vengeance by gratuitously noting that a recent article by Korovin 'is an example of a careless attitude to the reader . . . evidently composed in a hurry and . . . nothing but a compilation of sentences and facts covering a period of forty years.' He went on:

At the present time there are almost no educational establishments to train qualified propagandists in the field of international affairs. Humanity departments of higher schools either offer no courses on international affairs whatsoever or make these courses purely optional. Unfortunately, in 1956 the course on international relations and Soviet foreign policy was dropped from the curriculum of republican, territorial, and inter-regional party schools where many propagandists receive their training . . . Great anxiety is caused by the fact that current history (the most important and vital part of general history) is not taught at all in secondary schools and is only touched upon in the part of the syllabus covering the post-October period of the history of the USSR. Thus, knowledge of the most important contemporary events abroad is kept from millions of young people. Our historians should be ashamed of the fact that we have no textbooks on current history. A number of works on general history are carried only as far as 1917.

Sarcastically, he noted that 'work on a world history has been going on for about twenty years but so far only Volume I has been completed'.

It was now time for the historians and the provincial constituencies to be heard from. Professor Galkin, head of the Modern History Department of Moscow University, in turn accused the publishing houses 'of converting scholarly papers into popular, or at best popular science booklets, a practice which does not attract serious authors'.[1] Furthermore, 'repeated abridgements of history books have transformed them into a compendium of titles and brief sociological generalizations [in which] . . . history has been deprived of its pulse'. Conceding that 'training of post-graduates in the field of international relations has been stopped', he announced proudly that his department at least had one post-graduate in this subject.

This was the state of Soviet scholarship and teaching in the field of international relations and diplomacy some years ago. Since then, however, a veritable avalanche of books, monographs, symposia, reference works, and documentary collections has poured forth from Soviet universities, research institutes, and publishing houses, on all types of international and diplomatic subjects. In 1957 there appeared the first history of Soviet foreign policy, produced by Ivashin's Higher Party School, which was almost immediately attacked and criticized by other scholars for its superficiality.[2] A lively discussion on Soviet foreign

---

[1] Letters from Professors Galkin and M. Yanovsky (Assistant Professor, Tashkent State University) are in *International Affairs*, 1957, No. 2.

[2] *Istoriya mezhdunarodnykh otnoshenii i vneshnei politiki SSSR 1870-1957 gg.* (Moscow, 1957). An earlier outline, *Mezhdunarodnye otnosheniya i vneshnyaya politika SSSR 1917-1941 gg.*, had been published in 1955 for use in military academies.

policy ensued in the pages of *Mezhdunarodnaya Zhizn* in 1958-9,[1] and dozens of works on Soviet foreign policy alone have been published since 1957.[2] The number of books and monographs on other aspects of diplomacy run into hundreds, including numerous translations of western books.

The recent output is distinguished by its relatively high level of scholarship, sophisticated approach to ideological questions, and its varied use of foreign publications, though these are selected from among those western works which either present the Soviet position in a sympathetic light or represent extremely hostile positions which seem to confirm Soviet preconceptions and expectations of 'bourgeois' behaviour. Tendentious and stereotyped propaganda tracts, shorn of the more vulgar excrescences of the Stalinist era, continue to appear, but with diminishing frequency, and they must now compete for attention with the output of genuine scholars.

The publication of documents was inaugurated with the annual series of *Documents on Soviet Foreign Policy*, the first volume of which appeared in 1957.[3] In contrast to Stalinist practice, documents signed by former Soviet luminaries later consigned to oblivion appear with their original signatures. Soviet scholars and the Soviet public can now see for themselves the important parts played by personalities such as Trotsky, Krylenko, Joffe, Kamenev, Shlyapnikov, Karakhan, Rakovsky, Sokolnikov, and others during the early days of Soviet diplomacy, without benefit of gratuitous annotations explaining their subsequent 'treason'.

The change creates problems of adjustment for non-Soviet observers of the scene. Under Stalin, there was nothing to study but speeches by Stalin, Molotov, and their minions, the pages of *Pravda*, *Izvestiya*, and *Bolshevik*, and the few quasi-official texts and reference works on international law and diplomacy. Virtually anything in print could be safely assumed to be an expression of official attitudes. Things are different now. Books, periodicals, and even newspapers can no longer be accepted as automatic expressions of official thinking; increasingly they represent the views of individual authors writing within the bounds of official latitude, which are relatively broad and allow for considerable variation on a single ideological theme.

While the official textbook seems to be a relic of the past, the conceptual framework which is common to all Soviet scholars remains fixed in its essentials. It is the identical ideology which governed during the Stalinist period, but shorn of its excesses, rigidities, and dogmatic

[1] *International Affairs*, 1958, No. 2, pp. 63-70; No. 5, pp. 71-5; No. 7, pp. 59-64; No. 8, pp. 65-71.

[2] For a list of recent Soviet works on international relations, cf. the 400-page bibliographical handbook compiled by V. Yegorov, *Mezhdunarodnye otnosheniya: bibliograficheskii spravochnik: 1945-1960* (Moscow, 1961). Not a single work by Stalin is listed, although speeches and articles by Lenin and Khrushchev appear in profusion.

[3] *Dokumenty vneshnei politiki SSSR* (Moscow, 1957—in progress).

sterility. Even the new editions of the *Diplomatic Dictionary* and the *History of Diplomacy*, whose first volumes have appeared, will not enjoy the official standing of their predecessors, although they, too, are being compiled by a group of active and retired diplomats and distinguished scholars.[1] The announcement on the *History of Diplomacy* promised that 'great care will be taken to preserve the first edition's popular presentation, laconic style, and profoundly scholarly exposition.'[2] It is still too early to say whether this is a promise or a threat.

Soviet scholarship on international relations and diplomacy has been further enhanced by the resurrection of old research institutes and the creation of new ones. Within the Soviet Academy of Sciences, not only the Institute of History, but the new Institute of World Economics and International Relations,[3] and the Soviet International Law Association conduct research on international and diplomatic matters, while under the central committee both the Academy of Social Sciences and the Higher Party School sponsor quasi-scholarly works on diplomatic history and contemporary international relations. *Mezhdunarodnaya Zhizn* is published by the All-Union Society for the Dissemination of Political and Scientific Knowledge, but seems actually to be a quasi-official organ of the Soviet Foreign Ministry.

The teaching of international relations and modern history in universities, pedagogical institutes, and other establishments of higher learning has also experienced a renaissance since the twentieth CPSU congress, and in recent years many conferences on international relations, law and organization, and diplomatic historiography in general, have been held.

Soviet diplomatic scholarship operates within ideological limits set by Marxist-Leninist theoretical conceptions of diplomacy. For Marx and Engels, as for Lenin, diplomacy was essentially a bourgeois institution, either inappropriate or superfluous for a proletarian state. According to Trotsky, when the Bolsheviks met to organize their first government and the question of foreign relations was raised, Lenin exclaimed: 'What, are we going to have foreign relations?' And upon his own appointment as the first Foreign Commissar, Trotsky announced: 'I will issue a few revolutionary proclamations and then close up shop.'[4]

The failure of the world revolution to exfoliate according to expectations and the *de facto* survival of the Soviet state in a hostile world

---

[1] *Diplomaticheskii slovar*, edited by A. A. Gromyko, S. A. Golunsky and V. M. Khvostov, I (Moscow, 1960); II (1961). *Istoriya diplomatii*, edited by V. A. Zorin, V. S. Semenov, S. D. Skazkin and V. M. Khvostov, I (Moscow, 1959).

[2] *International Affairs*, 1958, No. 7, p. 115.

[3] Its monthly publication is *Mirovaya Ekonomika i Mezhdunarodnye Otnosheniya*. The institute continues the work of Varga's Institute of World Politics and World Economics, which was dissolved in 1949, as was its publication, *Mirovoe Khozyaistvo i Mirovaya Politika*.

[4] Leon Trotsky, *Moya zhizn* (Berlin, 1930), II, p. 64. Cf. L. Trotsky, *My Life* (New York, 1930), p. 341.

forced the Bolsheviks to re-appraise diplomacy as a means of conducting foreign relations with capitalist powers during the period of co-existence. Initially, Soviet diplomacy was overtly connected with the espionage, subversion, and propaganda carried on by the regime, but after 1924 the bulk of these operations was shifted to the Comintern and other agencies.

Soviet writers, like their western counterparts, draw a distinction between foreign policy and diplomacy, but also concede that frequently the two are confused and, indeed, at times barely distinguishable. Like the state itself, foreign policy and diplomacy are pre-determined and shaped by the structure of society, the nature of its inner conflicts, and the interests of its ruling classes.

I. D. Levin, in his book *Diplomatic Immunity*, defines foreign policy as:

a combination of the aims and interests pursued and defended by the given state and its ruling class in its relations with other states, and the methods and means it uses to achieve and defend these purposes and interests. The aims and interests of a state in international relations are realized by various methods and means: first of all, by peaceful official relations, maintained by a government, through its special agencies, with the corresponding agencies of other states, by economic, cultural, and other contacts, maintained by state agencies, as well as by public and private institutions (economic, political, scientific, religious, etc.), which provide a state with wide opportunities for exercising economic, political and ideological influence on other states; finally by using armed force, i.e. by war or other methods of armed coercion.[1]

This definition is unusually broad and frank, and would include, among other Soviet devices, the activities of foreign communist parties, the Comintern, Cominform, and cultural exchanges as instruments of Soviet foreign policy; although the *Diplomatic Dictionary*, Volume I of which appeared in the same year as Levin's monograph, carefully eschews any references to the activities of foreign communist parties or the Comintern in the long entry on 'Soviet Foreign Policy'. Diplomacy, however, Levin views more narrowly:

Diplomacy, on the other hand, is precisely the kind of state activity which consists in realizing the foreign policy aims and interests of a state by means of official relations maintained by a government, its special agencies, both within its own state and abroad, in the form of negotiations, correspondence, agreements, etc. Thus, the concept of diplomacy does not cover the concept of foreign policy, but is a part of it. Diplomacy is a method or means of foreign policy of states, and alongside it there exist other methods and means . . . Diplomacy is not merely one

[1] I. D. Levin, *Diplomaticheskii immunitet* (Moscow, 1949), pp. iv-v. Cf. also I. D. Levin, 'On the Question of the Concept of Diplomacy', *Sovetskoe Gosudarstvo i Pravo*, 1948, No. 9.

of the methods of foreign policy. Among all the methods of foreign policy, it is of primary importance in times of peace, and usually dominates over other methods, or their successful application depends upon it. The history of the diplomacy of slave-owning, feudal, and capitalist states reveals that diplomacy prepares for wars, trying to create an advantageous correlation of forces, to secure allies and to isolate the future enemy by the time war begins. Diplomacy completes wars by striving to secure the fruits of victory with the greatest possible advantage, or to mitigate the consequences of defeat . . . The correlation between foreign policy and diplomacy may to a certain extent be compared with the correlation between strategy and tactics.[1]

The Soviet view that diplomacy is inseparable from, and incapable of rising above the class character of the state and society which it represents, provides a deeper insight into its inner workings and functions than the views held in the West by the traditional practitioners of diplomacy. The Soviet concept is inextricably linked to the general socio-historical categories of Marxism, and differs from western notions in being overtly rooted in a systematic philosophy of social norms and objectives which not only inspire and guide the policies and diplomacy of the Soviet state, but in fact transcend them. What Soviet writers and statesmen consider to be the chief source of Soviet diplomatic successes is precisely what continues to baffle veteran western diplomats. Confronted with the arrogant assertion by Professor Tarle in Volume III of the *History of Diplomacy*, that 'Soviet diplomacy . . . wields a weapon possessed by none of its rivals or opponents . . . the scientific theory of Marxism-Leninism',[2] Sir Harold Nicolson wrote:

You will have observed that in these lectures I have made but slight reference to the diplomacy of the Soviet Union. Mr W. P. Potjomkin [V. P. Potemkin], in his History of Diplomacy, assured us that the Russians possess one powerful weapon denied to their opponents— namely 'the scientific dialectic of the Marx-Lenin formula'. I have not observed as yet that this dialectic has improved international relationships, or that the Soviet diplomatists and commissars have evolved any system of negotiation that might be called a diplomatic system. Their activity in foreign countries or at international conferences is formidable, disturbing, compulsive. I do not for one moment underestimate either its potency or its danger. But it is not diplomacy: it is something else.[3]

Nicolson's contempt for Soviet diplomacy derives from the misplaced

[1] Ibid., pp. v-vi. For virtually identical conceptions, cf. 'Diplomacy', in *Diplomaticheskii slovar*, I (1948), pp. 569-91. On the relationship between foreign policy and diplomacy and their theoretical constructs in general, no significant difference exists between the Stalinist period and the post-Stalinist. Cf. 'Diplomacy', in *Diplomaticheskii slovar*, I (1960), pp. 457-68.

[2] *Istoriya diplomatii*, III, p. 764.

[3] Sir Harold Nicolson, *The Evolution of Diplomatic Method* (London and New York, 1954), p. 90.

notion that the function of diplomacy is to improve international relationships, and since the dialectic has not contributed to this objective, it must perforce be worthless. The value of the dialectic to Soviet diplomats is indeed formidable, for it provides them with an integrated scheme of analysis and prognostication which, while frequently out of focus with reality and far from being as scientific as they claim, is at any rate an effective system of analysis and strategy in terms of Soviet objectives.

The frequent assertion by western diplomats and scholars alike that the so-called laws of the dialectic have little or no application to foreign policy and constitute a sort of ritualistic mumbo-jumbo, is a dangerous self-deception. In fact, the entire structure of the Soviet image of reality and international politics rests upon a dialectical analysis which furnishes Soviet decision-makers and diplomats with analytical categories, creates for them an integrated ordering of events, relating them to each other, no matter how widely dispersed in time and space, and co-ordinates the effects of the various and sundry conflicts within individual countries as well as the world as a whole. Through dialectical analysis, Soviet statesmen and diplomats see events and forces in motion and interrelation, not statically and in isolation; measure their direction and tempo; and above all are able to mobilize the energies of a world in ferment and movement, transmuting them into political power, subjecting them to the manipulation of Soviet policy. In short, Marxism-Leninism is a framework for the analysis, mobilization, and manipulation of social and political power under a variety of conditions and circumstances. Thus, according to a recent Soviet appraisal:

The foreign policy of socialism is based on science and founded on the only correct science of society, the theory of Marxism-Leninism . . . Marxism is a reliable compass for understanding reality and reconstructing society in a revolutionary manner in accordance with socialist principles. The strength of Marxism-Leninism lies in the fact that it gives the communist party and the Soviet state the possibility of discovering the objective laws of the historical process, of steering the correct course in accordance with the internal and external situation, of understanding the inner connection between events and of ascertaining not only how and in what direction events are developing in the present, but also how and in what direction they will develop in the future . . . However, the mere understanding of the objective laws of social development, and in particular of international relations, is not in itself sufficient to determine the correct course in foreign policy by which major victories can be won. The decisive source of the strength or weakness of foreign policy, of its historical prospects or lack of prospects, is the correlation of that policy and social progress, its conformity or non-conformity to the laws of development.

On the other hand, in the Soviet view, western diplomacy relies upon chance, personalities, opportunism, adventurism, sentimentalism and other subjective factors for its successes, and correspondingly attributes diplomatic failures to similar factors, over which western diplomats claim to have little control or understanding:

The bourgeois press attempts to explain the failure of imperialist foreign policy by psychological factors, individual features and miscalculations of certain bourgeois statesmen and diplomats, by the greed and envy of some of them, by 'communist propaganda' and the like. Thus Adlai Stevenson . . . maintains that the crisis of American foreign policy 'has its seat in the minds and hearts of Americans'. Some American bourgeois historians put themselves out to prove, for instance, that it was Truman's 'stinginess' in subsidizing the Chiang Kai-shek clique, Marshall's 'inflexibility', etc., that resulted in the defeat of American policy in China. But such arguments are untenable, for their authors, basing themselves on idealist conceptions, consider individual defeats and also the crisis of imperialist foreign policy in isolation from the acute and profound crisis of the whole capitalist system.'[1]

Now, it may be argued, and frequently is, that the 'scientific' discovery of 'contradictions' in international politics is a spurious claim, since contradictions are neither more nor less than conflicting state or national interests, such has have existed for ages, and that the Soviet exploitation of rivalries among their adversaries is a technique as hoary as politics itself. Even if this is true, the Soviets would not claim to have either discovered these conflicts or invented the device of exploiting them for diplomatic advantage. What distinguishes the Soviet view is that these conflicts are seen in qualitatively different dimensions, and in a condition of dynamic flux, moving to a foreordained conclusion, rather than being chance or fortuitous occurrences. Thus, whereas the traditional function of diplomacy is to seek adjustment, accommodation, and even the resolution of these conflicts to the maximum advantage of the state concerned, these conflicts are viewed by the Soviets as irreconcilable; the function of diplomacy is to facilitate a resolution by bringing about the annihilation, liquidation, absorption, or submission of one pole of the contradiction. The dialectical approach to international politics, furthermore, goes deeper than an examination of state or national interests in conflict; it seeks to uncover the more profound, passionate, and explosive animosities and resentments of social classes and submerged populations, which Soviet diplomacy then attempts to manipulate to its own advantage. It provides a scheme for relating conflicts in foreign policy to internal social conflicts, and for ordering these contradictions into a coherent frame, establishing priorities, differentiating and arranging them into social and power

---

[1] M. Airapetyan and G. Deborin, 'Foreign Policy and Social Progress', *International Affairs*, 1959, No. 2.

equations which can be added, subtracted, multiplied or divided as the occasion demands or the opportunity arises.

We can brush aside the claim that Marxist-Leninist dialectics constitutes the only valid scheme of analysis, but it is not so easy to ignore its effectiveness as a basis for action. Historical inevitability and scientifically derived laws of social change may indeed be intellectual residues of the nineteenth century, little more than sophisticated and sophistic nonsense, but this misses the main point. Reality, in whatever dimension, is plastic, and while its transformations may not be predetermined, the implacable voluntarism of fanatics determined to realize what they say is inevitable, may render the difference between 'objective inevitability' and the 'self-fulfilling prophecy' irrelevant; for no matter how successfully they may be distinguished in the intellectual processes of the mind, the distinctions in terms of consequences in the world of reality are essentially nil. A purely intellectual critique of Marxism inevitably wins the theoretical battle and loses the war on the plains of reality.

All theories of reality are approximations and can to a certain degree influence the development of reality in the direction desired by their sponsors; and a serious examination of Marxism-Leninism, not as a 'science', but simply as a mundane theory of reality, particularly as it applies to international politics, is long overdue. Its effectiveness as a guide to policy is necessarily relative, since it must be measured against the effectiveness of corresponding analytical systems employed by others. A true measure of its validity requires it to be compared, not with the great profusion of theories, models, systems, processes, and games devised by western scholars, but with comparable theories of reality and analysis employed by western statesmen and diplomats, whether implicit or explicit, eclectic or synthetic, ad hoc or systematic, pragmatic or dogmatic, empirical or a priori.

Soviet ideology is not simply a conglomeration of abstract norms, but an ideology cemented to state power, providing a framework for the execution of Soviet foreign policy. Consequently, whether it is, in fact, superior or inferior to the array of analytical devices contrived by western professors is almost totally irrelevant, unless, of course, they eventually enjoy the same relationship to state power as does Marxism-Leninism. The pertinent question is not: 'is Marxism-Leninism a science?', which has diverted attention from the real issue, but: 'how effective is it in providing Soviet leaders with a map of international reality, enabling them to see their way through the complicated and bewildering maze of events to their objectives, as compared with the effectiveness of the maps of reality implicitly or explicitly employed by their western counterparts?' Furthermore, in assessing the past forty years, have the expectations of the Soviet Union in world affairs, based upon the insights gained from their ideological prism, been more or less accurately fulfilled than those of their enemies?

Really, the Soviet leaders had little more than this map of reality called dialectics as a surrogate for experience, but it served their purpose and yielded immense returns, against heavy odds, within the span of a single generation. Like the hedgehog of the Greek poet, Archilochus, Soviet diplomacy 'knows one big thing', while the western foxes 'know many things', none of which, so far at any rate, has been able to cope with the one big thing that Soviet diplomacy knows. Since the Soviet dialectic has been so effective during moments of weakness in Soviet history, is it any wonder that Soviet leaders remain even more convinced of its 'scientific' character, now that their country is so strong?

A fundamental redistribution of power has taken place more or less in accordance with Soviet expectations. While Soviet predictions have not been borne out in all particulars and the record has been marked by reverses, defeats, and retreats, the overall pattern of expectations has been depressingly favourable. Thus, the following general expectations have been substantially realized: (1) The western world has shrunk in power, influence, and territory; (2) The United States has emerged as the leader of the western world; (3) The colonial empires have disintegrated in response to movements for independence supported by the Soviet Union; and (4) The communist world has expanded in territory and in power at the expense of the western world.

Thus, when we compare the balance-sheet to date of the 'successes' and 'defeats' of Soviet foreign policy, it is indisputable that the net balance is heavily weighted in favour of the Soviet Union and/or Soviet communism. In less than fifty years, Soviet communism has grown from an obscure Russian conspiratorial sect into a distinctive world civilization embracing more than a dozen states with a combined population of nearly one billion people, occupying about one-third of the earth's land surface. Communist parties, large and small, growing and diminishing, conspiratorial and legal, exist in seventy-five countries and command substantial electorates in France, Italy, Indonesia, and India. Soviet power and influence have intruded into South-east Asia, Africa, and Latin America, where only two decades ago the western powers were in complete control.

The Marxist view of diplomacy was summed up by Engels in 1890 in his essay on 'The Foreign Policy of Russia's Tsars', which was specifically restricted to the diplomacy of Imperial Russia and not to 'bourgeois' diplomacy in general.[1] The fate of this essay in Stalin's Russia is itself a commentary on the state of diplomatic history there. Although the essay was included in the Russian edition of the collected works of Marx and Engels, it did not have wide circulation. In 1934, the editors of *Bolshevik* naïvely planned to reprint the essay in a special issue, but were overruled by Stalin. In a letter dated July 19, 1934, but not made public until May 1941, Stalin criticized Engels for exaggerating the role of Tsarist Russia as the 'bulwark of European reaction', assigning it a

---

[1] Cf. K. Marx and F. Engels, *The Russian Menace to Europe*, edited by Bert Hoselitz and Paul W. Blackstock (Glencoe, 1952) for an English translation of Engels' essay.

monopoly in the 'policy of conquest' and imparting to its diplomacy a unique venality, which seemed to transcend history, classes, and ideology as the inseparable characteristic of an 'eternal' Russia.[1]

If Engels was correct, Stalin noted, then 'it must be clear that war, let us say, between bourgeois Germany and Tsarist Russia is not an imperialist war, not a war of plunder, but a war of liberation or almost of liberation'. As for the implication that a policy of conquest was 'a monopoly of the Tsars', Stalin said:

Everyone knows that a policy of conquest was also characteristic . . . of the kings and diplomats of all the countries of Europe, including an emperor of such a bourgeois cast as Napoleon, who . . . successfully practised intrigue, deceit, perfidy, flattery, atrocities, bribery, murder and arson in foreign policy. Obviously it could not be otherwise.

What apparently infuriated Stalin was Engels' grudging admiration for the unparalleled mendacity and effectiveness of Tsarist diplomacy, which, to give the devil his due, justified Stalin's observation that it was 'un-Marxist' in its analysis.

'One might get the impression,' Stalin wrote caustically, 'that in Russian history and foreign policy diplomacy was everything, while Tsars, feudal lords, merchants and other social groups counted for nothing or almost nothing,' and added that, far from being peculiarly Tsarist, 'perfidy, treachery, bribery . . . and similar "qualities" of diplomacy . . . are the characteristic sores of any . . . capitalist diplomacy'.

Apart from any anxiety that Engels' description of Tsarist diplomacy might appear too close an approximation to his own, the re-publication of the essay would have needlessly compromised Stalin's planned resurrection of Russian nationalism and the retrospectively re-interpreted 'progressive' character of Imperial Russian expansion, which came to dominate Soviet historiography.

Even before the revolution, Stalin's image of diplomacy had crystallized into its characteristic form. In a speech made in 1913 he said:

A diplomat's words must have no relation to action—otherwise what kind of diplomacy is it? Words are one thing, actions another . . . Sincere diplomacy is no more possible than dry water or iron wood.[2]

As a synonym for deceit, diplomacy was not restricted to foreign policy but was frequently employed by Stalin to characterize the speeches and actions of his critics and opponents, who were charged with being 'diplomatic and insincere'. At a conference of the party, held in 1923, he said:

One report diverged very widely from reality . . . It was not even a

---

[1] J. V. Stalin, 'On Engels' Article, "The Foreign Policy of Russian Tsarism",' *Bolshevik*, 1941, No. 9.

[2] Stalin, *Sochineniya* (Moscow, 1946), II, p. 277.

report, it was sheer diplomacy, for everything that is bad . . . was obscured, glossed over, whereas everything that glitters on the surface and strikes the eye was pushed into the foreground, for display . . . I think that we have gathered at this conference not for the purpose of playing at diplomacy with one another, of making eyes at one another, while surreptitiously trying to lead one another by the nose, but for the purpose of telling the whole truth.[1]

In Stalin's mind, this identification of diplomacy with deceit persisted until his death in 1953. At Yalta, for example, Stalin expansively ruminated with Churchill:

I am talking as an old man; that is why I am talking so much. But I want to drink to our alliance that it should not lose its character of intimacy, of its true expression of views. . . . In an alliance the allies should not deceive each other. Perhaps that is naïve? Experienced diplomatists may say: 'Why should I not deceive my ally?' But I as a naïve man may think it is best not to deceive my ally even if he is a fool. Possibly our alliance is so firm just because we do not deceive each other; or is it because it is not so easy to deceive each other?[2]

Theoretically, of course, in identifying diplomacy with deceit, Stalin was characterizing 'bourgeois' diplomacy and 'bourgeois' behaviour, but since Soviet diplomacy before the war was necessarily restricted to diplomatic contact with the capitalist world, it was forced into the same mould, for, in the words of the late dictator, it would be 'naïve to preach morality to people who do not recognize morality. Politics is politics, say the old, hardbitten bourgeois diplomats.'[3] Whereas deceit and deception were appropriate in dealing with the 'class enemy', they were not suitable forms of behaviour for communists, whose relations, according to Stalin, would be governed by absolute respect for sincerity, truth, trust, and confidence. According to this peerless master of simulation and dissimulation:

Either we are Leninists, and our relations one with another as well as relations with the sections with the Comintern, and vice versa, must be built on mutual confidence, must be as clean and pure as crystal—in which case there should be no room in our ranks for rotten diplomatic intrigue; or we are not Leninists.[4]

Implicitly, of course, relations based upon mutual trust and confidence would continue to prevail once other communist parties came to power in their own countries creating a new socialist type of diplomacy which

[1] Ibid., p. 338; cf. also pp. 331, 312.
[2] Winston Churchill, *Triumph and Tragedy* (Cambridge, 1953), pp. 362-363.
[3] J. Stalin, 'Report to the 18th Communist Party Congress," March 10, 1939.
[4] J. Stalin, *Stalin's Speeches on the American Communist Party*, p. 15.

would challenge and eventually supplant that of the bourgeoisie. Stalin, however, in his relations with his own colleagues, with satellite and other communist leaders, victimized them even more than his implacable 'bourgeois' enemies, yet he continued to subscribe verbally to a theoretical double standard of diplomatic behaviour. In 1948, Stalin, in effect, accused Tito of failing to observe this double standard in his dealing with the Soviet ambassador:

Tito and Kardelj . . . identify the Soviet ambassador . . . with an ordinary bourgeois ambassador; a simple official of a bourgeois state, who is called upon to undermine the foundations of the Yugoslav state. . . . They, therefore, put the foreign policy of the USSR on a par with the foreign policy of the English and Americans and feel that they should follow the same policy towards the Soviet Union as towards the imperialist states.[1]

Thus, the institutionalized deception which Marx and Engels ascribed to the bourgeois 'ruling class', and which Lenin converted into an instrument to be used only against the 'class enemy,' was personalized by Stalin and used against capitalist and communist alike, against friend and foe. Soviet diplomacy has inexorably evolved within the context of the Stalinist image of 'bourgeois' diplomacy; Engels' image of Tsarist diplomacy was universalized as 'bourgeois' diplomacy in general and served as the inverted model for Soviet diplomatic behaviour.

This view of diplomacy was carried over intact into the body of Soviet historiography. In Volume III of the *History of Diplomacy*, for example, there is a chapter entitled 'The Tactics of Bourgeois Diplomacy', written by Academician E. V. Tarle, whose unifying theme he claims he owes to 'one of the great masters of the diplomatic art', the seventeenth-century Swedish statesman, Axel Oxenstierna, who allegedly said:

Diplomacy always has at its disposal two obedient slaves: *simulation* and *dissimulation*. Simulate what is *not*, but that *which is* dissimulate . . . The diplomats of the seventeenth century, as well as their colleagues of the eighteenth, nineteenth, and twentieth centuries made profitable use of these two 'slaves': they affirmed what did not exist, but concealed what did, practising with skill both simulation and dissimulation (p. 702).

Professor Tarle proceeds to enumerate eleven discrete techniques of this dual tactic, embellished with historical illustrations from the diplomatic history of Europe, liberally interpreting 'bourgeois' diplomacy to include the writings of Machiavelli—to whom is attributed the device of inciting internal differences for diplomatic advantage—and the policies of Louis XIV. A caveat is issued that neither the list nor the historical

[1] *The Soviet-Yugoslav Dispute*, p. 42.

examples exhaust the rich and varied artifices of bourgeois diplomacy. Illustrations are selected almost indiscriminately, irrespective of century, form of government, or ideology, since in the Soviet view the bourgeois state can assume many forms, but remains the instrument of the ruling class. Thus, whether the states are autocracies, absolute monarchies, petty principalities, representative republics, parliamentary democracies, or fascist dictatorships, they are all classed as bourgeois.

Although the eleven tactics of bourgeois diplomacy are illustrated by examples from the diplomatic behaviour of Nazi Germany and Mussolini's Italy, Professor Tarle distinguishes the 'systematic employment of lies and extortion' as specific techniques of fascist diplomacy. Nevertheless, the eleven general tactics of bourgeois diplomacy are sordid enough, and are in fact easily recognized as the tactics of Stalinist diplomacy inverted to simulate those of the western powers and to dissimulate its own.

As reconstructed by Professor Tarle, they are:
1. Aggression masquerading as self-defence.
2. Aggression camouflaged by 'disinterested' motives.
3. Peace propaganda employed to deceive the adversary.
4. Concluding 'friendship' treaties for the purpose of subverting the vigilance of the adversary.
5. Aggressive plans disguised as a struggle against Bolshevism and the USSR.
6. 'Localized conflicts' disguised to facilitate the successive elimination of victims.
7. Diplomatic exploitation of internal antagonisms in the camp of the adversary.
8. The exploitation of national differences and conflicts of interest in the camp of the enemy.
9. Demogogic appeal to struggle against the hegemony of the victorious group of imperialist powers.
10. Systematic employment of threats to terrorize the adversary.
11. The 'protection' of weak states as a pretext for aggression.

Current Soviet literature on international relations and diplomacy continues to define and describe the diplomacy of the West within these tactical contexts, although in recent years new forms of 'bourgeois' simulation and dissimulation have been added. Perhaps the new edition of the *History of Diplomacy* will bring the list up to date.

The death of Stalin in 1953 had little impact on the foundations of Soviet ideology, but it did much to change the Stalinist emendations and extrapolations. The repudiation of the inevitability-of-war thesis, capitalist encirclement, the two-camp image, of the doctrine of the accelerated intensification of the class struggle as final victory approaches, the *de facto* abandonment of a communist orbit tightly controlled and directed from Moscow, and the recognition of a favourable shift in the world equilibrium of power, were bound to modify seriously Soviet conceptions of international relations and diplomacy and the historiography which they shape and support. Although doctrinal continuity persists, considerable variation, deviation, transformation, and even repudiation of Stalinist content, style, form, and methodology have taken place. Soviet conceptions of both diplomacy and historiography have benefited from Khrushchev's recognition of altered international conditions which Stalin was either unable or unwilling to acknowledge.

The first noticeable change in post-Stalinist literature on diplomacy and foreign affairs is the relative absence of abusive language, and the greater effort to bolster interpretations of the past with at least some outward display of scholarship and documentation. It has been largely shorn of its Stalinist distortions, arrant fabrications, and piercing invective. Some distortion persists, but omission of damaging facts and events is becoming more usual than the overt invention of falsehoods.

Post-Stalinist treatment of Munich and the Nazi-Soviet pact provides revealing glimpses of both contrasts and similarities to the Stalinist era. The unrelenting theme of Soviet historiography on pre-war diplomacy remains one of continuous conspiracy on the part of the Anglo-French imperialist camp to manoeuvre Germany into a war with the Soviet Union, and with a single stroke to weaken its imperialist adversaries and destroy the Bolshevik state. Thus, a commentary on a new Soviet history of the war being compiled by the Institute of Marxism-Leninism maintains:

It would be an over-simplification to say that the present policy of British ruling circles towards German militarism is an exact replica of the policy pursued with such tragic consequences in the 1930s . . . Nevertheless, those who rule Britain are largely following the pre-war pattern in their policy. Throughout the post-war years the British monopolies . . . have been guided by the desire to build up German militarism and imperialism as both a bulwark and an assault force against the forces of socialism.[1]

The major difference between pre-war and post-war western machinations against the Soviet Union stems, not from any change in the intentions of the western powers, but from the change in the world balance of power which imparts to western post-war policy an air of unreality. Whereas before the war it was possible to aim at the destruction of the Soviet Union, since the war this is so no longer.

How the Soviet Union managed to foil these conspiracies and stratagems is tediously recounted in terms of a simple morality play. Intervention, blockade, Leagues of Nations, *cordons sanitaires*, Young and Dawes plans, Locarnos, Kellogg-Briand pacts, Anti-Comintern pacts, and Munichs were fended off in a series of intrepid Soviet diplomatic

[1] M. Andreyeva and K. Dmitrieva, 'From the Pre-history of the Second World War', *International Affairs*, 1961, No. 5, p. 73.

strokes, such as Rapallo, non-aggression and neutrality pacts, the Lit-vinov protocols, disarmament conferences, collective security appeals, and, the most stunning coup of all, the Nazi-Soviet Pact, which, in the words of the old *Dictionary*, frustrated 'the double game of British-French diplomacy' and 'upset all the designs of the ruling circles of Britain and France'.[1] This remains the *leitmotiv* of post-war Soviet diplomatic historiography, increasingly buttressed by the publication of documents, old and new, the memoirs and diaries of western statesmen and diplomats, and accounts by 'bourgeois' historians, all cited to support the Soviet position. Recent Soviet literature has also quoted un-published material from the archives of the Soviet Foreign Ministry, which means that Soviet scholars have at last been given at least limited access to unpublished sources.

The theme of Volume III of the old *History of Diplomacy* was revealed in its title, 'Diplomacy in the Period of the Preparation of the Second World War'; Volume I of the new projected six-volume *History of the Great Patriotic War of the Soviet Union 1941-1945*, is called 'Prepara-tion and Unleashing of the War by the Imperialist States'. Virtually all Soviet general accounts of the diplomacy of the inter-war period carry a similar title.

A comparison of two pre-war episodes, the Czech crisis and the Nazi-Soviet Pact, in Stalinist and post-Stalinist literature, reveals interesting divergences. It should be noted that there was a sharp difference in tone, language, and degree of distortion between the *History of Diplomacy* and the *Diplomatic Dictionary*, particularly Volume II of the latter, which appeared in 1950. The former, which was compiled while the Grand Alliance was still intact, distinguished between the 'reactionary bour-geoisie' (Chamberlain, Halifax, the 'Cliveden set', etc.) and far-sighted members of the British ruling class (Churchill, Eden, Lloyd George, Duff Cooper), but no such distinctions are apparent in the *Dictionary*. In post-Stalin accounts the distinction is once again resurrected, although Churchill cannot be forgiven for his Fulton speech.

While historians do their best to present Soviet diplomatic behaviour at the time of Munich in the most favourable light, the 'dead rat' caught in the throats of Soviet historians, to use Khrushchev's phrase, remains the Nazi-Soviet Pact. Since the Soviet Union has not yet publicly acknowledged the existence of the secret protocols to the pact, while their existence is universally known outside the Soviet Union, Soviet historians are left with the impossible task of justifying something whose existence is not admitted. They are reduced to pleading that the Soviet Union signed a treaty of non-aggression in self-defence, as a result of the acknowledged equivocation of Britain and France; but their arguments cannot support the entire structure of Nazi-Soviet negotiations, agree-ments, and discussions during the period April 1939-June 1941.

In Soviet historiography Munich and the Nazi-Soviet Pact are linked, Anglo-French behaviour at Munich being the moral justification for the

[1] *Diplomaticheskii Slovar*, II, p. 176.

Pact. Every effort is made to show that the Soviet Union was the only country sincerely willing and ready to act against fascist aggression. The joint publication of Czech-Soviet documents on Munich,[1] and the Soviet transcript of the ill-fated Anglo-French-Soviet military negotiations, were both designed to supply documentary ballast to an old position.[2] The first does throw new light on the Munich crisis, but the latter adds little more than trivia to the record.

Although the point was not mentioned in Volume II of the *History*, Volume II of the *Dictionary* asserts that Stalin asked Gottwald to assure Beneš that the Soviet Union was ready to aid Czechoslovakia, even if France failed to fulfil her treaty obligations, but 'the ruling clique of the Czechoslovak bourgeoisie, afraid for its class interests, preferred capitulation', and Beneš spurned the offer (p. 198). No further details are offered. The documents published in 1960, however, prove, according to the Soviet commentator, that:

In the middle of May 1938 Klement Gottwald, who was in Moscow at that time in connection with the activities of the Comintern, had a long talk on the Czechoslovak question with J. V. Stalin, who stated that the Soviet Union was ready to help Czechoslovakia even if this was not done by France, but only on condition that Czechoslovakia defended herself and asked for assistance. J. V. Stalin authorized Gottwald to communicate this to President Beneš.[3]

The most interesting thing about this revelation is the uninhibited manner in which the Comintern (not mentioned in the *Dictionary*) is implicated in Soviet foreign policy. Why this so-called assurance was never given through official diplomatic channels is not explained. At the time, Stalin held no official position in the Soviet Government, and since the assurance did not constitute an official act, verbal or written, it could hardly commit the Soviet Government.

The documents do not shower much credit on the British or French; but neither do they prove that the Soviet Union was ready or able to go beyond its commitments if Beneš would only give the signal. In its official and public diplomatic activity, amply supported by the record, the Soviet Union made much of the fact that neither Poland nor Rumania was ready to facilitate Soviet assistance to Prague (after all, Poland was also making territorial demands on the Czechs), but no explanation is offered as to how Stalin's assurance to Gottwald could possibly negotiate the geographical barrier.

The first public Soviet admission of the secret Nazi-Soviet negotia-

[1] *Novye dokumenty iz istorii Myunkhena* (Moscow, 1958).

[2] Cf. *International Affairs*, 1959, No. 2, pp. 107-23 and No. 3, pp. 106-22 for a transcript of the military negotiations, and a commentary on their significance.

[3] I. Zemskov, 'New Documents on the History of Munich', *International Affairs*, 1958, No. 10, p. 70. Cf. also V. G. Polyakov, *Angliya i Myunkhenskii sgovor* (Moscow, 1960).

tions preceding the Hitler-Stalin Pact, and a hint at the possible existence of the secret protocols, seems to have been made in Volume I of the new *History of the Great Patriotic War*. Only the most tantalizing of outlines is provided, combined with the deliberate omission of embarrassing material and a perceptible, but not scandalous, bending of the truth. Up to this time, all Soviet accounts had conveyed the impression that the Pact suddenly materialized out of thin air.

The Soviet version, as given by this source, deviates sharply from that in the German documents. According to this sketchy chronology, negotiations started on May 30, 1939, with a meeting between Astakhov and Weizsäcker; the non-aggression pact was a German idea, and Moscow twice spurned German offers to sign a secret protocol (thus leaving the impression that no secret agreements were in fact signed). The German documents show, on the other hand, that the story actually began on April 17th, with a meeting between the Soviet ambassador, Merekalov, and Weizsäcker, and that the Soviet attaché, Astakhov, had two meetings with a German official, Schnurre, and another with Weizsäcker prior to May 30th. Furthermore, a meeting between Molotov and Schulenberg on May 20th is not mentioned. The German documents also show that, whereas the Germans took the initiative in proposing a deal, the specific form and execution of the arrangements were all suggested from the Soviet side: the non-aggression treaty and the special protocol, as well as a preparatory trade and credit agreement, were all first advanced by Moscow.

The Soviet account leaps from May 30th to August 3rd when, according to this version, Ribbentrop told Astakhov that no 'insoluble' question between the two countries existed, and 'suggested a secret German-Soviet protocol to delimit the interests of the two powers "all along the line from the Black to the Baltic Sea" ', but the Soviet Union was 'unwilling to enter into such an agreement' (p. 174); neither contention is supported by the German documents. The next date mentioned is August 14th, when Schulenberg makes a second 'verbal offer' of a non-aggression treaty and a secret protocol to Molotov but 'the Soviet Government again declined the German proposal' (p. 175), which again is not supported by the German evidence. The German documentation shows that both the non-aggression treaty and a special protocol as well as a trade and credit agreement were all suggested for the first time on August 17th by Molotov, who furnished the German ambassador with a Soviet draft treaty two days later—all of which elated the Germans, because they themselves were not yet ready to formulate such a daring proposal.

The Soviet account then records Hitler's anxiety to make an agreement immediately, on the ground that a crisis was likely to break out any day, possibly involving the Russians, expressed in the telegram he dispatched on August 20th insisting that Ribbentrop be received in Moscow on the 22nd or 23rd (all of which is supported by the German documents); but Stalin's personal reply to Hitler the next day accepting Ribbentrop is not mentioned. 'The Soviet Union was left with no choice', the book relates, 'because an attack by Germany upon the Soviet Union could well have developed into a "crusade" of the capitalist world against our state . . . The only thing that could still be done was to deliver the western Ukraine, western Belorussia, and the Baltic countries from German invasion. With this in mind, the Soviet Government succeeded in obtaining a German commitment not to cross the rivers Pissa, Narew, Bug and San' (p. 176).[1]

The reader is thus left with the impression that secret treaties were offered and spurned twice, but finally some sort of agreement (which was never made public) establishing a territorial delimitation between the two countries was reached, the main purpose of which was to deliver the peoples of eastern Poland and the Baltic States from Nazi tyranny. This also makes it just a little bit easier for Soviet historians to persist in their tedious assault on the pernicious 'secret' diplomacy of the 'bourgeoisie', for they can now concede the existence of an unpublicized agreement, and continue to deny that it was 'secret'.

One new development is the discovery by Soviet historians of Soviet foreign policy as a distinct field of diplomatic study. The first general history of Soviet foreign policy, *History of International Relations and Foreign Policy of the USSR (1870-1957)*, appeared in 1957, edited by F. G. Zueva and bearing the imprimatur of the Higher Party School of the central committee.[2] The work was almost immediately criticized for faulty 'periodization'. One of the main obstacles in the past to a work on Soviet foreign policy was the completely justified fear on the part of Soviet historians that they might unwittingly devise heretical 'periodizations', to say nothing of the perplexities and embarrassments of having to deal with a subject in which most of the principals and personalities had been purged and liquidated. As it is, even post-Stalinist literature avoids mentioning Soviet personalities, apart from Lenin and occasional references to Stalin, although bourgeois statesmen and diplomats flit through its pages with relative abandon. General Mac-Arthur comes into the picture several times, but Litvinov is not mentioned once, either in connection with the famous Litvinov protocols following the Kellogg-Briand Pact, or during the period 1930-9, when he was People's Commissar for Foreign Affairs. All his statements and

[1] Molotov's meeting with Hitler and Ribbentrop in November 1940 in Berlin is not mentioned.

[2] Actually an outline had appeared two years earlier with a terminal date set at 1941. The 1957 work was followed in 1958 by I. F. Ivashin's *Ocherki istorii vneshnei politiki SSSR* (Moscow, 1958), which was equally unsatisfactory. A new work on the same subject, *Mezhdunarodnye otnosheniya i vneshnyaya politika Sovetskovo Soyuza, 1950-1959*, 2 vols., edited by V. P. Nikhamin, appeared in 1960, but it was restricted to one decade. In 1961, the three authors joined forces to edit a new general work on Soviet foreign policy, *Mezhdunarodnye otnosheniya i vneshnyaya politika SSSR 1917-1960* (Moscow, 1961). This work was also issued by the Higher Party School of the central committee.

activities are ascribed to anonymous Soviet representatives or to the Narkomindel. Neither is Molotov's replacement of Litvinov in 1939 mentioned, although the *Dictionary* called this a significant move.

Although the 'periodization' fear has evaporated and Soviet historians are now free, within limits, to discuss the 'periodization' of Soviet foreign policy, the role and influence of personalities still create complications.[1] This is never stated explicitly, however; no hard party line

[1] Although only the first two volumes of the new edition of the *Diplomatic Dictionary* (A-I and K-P) had been published when this essay was written, the general contours of the new retrospective historical treatment of Soviet diplomatic personalities have been set. The criteria established for those to be resurrected, those to remain in oblivion, and those to be consigned to the ranks of obscurity never fail to arouse the curiosity of both Soviet and non-Soviet historians. Comparing biographical entries in the new edition with those in the old is not necessarily conclusive in its implication, since the new edition is much less ambitious in scope than the old. All biographical entries have been shortened and the colourful language (whether invective or panegyric) has been substantially excised. The entries for active Soviet diplomats are extraordinarily meagre, particularly the new diplomats drawn from the party apparatus, who often have no more than three or four lines. Foreign Minister Gromyko is given barely a half-column. 'Bourgeois' diplomats, however obscure, fare much better: Joseph Beck, for example, is awarded nearly three times as much space as Gromyko; Imperial Russian diplomats are generously treated; and the late John Foster Dulles is awarded three full columns. In contrast, V. M. Molotov, who was head of the Soviet Foreign Office for longer than any other individual, is not even entered, while Vyshinsky is given a curt half-column and Litvinov a skimpy fourteen lines. Of the pre-purge diplomats, S. S. Aleksandrovsky (Soviet ambassador to Czechoslovakia at the time of Munich), Antonov-Ovseyenko and L. M. Karakhan (twenty-three lines), are among those rehabilitated, whereas veteran pre-purge diplomats like Jan Berzin, I. Joffe, D. V. Bogomolov, Davtian, Arosev, Aralov, Krestinsky, and Bekzadian remain in limbo, although documents bearing the names of both Joffe and Berzin appear in *Dokumenty vneshnei politiki SSSR*. Manuilsky has also been excluded from the new edition, although he was in the old. Since most of the first volume of the new history of the war is simply a survey of the diplomacy of the inter-war period, and its format indicates that it is destined to be the definitive history produced by the current regime, it is interesting to make a quantitative check of the number of entries various personalities, Soviet and non-Soviet, have been given in the index. Of the Soviet personalities, Lenin leads with 50, followed by Khrushchev with 24, Stalin with 22, and Voroshilov with 12. Khrushchev is the first to be mentioned, on the first page of the introduction, with a quotation on the significance of the war, whereas Stalin appears only five pages later and then only as a name in another quotation from a Khrushchev speech; this is his only appearance in the introduction. Altogether Khrushchev is quoted five times in the introduction and has four other entries in the introductory section. Stalin is not quoted at all, while Lenin merits four entries, of which two are quotations. Bulganin, Kaganovich, and Malenkov do not appear in the index at all, whereas Engels has 8 entries, Marx 7, and Mao Tse-tung 6. Kalinin has 5 entries, Kollontai, Marshals Blyukher and Timoshenko, 3 each. Gomulka and Gottwald also merit 6 apiece, while Vyshinsky and Chicherin go unmentioned. Ordzhonikidze, Potemkin, and, strangely enough, L. P. Beria have 2 entries each, while a sprinkling of military figures have 1 apiece. A. A. Kuznetsov and Antonov-Ovseyenko have 1 entry each, while Voznesensky is given 2. Molotov, Mikoyan, Zhdanov, and Litvinov have 1 entry each. Of the non-Soviet personalities, who on the whole get much more coverage than Soviet figures, Hitler leads all entries with 117, followed by Chamberlain with 33, Mussolini with 24, Ribbentrop with 23, Goering with 22, Churchill with 22, Hull with 17, Halifax and Roosevelt with 11 each, and de Gaulle and Bullitt with 10.

has been established on periodization and none seems likely. The job is visualized as essentially the responsibility of historians, who still betray the caution and prudence of their craft.

A general discussion of the problem was initiated in the pages of *Mezhdunarodnaya Zhizn* in February 1958 by M. Airapetyan, in an article entitled 'The Periodization of the History of Soviet Foreign Policy'. Fundamental importance is assigned to periodization, because:

To define the historical periods of Soviet foreign policy correctly and scientifically is of paramount importance in understanding its basis and the place in history of each stage in the struggle for peace and the creation of favourable international conditions for the building of socialism and communism in the USSR, and in clarifying the ever-growing influence of our foreign policy on the whole course of international development and its transformation into a decisive factor of contemporary world history. It enables us to understand the social laws governing the transition from one stage of foreign policy to another and permits a better understanding of the nature of historical turns in Soviet foreign policy, reveals their causes and consequences, and demonstrates the many-sided role played by the communist party of the Soviet Union as the leader and guiding force of Soviet foreign policy.

The basic principles of Soviet foreign policy, 'proletarian internationalism' and 'peaceful co-existence', he writes, do not vary, but 'the specific forms and methods of their application change as the international situation and the world balance of forces change', and 'the transition from one stage of Soviet foreign policy to another is determined not by chance combinations of circumstances or diplomatic tactics, but by objective economic and political factors both at home and abroad'.

Airapetyan divides the entire history of Soviet foreign policy into 'two basic strategic stages', the first stretching from the revolution to the end of the Second World War, when socialism was transformed into a world system. The second period covers the years from 1945 to the present. Each is then divided into periods, the two most interesting of which are those called 'The Early Stages of the Second World War (September 1939-July 1941)', i.e. the years of the Nazi-Soviet honeymoon, and 'The Period of the Emergence and Consolidation of the World Socialist System (1945-1953)', whose terminal point is, of course, the year in which Stalin died. Whether coincidental or not, every year in which an important personality shift occurred appears as the terminal point of a period, although not all of his periods are defined by this criterion. What is interesting is that the year in which Stalin died, 1953, has been proposed as a dividing line rather than 1956 (the twentieth party congress). The major event of the former year is obvious to everyone even though its significance cannot be explicitly recognized. 'The tremendous impact of Soviet peace policy after 1953', wrote Academician Khvostov, 'and the extension of the Soviet peace effort, justify its choice

I*

as an important milestone on the straight road of development of the Leninist peace policy'.[1] Yet the major shifts in foreign policy actually took place after 1955.

Airapetyan's article was offered as 'a basis for discussion' and re-actions were solicited. Aside from quibbling about periods, and the implied question of the relationship between personalities and periods, two other issues emerged as continuing problems for Soviet historians of Soviet foreign policy. The first is the Nazi-Soviet Pact. Khvostov, in his outline published in 1957, frankly suggested that the period September 1939-July 1941 be called the 'Period of the Soviet-German Pact', but Ivashin of the Higher Party School thought this 'an unhappy and narrow definition'.[2] Virtually all Soviet scholars now subsume it under some variation of 'The Early Stages of the Second World War', which is appropriately innocuous.

More serious methodologically is the co-ordination of Soviet foreign policy with internal developments, in accordance with the doctrine that foreign policy is an extension of internal policy. The chief problem here is that, whereas 1936 constitutes, in the official mythology, the most fundamental dividing-point in Soviet internal development, it does not correspond with any comparable development in Soviet foreign policy. Some of Airapetyan's critics pointed out that the year in which socialism was established in the USSR failed even to produce a ripple in his period-ization. The underlying difficulty is, of course, that whereas Stalin could unilaterally declare the existence of a 'fundamental' internal trans-formation by ideological fiat, he could hardly decree a corresponding change in foreign policy.

It is not always recognized that, while certain externals of diplomacy seem to transcend both ideologies and centuries, they are in fact given new content and often serve other purposes than those for which they were originally conceived. Each historical era has its own specific diplomacy, the features of which are determined not only by the given state of technology and geographical communication but also by the socio-economic and political order which prevails within a given civiliza-tion, and the ideological consensus which binds it together. Diplomacy, as a part of the prevailing customary inter-state legal system, no matter how nebulously conceived and ambiguously executed, can function effectively only when fundamental ideological and social questions are no longer a matter of dispute. It functions to preserve the given ideo-social system by seeking to accommodate and adjust conflicts which are bound to arise within it. Diplomacy is thus most effective when it serves to lubricate frictions and resolve conflicts between states in such a way

---

[1] *International Affairs*, 1958, No. 8, p. 71.

[2] *International Affairs*, 1958, No. 7, p. 62. Cf. also *Novaya i Noveishaya Istoriya*, 1957, No. 4. Khvostov's outline covered only the first forty years of Soviet foreign policy and constituted the framework for his short book, *40 let borby za mir* (Moscow, 1958).

that the system itself is never brought into question. Even when force is employed to resolve issues, the unwritten premiss guarantees that it will simply result in the re-arrangement of a new political mosaic within the existing order, which itself is never at stake.

Immanuel Kant, in his essay on *Eternal Peace*, expressed much the same idea when he wrote that 'no state shall, during war, permit such acts of hostility which would make mutual confidence in the subsequent peace impossible', for 'it follows that a war of extermination, in which the destruction of both parties and of all justice can result, would permit perpetual peace only in the vast burial-ground of the human race'.[1] These maxims apply only if there exists a consensus to preserve the given order, but if that order itself is challenged they are invalidated. The distinctive feature of a world without an international ideological consensus is precisely that conflict can be resolved only within the framework of 'extermination' and 'annihilation', not necessarily in the physical sense, but certainly in the ideological and spiritual. This international consensus is absent from the world today; the old order has been challenged now for over four decades and the challenger repeatedly and without reservation asserts that its ultimate objective is to replace the existing consensus by a new one.

It is an intrinsic tendency of a diplomatic system to universalize its premises in order the better to perform its function of preserving the basic elements of the civilization it serves. By nature it cannot and does not tolerate or endure for any length of time a rival diplomacy representing another system or civilization, which it always seeks to subordinate to its own forms and rules. This happened when the European diplomatic system collided with those of the Ottoman Empire and China; both systems were eventually subjugated and subordinated to the European system by means of the peculiar diplomatic institutions known as capitulations and extra-territoriality.

In the absence of basic challenges to its supremacy, the diplomacy of a given order tends to assume that it is eternally valid and universally applicable, as the unwritten presuppositions of its existence recede into invisibility. Since nothing fundamental is at stake, variations in form, technique, style, and tempo are exaggerated out of all proportion to their intrinsic importance; ritual and ceremony assume greater superficial prominence. The art of diplomacy becomes the manipulation of externals to maximum advantage and the avoidance of fundamental controversy. At its best, such a diplomacy functions in an atmosphere of good faith and tact, but it is frequently forgotten that these qualities in large measure apply to relations between social equals. Characteristically, only those who are excluded from the consensus are conscious of their non-universal character. These values are exposed as ephemeral in their operative sense only when different social orders or ideologies come into collision, for each devises its own framework within which

[1] Immanuel Kant, *Critique of Practical Reason and Other Writings in Moral Philosophy*, edited by L. W. Beck (Chicago, 1949), p. 309.

these identical qualities and virtues are defined. In a world where the conception of 'truth' is in dispute, where the existence of 'facts' is subject to contradictory epistemological doctrines, and a common definition of 'lying' does not exist, the values resting upon differing social perspectives may lose all relevance in judging diplomatic behaviour between rival civilizations. While the Bolsheviks made it explicit that they would endeavour to deceive and cheat the 'bourgeoisie', it is not often recalled that, in its reaction to the Bolshevik revolution, the West confirmed Lenin's contention that the existing international order was 'bourgeois' by casting the Soviet republic outside the framework of the western pattern of law and ethics for its refusal to be bound by prevailing norms of property law; the Bolshevik regime was declared more than once an outcast government and hence outside the protection of international law. In short, no holds were barred in dealing with the Bolsheviks, since they were 'outlaws' and the normal restrictions of international law governing intervention and retaliation were suspended in dealing with the Bolshevik state. The refusal to recognize the Soviet Government during the early years of its existence—and the refusal of the United States to recognize communist China since 1949—reflect the belief that rules of international law and diplomacy are essentially based upon an international ideological consensus. Many aspects of current American policy with respect to countries in the Soviet orbit and to Cuba operate upon the unstated assumption that these countries are really outside the framework of the law, and hence the normal restraints do not apply. No attempt is being made here to justify or condemn these attitudes, but merely to show that they confirm the ideological basis of a given diplomatic and international order—a point that is only too rarely recognized.

Thus, while a diplomacy which governs relations between members of a common ideo-social order must rely upon a fund of good will and a reservoir of trust which transcends their conflicts, the diplomacy which governs relations between different ideo-social systems often ignores these factors, since the ultimate issue at stake is the existence of this or that civilization itself. A triumphant ideological bloc will write its own history and pass ethical judgement on its own conduct independently of the standards or values of the vanquished order.

The Bolshevik revolution not only rejected the prevailing ideo-social system and repudiated its fundamental values and ethical principles, but declared eternal war against it, undertook to overturn it, and to supplant it with a radically new order. Since the prevailing diplomatic system functions to preserve the order it was rejecting the Soviet regime refused to re-establish relations on the basis of existing diplomacy but demanded and received certain modifications and adjustments of existing diplomatic institutions and processes to accommodate its entry into the diplomatic community. In the initial phase of collision between the old and the embryonic new, it was the old system which made adjustments to accommodate the Soviet Union. Thus, from the very beginning, the Soviet Union was able to impose its radical diplomatic norms upon traditional diplomacy; and this pressure has steadily increased until today the full complement of western diplomatic norms applies to an ever-shrinking geographical area.

The Soviet conception was bound to increase in influence in proportion to the country's increase in power, and today it has wider application than the western. Western spokesmen continually vow not to engage in summit or public diplomacy; to operate through normal diplomatic channels rather than through propaganda media, but it becomes a futile endeavour unless the Soviet Union 'co-operates'. As long as the methods which the West finds anathema remain congenial and advantageous to the Soviet Union, the Russians will continue to call the diplomatic tune, because the West finds itself at a disadvantage whether it refuses to deal on Soviet terms or conducts business at the Soviet pace.

The ideo-social consensus which prevailed before 1917 and the diplomacy which it reflected have since 1917 been shattered, but only after the Second World War has this been generally recognized in the West. Two competing social and ideological systems have arisen where before there was one, and each has its diplomatic projection, but instead of only two diplomatic systems, there are in fact three: (1) Western diplomacy ('bourgeois' in the Soviet version), which is now restricted by and large to the NATO powers and those countries associated with them. (2) 'Socialist' diplomacy, which governs relations among the states of the Soviet orbit and which is still in the development stage and not yet a fully integrated system. (3) The diplomacy of 'co-existence', which governs relations between states of the Soviet and western worlds and the 'neutralist' universe of states, which accept neither the communist nor western norms in their totality and deal with those of each system. These states do not constitute an ideo-social system nor do they have their own distinctive diplomatic projection. In the Soviet view, these three diplomacies are closely inter-related and in dynamic flux, in accordance with their dialectical framework, whereby the new (communist diplomacy) is in a continuous state of expansion at the expense of the old (western diplomacy) through the medium of a transitional phase (co-existence diplomacy).

Interestingly enough, the post-Stalinist image of 'bourgeois' diplomacy has mellowed considerably and the old vulgar invective and clichés have noticeably diminished. But the basic ideology has not changed; neither has the view taken of 'bourgeois' diplomacy. It is in fact now bolstered by sociological analyses of the 'bourgeois' states and their external functions, as they relate to internal purposes. Bourgeois diplomacy persists in the Soviet version as the instrument of capitalist 'ruling circles' in the representation of their class interests abroad, but clearly as a diplomacy in an advanced state of degeneration corresponding to the decline of the system which it represents. Hence it is no longer viewed as a serious threat, although its capacity for mischief is continually emphasized. The entry on 'Diplomacy' in the first volume of the second edition of the *Diplomatic Dictionary* has been completely re-written and shorn of much of its crudity in favour of a more 'objective' Marxist description. Bourgeois diplomacy is no longer linked with fascist diplomacy; the Stalinist image of bourgeois diplomacy is now ascribed to the diplomacy of feudal absolutism, but with the observation that some of its features were inevitably carried over into the bourgeois era. Diplomacy is defined as

the official activity of heads of states, governments and special agencies engaged in foreign relations . . . designed to accomplish the aims and purposes of the foreign policy of a state as determined by the interests of the ruling class, and also to uphold the rights and interests of the state concerned.[1]

Soviet writers now view bourgeois diplomacy as a once great institution in decline. There is even a certain patronizing nostalgia which reflects the smug conviction that history is moving in Moscow's direction and that therefore a more generous and charitable tone can be used in describing bourgeois diplomacy in the final phases of its agony. Whereas its objective before the war was to isolate, encircle, and destroy the USSR, it can now do no more than put up futile rearguard actions and fight desperately for survival against the relentless advance of communism. Instead of denunciations, Soviet writers offer more 'critiques' and 'analyses' of bourgeois diplomacy, exposing its frailties and errors and taunting its practitioners for not being able to rise to the brilliant heights of their 'illustrious' predecessors, Metternich and Talleyrand, Bismarck and Canning, Disraeli and Gorchakov, and the writer-practitioners Satow, Nicolson, and Cambon, all of whom are presented in a favourable light in contrast to their inept and fumbling contemporary counterparts. Instead of following the sage counsel of the illustrious diplomats of the past to use intelligence, tact, compromise, common sense, and decency in diplomacy, and to avoid involvement with general staffs, espionage establishments, and the use of deceit and trickery, modern bourgeois diplomacy increasingly subordinates itself to military strategy, espionage, and sabotage to achieve its purposes. Soviet writers and historians are now indulging in the luxury of dispensing gratuitous advice to the 'bourgeoisie' on how to view their own interests—that is, to join up with history instead of futilely resisting its implacable mandate—much in the same way that western

---

[1] *Diplomaticheskii slovar*, I, 1960, p. 457. The new *Dictionary* continues to emphasize deception as an important 'objective' characteristic of 'bourgeois' diplomacy, but its effectiveness is said to have been blunted because of its exposure by the Soviet Union. The might of the socialist camp, it is held, has forced bourgeois diplomacy to employ new devices, which are becoming increasingly difficult to contrive, forcing it to become less dishonest contrary to its own will.

scholars define the interests of the Soviet Union for the benefit of the Kremlin, imploring it to renounce its childish notion that an outmoded social doctrine like Marxism can have any real relevance for the present or the future, and to accept the permanence of a non-Soviet world. The wheel of history has made a complete revolution, in the view of Soviet writers, for only a generation ago the bourgeoisie was refusing to acknowledge that the Soviet system had any claim to permanent existence, but now the bourgeoisie is itself pleading for survival.

With respect to the international relations and diplomacy of the communist orbit, three main innovations have been introduced, corresponding to the transformation of socialism from a system restricted to one country into an international system: (1) The restoration of the so-called Leninist norms of behaviour between communist parties and states, which were consistently violated by Stalin, although repeatedly re-affirmed doctrinally, as the basis of inter-communist relationships. (2) The transformation of the principles of 'proletarian internationalism' from a norm of inter-party relations into a diplomatic norm of inter-state relations. (3) The transformation and expansion of Soviet diplomacy into 'socialist' diplomacy and the appearance of a new parallel and self-contained diplomatic and international order, bound by a common ideology, in which inter-state and inter-party relations have been virtually merged.

One of the most striking innovations is the retrospective assimilation of pre-war inter-party relations and institutions in diplomatic history. Since the communist states are now governed by parties which were out of power before the war, pre-war inter-party activities have been, *mutatis mutandis*, retroactively extrapolated into the past as part of the diplomatic history of the communist orbit. The old pretence of a dichotomy between party and official relations has been abandoned. Corresponding institutional changes have also been made in the diplomacy of the communist universe. The Soviet ambassador, for example, now functions overtly as both a party and state representative and in the first capacity attends communist functions in the state to which he is accredited. All Soviet diplomatic emissaries to communist capitals are now career party functionaries rather than professional diplomats such as those who serve outside the communist orbit.

The idea of a communist system of international relations was not ideologically orthodox under Stalin, who tried to maintain the artificial distinction between state and party relations because of certain advantages that accrued to his rigid control over the satellite states. 'Proletarian internationalism' remained a party principle. Its essence was that all communists, whether in or out of power, owed first loyalty to the Soviet party and state just as if no change had taken place since before the war. Consequently, during the Stalin era a 'communist' diplomatic system did not exist, but only Soviet diplomacy. In contrast to the mendacity of bourgeois diplomacy, Soviet diplomacy, according to a 1948 account:

cannot use the amoral and anti-popular methods practised by the diplomacy of absolutist and bourgeois states; it cannot have recourse to deceiving its own and other peoples . . . since its aims meet with the sympathy of all progressive mankind . . . The art of Soviet diplomacy . . . differs fundamentally from the diplomatic art of the bourgeois states . . . in the realization of its declared principles, clearness and straightforwardness in the formulation of its demands . . . It is alien to 'combinations' . . . to unscrupulous transactions, intrigues, intimidation, or disguising real tendencies by false formulas and 'doctrines' . . . Not resorting to the traditional . . . methods of the 'diplomatic game'— threats, perfidy, and lies—the Soviet diplomatic art invariably insures the realization of all the foreign policy aims of the Soviet state, and at the same time wins deep moral support.[1]

The absurdity of this description merits neither elaboration nor extensive documentation, but it remains substantially unaltered as the contemporary Soviet description of communist diplomacy which is simply the internationalization of the Soviet version of Soviet diplomacy. These principles apply only among socialist states and are not extended to the 'bourgeois' world; and then only to parties and states which accept the ideological consensus of the Soviet orbit; they cease to apply in the event of heresy (the Nagy regime) or non-acceptance (Tito).

The Sino-Soviet conflict, however, added, by implication, a new element to the Soviet perception of the problem of international relations. Stalin could avoid recognizing 'contradictions' between the socialist states by declaring Tito's Yugoslavia a non-socialist state. Since Moscow still considers Albania and China to be socialist states, Soviet leaders are hoisted upon their own ideological petard. They are faced with a problem which is not explicable either in terms of the principle of 'proletarian internationalism', nor that of 'peaceful co-existence'. At present, the Soviet theory asserts that while the principles of 'proletarian internationalism' govern relations in the Soviet orbit, the principle which governs relations with the non-Soviet world is 'peaceful co-existence', which in the Soviet view is no longer a tactical expedient but a distinct historical phase of transition from one ideo-social system to another, and hence is characterized by the simultaneous existence of contradictory systems which must establish some form of relationship with one another. It is, in effect, a period in which a single ideo-social system does not prevail, and the diplomacy it reflects is correspondingly provisional in character and a diplomacy of non-consensus. It is a diplomacy which does not seek to resolve disputes within the given order or orders—as is the case with both 'bourgeois' and 'socialist' diplomacies—but rather seeks to resolve them within the framework of annihilating, liquidating, or assimilating one pole (capitalism) to the other (communism), not necessarily physically or through the use of external force (which has been rendered impractical by technological

[1] I. D. Levin, op. cit.

developments), but its elimination nevertheless. Soviet spokesmen, from Khrushchev down, are vociferous in their condemnation of the view that peaceful co-existence is based upon the *permanent* as opposed to the *temporary* co-existence of different ideo-social systems:

The principle of peaceful co-existence is a most important principle governing the relations between the socialist and capitalist countries. Peaceful co-existence does not presuppose any similarity between the social systems of co-operating countries; on the contrary, as emerges from the phrase itself, it means that on our planet there simultaneously exist countries with differing social and economic systems. The principles of proletarian internationalism are much wider and deeper than the principles of peaceful co-existence. They express the interests of the working class, the class interests of the workers of the socialist countries.[1]

The temporary character of peaceful co-existence is dictated by the inexorable laws of history, which preclude any resolution on the basis of the permanent existence of differing ideo-social systems. Co-existence is simply another way of defining the class struggle on the international level. In no case does it permit any relaxation of the ideological struggle to extirpate capitalism.

Co-existence also implies a double standard of diplomatic behaviour, for international legal and diplomatic norms may have diametrically opposite effects, depending upon whether they are applied to the communist orbit or to the capitalist states.

A legal norm that has positive (progressive) value in relations between capitalist states may, in a number of cases, acquire the opposite (reactionary) character when transferred to the relations between socialist states.[2]

Thus, the Soviet Union has managed to transform norms designed to preserve the *status quo* into instruments for digging its grave, by first changing their content and then universalizing their application. It relies on non-communist states continuing to be bound by the norms of international law which they consider sacred; should they violate their own ethical and legal norms, they can then be denounced as hypocritical and their norms exposed as no more universal than those of the Soviet orbit. On the other hand, the Soviet Union can freely violate 'bourgeois' norms of international law and diplomacy because

[1] Sanakoev, op. cit., p. 30. Cf. also Korovin, 'Mirnoe sosushchestvovanie kak osnova sovremennykh mezhdunarodnykh otnoshenii i mezhdunarodnogo prava', in *Osnovnye Problemy*; and V. Vasileyev, 'Peaceful Co-existence—the Basis of International Relations', *International Affairs*, 1958, No. 3.

[2] Korovin, op. cit., p. 77.

it has renounced them and thus is not committed to their sanctity. Thus the Soviet Union can simultaneously observe and violate norms of international law and diplomacy, since it will be observing them in the 'socialist' sense and violating them in the 'bourgeois' sense.

The catastrophic impact which Soviet conceptions of international relations and diplomacy have had upon the western world and its diplomacy raises two fundamental questions: (1) To what extent do western statesmen and diplomats realize that a single diplomatic order no longer exists, and that the traditional diplomacy for which they yearn is beyond resurrection? (2) If the rupture of the diplomatic consensus is recognized, as well as its implications, to what extent has any serious thought been given to the development of a specific non-consensus diplomacy as a medium of diplomatic communication and negotiation with the Soviet orbit? Or has the Soviet norm of a non-consensus diplomacy (peaceful co-existence) been accepted by default? Peaceful co-existence, it should be recognized, is in its Soviet form essentially a formula designed to facilitate as painlessly as possible the self-liquidation of the non-communist world. There is the view in the West that peaceful co-existence can be given a new non-Soviet content and should therefore be retained because of its propaganda and psychological value. This is possible, but it is likely to be a rather formidable operation, since the Soviets are past masters at converting devices invented by others to their own purposes and are always alert to the possibilities in reverse. Thus Khrushchev betrayed both dismay and chagrin that President Kennedy did not understand the proper meaning of peaceful co-existence, which was simply a courteous way of informing the President that Moscow was in no mood to accept re-definitions of its own formulas.

There is much to be said for using the peaceful co-existence formula in a way which exposes the spurious peace posture of the Soviet Union by provoking it into repeated and increasingly aggressive re-affirmations of the ideological struggle, but this cannot serve as a substitute for a more systematic and unified approach to international relations in a world searching for a new consensus. As Isaiah Berlin has so perceptively demonstrated, ideologies of determinism develop attitudes of moral irresponsibility by assigning the burden of responsibility for the behaviour of individuals to the impersonal forces of history.[1] Dealing and negotiating with the Soviet Union is so frustrating because its representatives deny all personal responsibility for their inflexibility, assigning it to the inexorable laws of history, forcing western statesmen to negotiate not with Moscow but with the dialectic, to which the West is advised to lodge all its complaints concerning the class struggle and the inevitable doom of capitalism. Clearly, western diplomacy in its traditional garb is no match for manoeuvres of this character.

[1] Isaiah Berlin, *Historical Inevitability* (London, 1954).

DISCUSSION

Professor Aspaturian opened the discussion; he noted that before 1955 there was not a single book on Soviet foreign policy in the Soviet Union; the closest thing to scholarly work in this field had been a long article in the first edition of the *Diplomatic Dictionary*. The avalanche of books on Soviet foreign policy which had appeared since 1957 was a welcome departure from the past, but it had its limitations: the history was very skeletal, devoid of individuals and personalities. Even Litvinov, Molotov, and Chicherin, who dominated Soviet diplomacy for more than thirty years, were barely mentioned. One could read extracts from Litvinov's speeches or commentaries about the Soviet protocols to the Kellogg-Briand Pact, but one looked in vain for the name of Litvinov who was so closely associated with them. Some of the new documents were interesting, often more because of the way they had been published rather than in themselves, and additional documentation was promised. However, favourable comparisons with the past were entirely relative. It would be wrong to create the impression that suddenly there was a tremendous, highly sophisticated development of scholarship in this area, except in relation to what had gone on before.

The Nazi-Soviet Pact still constituted the 'dead rat' in the throats of Soviet historians. In essentials, Munich was taken as its justification; the difficulty of the Soviet historians was that they had to justify what they could not even acknowledge: the secret negotiations and the secret protocols. These were alluded to for the first time in the first volume of the new history of the war. The Soviet version contradicted the German documentation at almost every point. Even allowing for some genuine discrepancies between the material of the Soviet Foreign Ministry archives and the German documents, the Soviet version was clearly guilty of bending the truth by omitting damaging evidence.

The main development in Soviet diplomatic history was the opening up of Soviet foreign policy as a field of scholarship; Soviet historians were still manifestly troubled by the problem of how to deal with the role and influence of individuals. The debates on the periodization of Soviet foreign policy showed that, in most cases, the proposed demarcations between periods coincided with a change in personality either in the Foreign Ministry or at a higher level. But nowhere in the discussions was it admitted that the change of personalities affected the development of Soviet foreign policy. Thus for instance 1953—the year of Stalin's death—had been mentioned by all participants in these discussions as an important terminal date, even though the significance of Stalin's death as a dividing line could not be explicitly recognized.

Professor Aspaturian had long been disturbed by the ease with which professional diplomats in the West dismissed the Soviet claim that the primary cause of the successes of their diplomacy was their use as a tool of analysis of Marxism-Leninism, an advantage denied to their western counterparts. To argue, as Harold Nicolson did in his book on the evolution of diplomacy, that Marxism-Leninism had never contributed anything to international agreements or the improvement of international relations, was to miss the point. That was not its purpose in Soviet diplomacy or foreign policy. It was futile to disprove Marxism-Leninism as a science. The dialectical system constituted a theory of reality, and the important question to ask was how effective it was as such, i.e. in terms of Soviet diplomatic purposes. In Professor Aspaturian's view it had been highly effective. The sooner this was recognized, the sooner we would be able to cope with it.

Professor Rubinstein thought that Soviet writing on foreign policy and international relations had improved in recent years. In this field at least the party leaders did not seem to want the past re-written in order to enhance their present power and prestige, but rather sought from historians information and interpretations which could be used to increase the effectiveness of their foreign policy.

He had been particularly interested in the relation between ideology and policy. How did ideology affect historiography, which mirrors official policy and seeks to interpret it to the population at large and to foreign communist parties? It could be seen as acting on concentric circles: the inner circle was most resistant to change and, in this period of growing Soviet power, was characterized by a conception of the enemy in close accord with ideological preconceptions and categories. The outer circles were more susceptible to change because they were further away from the fundamentals of national security and threats to communist party power.

Thus the unchanging character of the Soviet image of the West indicated that it represented the inner core of Soviet belief; hence the continuing Soviet hostility to all western efforts at integration. So long as Moscow had a stake in a divided and weak Europe, and so long as there were sufficient indications of western weakness, Soviet leaders would act as if these were permanent features of intra-western political and economic relationships. Their ideological concepts were reinforced by observable political phenomena and *vice versa*.

In dealing with the under-developed world and the United Nations we moved further away from primary security considerations. Hence the relative flexibility of the Soviet leaders in terms of ideology and tactics. The changed Soviet attitude to under-developed countries since 1953, and Moscow's moderation on the question of communist policy towards the national bourgeoisie, suggested that in areas not involving vital security interests the ideology factor as a policy determinant responds more readily to changed circumstances. No hint of Moscow's impending change of approach to the under-developed countries appeared in Soviet writings on the United Nations—the tentative moves of Soviet officials in the economic organizations of the United Nations had been far more revealing in this respect.

Commentaries in journals such as *New Times* and *International Affairs* were usually a more valuable guide to changes in Soviet policy and thinking on specific issues than those appearing in the scholarly journals.

The treatment of disarmament questions by Soviet writers from 1956 to early 1961 showed a high level of understanding both of the western position and of the technical problems involved.

Early in 1961 Professor Yemelyanov raised for the first time the problem of coping with nuclear stockpiles secreted away after a disarmament agreement had been put into effect, and he discussed quite fairly the legitimate doubts of western participants at the sixth Pugwash conference in Moscow in November-December 1960.

Professor Freymond could not agree with Professor Aspaturian's contention that 'the more powerful and confident the Soviet Union has become in the post-Stalin era, the more its diplomatic behaviour tends to abjure the hypocrisies and deceits of the past in favour of more forthright postures in both external and internal policy'. He agreed that Soviet diplomats and politicians were using the dialectical method to explain the evolution of the world. Those who had read some of the resolutions and manifestos of the Comintern in the twenties could not help being impressed by the kind of analysis made in them, and there was no doubt that the rank and file were prepared to follow the conclusions and recommendations deduced from these analyses. But that did not prevent the Soviet Government from making quite a number of mistakes—the method was not as sure as it appeared.

Was Soviet diplomacy really a new kind of diplomacy? This was its claim; but once one got beyond the first impression created by speeches and textbooks, one came to the conclusion that it was a revolutionary foreign policy served by a diplomacy of the most traditional aspect. It was a secret diplomacy—in this the Soviets had a great advantage over the West. It was a diplomacy which tried to mobilize public opinion in order to immobilize the government with which it was dealing. That too was nothing new—the sixteenth century offered quite a number of similar examples. That the Soviets were more successful in applying this kind of diplomacy to others and more successful in parrying it when it was applied to them was due to the difference of regime. The use of the communist parties in other countries, this *enveloppement par l'intérieur*, was also something traditional. In the sixteenth and seventeenth centuries there had been the Spanish party at the French court, and the French party at the Spanish court. The Soviets were merely using systematically the methods which all diplomats and all powers had used in the past.

Professor Freymond agreed that there was a difference between the traditional Tsarist policy and Soviet foreign policy, just as there had been one between the policies of Vergennes and those of the French revolution. What had to be analysed, however, was the real content of Soviet foreign policy. The outsider seemed to be in a better position to do this than the Soviet historian, who, even though he might give us some of the facts and use some of the archives, left too many vital gaps unfilled. A study of the Comintern could be very useful for the interpretation of Soviet foreign policy, because it would illumine some of the problems that were not even mentioned in the Soviet Union. Similarly, a careful comparative study of the history and the actions of the communist parties, front organizations, and foreign policies of other states in the communist orbit could help to throw light on the real intentions of the Soviet Government.

Professor Lowenthal raised the relation of ideology to foreign policy, with particular reference to the post-Stalin period. Two notions in this context he discarded at once: that of ideology as an unchanging recipe for gaining power; and that of ideology as a mere verbal disguise for traditional power politics. Ideology seemed to him to have been all the time the way in which the Soviets conceived reality and their own objectives. In this revolutionary conception of the outside world there were several distinctive elements. To begin with, ideology made the gulf between the Soviet Union and the non-communist powers unbridgeable, in a way in which gulfs in traditional politics are not. There was an element of the wars of religion here. To Professor Freymond, who referred to the diplomatic conflicts of the seventeenth century, he would say that that too was an ideological period—in the eighteenth century, a non-ideological century, one would find no such parallels.

It was implied in this ideology that it must conquer the world; the ambiguity—whether it meant conquest by empire or by world revolution, was eliminated during the Stalinist period, when the two were identified by definition. Because of the delay in world revolution, Stalin became convinced that the expansion of Soviet state power and the expansion of communism were identical, and that independent revolutions were neither likely nor desirable from a Soviet point of view. Now this Stalinist identification had broken down again, because we lived once more in a revolutionary world (though not necessarily a communist revolutionary world); because it was a world in revolutionary flux, in which other communist powers had arisen, the Stalinist synthesis of the two objectives had given way to a more ambiguous interpretation. Some of the successes and some of the problems of Soviet foreign policy in our time were due precisely to the fact that it was no longer simply a question of military expansion.

Since Stalin, Soviet foreign policy had freed itself from certain rigidities not only in relations with the under-developed countries, but also as regards relations among communist states. One of the major revisions was the new concept of the socialist world system. It implied the idea of an approach to equality among communist states, especially with regard to China, potentially with regard to Yugoslavia, and was expressed in a loosening of the reins holding the satellites. This in itself meant that Soviet state expansion and communist expansion were no longer simply identical. It made for contradictions and problems, but it also created a double kind of expansion. Soviet policy was a dual policy again, as it had been under Lenin.

Another concept, basic to Stalinist foreign policy, which had been thrown overboard was the concept of capitalist encirclement. The notion of being isolated in a hostile world was discarded as a result of the changed balance of power. Mr Lowenthal would not agree that there had been no change in the Soviet analysis of the western world. The Soviets still emphasized contradictions within NATO, but on the whole it seemed an under-emphasis. Stalin would have made the Suez crisis the central proof of an irreconcilable conflict between Britain and France on one hand and the United States on the other. Under Khrushchev the Soviets underplayed this conflict, because their chief aim was to tar the United States with the colonialist brush in the eyes of the uncommitted world. It was far more important for them to play on the potential conflicts between the third world and the capitalist world than to exploit the internal conflicts within the capitalist world.

The liberation from Stalinist rigidity, with its attendant expansion of ideologically informed activity all over the world, had created a number of new problems for the Soviets. The problem of polycentrism, of the relations within the communist camp, had already been mentioned. Another problem was the difficulty of reconciling their basic analysis with the shift of activity to the under-developed world. This shift had occurred repeatedly in the history of Soviet foreign policy: whenever the Soviets came to a stop in Europe, they shifted to Asia. In 1924 they shifted to China; in 1948-9, after they had been forced to a standstill in Europe, they shifted to the guerrilla wars in Asia, Korea, and so on. And yet, they could not abandon the idea that their revolution was linked to the class struggle of the proletariat in the advanced industrial countries, although in this field they had been consistently unsuccessful.

Mrs Degras said this discussion about ideology recalled the big debate at the sixth Comintern congress in 1928 on the role of the national bourgeoisie and de-colonization. Then one of the speakers had argued that acceptance of the theory of de-colonization would undermine the case against imperialism which was an integral part of Soviet foreign policies. The original concept of the international proletarian revolution was probably abandoned in 1920, when Lenin confessed to Clara Zetkin after the defeat of the Red Army before Warsaw that he had thought the Polish workers would welcome them as liberators, but found that they did not. It certainly was not maintained after the 1923 fiasco in Germany. Now the support of a non-existent proletarian revolution either in the West or in countries where there was no proletariat to make a revolution, had been replaced by patronage of whatever movement promised success, in the hope that the regime established as a result of this new movement could be brought into the communist or Soviet sphere. In this respect the Soviets had a great advantage, as most of such movements were anti-western in character.

Ideology had, of course, often misled the communists, sometimes seriously. If the policies of other communist parties reflected the foreign policy of the USSR, then the entire policy of the German communist party between 1928 and 1933 was a glaring example of mistaken theoretical assumptions—or rather, of ignorance of the true nature and scope of the Nazi movement.

Whenever there had been a conflict between ideology or communism in its theoretical sense and foreign policy, foreign policy had taken precedence. As early as 1921 Russia had chosen to ignore the persecution of communists by the Turkish Government, because in relation to the West and the negotiations over the regime of the Straits it was in her interest to support Turkey. Today the same attitude was evident with regard to the United Arab Republic and Nasser's persecution of the Egyptian communist party.

The criterion for judging a foreign policy should be whether it used all the opportunities open to it. What one could say of Stalin was that he had not exploited all the possibilities open to the Soviet Union as a result of Soviet military prestige, the dissolution of empires, and all the other post-war changes.

As to the Comintern seen in the mirror of Soviet historiography, the changes were very difficult to evaluate, because there was no basis for comparison: since 1943, when the Comintern was dissolved, until a couple of years ago, virtually nothing was written by Soviet historians on this subject. The series of articles and the chapters in books that had appeared since were at an appallingly low level. None of the authors seemed to have had any access to the documents, as could be surmised from the footnotes; nothing whatever was to be learned from these writings, but they did indicate what problems were to be avoided. For example, there was no attempt to explain why there had been no proletarian revolution in the developed countries; in most of these articles the term 'revolutionary proletariat' had been dropped and replaced by phrases like 'fighters for peace', 'supporters of the peace camp', 'the progressive element', etc. Soviet historians were clearly not being encouraged to venture into this field, although as late as 1961 *Kommunist* had complained in a long article that nobody had written anything on the role of the CPSU in the *Communist International* and the impact of the experiences of the Soviet communist party on other parties.

Mr Wolfe took up Professor Freymond's point that Soviet diplomacy was not new in principle, but merely more systematized. He thought that raising traditional methods to a system in itself implied a fundamental qualitative difference. Extending your ambitions to all lands and continents was another such fundamental difference. In this respect Stalin had been closer to Tsarist diplomacy than Khrushchev.

It was true that in the religious wars and the Napoleonic wars there was something resembling the modern fifth column, but never had there been such a universal doctrine, such organization, and such discipline. Here, too, Leninism had introduced a new element.

The history of Russian expansion before communism showed that the growth of the Russian empire had little to do with a predictive ideology: at the beginning of the nineteenth century one European in seven was under Russian rule, at the end of the nineteenth century one European in four, and at the middle of the twentieth century one European in approximately two. The rate of growth of industry under the last two Tsars bore out the same conclusion: though neither of them was in any way outstanding, under their rule there were striking economic advances.

What had saved Stalin from total defeat was England's courage in holding out alone; America's unconditional aid without any strings; America's naïve withdrawal from Europe the moment the war was over; America's misjudgement of Stalin's purposes and aims; Hitler's over-extended military strategy and his occupation policy. All these things had little to do with predictability on the basis of ideology, nothing to do with the social order.

Turning to the question of the advantages of revolutionary over conventional diplomacy, Mr Wolfe stressed that the aim of revolutionary diplomacy was not agreement. Whereas conventional diplomacy tried to reach agreement over a disturbed *status quo* and to secure a return to the *status quo*, revolutionary diplomacy regarded conferences as sounding-boards, and agreements, if entered into, as spring-boards for further thrusts. The nature of Soviet 'compromises', the fundamental principle in all Soviet negotiations, was a simple one: first, to make startling and extravagant demands; then, when these had stirred up sufficient anxiety, to withdraw some of them, and to demand a concession in return.

The Soviet interpretation of the world as divided into two ideological camps also placed the West at a disadvantage: we accepted their view that the world's peace should not be disturbed in the areas under their control and equally accepted the view that any disturbance in our areas or in the outside world was an issue for the United Nations and for adjudication.

Professor Scheibert thought that in evaluating Soviet foreign policy and diplomacy, one should think as long as possible in terms of traditional Russian politics. After all, the so-called ideological drive in Soviet policy had never at any time involved a risk which might in any way endanger the integrity of the Soviet empire. Traditionally, Russian power politics were based on the inferiority complex of the land power towards the sea power. Hence the obsession about being encircled and the pursuit of policies that would bring the Baltic Sea, the Black Sea, and the Sea of Japan under Soviet domination.

Another traditional aspiration of Russian power policy was the idea of imposing a *pax russica* on the European continent, with Russia's role as benevolent guardian of European peace and arbiter of European policies assured by superior forces. A thorough history of Russian thinking on disarmament could contribute greatly to our understanding of what we were facing.

Answering the point raised by Professors Freymond and Halle, Mr Labedz admitted that Professor Aspaturian had perhaps overstated his case, though he thought it difficult not to do so in face of the general complacency about the nature of Soviet foreign policy in the western world. After all, we were facing the problem of the shifting balance of power, and until now the shift was not in our favour. What factors accounted for this? Were there any weaknesses in our understanding of the motivation of Soviet foreign policy and what could be done about it? He believed such weaknesses to be rooted in the western empirical tradition, which again and again induced people to try to understand the motivation of Soviet foreign policy in traditional terms.

Some historical parallels which had been invoked in the discussion were fallacious. The existence of the Spanish party at the French court had been mentioned as the old counterpart of the present fifth-column techniques. But the Spanish party had no universal aspirations; the ideology reigning in the seventeenth century had been traditionally limited. The current form of ideology was universal. From this point of view the parallels with Nazi Germany were also irrelevant. Nazi Germany possessed no universal ideology. The German Bund in America had few counterparts in other countries, and one could not compare the operations of the communist movement all over the world with the rather limited operations of Nazi fifth columns. The argument based on such a parallel was therefore fallacious.

Tocqueville's prophecy had been quoted as proof that Soviet success could be explained without invoking dialectics and ideology. Tocqueville happened to be one conservative thinker in the nineteenth century who understood the revolutionary process—as much could not be said of his followers in the twentieth century, who tried to apply his reasoning in a revolutionary age without grasping the revolutionary process itself.

Professor Aspaturian had raised the question: has Soviet foreign policy something in the form of a unified point of view which gives it a dynamic, despite theoretical flaws, failures in predicting developments, fundamental mistakes like the misjudgement of Hitler, etc.? The point was that the Soviets were in a position to correct these mistakes, because they had a foreign policy based on a long-term view, however mistaken and fantastic its premises, while the West was going from one crisis to another, without really relating the separate incidents, basing its policy in the best empirical tradition on adjustment to events as they happen to occur.

Mr Lasky was less prepared to dump overboard the empirical tradition of the West in favour of the type of total organic approach to foreign policy outlined in Professor Aspaturian's paper. It was a monumental *post hoc propter hoc* fallacy to believe that, because of the successes of a vast empire over forty years, the dialectical method of analysis in foreign policy had been the correct one. Four permutations of this problem should be taken into consideration in any appraisal of Soviet foreign policy. One: there could be a correct analysis and a wrong decision. In regard to the post-war approach to Germany, Soviet analysis had by and large been correct, despite the rhetorical and verbal excesses in which it was couched. Yet the Soviets made a wrong decision, because although they foresaw the establishment of a separate West German republic, propped up by American economic power and politically and militarily related to the West, they were unable to do anything effective against it and, in fact, missed several opportunities to prevent it. Second: there could be an incorrect analysis and a right decision. This, by and large, had been the case of the Soviet approach to Austria. Despite their belief that in the heart of Europe neutrality could not be effective, the Soviets nevertheless signed an Austrian treaty and thus succeeded in eliminating some of the American influence in Austria. Third: there could be a correct analysis and a correct decision resulting in failure. There were many contingent factors unaccounted for in any Marxist-Leninist version of history. The Russians were correct in assessing West Berlin as an intolerable thorn in the flesh of their eastern empire. From that point of view their decision, from 1948 onwards, to use all means short of war to dislodge the West from its positions in Berlin was equally correct. And yet they failed in 1948-9 because of a few accidents: a cabinet meeting in Washington at which a decision was made which could not have been predicted, the mobilization of certain aeronautical and other techniques which maintained the western position there. Finally, to round the argument off pseudo-dialectically, there could be an incorrect analysis and incorrect decision resulting in success. Soviet foreign policy in 1939 was based on the incorrect assumption that the western powers would not resist Hitler. Stalin's decision to insure himself against Hitler's invasion was faulty because based on a wrong analysis. Yet within five years he had emerged as master of half Europe.

In his reply Professor Aspaturian denied that he advocated the abandonment of the empirical tradition; he only hoped that we could adjust it to make it more effective. He did not maintain that Soviet ideology was infallible; in fact, he had stated repeatedly that the Soviet record of diplomacy was full of failure. The Soviets were unlikely to dismantle their system because the tenets of Marxism-Leninism could be refuted. If they maintained that their successes were due to their ideology, then we should take that claim seriously and investigate it, and if we found that it had any validity, that would react to our benefit.

If, on the other hand, they remained addicted to a false ideology, it might ultimately lead them to disaster, although the system had a built-in way of rectifying its mistakes.

The accidental and the unforeseen were, indeed, very important, but the point about Soviet ideology was that it enabled the Soviet leaders to take advantage of accident and to exploit opportunities, whereas the West had let many opportunities slip.

To Professor Scheibert he would reply by pointing out that before 1939, Soviet foreign policy had been of marginal importance in international relations. The fundamental decisions that affected war and peace in the world at large were not made in Moscow, nor were they influenced in any decisive way by what Moscow did or said. The treaty with Germany in 1939 was certainly a gamble, but it was quite possible to develop a plausible ideological interpretation for their decision to sign the Pact. True, since 1945 the Soviets had not made any moves that were conditioned primarily by ideological considerations that might at the same time threaten their security. But we should be careful not to remain prisoners of past concepts and standards that no longer had validity in the present.

To Mr Lasky he would say that possibly the Soviet leaders, looking at the broad picture, might feel that the outlines of their policy had been correct and that its success was due not merely to military power, but to the ideological framework of their analysis. In that sense the list of the successes of the past forty years might serve to reinforce psychologically the Soviet view of the world.

As to the nature of Soviet objectives, he believed these to be the expansion of Soviet and/or communist power in whatever combination. Whether or not this objective was faithful to Marx or Lenin was as irrelevant as the moral character of Soviet aims. Their expectations forty years ago had been that Soviet power would become universal, while capitalism would shrink and gradually disappear. Could one deny that this was the way things were moving, and if not, what could we do to prevent their predictions from coming true?

The question of the connection between ideology and foreign policy was very important in this context. Of course, we were at liberty to attribute Soviet successes to anything we chose—Buddhism, or geography, or the traditional policies of a land power. But we could only begin to thwart Soviet successes if we found the true explanation for them. As Professor Rubinstein had pointed out, the diplomatic successes of the Soviets constantly reinforced their faith in their system. If their system was a false one we need not worry, for it would turn to our advantage in the long run. (Hitler's reliance upon a false philosophy, in terms of power calculations, and his conviction that his personal intuition transcended any system of analysis, ultimately worked in our favour.) But, in Professor Aspaturian's view, there were sufficient elements of validity in the social analysis of the Soviets to guarantee them a sufficient measure of success.

Finally, in respect to the nature of Soviet ideology as a self-fulfilling prophecy, Professor Aspaturian thought this was one area in which we could use the Soviet predictive apparatus to our own advantage, provided their prophecies stimulated us into effective counter-action. Too often western statesmen and diplomats had dismissed Soviet declarations of what they intended to do as ideological hocus-pocus, on the grounds that what was really guiding them were traditional foreign policy objectives. If these predictions had been taken seriously, their fulfilment could have been thwarted.

XIII. Soviet Historiography and America's Role in the Intervention

GEORGE F. KENNAN

The post-war years, and particularly the last decade, have witnessed the appearance in Russia of a considerable body of historical literature devoted either directly or indirectly to Soviet-American relations in the initial period of Soviet power. This literature has been concerned primarily with the role of the United States in the Allied intervention and in the Russian civil war. The attention given to this subject by Soviet historians over the period in question has, in fact, considerably exceeded that which the subject has received in the West during the same years.

While there are significant variations in the degree of ideological coloration, all of this material is written in communist terms and involves frequent use of expressions that would not be accepted in western scholarly circles as having any clearly established scientific meaning. Though this naturally complicates the use of the material by western historians and impedes the normal process of international scholarly discussion, it would not, in itself, constitute an insuperable barrier to the achievement of a certain community of effort, designed to establish at least a body of factual material on which both sides could agree as a starting-point for interpretation. But for this there would also be necessary something like a common standard in the treatment and use of historical evidence, and in particular a common willingness to respect not only the individual fact but the preponderant and obvious weight of available factual evidence as the supreme arbiter of historical controversy.

It is this common standard that frequently appears to be lacking. Occasionally, in the perusal of Soviet historical material, one does indeed seem to feel oneself in the presence of people from whom one is divided by no very deep and significant gulf in this respect. This is particularly the case when one is dealing with phases of history in which the Soviet Union or the Russian communist party were not directly involved. Even with reference to the history of the early period of Soviet foreign

This essay was first published in The American Historical Review *(January, 1960) and is re-published here with the kind permission of its editors.*

relations there have been Soviet historians whose practices in this regard did not differ too widely from those of western scholars, or, for that matter, of the great Russian historians of the past. But generally in these recent years—especially before 1953 and after 1956—Soviet historiography on this latter subject has been marked by an attitude towards the rules of historical evidence that has brought deep discouragement to those on the western side who had hoped, in turning to the works of their Soviet colleagues, for aid and enrichment in their own efforts to understand and illuminate the period in question. The purpose of this essay is to illustrate why this is so.

The volume of the relevant material is great, and random examples would probably not suffice to indicate the intensity of the practices to which a western historian might have to take exception. For this reason I have chosen, by way of example, a single, relatively brief document that is both recent and authoritative and touches closely on subjects with which I am particularly familiar. My selection is the chapter entitled 'Concerning the Role of the Imperialists of the USA in Carrying Out the Intervention in the USSR in the Years 1917-1920', from the volume *Concerning Certain Questions of the History of the Civil War in the USSR*, by S. F. Naida.[1]

Naida is a military historian and a prominent and responsible figure in the Soviet academic community. A doctor of historical sciences, a leading member of the historical faculty of Moscow University, and reportedly a major-general by rank, he has specialized in the history of the Russian civil war of 1918-20. In 1956 he was director of the section for the History of the Civil War in the Institute of Marxism-Leninism, under the central committee of the communist party. He is one of those who have been completing the official history of the civil war. He has been an active critic of the work of other Soviet writers on the civil war and the intervention. Until 1960 he served as chief editor of *Voprosy Istorii*. These facts would suggest that he stands relatively high in the ranks of Soviet historians in point of experience, erudition, and authority.

Naida's article contains numerous sweeping statements for which no detailed argument is offered. The 'American imperialists', we are told, repeatedly tried to strangle the Soviet state in its infancy, to take merciless reprisals on the workers and peasants, to turn Russia into an American colony. They tried, it is said, to prolong the world war in 1917-18. They secretly sought the strengthening of Germany as a result of the war. In particular, they were, we are assured, the *principal* organizers 'of *all* the forces of external and internal counter-revolution [in Russia] . . . the *leading* initiators of anti-Soviet intervention and the incendiaries of the civil war . . .' They were 'the initiators of *all* the campaigns of the Entente and *all* the more important anti-Soviet conspiracies, diversionary actions and blockades of Russia, of her partition,

[1] S. F. Naida, *O nekotorykh voprosakh istorii grazhdanskoi voiny v SSSR* (Moscow, 1958), pp. 70-105.

and of the creation on her territory of a series of small states . . . (p. 88. My italics—G.F.K.).

With allegations of this order one obviously cannot deal in the space of a single article. There is, however, one general feature of Naida's chapter of which special mention must be made. In the course of thirty-five pages, he uses some eighty times the phrase 'American imperialists'. In addition, a number of similar expressions of equal vagueness—'the American reactionaries', 'the American capitalists', 'imperialist circles of the USA', 'American bourgeois politicians', 'the interventionists', 'aggressive imperialist circles', 'the American millionaires', 'American leading circles'—are employed. I cannot refrain from pointing out that these expressions are not sufficiently precise to serve a serious historical purpose. They are so imprecise, in fact, as to impede serious evaluation of statements in which they are used.

Whom does Naida mean when he refers to the 'American imperialists'? In some instances the reference is apparently to the United States Government; in others the context would suggest that he has private American business concerns in mind. In one case the expression is evidently used to refer to the American Relief Administration. To judge the accuracy of many of his statements one would have to know precisely which of the organizations or categories he is considering.

So much for generalities. Let us now examine a small selection of the detailed points made in Naida's article.

1. *The statement* [*p. 82*]:
In the first days after the establishment of Soviet power, the American Military Mission at the General Field Headquarters addressed itself to General Dukhonin and other Tsarist generals with a summons not to recognize the Soviet regime but to employ the resources of the headquarters for the creation of an all-Russian bourgeois government.

The facts:
Major Monroe C. Kerth, the United States military representative at headquarters, addressed to General N. N. Dukhonin on November 27, 1917, a protest against the conclusion by the Russians of a separate armistice with the Germans. The key passage in this one-sentence communication reads as follows:

. . . since the United States of America and Russia are united in fact in a war which is essentially a struggle of democracy against autocracy, my Government protests categorically and vigorously against any form of separate armistice that might be concluded by Russia . . .[1]

The letter contained no reference to the question of recognition or to the creation of an all-Russian bourgeois government.

[1] From a French translation included in the article 'Nakanune peremiriya', *Krasnyi Arkhiv*, 1927, XXIII, pp. 199-249.

Naida could have found the text of Kerth's letter. It appears verbatim in the third volume of the *History of the Civil War in the USSR*, prepared by a group of scholars of whom Naida was one, under the supervision of an editorial commission among the members of which his name appears in first place.

2. *The statement* [*p. 83*]:
At the same time [around the time of the October revolution] the foreign imperialists and particularly the imperialists of the USA attached great importance to the organization of counter-revolutionary bourgeois-nationalist governments, intending to utilize them as weapons for the overthrow of Soviet power.

Thus Smith, the American consul in Tiflis Ambassador Francis, and the consul-general in Moscow, Summers, tried as early as 1917 to create a federation of Transcaucasia, the Kuban, Terek and Don regions, and the Ukraine, headed by bourgeois-nationalist governments, in order to obtain in the south of Russia a theatre of action for the struggle against the Soviet state.

At the direction of Francis and of the State Department of the USA, Consul Smith participated in the creation in 1918 of the counter-revolutionary bourgeois-nationalist governments of Georgia, Armenia, and Azerbaidzhan.

The facts:
Throughout the period under reference, American Consul F. Willoughby Smith, stationed at Tiflis, bombarded his superiors in the United States Government with somewhat confused requests that he be authorized to encourage the establishment of an autonomous regional administration in that part of Russia and the utilization of native units from this region in the Russian Army on the Turkish front. When, after the communist seizure of power in Petrograd, this latter army began to disintegrate under the demoralizing impact of the Soviet move for an armistice on the European front, Smith asked for money to help hold the army together and to support whatever continued military efforts might be possible.

All of these requests were plainly motivated by the belief that they would serve the overall military interests of the Allies in the war against Germany. Some pre-dated the October revolution, and therefore could scarcely have been directed to the overthrow of Soviet power. None was granted. The American ambassador at Petrograd, David R. Francis, on October 5, 1917, notified Smith that the step he was then recommending (assignment of local territorial units to the Turkish front) was considered to be 'one relating to internal affairs in which the Embassy can take no action'.[1]

So far as I can ascertain, Smith received four instructions from the

---

[1] *Papers Relating to the Foreign Relations of the United States, 1918, Russia,* 3 vols. (Washington, DC, 1931-2), II, p. 578. Hereafter cited as *FR*.

K

State Department during this period. On November 26, 1917, he was told that the Department 'cannot encourage tendencies in any of these directions'. On December 15th the Department wired: '. . . do not commit this Government'. On December 28th it stated: 'Only instructions for you for present are to keep us informed'. Similarly, on March 30, 1918: 'The United States is not in a position to support active military operations on Caucasus front'.[1]

Smith's tendency to exceed his authority was the subject of much anxiety to his superiors both in Russia and in Washington, among others to his immediate supervisory chief, Consul-General Maddin Summers in Moscow. On January 10, 1918, Summers wrote privately to the counsellor of the American embassy at Petrograd, J. Butler Wright, to confirm his own impression that Smith had been exceeding his instructions in his various initiatives.[2] Wright, in his reply, concurred with Summers' judgement, and expressed his own concern over the situation. There is no evidence whatever of an instruction from either Summers or Francis or the Department of State to Smith, encouraging him along the lines of his own recommendations.

One is constantly struck, in reading Soviet diplomatic history, by the freedom with which the recommendations or personal views of individual junior officials of 'bourgeois' governments are cited as evidence of official policy, regardless of whether they were approved and supported by the responsible superiors of these officials. There seems to be no recognition of the fact that people could honestly disagree, and honestly express this disagreement.

3. *The statement* [*p. 83*]:
The American imperialists in 1918 established contacts with the Ukrainian bourgeois-nationalist Central Rada; and at the beginning of 1919, having extended to the Petlyurites major aid through the French, they suggested the recognition by the Entente of the counter-revolutionary Petlyura Government—the Directorate.

The facts:
In the summer of 1917, before the establishment of the Soviet Government, the United States Government had taken up with the Provisional Government the question of opening a United States consulate at Kiev. Before a reply was made, the communist seizure of power occurred in Petrograd. A few weeks later, in mid-December 1917, the Ukraine being still effectively outside the control of the new Soviet Government, Ambassador Francis detailed Consul Jenkins to Kiev to find out what could be done about opening the consulate. He specifically (these are his own words) 'cautioned Jenkins against recognizing any government' in that part of Russia.[5] Jenkins went to Kiev

[1] Ibid., pp. 582, 590, 601, 623.
[2] Petrograd Embassy, File 800, 1918. National Archives, Washington, DC.
[3] See Francis' telegram to the Secretary of State, No. 2090, December 12, 1917. *FR, 1918, Russia,* II, pp. 649-50.

and spent some weeks there waiting for the situation to clarify itself. Fearing that a political interpretation might be given to any contacts he might have with the Ukrainian authorities, he refrained for a period of several weeks from even making a courtesy call at the 'foreign office' of the Ukrainian Rada in Kiev. Only on January 23, 1918, when forced to do so by a governmental order (to which he would otherwise have been subject) to the effect that all non-residents should leave Kiev, did he call on the foreign minister of the Rada in order to ask permission to remain. The report of the conversation, as given by Jenkins to the Department of State in a confidential dispatch, was as follows:

Mr Schulgin met me pleasantly and said there would be no objection whatever to my remaining in Kiev. He said some pleasant things about the United States and I talked about the attractiveness of Kiev and the very evident possibilities of great agricultural and industrial development in the Ukraine.[1]

This is as close to the sinister as Jenkins' mission ever came. Shortly thereafter the Rada made a separate peace with the Germans. Kiev was swallowed up by the renewed German military advance, and all Allied representatives were obliged to leave. No exchange of views on a political subject took place between the United States Government and the Rada. There is no evidence of any political interest being manifested in this body at any time by any responsible American statesman.

As for Simon Petlyura and the Directorate (the regime which took over briefly in the Ukraine following the departure of the Germans in the fall of 1918), I am unable to imagine where Naida could have found evidence indicating that recognition of Petlyura was 'suggested' by the United States Government at the beginning of 1919. The major American statesmen were at that time attending the Paris Peace Conference. Their concern at that moment was to clarify the question of possible Russian representation at the Conference; and pending such clarification they were wholly disinclined to take any unilateral action with regard to any of the competing factions in Russia.

Could Naida have had in mind here the Prinkipo proposal? It would be a curious flight of imagination to describe Wilson's acquiescence in this proposal as a suggestion for recognition of Petlyura. It could just as aptly be described as a suggestion for recognition of the Soviet Government.

The representatives of the Ukrainian Directorate in Paris had dealings (if their memoirs may be believed) with only two responsible American figures at the Peace Conference: with Professor Robert H. Lord of Harvard University and (in a single interview of June 3, 1919) with Secretary of State Robert Lansing. In the memoirs of one of these Ukrainian representatives, Arnold D. Margolin, it is stated that

[1] Petrograd Embassy, File 800, 1918, dispatch from Jenkins of January 23, 1918, to the Petrograd Embassy. National Archives.

K*

Professor Lord 'as a rule . . . refrained from expressing his views and limited himself to asking us questions'. Lansing, Margolin relates, showed himself 'lamentably misinformed' about the situation in eastern Europe and frankly hostile to the establishment of an independent Ukrainian regime.[1] The Ukrainians received from him not the slightest encouragement in their quest for recognition by the Allied powers.

As for the alleged extension of major aid to the Petlyurites by the United States through the French, the source of this charge is again not indicated. What the French themselves did is another matter, but that they were in any way encouraged by the United States Government to assist Petlyura seems most improbable. When, in the autumn of 1919, the Department of State discovered that the American Liquidation Commission in Paris, charged with the disposal of surplus army clothing and supplies, had contracted to sell certain of this material to the representatives of the Ukrainian Directorate, it at once remonstrated with the Commission and asked that the contract, if possible, be annulled. The Department expressed itself, in this connection, 'disposed to regard the Ukrainian separatist movement as largely the result of Austrian and German propaganda seeking the disruption of Russia'.[2] The materials, so far as I am able to ascertain, got no nearer to the Ukraine than a warehouse in Marseilles.

4. *The statement* [p. 83]:
On December 3, 1917, on the initiative of the American imperialists, there convened a special conference in which the USA, England, France and allied countries participated, and at which it was decided to organize in the immediate future an open, anti-Soviet military intervention, in which connection the participants in the conference distributed among themselves the roles to be played in this dirty business. The principal role in the Far East, in Siberia, and to a considerable degree in the north, the USA took upon itself. They expected, having once seized the basic regions of Russia, to gain a foothold, with the help of the White-Czechoslovak Corps and the adherents of Kolchak, to seize positions in the Urals as well, to push through to the Volga, to penetrate to the south, and, having thus created a wide theatre of operations, to put an end speedily to Soviet power.

The facts:
It is difficult to know to what conference Naida is referring. The date given was before the abandonment by the Soviet Government of the old Julian calendar. In other instances, Naida employs the double date; but in this instance he gives no indication whether his December 3rd is based on the old calendar or the new.

The contents suggest that if the old calendar was used, the reference

[1] Arnold D. Margolin, *From a Political Diary: Russia, the Ukraine, and America. 1905-1945* (New York, 1946), pp. 47-8.
[2] *FR, 1919, Russia* (Washington, DC, 1937), pp. 783-4.

might conceivably be to the Anglo-French diplomatic discussions that took place in Paris on December 22nd-23rd (by the western calendar), and at which indeed the participants did agree on a rough allotment of the areas in southern Russia in which each should do what could be done to restore local resistance to the Germans. But the Old Style dates of these discussions are correctly given in the official *History of the Civil War in the USSR*, on which Naida collaborated, as December 9th-10th, not December 3rd. This meeting, furthermore, did not take place on American initiative. The United States did not participate, nor did any other of the Allied powers aside from the French and British. The idea of promoting a counter-revolution in Russia, incidentally, was specifically repudiated by the participants.

We are left to conclude, therefore, that Naida's date was based on the new calendar, in which case the reference could have been only to an informal meeting on December 3, 1917, at the French Foreign Office, of a number of the senior Allied statesmen who happened to be in Paris at that time for the sessions of the Inter-Allied Conference and the Supreme War Council. The meeting in question was one of a series of such meetings held in the last days of November and the first days of December. The need for these conferences as a means of co-ordinating the war-time policies of the Allies was obvious, and the presence of the various statesmen in Paris provided a natural occasion for them. It would be inaccurate to attribute them to the 'initiative' of any particular power, particularly the United States. The French were of course the official hosts. The American representative was the personal emissary of President Wilson, Colonel Edward M. House.

At the meeting on December 3rd, Colonel House did not initiate in any way the discussion of Russian matters. Marshal Foch, however, introduced a number of resolutions, the first of which envisaged Allied occupation of the Trans-Siberian railway as a means of assuring a line of communications to the Rumanian army, which had been placed in an extremely precarious situation by the Bolshevik peace move. The Japanese representatives, British Foreign Minister Balfour, and Colonel House all spoke in opposition to this resolution, and it was not accepted. Writing in his diary that evening, Colonel House referred to the meeting as follows:

I sat in with the Prime Ministers at eleven o'clock . . . General Foch was there and introduced one foolish resolution after another. It has lessened my good opinion of him. Balfour leaned over and said to me: 'Did you ever hear of such proposals?'[1]

It is abundantly plain, not only from the record of this meeting, but from the evidence of his personal views, that House was strongly opposed at that time, and for months afterwards, to any form of Allied intervention in Russia, fearing that any such action would tend to throw

[1] Diary, December 3, 1917. Edward M. House MSS, Yale University Library.

the Russians into the arms of the Germans. He was fully aware, further-more, that President Wilson had similar views. He would not, therefore, have been in a position to encourage any schemes of this nature during the period of his visit to Paris in November-December 1917.

Even had Foch's proposal been approved, Naida's statement would still be wide of the mark. No division of roles such as he alleges was discussed at this meeting. Particularly absurd is the charge that the 'American imperialists' were scheming to use the Czechoslovak Corps and the 'Kolchakovites' to gain a foothold in the Urals. The Czechs were at that time still in line on the eastern European front. The idea that they should be evacuated through Siberia had not yet been seriously dis-cussed. Admiral Aleksandr Kolchak, for his part, was at that moment in Yokohama, attempting to return to Russia from the United States. He had heard of the Bolshevik seizure of power only on the day he sailed from San Francisco. He was now wholly uncertain as to his plans, and had discussed them with no American official. Neither he nor any-one else could conceivably have guessed that one year later he would be in a position to play a political role in Siberia.

5. *The statement* [pp. 84, 85]:
Above all, the Government of the USA promised the Soviet Government economic and military aid, on condition that it continue the war with Germany.

In promising aid to the Soviet Government, the American imperialists advanced a number of conditions. Thus they demanded, for example, that the Soviet Government permit the USA, England, and France to bring troops into Soviet Russia for 'the common struggle' against the Austro-German and Turkish troops, and that the military training of the formations of the Red Army and Fleet should be placed in the hands of American, English, and French 'instructors' as well as of Tsarist generals, admirals, and officers, in which connection the institu-tion of [military] commissars should be abolished . . .

The facts:
At no time did the United States Government promise military or economic aid to the Soviet Government during the First World War. The efforts of American representatives in Russia to induce the United States Government to do just this were without exception unsuccessful. The nearest the United States Government ever came to a communica-tion to the Soviet Government on this subject was the message addressed by President Wilson to the Fourth Special All-Russian Congress of Soviets, convened in March 1918 to consider ratification of the treaty of Brest-Litovsk. In this message the President, after expressing sympathy with the Russian people, went on to say:

Although the Government of the United States is unhappily not now in a position to render the direct and effective aid it would wish to render,

I beg to assure the people of Russia through the Congress that it will avail itself of every opportunity to secure for Russia once more complete sovereignty and independence in her own affairs . . .[1]

Shortly after the dispatch of the President's message, meetings of the Allied chiefs of mission and military attachés in Russia took place in Vologda. Here various questions of Allied policy towards the Soviet Government were discussed, including the question as to the terms on which military aid to the Soviet Government should be extended, in the event it were to be extended at all. On April 3rd the French representatives brought to one of these meetings the draft of a *procès-verbal* devoted to this question. The draft's contents would suggest that it was this document which served as the basis for Naida's statement concerning the conditions the 'American imperialists' are supposed to have placed on their alleged offer of military assistance.[2]

Francis never forwarded this document to the State Department, nor did he even specifically mention its existence. It is clear that he did not accept it, for he cabled Washington that on two points (both at issue in the French draft) he had not been able to accept the views of his colleagues and that they had consented to defer such demands for the present. Nevertheless, the State Department, worried lest Francis go too far, wired him: ' . . . do not give Soviet promise military support as requested in queries submitted through you and through military attaché . . .'[3] This put an end to further American participation in the discussion. No such proposal for aid was ever made to the Soviet Government in the name of the Government of the United States.

6. *The statement* [p. 86]:
The American imperialists took a most active part in the organization of the mutiny of the Czechoslovak Corps . . . Thus, as early as the autumn of 1917 in Kiev, and then in December in Jassy, American representatives conducted negotiations with representatives of . . . Masaryk concerning the use of this Corps for the struggle against the Soviet Government. Masaryk's agent, the officer Cherzhensky, was asked point-blank the questions: '. . . is the Czechoslovak Army prepared for an armed uprising against the Bolsheviks and will it be able to occupy the region between the Don and Bessarabia?' American representatives also met with Masaryk himself, who was in Russia in the winter of 1917-18. From March 1918 these negotiations were continued in

[1] The text of Wilson's message to the Soviet Congress will be found in *FR, 1918, Russia*, I, pp. 395-6.

[2] The French text of this document will be found in Joseph Noulens, *Mon ambassade en Russie soviétique, 1917-1919*, 2 volumes (Paris, 1933), II, pp. 56-7. An English text was sent to the War Department by the American military attaché in Russia. A copy can now be found in the State Department File 861.00/1730 1/2, National Archives.

[3] *FR, 1918, Russia*, I, pp. 494-5.

Washington, where Masaryk had gone in order finally to sell the soldiers of the Czechoslovak Corps to the American imperialists.

The facts:
That Thomas Masaryk should have occasionally met with Americans in Russia in 1917-18 is in no way surprising and proves nothing. He was a highly respected Allied statesman, and he had normal social relations with his Allied colleagues in Russia. How such relations could be taken as evidence that he and these Americans conspired to use the Czechoslovak Corps for an armed action against the Bolsheviks is wholly unclear.

Masaryk was personally, throughout this period, firmly averse to any schemes that involved the retention of the Corps in Russia. The desire to assure its evacuation to the western front was the guiding motive of his entire activity in Russia in 1917 and 1918. The disintegration of the Russian army and the Bolshevik peace move in late 1917 made evacuation from the eastern front urgently necessary. These events meant, as Masaryk related in his autobiography, 'that we could no longer fight against our enemies in Russia; hence all our effort was concentrated on getting to France'.[1] Of the efforts made to involve the Corps at that time in the Russian civil war he said:

Ranged against our departure were the politicians and military commanders of Tsarist and pre-Bolshevik Russia. Generals [L. G.] Kornilov and [M. V.] Alekseyev, and also [Paul N.] Milyukov, among others, pressed me to join them in the fight against the Bolsheviki. The Bolsheviki and the Ukrainians were also against our departure in so far as they both hoped to win our army over to their side . . . All these plans I rejected.

When Masaryk left Russia in March 1918, he did so in the confidence that the evacuation of the Corps through Siberia was arranged and assured. His ensuing visit to the United States was motivated largely by his desire to complete these arrangements at the western end. Neither in the statement for the American ambassador in Japan which he prepared while *en route*, nor in his informal meeting with State Department officials on May 16th (his first real discussion with responsible American Government representatives in Washington). nor in his meeting with Secretary of State Lansing on June 3rd (ten days after the uprising of the Corps in Siberia), nor in the interview which he finally succeeded (after long delay) in obtaining with President Wilson on June 19th, did he show any enthusiasm or interest either for intervention generally or for the suggestion that the Corps should remain in Russia.

The Czechoslovak uprising itself, occurring in late May 1918, was, as is known, the outcome of orders given by the commanders of the

[1] T. G. Masaryk, *Die Weltrevolution* (Berlin, 1925), p. 198.

Corps on the spot. The course followed by these commanders in authorizing the revolt against Soviet authority not only ran counter to the expressed wishes of Masaryk and the Czechoslovak National Council, but was conceived as a means of avoiding compliance with a directive received from the Council which the commanders considered dangerous to the security of the Corps. It was opposed by the French military liaison officers (the official representatives of the Allied military command in France) attached to the Corps.

The United States Government knew nothing of the circumstances out of which the Czechoslovak uprising arose and had not the slightest relation to its outbreak.

In support of his charge that the Americans were conspiring with Masaryk as early as autumn 1917 to use the Corps to overthrow the Soviet Government, Naida cites a question said to have been asked by an unnamed person (he does not say this was an American, but allows his readers to infer that it was) of a Czechoslovak officer on an unnamed occasion and in a context unspecified. For this he gives a footnote source which, when pursued, brings the reader to a Soviet book published in 1922, now long out of print and apparently unavailable in the United States.[1] The incident in question, if it occurred at all, presumably took place at a conference of Allied military attachés in Jassy in November 1917, at which were discussed a number of rather desperate possible expedients for rescuing the Rumanian army from the impossible position in which it had been placed by the Soviet peace move. The French had an idea at that time of using the Czechoslovak Corps and other non-Russian units loyal to the Allies to form, together with the Rumanians, a nucleus of continued military resistance to the Central Powers on the eastern front. This would have necessitated opening and maintaining a supply route through southern Russia, which was as yet only partially in Bolshevik hands. Any such undertaking would certainly have encountered Soviet opposition and could to this extent have been described as incidentally 'anti-Soviet', though its main motivation would have been to prosecute the war against Germany. The idea was presumably discussed, among others, at the Jassy conference. That questions should have been put to the Czechs, in this connection, about their ability to hold territory in southern

---

[1] The source referred to in Naida's book was Volume III of the above-mentioned *History of the Civil War in the USSR*, p. 182. This referred, in turn, to B. Shmeral (Šmeral), *Chekhoslovaki i Esery* [The Czechoslovaks and the SRs] (Moscow, 1922). A book published in Russia at a somewhat later date (F. Popov. *Chekhoslovatskii myatezh i Samarskaya uchredilka* [The Czechoslovak Revolt and the Samara Constitutional Assembly]) (Moscow, 1932), cites at greater length the passage in question from Šmeral's book. This quotation suggests that Šmeral himself did not name or describe the questioner to whom he refers. If this is true, then Naida himself did not know any more than do his readers who put the question. None of this dissuaded him from weaving the quotation into the passage in such a way as to suggest that it came from American lips and was proof that the Americans were scheming at that time to use the Czechs for the overthrow of the Soviet Government.

Russia against the assumed opposition of the Soviet Government is not surprising. If true, however, it would not constitute evidence that the Americans had conspired with Masaryk to overthrow the Soviet Government.

7. *The statement* [p. 92]:
In 1919 the State Department of the USA fabricated a map which reflected the schemes of the imperialists for the dismemberment and enslavement of Russia. By way of elucidation of this map it was stated: 'All of Russia should be [*sleduyet*] divided into large natural regions, each with its specific economic life. In this connection no single region should be sufficiently independent to constitute a strong state.' [The source for this statement is given as: D. N. Miller, *My Diary of the Conference of Paris. With Documents* (New York, 1924), IV, pp. 214-20.]

The facts:
The reference here, as shown by Naida's footnote, is to an 'Outline of Tentative Report and Recommendations', prepared not by the State Department but by the intelligence section of the United States delegation to the Peace Conference for guidance of the President and the delegates. This document was only in the nature of a recommendation. There is no evidence that it was ever formally approved by the President.

The text of the recommendation itself was as follows:

It is recommended:
1. That encouragement be given, at opportune times, to the reunion with Russia of those border regions of the south and west which have broken away and set up their own national governments, particularly the Baltic Provinces and the Ukraine, if reunion can be accomplished within a federalized or genuinely democratic Russia.

2. That there be excepted from the general application of the principle above mentioned Finland, Poland, the Armenians in Transcaucasia, and probably Lithuania. See map 4.[1]

In the subsequent 'discussion' the following passage occurred:

Russia may be divided into great natural regions, each with its own distinctive economic life. No one region is self-sufficient enough to form a strong state. The economic welfare of all would be served by reunion on a federal basis, which would, of course, also have other evident advantages.

As will readily be seen, the recommendation was that with the exception of four specific border areas (in two of which the Soviet Government

[1] David Hunter Miller, *My Diary at the Conference of Paris, with Documents*, 22 volumes (New York, 1924), IV, p. 219.

had itself already recognized the creation of an independent state) American policy should be *opposed* to the permanent dismemberment of Russia and should favour reunion of the country on a liberal basis, allowing reasonable opportunity for the expression of the will of the respective peoples. This Naida has contrived to portray as a decision *in favour of* the dismemberment and enslavement of Russia. To support his thesis he has neglected to mention the recommendation itself and has selected for quotation two sentences from the accompanying discussion, into each of which has been inserted a verb with an imperative connotation (in one case *sleduyet* [should be]; in the other, *ne dolzhna byt* [should not, or must not, be]) to replace, respectively, the verbs 'may be' and 'is', which were actually there and which had no such connotation. This cannot be described otherwise than as a direct mistranslation. By no stretch of the translator's licence can the phrase 'may be divided' be properly rendered in Russian by *sleduyet razdelit*, or the phrase 'no one region is self-sufficient enough' by *ni odna oblast ne dolzhna byt nastolko samostoyatelnoi.*

I do not mean to suggest that Naida was personally guilty of this mistranslation. It appeared at the height of the anti-American campaign of the years 1950-2 in the works of two Soviet historians, A. Ye. Kunina and A. I. Melchin.[1] Each of these at that time attributed the passage, as does Naida in the present instance, directly to David Hunter Miller's *Diary at the Conference of Paris*. It is worth noting, however, that in the second and more extended edition of her book, which was published in 1954, Madame Kunina had the prudence to omit this quotation altogether, restricting herself on this occasion to comments on the accompanying map. Melchin, similarly, in another work published in 1953,[2] included the passage but took pains to attribute it this time to Madame Kunina and not directly to the Miller diary. Surely these circumstances should have been sufficient to warn Naida against uncritical acceptance.

8. *The statement* [p. 100]:
The secretary of the American YMCA Ralph Albertson wrote that in the Russian north: 'Every night American detachments led their victims out in batches and destroyed them,' that on one occasion a convoy detachment of Americans shot more than thirty prisoners, that Americans used against Soviet people shells with poisonous substances. Ralph Albertson noted that the American interventionists dealt in a particularly bestial manner with communists, commissars, and political

[1] A. Ye. Kunina, *Proval amerikanskikh planov zavoevaniya mirovovo gospodstva v 1917-1920 gg.* [The Failure of the American Plans for the Achievement of World Domination, 1917-1920] (Moscow, 1951); A. I. Melchin, *Amerikanskaya interventsiya na sovetskom Dalnem vostoke* [The American Intervention in the Soviet Far East] (Moscow, 1951).

[2] A. I. Melchin, *Razgrom amerikano-yaponskikh interventov na sovetskom dalnem vostoke v 1920-1922 godakh* [The Smashing of the American-Japanese Interventionists in the Soviet Far East, 1920-1922] (Moscow, 1953).

workers, ordering the soldiers not to take them prisoner but to kill them even when they were apprehended unarmed.

The facts:
This is not what Albertson said. These statements are obviously taken from pages seventy-one, eighty-six, and eighty-eight of Albertson's book *Fighting without a War*.[1]

With respect to the shooting of people in batches at night, what Albertson actually wrote was this: (p. 71):

The execution of suspects made Bolsheviki right and left. The inquisitorial processes of the Russian puppets of the Military Intervention were necessarily so much like those of the old regime that they went far to dispel all illusions about the Military Intervention that might have remained in the peasant mind.

When night after night the firing squad took out its batches of victims it mattered not that no civilians were permitted on the streets. There were thousands of listening ears to hear the rat-tat-tat of the machine guns . . .

This passage, it will be noted, not only makes no reference to Americans but plainly and specifically refers to the activities of the Russian units associated with the Allied command.

The remaining statements in Naida's paragraph cited above are all taken from the chapter of Albertson's book entitled 'Atrocities.' In this chapter there is not a single reference to Americans, nor is there anything that would permit the reader to associate the alleged incidents with American troops. Albertson did *not* say that it was a convoy detachment *of Americans* which shot more than thirty prisoners. He did *not* say that *Americans* used shells with poisonous substances. He did *not* say that *Americans* ordered the men to kill prisoners. I cannot find that Albertson said at any point that Americans or anyone else dealt in a particularly bestial manner with 'communists, commissars, and political workers'.

Albertson was at the front both during the period when the Americans were participating and after their departure. He was, in fact, one of the last Americans to leave. That his reference to 'our' atrocities did not necessarily mean Americans is clear from the following fact. The paragraph from which some of Naida's examples are taken also included a passage, omitted in Naida's charge, alleging that in taking the village of Borok 'we' killed the civilian commissar in that town and left his bayoneted body lying in the street. Borok was actually taken by the British in the course of their final offensive on the Dvina front, in late summer 1919, designed to cover their evacuation. This was well after the departure of the last American troops.

[1] Ralph Albertson, *Fighting without a War* (New York, 1920).

No Americans participated in the senior command of the north Russian intervention or had any part in determining its policies.

As Naida is aware, the method of dealing with prisoners varied in the civil war in the north according to the individual fighting front, the type of unit employed, and the status of the prisoner. On certain fronts, at certain times, and in certain circumstances, the killing of prisoners was the common practice on both sides. On the fronts where the Americans were involved, this was, as Naida should also know, not generally the case.

9. The statement [p. 101]:
Together with the English and French interventionists, the American plunderers took part in the establishment in the north of a concentration camp on the island of Mudyug . . .

A no less terrible camp was established at Iokange, where the American interventionists, together with the British and the French, perpetrated bestial atrocities on the prisoners.

The facts:
The Americans, not participating in the command of the Archangel expedition, had nothing to do with the establishment of either of these places of detention. I cannot find that either was ever visited by an American during the period in question.

The use of Mudyug Island by the Archangel regime as a place of detention for political prisoners began in August 1918. The first group of prisoners was sent there on August 23rd. This was twelve days before the arrival of the American troops in the Archangel area. Thus the Americans could scarcely have taken part in the establishment of the prison camp there. It was guarded and in part administered, in the first months, by naval personnel from the French men-of-war stationed at Archangel. Later this task was taken over by White Russian detachments.[1] At no time did Americans participate in any of this work.

The place of detention at Iokange appears to have been originally established in 1918 by the Russian authorities at Murmansk, for prisoners from that place. No American had anything whatsoever to do with this. The Iokange camp was not used by the Archangel authorities at all until the late summer of 1919. This was well after the departure of the last American forces from the Archangel area.

10. The statement [p. 100]:
American troops participated in the cruel repression of the partisan movement in the Ussuri valley in August-September 1918 and in the summer of 1919. Here the American interventionists in the most bestial manner obliterated the entire population of entire regions, acting in

---

[1] See P. Rasskazov, *Zapiski zaklyuchennovo* [Notes of a Prisoner] (Archangel, 1928).

L

the same manner as the bands of Semenov, Kalmykov, the Kolchakovites and the Japanese.

Having occupied the railway branch Vladivostok-Suchan and having
seized the Suchan mines, the American interventionists began a merciless persecution of the population, particularly the partisans and their
families. At the Skidelsky mine one of the American detachments,
headed by a certain Pedders, succeeded in seizing partisans from among
the local workers. The prisoners were subjected to unbelievable torture.
The American bandits, as was said in the newspaper *Krasnoe Znamya*
of March 28, 1920, 'tortured them one by one, inflicting burns on their
bodies, breaking the bones of their hands and feet and then dragging
them out in broad daylight to the bushes and shooting dead the half-
living people'. On another occasion this same Pedders with his band
got up a 'peasant hunt'. In the case of one peasant, the bandits cut off
his nose, lips, and ears, broke his jaw, put his eyes out, and pierced him
with bayonets.

The facts:
The allegation about the cruel suppression of the partisan movement in
the Ussuri valley in August-September 1918 could scarcely refer to
anything other than the participation of a portion of the Twenty-
seventh Infantry Battalion, USA, under Colonel Henry D. Styer, in a
combined action with Japanese and Czechoslovak forces, under
Japanese command, against what the American commander understood
to be a force of Bolsheviks and German prisoners of war. The Twenty-
seventh Infantry was the first American unit to arrive in Siberia, landing
in Vladivostok on August 16th. Its participation in this action was the
result of a misunderstanding on the part of its commander. The
Americans were kept by the Japanese in the rear echelons, presumably
in order that they should not have the opportunity to check Japanese
statements about the nature and strength of the enemy; and they took
no part in any of the fighting.

This seems to be as close as any Americans came to participation in
'the cruel repression of the partisan movement in the Ussuri valley in
August-September 1918'. On the arrival of the commander of the
expeditionary force, General William S. Graves, on September 1st, the
Twenty-seventh Infantry passed entirely under his command. All
American forces acted from that time on under strictest orders in
implementation of General Graves' policy, which was not to involve
his force in any way in Russian internal affairs, but to limit it to guarding
those segments of the Trans-Siberian railway and supporting services
entrusted by inter-Allied agreement to his protection.

In the pursuit of this policy, an American detachment participated,
beginning September 11, 1918, in the guarding of the coal mines at
Suchan, near Vladivostok. General Graves did not seek this responsibility; it was wished on him by the other Allied commanders. He made

no changes in the ownership of the mines. The latter, therefore, were not 'seized'. In addition to the Americans, Japanese and, for a time, Russian Cossack troops were also involved in the protection of the mines.

Up to May 1919 relations between the American detachment at Suchan and the Russian partisan groups in near-by villages remained amicable. The Americans were even called upon on certain occasions by the villagers to act as witnesses to the truly abominable atrocities perpetrated by the local Russian Cossack detachments. As a result, General Graves did what he could to achieve the removal of those detachments from the vicinity. In May and June 1919 the partisans, who had now come under closer communist control, began to interfere with the operation of the mines and of the branch railway by which the mines were connected with the main line of the Trans-Siberian. In early June one American platoon suffered what its members considered to be a treacherous early morning attack in its barracks, involving severe American casualities. By the end of June the Americans found themselves obliged to take action against the partisans and to clear them out of some surrounding areas.

I am unable to find the faintest confirmation of an incident such as that described by Naida. The newspaper to which he refers (it is presumably the Vladivostok paper of the name given above, though he does not make this plain) is not available in this country. At the time this issue of the newspaper appeared, the American detachment had long been withdrawn from Suchan. The story thus must have referred to something supposed to have transpired at least several months before the story was written; but no date for the incident itself is indicated.

Other Soviet historians have also referred to atrocities said to have been perpetrated by an American by the name of Pedders; in one case he is referred to as Major John Pedders.[1] The roster of the Thirty-first Infantry Regiment, which provided the mine guard at Suchan, shows no officer by that name or any similar name. The United States Army records, in fact, fail to show anyone of this name, of any rank, as serving in Siberia at that time. In the examination of hundreds of documents from the official files of the Mine Guard Detachment,[2] I have been unable to find a reference to anyone with such a name or, indeed, to any incident resembling that which Naida relates.

There is reason to suppose that this anecdote, like others recited in various works of Soviet historians on this period, was derived from the tales told by members of the partisan movement at the second congress of the Toilers of the Olginsk Raion of the Maritime Province, which took place in March 1920, just as the Americans were leaving Siberia. A comparison of these stories with what is known of the actual operations of the American force in Siberia suggests that the partisans were

---

[1] A. I. Melchin, *Razgrom amerikano-yaponskikh interventov . . .* , p. 21.
[2] American Expeditionary Force to Siberia, Suchan Mine Guard Detachment, War Department Records, National Archives.

themselves the victims of much confusion, particularly when it came to distinguishing between the American forces, on the one hand, and the Japanese and White Russian forces (some of whose members wore British uniforms) on the other.

Only in one instance (July 3, 1919, in the villages of Kazanka and Novitskoe) are there known to have occurred serious violations of the rules of war on the part of one American detachment. These violations, all of which were incidental to combat, involved the shooting of at least one unarmed civilian and some unnecessary destruction of property. They flowed from orders issued by a second lieutenant who apparently lost his head in the heat of battle. His action met with most emphatic disapproval and condemnation on the part of his superior officers. This is the only episode of this sort I have been able to discover in the records of the operations of the American Expeditionary Force in Siberia. It obviously is not the one that Naida describes. It involved no torture. It did not occur at the mine.

There may, of course, have been substance of some sort behind the tale Naida relates. Presumably, there is some reason why the name Pedders is mentioned instead of any other. But diligent search of the records available in this country fails to reveal what this substance might be; and nothing in the words of Naida and other Soviet historians suggests that any of them took the trouble to go beyond the Vladivostok press stories in the effort to find out what really happened.

These are only a few examples of Naida's practices in the use of historical materials out of a considerably greater number that could be cited from this one chapter, to which I, for one, would have to take exception.

In the foreword to his book, Naida calls for a 'merciless struggle . . . against bourgeois objectivism in science'. He defines 'bourgeois object-ivism' as something that occurs 'when certain authors, ignoring the concrete historical setting, attempt to argue this or that proposition, arbitrarily selecting isolated factlings [*faktiki*], citing them out of context, without relation to the whole'. One suspects that for Naida 'facts' are historical circumstances, or alleged or suggested circumstances, which serve a preconceived ideological interpretation of the historical process and are therefore to be treated with respect, whereas 'factlings' are circumstances which, though they may be marked by the awkward quality of having actually occurred, fail to serve this preconceived interpretation, and are therefore to be despised. One must ask forgive-ness if one finds it impossible to accept this significant and revealing distinction.

To anyone with a serious interest in the eliciting of historical truth it can only be a source of sadness, and by no means of satisfaction, to be obliged to make these observations. As one who has had occasion to see something of contemporary Soviet historiography, I am happy to note, along with much that is unacceptable to me, evidence of much else that commands respect: of seriousness of purpose, of hard work, of talent which not even the strictures of a rigid ideological discipline can wholly conceal. It is a source of deep satisfaction that we are beginning to see more of our Soviet colleagues at international gatherings of historians and to greet them as visitors to western institutions. I am sure they will continue to find a warm welcome, even S. F. Naida, if he cares to come.

In particular, one does not object to being confronted with a different point of view. Among those of us who work in Naida's field of historical study, there is none, I am sure, who would not be free to admit that the western countries have from time to time made serious mistakes in their relations with the Soviet Union. I know of none of us who is committed to proving that our side was without fault and that the diplomacy of the other side consisted exclusively of villainy.

If a corresponding forbearance could only be shown on the other side, I for one could hope that the study of history might yet be, as it should be, one of the means by which each of our countries could gain a measure of perspective with regard to itself and by which we could begin to reduce the differences of outlook that now divide us.

xiv. Soviet Historians and American History

MAX BELOFF

Selections from a recent group of Soviet writings on topics of American history, and on the political institutions of the United States, raise a number of general questions of greater interest than the books themselves. Most of the works under consideration are written for specific instructional purposes at a secondary-school or university level. One would imagine that, in dealing with countries of so great an importance to the Soviet Union, the essential thing would be to give the readers the factual information necessary for such dealings with these countries in the political, cultural, or economic spheres as their subsequent careers may require of them. While one would naturally expect the approach to be conditioned by the ideological framework of Soviet thinking, one would feel that even on matters of history and political institutions there would be a common ground in matters of hard fact, and that it would be no more desirable for Soviet executives to be unaware of these than it would be for the designers of Soviet aircraft to be unaware of the data of aerodynamics.

These would not only seem to be reasonable expectations; they would also seem to be the assumptions held by protagonists of the theory of 'cultural exchanges' with the Soviet Union, who believe that there should be this common ground of factual knowledge and that it is one of the aims of international contacts to increase and deepen this common store. It cannot, therefore, be said too emphatically that, whatever may be the case regarding Soviet historiography where earlier periods of history are concerned, or other scholarly subjects, this particular field is one in which the necessity of proving ideological points is so strong that it takes precedence over the need for giving Soviet citizens this desirable minimum of practical information. Nothing could be a better corrective to the view that a mere diminution of political tension would suffice to break down the ideological iron curtain than the publication of a few direct translations of these Soviet works.

No doubt the defects of Soviet writings on American history are partly the outcome, not of deliberate prejudice, but of genuine ignorance. These historians and political scientists are working on the basis of the available literature in the field, and the footnotes and bibliographies they provide suggest that, by and large, their facilities for doing this are quite adequate. But there are genuine difficulties in the way of any foreigner studying the institutions of a particular country without the experience of direct contact—one has only to think of French attempts to understand or describe the British Commonwealth. These genuine difficulties are obviously enhanced by the fact that their experience is so wholly different from that of citizens of Great Britain or the United States. If a Soviet writer is unclear about, say, the working of party primaries, it is not altogether surprising.

Quite apart from this dilemma about the use and reliability of sources, there is the obstacle which the Marxist-Leninist doctrine appears to place in the way of precisely that kind of description and analysis which this particular category of literature involves. Marxists seem unable to appreciate that there are such things as technical problems in government and administration which are quite irrelevant to the political content or bias of the regime. Historically, for instance, the problem of bringing into cultivation vast new areas, which has been a central theme in American development, does present a number of technical, economic, and administrative questions which could not be avoided under any imaginable social or political system. Or again, the mere problem of governing a country the size of the United States involves questions of administration which must be different from those of more compact countries. Issues of this kind are passed over in total silence.

My own view would be that this lack of ability to analyse economic and governmental questions is the major weakness of current Soviet literature in these fields, and that this is a much more important aspect of the matter than the more obvious use of historical writing to back up whatever may be the current line in foreign policy—for instance, the attempt over the last few years vastly to inflate the American role in the intervention during the civil war period in Russia, or even the assertions about the alleged Machiavellianism of the western Powers' policy in the 'appeasement' period. One is confronted, of course, both in regard to these obvious distortions and in regard to the wider questions already raised, with the familiar problem as to the extent to which this literature should be taken at its face value. Is it written by people who, even if uncertain about details, in fact have in their minds a much more realistic picture of the situation—or are we dealing with a generation in whose minds myth and reality are now hopelessly and inextricably confused? One is tempted at times to believe that perhaps there is another range of literature which is kept wholly secret from us, and that those upon whom real responsibility rests are not working under the handicaps which accepting these writings at their face value would imply. This may be very far-fetched, but the question of degrees of knowledge is one which is inescapable for students of totalitarian literature, from whichever angle they approach it.

In default of such wholesale translations as I have suggested, it would seem useful to illustrate the argument by a number of particular instances which, if not of overwhelming importance in themselves, do build up a certain picture in one's mind.

On the historical side we might have expected some sympathy for the near-Marxist approach of Charles Beard and his school. But in the introduction to Yefimov's *Outlines of the History of the USA (from the Discovery of America to the end of the Civil War)*, we learn that this is not the case. It is admitted that Beard and his 'economic school' were ready to recognize the revolutionary character of the Civil War and to treat it as the 'second American revolution'; but they underestimated the important contribution to it of the working class and especially of the struggle of the Negroes themselves. Incidentally, the communist attempt to capture and direct the political energies of the American Negro is mirrored in all their historians' treatments of the American scene. Thus Deborin, in dealing with the doctrinal basis of the American revolution—a period when the problem of slavery as such was pushed into the background by nearly all the writers he is treating—devotes a quarter of his space to dealing with slavery, even though this forces him to go right outside his chronological framework by bringing in Lincoln and the Civil War. In the same way, Kaverin's account of the impact of the great depression immediately leads to a discussion of the particular hardships admittedly suffered by the Negroes and other minority groups.

To return to Beard and his followers, they appear in Yefimov's treatment as the vanguard of the struggle against Marxism. Again, an American historian such as Philip Foner, whose left-wing sympathies are well known, is congratulated for his contribution to the history of the American working class in the pre-Civil War period, but criticized for idealizing some of the leaders of the 'bourgeois slave-holding democracy', in particular Jefferson and Jackson.

The Declaration of Independence cannot, of course, be denied its 'progressive' character, because it embodies the idea that the people must decide its own fate, but the references to man's Creator and the attention to natural rights have to be stigmatized as incorrect. And even the sovereignty of the people—in itself a new idea—was not carried into practice, since the bourgeoisie wrongly identified itself with the people.

After criticism of formal bourgeois democracy on familiar Marxist lines, with further emphasis on the denial of democracy inherent in slavery, Yefimov goes on to point out that it was in the name of popular sovereignty, that is, by appealing to Jeffersonian principles, that the southern slave-holders justified secession in 1860-1.

It is not surprising that the Constitution should be treated along Beard/Merrill Jensen lines as a reactionary document designed to protect propertied interests; some points are taken direct from Beard without acknowledgement; but Jensen's work is not referred to. All this is a matter of interpretation. What the Soviet reader has the right to expect is a description of the Constitution itself that would help to explain the subsequent workings of the American Government. This is not achieved by an author who begins by describing the President as the head of the 'Cabinet'—a body unknown to the Constitution—and then describes the Secretary of State as his 'deputy' in the Cabinet. The statement that the President can dismiss any 'minister' provided that he has a two-thirds vote in the Senate is totally incorrect (he requires such a vote for appointments only—dismissals, it has long been settled are for him alone).

While it is true that the Constitution differed from the Articles of Confederation in that the executive power could now reach directly into the States, the statement that the President has such power is meaningless without an explanation as to the particular spheres in which such action was permitted. Although a good deal is said about the class features of the Constitution and the reactionary role of the Senate —Stalin having laid it down that second chambers are necessarily reactionary—and of the Supreme Court, there is no analysis of the principal features of the Constitution itself, such as the distribution of powers between the States and the central government or the separation of powers at the centre. There is no analysis of the *Federalist* papers, which are only referred to in a brief sketch of the life of Madison.

On the Bill of Rights Yefimov finds himself in some difficulty; many of its provisions cannot be denied their 'progressive' character. He is therefore put into the absurd position of accusing bourgeois historians of concealing the fact that the Bill of Rights was not included in the original Constitution and only came in as a result of pressures exerted during the ratification process. Then he has to say that although the Bill of Rights, like the Constitution, is a weapon in the hands of the people in its struggle against the bourgeoisie, the formal recognition of these Rights by the bourgeoisie has been a means of deceiving the popular masses.

In examining the Monroe Doctrine the role of Russian expansion in bringing it about is played down, since it has to be defined as the doctrinal cover for United States domination in Latin America. When we come to the beginning of the slavery struggle and the Missouri compromise, we learn that as a part of Maine's admission to the Union, and as a balance to Missouri, slavery was abolished there; it had in fact been prohibited in Massachusetts, of which Maine was part, by its constitution in 1780. Although it is true that there was a tendency to admit free and slave States in pairs after 1820, no agreement to this effect was made in 1820, nor is it easy to see how it could have been. This lack of attention to constitutional and legal issues makes it impossible to give a coherent narrative of the actual events. It is correct that the provisions about fugitive slaves in the 1850 compromise were offensive to the free States; but it is not true that prior to this any Negro who got to free soil was automatically considered free—this was only the case when he went there with his master's consent. Indeed, the Constitution specifically provided for the return of fugitives. Even more confusing is the author's total inability to distinguish between 'State'

L*

and 'Territory' in the United States Constitution, which makes it impossible for him to give a coherent account of the Kansas/Nebraska bill, or correctly to present the significance of the Dred Scott decision. Indeed, the effect of judicial review upon the Constitution in any of its aspects is totally ignored. Neither Marshall nor Taney figures in the index of names.

This inability to describe and analyse the actual working of institutions is even more remarkable in a book like E. B. Chernyak's *The Governmental Structure and Political Parties of the USA*, despite the fact that its footnotes often refer to standard American works. The historical sketch with which it begins has the same weaknesses as Yefimov's. Like Yefimov, Chernyak has to equivocate about the position of the masses: they cannot be denied a leading role, yet they have to be represented as continually thwarted. For instance, the masses are pictured as having demanded the condemnation of the institution of slavery in the Declaration of Independence and having been thwarted by the planter interests. They are again credited with winning the Bill of Rights and thus strengthening the democratic character of the Constitution. The author's need to make the case against American imperialism leads him to refer to the acquisition of the Philippines but to omit the steps leading to their independence. But the main point again is the lack of precision where constitutional questions are concerned. The essence of the Missouri compromise and its relation to the problem of Congress's power in the Territories again baffles the author.

On more recent questions the anti-trust legislation is treated only in relation to trade unions. The Taft-Hartley Act is listed among other reactionary measures, but its content is not described—this is the more pertinent in that it figures as a major political issue in the period from its passage until 1956. Various acts of Congress are denounced as being contrary to the provisions of the Bill of Rights. But what is the Soviet reader to make of the author's summary of the Fifth Amendment 'by which an innocent man may not be compelled to make false accusations against himself'? In what context could a constitutional provision of this kind be meaningful?

Voting rights are another source of confusion—how far wilful it is perhaps hard to say. Chernyak picks up from an American textbook the statement that only a little over 50 per cent of the population have the right to vote, overlooking the fact that most of the remainder are children. Voting in the United States is not 'free', we learn, since the governments of most States demand of the voter that he state in advance for whom he is going to vote—no indication is given that this provision is directly related to the system of primaries.

In dealing with procedure, there is of course the further problem that although bourgeois democracy has to be exposed and the two American political parties represented simply as the agents of monopoly capitalism, it must be admitted that the political system can produce progressive legislation; otherwise there would be no point in stating, quite correctly, that the Senate's lack of a closure rule means that filibustering is one of the main weapons of reaction.

Chernyak cannot escape the problem of federalism. He has to account for the increasing centralization of power, to show that the rights of States are more formal than real, and so far as they exist may be exploited for reactionary purposes. But in order to explain the system, Chernyak does not follow the normal method of showing what the federal powers are under the Constitution and how they have been expanded, but instead lists the powers of the States.

The States may not, we learn with surprise, lay taxes on property, which are reserved for the Federal Government (what, then, of the whole controversy over the income-tax amendment?) The States can, we learn, make laws about commerce within their own boundaries, but there is no discussion of what this means in the light of the inter-State commerce clause. After listing the residual rights of the States to deal with such matters as health, education, roads, etc., Chernyak makes the breath-taking statement that 'it is obvious that all this activity of the States in fact takes place under the control of the Federal Government'—how and in what sense? It is impossible to see how the Soviet reader, with only his own experience to guide him, could possibly understand what is involved here—or, to take a concrete case, follow the legal issues involved in de-segregation.

This question is mentioned in passing in the account of the Supreme Court. The court's constitutional functions are treated with distaste, and it is pictured as a bulwark of reaction. But it is admitted that under pressure of public opinion, and after the introduction by Roosevelt of a few more liberal figures, it did in 1954-5 take some steps against segregation.

The problem of the political parties is of course an acute one for Soviet analysts of the United States. If both represent the forces of finance capitalism, why are two needed? Is one even more reactionary than the other, or is Democratic 'liberalism' a mere device for winning votes? If so, why are the masses taken in? How is the allegiance of so much of the trade-union movement to the democratic party to be explained? To none of these questions does Chernyak contrive to give an answer. The discussion is trenchantly disposed of by A. Gromyko in his book *The Congress of the United States*. He writes: 'However hard the apologists of monopoly capitalism may try to put forward concrete differences between the two American bourgeois parties, it is impossible to hide the fact that at bottom they are simply the double face of monopoly capitalism.' Gromyko criticizes some previous Soviet authors for paying too much attention to the formal antithesis between President and Congress, and in particular to the growing predominance of the executive branch; this obfuscates the real unity in the system, which derives from the fact that the whole government apparatus is the scene of a conspiracy between the great capitalist monopolies and that the conflict between executive and legislature is only a very secondary one.

More scholarly works reflect the same basic weaknesses. In the first volume of his *Social and Political Doctrines of Modern and Recent Times*, A. M. Deborin devotes a chapter to the American revolution of the eighteenth century and its political ideas. Although he emphasizes the historical significance of the American revolution, Deborin is limited in his study by the necessity of describing the revolution as the result of a 'national-liberationist and bourgeois-democratic movement of the American colonies'. That is to say, he plunges into the arguments by which the colonial pamphleteers justified the colonists' resistance to the claims of the British Parliament without examining the nature of the imperial problem itself or the different answers to it that divergent developments dictated to the two sides. There is no appreciation of the work done by British and American scholars in recent decades in order to illuminate the nature of the relationship between the mother-country and the colonies, nor any evidence of a direct study of the documents the author is dealing with. Indeed, those quoted are from translations that occur in works by pre-Soviet Russian historians.

This lack of acquaintance with the sources makes it more plausible to argue, as Deborin does, that the ideological roots of the American revolution can be traced directly to the English revolution of the seventeenth century, and in particular to the Levellers. Anyone more familiar with the documents would have noted rather the surprising absence of reference by the colonists to the last great outpouring in English of basic political arguments.

The difficulty of working within the formula comes up again in dealing with the constitutional Convention. Deborin points out the class character of its composition, and the fact that it did not contain a single representative of the workers, who in fact 'made the revolution'. He stretches the point even further by ascribing an outstanding role to Alexander Hamilton with his 'monarchical sympathies'. As a result, he sees the Constitution as the product of a secret compromise between sections of the ruling class carried out behind the backs of the people. It was fear of the people that led the Convention to meet in private and its records to be kept in conditions of the greatest secrecy in Washington [*sic*]. The records of the actual discussions have in fact been available to historians for 120 years.

The essays in the collection *Questions of Modern and Recent History*, edited by E. M. Zhukov and others, are only in part concerned with the United States. There is an essay by G. I. Kaverin on the working-class question in the United States between 1933 and 1936. The general line is indicated from the outset by the picture of Roosevelt as the instrument of monopoly capital—the 600 acres of Hyde Park are also brought in to identify him with large-scale property interests. Since no one (outside a Republican fringe) disputes Kaverin's main point that the New Deal was designed to save capitalism, not to overthrow it, his subsequent interpretation is less radical than he may believe. But his ostensible subject—the role of the working class and trade unionism—cannot be properly handled by someone who cannot look at their development as part of the changing American scene, nor appreciate the importance of the accretion to their countervailing power which New Deal legislation helped them to achieve. Thus Section 7A of the NRA is described (on the authority of the New York *Daily Worker*) as 'a new instrument in the hands of the capitalists for building up company unions'. What happened next can only be explained in the familiar way: first, that Section 7A, although enacted under pressure from the United States working class, did not alter its fundamental situation, and second, that it was nevertheless used by the working class, against the intentions of its authors, to pursue its own struggle.

More striking is the attempt to make the measures of the early New Deal period appear as an attempt to increase the United States' military resources. The Civilian Conservation Corps is thus seen as part of a programme to militarize the labour force. Even more important was the intention to insulate American youth from exposure to revolutionary ideas that might have led it to overthrow capitalism.

The Tennessee Valley Authority, that so fascinated European observers of the New Deal, is condemned outright as being wholly in the interests of monopoly capital and great landowners (shades of the power companies' lobby!).

The more significant fact is that the formula, in what is meant to be a piece of original historical writing, not vulgarization, is just the same—communist sources for the most part, with a couple of 'bourgeois' historians quoted when convenient. Incidentally, the number of errors in spelling, etc., in the footnote references to English language sources is very striking.

An essay by V. P. Androsov follows on the 1955 merger of the A.F. of L. and the CIO. The leaders of the joint organization are accused of concealing, under the cover of anti-communism and anti-racketeering, its role as the agent of reaction in preparing the new onslaught against the working class which the deepening crisis of United States capitalism must inevitably bring about. An article on the European Defence Community and on United States responsibility for the idea follows familiar lines.

V. Ya. Leede, in dealing with American-German relations between 1939 and 1941, is concerned to show that both the orthodox school of American diplomatic historians and the Beard 'revisionists' omit to stress the fact that United States policy was dictated by the conflict between those American monopolists with British interests and those with German interests. He treats the Nazi moves after the fall of France to secure the continuation of United States neutrality, on the basis of the United States disinteresting itself in Europe, as evidence for a plot between the Germans and the pro-Nazi elements in American big business for co-operation against the Soviet Union, which had always been the main purpose of United States policy. This was only unsuccessful because of the threat to United States markets and other American interests from the advance of German power. No evidence is produced for this version of American policy and there is no reference, needless to say, to the fact that the Soviet Union at the time was actually collaborating with the Nazi Government. This omission deserves extra emphasis in that American historians of the period are specifically blamed for neglecting the role of the USSR in the diplomacy of the time.

The current analysis of United States policy in the collective work *Questions of the Foreign Policy of the Soviet Union and Contemporary International Relations* is along conventional lines. Two essays deal respectively with the United States' 'colonial' policy in Asia and its 'monopoly' in Latin America. The latter theme is expanded in the separate volume by Grechev. Another more general essay expands the thesis that American foreign policy is wholly motivated by the pretensions of United States capitalism to global mastery.

The current emphasis on American imperialism makes the Spanish-American War of 1898 of particular interest to Soviet historians. The book by Vladimirov is based on some of the standard sources and makes some use of unpublished Russian dispatches of the period. Slezky's slighter work makes some use of writers in Spanish to emphasize the role of the Filipinos and the Cuban insurgents.

SOURCES

A. V. Yefimov, *Ocherki istorii SShA* (Moscow, 1955).

E. B. Chernyak, *Gosudarstvennyi stroi i politicheskie partii SShA* (Moscow, 1957).

A. Gromyko, *Kongress SShA* (Moscow, 1957).

Voprosy vneshnei politiki SSSR i sovremennikh mezhdunarodnikh otnoshenii, ed. L. F. Ilyichev and others (Moscow, 1958).

L. Yu. Slezky, *Ispano-Amerikanskaia voina 1898 goda* (Moscow, 1956).

L. S. Vladimirov, *Diplomatiya SShA v period Amerikano-Ispanskoi voiny 1898 g.* (Moscow, 1957).

M. A. Grechev, *Imperialisticheskaya ekspansiya SShA v stranakh Latinskoi Ameriki posle vtoroi mirovoi voiny* (Moscow, 1954).

Voprosy novoi i noveishei istorii, ed. E. M. Zhukov and others (Moscow, 1958).

A. M. Deborin, *Sotsialno-politicheskie ucheniya novovo vremeni* (Moscow, 1958), I.

Index

(Note—*Contributors' essays and interventions in the conference debates are indicated by heavy type.*)

Academy of Sciences, Chinese, 184
Academy of Sciences, Polish, 133
Academy of Sciences, Soviet, 94, 134, 143, 155, 224; Scientific Councils of, 120 f.; Historical Section of, 29, 59, 121, 123, 126; Archaeographic Commission of, 119;
—— , Institute of Economics, 131; of History, 40, 118, 120 f., 122 f., 131, 148, 245, 248; of Law, 115; of Oriental Studies, 131, 180, 182, 187, 198; of Peoples of Asia, 182, 184; of Sinology, 182 f.; of Slavonic Studies, 133; of World Economics and International Relations, 248
Academy of Social Sciences (Moscow), 248
Adoratsky, V. V., 219
Adzhariya: *see* Caucasus
Afghanistan, 160 n.
Africa 17, 155 f., 171, 174; Sov. historians on, 11, 28, 165
air force, Soviet, 227 f.
Airapetyan, M., 252, 265 f.
Albertson, R., 299 f.
Aleksandrov, A., 24
Aleksandrov, G., 43, 88
Aleksandrovsky, S. S., 264 n.
Alekseyev, Gen. M. V., 139, 296
Alekseyev, V. M., 180 f.
Algeria, 110, 176
All-Union Society for Dissemination of Political and Scientific Knowledge, 248
Amanullah, Emir, 160 n.
Andreyeva, M., 259
Androsov, V. P., 313
Anikeyev, V. V., 72, 75
Antonov-Ovseyenko, V. A., 21, 264 n.
Aptheker, H., 38
Aralov, S. I., 264 n.

archives, Soviet: guides to, 119, 130, 148; organization of, 118, 131, 146; use of, by Soviet historians, 11, 14, 19 f., 27 f., 30, 33, 37, 43, 72, 118 f., 126 n., 129, 144, 149 f., 260; by Western historians, 130, 148; cf. documents, Smolensk
Arctic and northern regions, 31, 131, 299 ff.
Aristov, A. B., 40
Arkhiv Russkoi Revolyutsii, 140
Armenia: *see* Transcaucasia
army, Soviet, and Party 225 ff., 232 f., 236, 240, 242; Sov. historians on, 11, 136, 140, 151, 223, 240; cf. World War II (eastern front)
Arosev, A., 264 n.
art, history of, 29
Arutyunyan, Yu. V., 128
Asia, history of: *see* decolonization, nationalism, Oriental studies
Aspaturian, V. V., 17, **88,** 111, **112, 116, 150 f.,** 171 ff., **243–74, 275 f.,** 277, 282, **283 ff.**
Astakhov, G., 236, 262
Ataturk, Kemal, 159, 170
atrocities, 299–304
Attlee, Lord, 103
Aveling, E., 209
Azerbaidzhan: *see* Transcaucasia

Bakhrushin, S. V., 145
Baku, 32
Bakunin, M. A., 25, 200
Balabusevich, V. V., 158 n.
Balfour, A. J., 293
Baltic Sailors in Revolution of 1917, 139 f.
Baltic states, 57, 263, 298
Baranovsky, M. I., 186 f.
Barghoorn, F. C., 106

Basso, L., 213
Baturin, N. N., 47 n.
Bauer, O., 155 n.
Bazilevich, V. V., 145
Beard, C., 39, 308, 313
Beck, J., 264 n.
Bekzadian, 264 n.
Belinsky, V. G., 128, 181 f., 200
Beloff, M., 306–314
Belorussia, 132, 238, 263
Belov, G. A., 131, 133, 142 f.
Belyaev, N. I., 55
Beneš, President E., 238 f., 261
Beria, L. P., 54, 118, 124; as historian, 40, 66, 147; Sov. historians on, 53, 58, 77, 264 n.
Berlin, Sir I., 9, **40 f., 89,** 91, **220,** 274
Bernstein, E., 205, 207–14, 217, 220
Berzin, J., 264 n.
Bessarabia, 238, 295
Bichurin, N. Ya., 181
Bill of Rights (USA), 309 f.
Blanqui, A., Blanquism, 203, 208
Blum, L., 207
Blyukher, Marshal V. K., 264 n.
Blyumkin, 142f.
Bogomolov, D. V., 264 n.
Bograd, Z. M., 201
Bolshevik: see *Kommunist*
Bolshevism, origins of: *see* Populism
Bolsover, G. H., 39, 83, **111,** 112, **147 f.**
Boltin, Maj.-Gen. E. A., 227, 233
Bonnet, G., 238
Borisov, Yu. V., 239
Bose, S. Chandra, 158 n.
Bubnov, A. S., 47 f.
Budenny, Marshal S. M., 232
Budovnits, I. U., 153
Bugaev, E. I., 22 f., 24 f., 34, 40, 42, 70 f., 74 f., 80
Bukharin, N. I., 30 f., 62, 151
Bulganin, N. A., 54, 59, 264 n.
Bullitt, W. C., 264 n.
Bund (General Union of Jewish Workers), 50, 78
Burdzhalov, E. N.: appointed editor of *Vop. Istorii*, 121; unorthodox views of, 22, 69 f., 74, 204; support for, 34, 37; motives of, 34, 36, 38–41, 215; attacks on, 22 ff., 70, 74 f.; dismissal of, 14, 26, 70, 73; significance of, 13, 35, 40 f.; later career of, 14, 122; 111, 148
Burma, 159, 162 f., 196
Bushuev, S. K., 25

Cambon, P., 270
Carr, E. H., 15, 65
Castro, F., 166
Caucasus: in World War II, 229; Sov. historians on, 21 f., 25, 32, 132
Central Asia, 27, 131 f., 179, 184, 190
Central Party Archive, 119 n., 131
Central State Archive of Soviet Army, 131 f.
Central State Archive of Soviet Navy, 131
Central State Archive of October Revolution and Socialist Construction, 131, 133
Central State Military-Historical Archive, 139
Ceylon, 162 f.
Chagin, B. A., 208 f.
Chamberlain, N. S., 235, 241, 260, 264 n.
Chamberlin, W. H., 139
Chartism, 205, 211
Chavannes, E., 180
Cheka: *see* police (political)
Ch'en Po-ta, 183
Cheremisov, Gen. V. A., 140
Cherepnin, L. V., 145
Chernomorsky, 146
Chernyak, E. B., 310 f.
Chernyshevsky, N. G., 128, 181 f., 187, 217
Cherzhevsky, 295
Chiang Chung-fang, 192
Chiang Kai-shek, Marshal, 168, 252
Chicherin, G. V., 152, 264 n., 275
China, 168, 268; revolution and communism in, 85, 156 f., 171 f., 175, 177, 186, 279; historiography in, 64, 85, 87 f., 177, 184, 192 f.; Lenin and Stalin on, 156, 171, 183, 185; Sov. historians on, 171, 183 ff., 187 ff., 190 f., 197, 252;
— , relations with USSR (to 1949), 177, 184 f., 190; (1949–), 18, 85, 175, 177 f., 189, 195 f., 197, 214, 272, 278; Sov. historians on, 133, 177–92, 195 f.
Chinese Eastern Railway, 190, 192, 197

Chubar, V. A., 21
Chuikov, Marshal V. I., 241
Chukotka, 131
Churchill, Sir W., 111, 256, 260, 264 n.
civil war, American, Sov. historians on, 308; Russian, Sov. historians on, 25, 52, 54, 131 f., 191 f., 286–305
Clemenceau, G., 238
co-existence, peaceful: defined, 272 ff.; 18, 23, 25, 39, 111 f., 245, 258 f.
Cole, G. D. H., 216, 219
collective work, by Sov. historians, 125, 135 f., 151
collectivization of agriculture, Sov. historians on, 30 f., 34, 36, 57, 77 f., 83, 132
Collingwood, R. G., 39
Comintern: see International (Third)
Commonwealth, British, 107 f.
communism, as objective in USSR, 18, 90, 125 ff., 133, 210
Communist Academy (Moscow), 153
Communist Party of Soviet Union:
    conferences of: VII (1917), 22, 24, 29, 147; XV (1926) 21; XVI (1929), 21;
    congresses of: I (1898), 78; IV (1906), 79; V (1907), 79; VI (1917), 29 f., 203; XIII (1924), 77; XVIII (1939), 238, 256; XIX (1952), 54, 58, 120; XX (1956), 10, 21 f., 34, 56, 58 f., 73 f., 124, 183, 195, 224, 265; XXI (1959), 55 f., 59, 94, 125, 134; XXII (1961), 10, 54, 56, 64, 81, 126, 227;
    decrees and resolutions of: (1938), 71, 82; (1956), 22, 39, 41, 226; (1957), 70 f., 73, 80, 124, 200; (1960), 32 f., 72, 125;
    history of: significance of, 61, 63 f., 66 f.; Sov. historians on (to 1953), 47–51, 200, (cf. Stalin); (1953–   ), 20, 29, 43–7, 51–62; on period 1903–17, 22 ff., 29, 37 f., 44 ff., 66, 70, 72 f., 79, 87, 109; on period 1917–28, 21, 26, 29, 54 f., 77; on period 1928–53, 21, 31, 53, 56 ff.;
    organizations of: central committee (to 1917), 66, 79; (1917–8), 37, 79, 141, 147, 204; (1929), 32; (1957–   ), 126, 225, 227; secretariat, 40; Agit-prop, 51 f., 64, 71, 76, 148; Moscow bureau, 40, 58; committees, 31,
    204; cf. Higher Party School, Inst. of Marxism-Leninism;
    programmes of: (1919), 62; (1961), 56, 62, 126;
    role of, in Soviet society, 14, 16, 18, 63, 83, 89 f., 214;
    cf. ideology
'compradore bourgeoisie', 160 f., 164
concentration camps, 31, 34, 301
Concise Account of History of CPSU: see History of CPSU
Congress party (India), 156, 162 f.
Conservative party, 104
Constitution, USA, 111, 308–312
constitutional government: see democracy
'contradictions', capitalist, Sov. historians on, 96 f., 106–9
Cooper, Duff, 260
Crimean War, 41
Croce, B., 39, 193
Cuba, 166, 173, 268, 314
'cult of the individual': see Stalin, Khrushchev
Czechoslovakia: and Russian civil war, 292, 294–8, 302; and Munich crisis, 238 f., 260 f., 264 n., and USSR, 133

Dagestan: see Caucasus
Daladier, E., 235
Danilov, V. P., 127
Danilova, 38
Davtian, Ya. K., 264 n.
Deborin, A. M., 308, 312
Deborin, G., 252
Decembrists, 128
Declaration of Independence (USA), 88, 308, 310
decolonization, 254; Sov. historians on, 111, 113 ff., 172 f.
De Gaulle, Gen. C., 264 n.
Degras, J., 113 f., 151, 151, 279 f.
democracy (Western), 93; Sov. historians on, 102–6, 310 ff.
Democratic Centralists, 55
Democratic party (USA), 311
Deutscher, I., 83
Dewey, J., 114
dialectical materialism, 89; and Sov. foreign policy, 250 ff.
dictatorship of proletariat, 80, 102

diplomacy, 266 ff.; Sov. definitions of, 249 f., 270; *see* foreign policy
Diplomatic Dictionary (1948), 243, 249, 260 f., 264, 275; (1960–1), 248, 264 n., 270
disarmament, 277, 282
Dmitriev, S. S., 150
Dmitrieva, K., 259
Dobrolyubov, N. A., 128, 181
Documents on Soviet Foreign Policy (1957–), 133, 150, 152, 247, 264 n.
documents, publication of, 27 f., 29 f., 33, 118 f., 127, 130–44, 146 f., 150 f.; significance of, 37, 41, 130; rules for, 72, 133, 134, 146, 150; non-observance of, 141 f., 147; extent of bias in, 37, 65, 72, 134, 138, 143 f., 147
Doerr, H., 229
Drabkina, F. I., 24, 36 f.
Druzhinin, N. M., 59, 145, 150
Dukhonin, Gen. N. N., 288
Dulles, J. F., 264 n.
Dzerzhinsky, F. E., 142 f.

economic development, Western, 92, 95 ff.; Soviet, 133
Economic Problems of Socialism (Stalin), 88, 111, 120, 122, 201
Economism, 45
Eden, Sir A., 260
education, history of, 128
Egypt, 156, 162 f., 166 f., 173, 280; Sov. historians on, 159, 166 f.
Eisenhower, President D. D., 104
elections (in West), Sov. historians on, 103 f.
Encyclopedia, Large Soviet, 181 f., 186, 195, 227 n., 244; *Philosophical,* 161; *Small Soviet,* 161; *Soviet Historical,* 29
Engels, F., 21, 156, 181, 202, 209, 220, 254 f., 264 n.
Essays on History of Great Patriotic War (1955), 224 n., 233
'expropriations', Bolshevik (1905–7), 53

Fabian Society, 209
Fadeyev, A., 224
Fainsod, M., 13 f., 18, **19–33, 34 f., 36, 39, 41, 63 f., 90,** 90, **115 f.,** 144

Far East, 174, 197; *see individual countries*
feudalism, 45; Russian, 38, 45; Asian, 172, 188
fictions: *see* myth
Finland, 57, 147, 298
Foch, Marshal F., 293 f.
Foner, P., 308
foreign policy, Soviet, 106, 112 f., 157, 160, 170, 177, 250 ff., 254, 268 f., 277 ff., 282; Sov. historians on, 133, 150, 152, 235, 243–8, 257–66; and pre-revolutionary Russian policy, 255, 277, 280 f.; and Western policy, 269–76, 281
Foster, W. Z., 38
Fourier, C., 217
France: socialism and communism in, 176, 208, 218 f.; and Russian civil war, 290, 292 f., 295, 297, 301; and Munich crisis, 238 f., 261; 133, 279
Francis, D. R., 289 f., 295
Freymond, J., 9, **277 f.,** 278, 280, 282
From the History of the Cheka: cf. *Iz Istorii VChK*

Galkin, I. S., 246
Gallagher, M., 110 f., 112, **148, 222–36, 236 ff.,** 239, 240, **241 f.**
Galperin, A., 184
Gandhi, Mahatma, 158, 170
Ganetsky (Fürstenberg, J. S.), 37, 141, 147
Garthoff, R., 241
Gates, J., 207
Georgia: *see* Transcaucasia, Guria
Germany: socialism and communism in, 48, 104, 218, 280; Sov. historians on, 209 ff., 213, 216; historiography in, 65 f., 152, 163 n.; Nazism in, 66 ff., 166, 234, 313 f.;
— —, and Russia (1917–8), 37, 141, 147, 287 f., 294, 302; (1922), 152; (1939–41), 159, 283 f.; Sov. historians on, 78, 83, 222, 235 f., 238 f., 239 f., 262 f., 265 f., 275; (1941–5: *see* World War II); (since 1945), 133, 283
Gershuni, G., 50
Giolitti, G., 212 f.
Goering, Marshal H., 264 n.
Golikov, G., 133 f.

Gomulka, W., 264 n.
Goncharov, I. A., 187
Gorky, M., 128
Gospolitizdat: *see* State Publishing House of Political Literature
Gottwald, K., 239, 261, 264 n.
GPU: *see* police (political)
Grand Alliance (1941–5), 260; Sov. historians on, 222, 224 f., 233, 235
Graves, Gen. W. S., 302 f.
Great Britain: communism in, 104, 207 f., 218 f.; Sov. historians on, 95, 98 f., 103, 205, 235; and Russia (1917–8), 292 f., 300; (1939–41), 78, 241, 260 f.; and United States, 107, 111, 279
Great Patriotic War: *see* World War II (eastern front)
Grechev, M. A., 314
Grechko, Marshal A. A., 231
Grekov, B. D., 120, 129, 145
Gromyko, A. A., 264 n., 311
Guber, A. A., 121, 244 n.
Guchkov, A. I., 139
Guinea, 165
Guria, 147
Guseinov, 32

Halifax, Lord, 260, 264 n.
Halle, L., 113, 282
Hamilton, A., 312
Hanecki: *see* Ganetsky
Harbin, 190
Hegel, F., 193
Helbig, H., 152
Helsinki, 147
Herzen, A. I., 128, 200
Higher Party School (Moscow), 94, 104, 245 f., 248, 263, 266
Hilferding, R., 155 n., 213
historians, historiography, Soviet:
appeal of, 17, 169;
classification of, 35;
Communist Party control of, 10, 12–17, 19–28, 32–7, 40, 43–68, 69–91, 94 f., 109, 114 ff., 117–29, 133 f., 138, 143–7, 149 f., 152 ff., 155, 158 ff., 178, 199, 205, 207, 213, 223, 243 f.;
crisis in (1955–7), 16, 19–28, 73 f.,
76 f., 116–21, 123–9, 148, 183, 195, 199–213, 215, 223, 237; significance of, 35, 202, 215;
discussions and conferences of, 25; (1952), 195; (1956), 20, 23 f., 34, 163 n.; (1957), 124, 233; (1958), 65 f.; (1961), 126; (1962), 12 f., 14, 81, 126;
ethical and psychological attitudes of, 14–17, 20, 31, 33, 35, 78, 83, 109, 115, 123 f., 217;
and evidence, 32, 113 f., 123, 222, 238, 240, 287;
freedom among: *see supra,* Communist Party control;
future of, 18, 41, 217;
organization of, 120 f., 145, 247 f.;
physical expansion of (1953–), 11 ff., 20, 27 ff., 109, 119 f., 145, 246 f., 275;
professionalism among, 13 f., 19, 27 f., 35;
scholarly value of, 9, 11 f., 19, 34, 38, 40, 127, 144, 149, 164, 193 ff., 247, 259, 286 f., 304 f.;
study of (in USSR), 129; (in West), 117, 144, 148;
and western historians, 12, 19, 28, 38, 65, 83, 94, 111, 117 f., 121, 123, 148, 151, 213, 220, 240;
see purges
history, philosophy of, 11, 15 ff., 121, 148 ff., 253
History of Civil War in USSR (1947), 289, 293, 297 n.
History of CPSU (1959), 52–61, 71 ff., 75–82, 87, 90, 204, 241; compared with Stalin's *Short Course*, 52, 53 f., 57 ff., 62 f., 67, 69, 71, 76, 77–82, 82–5, 88 f.; revised edition (1962), 60; 6-vol. edition, proposed, 55 f., 60 f., 73, 81 f.
History of Diplomacy (1945–50), 243, 250, 260; (1959–), 29, 248, 257
History of Great Patriotic War of Soviet Union (1960–), 225, 227, 231 f., 235, 238 f., 259–62, 275
History of . . . Soviet Foreign Policy (1957), 246, 263
History of USA (1959–60), 94, 98 f., 104 f.
History of World, 246

Hitler, A., 66 f., 78, 167, 234, 241, 263 n.,
    264 n., 284
Hoover Library, 142
House, Col. E. M., 293
Hudson, R. S., 241
Hull, Cordell, 264 n.
Hungarian revolution (1956), Sov. his-
    torians on, 57, 272; effect on Sov.
    historiography, 25, 34, 70, 73, 118,
    206, 219, 223

ideology, Marxist-Leninist: nature and
    function of, 89 ff., 116, 219, 274;
    appeal of, attempt by Party to sustain,
    87, 89, 112, 174, 200 f., 206, 210,
    215 f.;
— —, and Sov. historiography 12–17,
    19, 26 f., 43, 61, 64 ff., 81, 89, 93, 112,
    126, 148 ff., 153, 179, 200, 223, 247,
    306 f.;
    and diplomacy, 248, 250–3, 275–85
impoverishment of proletariat: see
    living standards (Western)
India, 156, 162 f., 167, 196; Sov. his-
    torians on, 111, 114, 158, 170; and
    USSR, 133
Indonesia, 162 f., 166 f., 176, 196
industrial conditions (in West), Sov.
    historians on, 101
Industrial party, 57
industrial unrest (in West), Sov. his-
    torians on, 105
industrialization (in USSR), 57, 132
industry, nationalization of: in USSR,
    203; in West, 92; Sov. historians on,
    98 f.
Institute of Historical Archives, 130
Institute of Marxism-Leninism (Mos-
    cow), 40, 71, 81, 119 n., 131, 133,
    233 f., 259, 287
Institute of Red Professors, 153
Institute of World Politics and World
    Economics, 248 n.
integration, Western, 93, 108 f.; Sov.
    historians on, 106–9, 276
intelligentsia, role of, in under-developed
    societies, 166, 173, 175
International, Socialist, First, 63;
    Second, 46; Third (Communist), 46,
    62, 156 f., 159 f., 163, 165, 170, 184,

243, 249, 261; Sov. historians on, 151,
    278 ff.
International Affairs (Moscow), 276
International Congress of Historians:
    X (Rome, 1955), 12, 117 f., 124;
    XI (Stockholm, 1960), 12, 59, 118,
    125, 141
International Institute for Social His-
    tory (Amsterdam), 219
international law, Sov. attitude to,
    268 f., 273 f.
International Law Association of USSR,
    248
International Relations in Far East (1951,
    1956), 197
Iokange, 301
Iraq, 162, 166, 173
Iskra, 45 f., 50
Islam, 157, 197
Israel, 160
Istoricheskie Zapiski, 119, 146
Istoricheskii Arkhiv, 118 f.
Istoricheskii Zhurnal, 222 n.
Istoriya SSSR, 28, 30, 119
Italy, 212 f., 216 ff.
Ivanov, G., 143
Ivanov, Col.-Gen. S. P., 231
Ivashin, I. F., 245 f., 263 n., 266
Iz Istorii VChK (1958), 142

Jackson, President A., 308
Japan, 161, 174, 185; and Russian civil
    war, 293, 296, 302; Sov. historians on,
    184, 187 ff.
Jassy, conference at (1917), 295, 297
Jefferson, President T., 308
Jenkins, D., 290 f.
Jensen, M., 308
Joffe, A. A., 247, 264 n.
journals, Soviet historical, 11, 28 f., 70,
    119 f., 244

Kadets (Constitutional Democrats),
    44 f.
Kaganovich, L. M., 53 f., 58, 207, 264 n.
Kalinin, M. I., 31, 132, 264 n.
Kamenev, L. B., 22, 30, 204, 247
Kandel, E. P., 207 f.
Kant, I., 267
Karakhan, L. M., 247, 264 n.

Kardashev, D. I., 47
Kardelj, E., 257
Kassem, Gen. A. K., 162, 166, 173
Katkov, G., 11, **36 f., 88 f., 111 f.,** 112, 130–44, **146 f.,** 150, 152, **240**
Kautsky, B., 213
Kautsky, K., 24, 155 n., 209, 211, 213
Kaverin, G. I., 308
Kazakevich, E., 37, 40, 147
Kazakevich, R. A., 146
Kazakhstan, 31
Kazan, 126 n.
Kechekyan, S. F., 129, 145
Keep, J. L. H., 9–18, 86 f., **92–109,** 109 f., 112, 113, 146, **239 f.**
Kellogg-Briand pact, 259, 263, 275
Kemal, Mustafa, 156, 159 f.
Kennan, G. F., 286–305
Kennedy, President J. F., 274
Kerensky, A. F., 140
Kerth, Major M. C., 288 f.
Kerzhentsev, P. M., 47
Kharkov, battle of, 240
Kheifets, A. N., 191 f.
Khrenov, I. A., 26
Khrushchev, N. S., 14, 18, 21 f., 52 f., 172, 202, 206, 218 f., 273; on history, 43; as historian of Party, 52–64; — —, historical role emphasized, in recent Party histories, 36, 54 ff., 58–61, 67, 83 f., 88, 125; in histories of World War II, 231 f., 238, 241 f., 264 n.
Khvostov, V. M., 121, 265 f.
Kiev, 23, 140, 290 f., 295; battle of (1941), 231 f., 237 f.
Kim, M. P., 126 f.
Kirichenko, A. I., 55
Kirov, S. M., 53
Kiryaev, N. M., 232
Klyuchevsky, V. O., 29, 39
Knorin, V., 47, 48 f., 52
Kolakowski, L., 207
Kolchak, Admiral A. V., 292, 294, 302
Kollontai, A., 264 n.
Kommunist (formerly *Bolshevik*), 22, 24, 26, 39, 70, 73, 87, 122 f., 133, 226, 230, 233 f., 254, 280
Kon, I. S., 40
Konev, Marshal I. S., 227
Korea, 191, 195
Kornilov, L. G., 296

Korovin, E., 244 f.
Kosarev, A. V., 21
Kossior, S. V., 21
Kostomarov, G., 70, 201
Kovalev, 186
Kovalevsky, M. M., 145, 153
Kozlovsky, M. Yu., 37, 141, 147
Kozmin, B. P., 63
Krachkovsky, I. Yu., 180
Krasnaya Nov, 139
Krasnaya Zvezda, 226
Krasnov, Gen. P. N., 140
Krasnyi Arkhiv, 139 f.
Krestinsky, N. N., 150, 264 n.
Kronstadt, 54, 139
Krutikova, N. I., 24
Krylenko, N. V., 247
Krylov, S. B., 243
Kuczynski, J., 213
Kühlmann, R. von, 147
Kuibyshev, V. V., 201
kulaks, 30 f., 78
Kulik, Marshal G. I., 227
Kunina, A. E., 299
Kuo Mo-jo, 184
Kurochkin, Col.-Gen. P., 224 n.
Kursk, battle of (1943), 229
Kutuzov, Field-Marshal M. I., 229, 237
Kux, E , 65 f.
Kuznetsov, A. A., 264 n.
Kuznetsova, S. I., 25
Kyakhta, treaty of (1727), 184

Labedz, L., 16, **39 f., 64, 84 f., 89 f.,** 112 f., 114, **219 f., 282**
Labour party, 104, 208
La Croix, V. L. de, 238 f.
Landshut, S., 208
Lansing, R., 291 f., 296
Laqueur, W. Z., 40, 65, 155–69, 169 ff., 174
Lashevich, M. M., 40
Laski, H., 207 f., 216
Lasky, M., 66, 282 f., 284
Lassalle, F., 25, 200
Latin America, 28, 166 f., 174, 309
Latsis, M. Ya., 142
Leede, V. Ya., 313
Leipzig, conference at (1959), 163 n., 167

Lenin, V. I., 21, 66, 172, 203, 218, 248, 257, 279; in 1917, 22, 37, 70, 141, 204; and Asia, 155 n., 156 f., 170; — —, as historian, 44 ff., 61 f., 123, 202; Sov. historians on, 24, 26, 36, 53, 62, 73 f., 76 f., 147, 209, 264 n.; — —,Testament of, 77; works of, 119; cf. Leninism
Lenin Library (Moscow), 149
Leningrad, 23 f., 34, 44, 74 ff., 120, 140, 204; University of, 119, 180 f.; group (in CPSU), 40; treaty of St. Petersburg (1896), 191
Leninism: and Marxism, 82 f., 87, 89 ff., 93, 103, 108 f., 110, 113, 116, 202, 204, 218; and Populism, 36, 38, 44, 86 f.; and Stalinism, 38, 116, 218
Leninskii Sbornik, 141
Levin, I. D., 249
Liberation of Labour group, 73
Liebknecht, K., 209
Lincoln, President A., 308
Litvinov, M. M., 260, 263 f., 275
Liu Shao-ch'i, 192
living standards, Western, 92 f., 100; Sov. historians on, 95, 99–102, 110, 113, 212 f.
Lloyd George, D., 260
Lomonosov, M. V., 128
Lord, R. H., 291 f.
Lossky, N. O., 121
Lowenthal, R., 150, 153, **174 ff., 217 f.,** 219, **278 f.**
Lozovsky, S. A., 243
Lurye, Ya. S., 154
Luxemburg, R., 155 n., 209, 213 f., 216 f.
Lyadov, M. N., 47, 62
Lysenko, T. D., 128
Lyubimov, N., 244 n.
Lyubimova, V., 101
Lyubosh, 140

MacArthur, Gen. D., 263
Madison, President J., 309
Magadan, 131
Main Archive Administration, 130–4, 142 f., 146, 148
Main Political Administration of Red Army, 227 n.
Makarenko, A. S., 128

Makintsian, P., 142
Malenkov, G. M., 53 f., 58, 77, 207, 242, 264 n.
Malinovsky, Marshal R. Ya., 225 f.
Maltzan, Baron A. von, 152
Mancall, M., 18, **85,** 87, **174, 177–92, 192–6,** 196, 197, **197 f.**
Manchuria, 190, 192, 197
Mandelshtam, O. E., 143
Manfred, A., 244 n.
Manuilsky, D. Z., 264 n.
Mao Tse-tung, 85, 164, 172, 175, 184, 186 f., 192, 264 n.
Margolin, A. D., 291 f.
Marr, N. Ya., 122, 147
Marshall, Gen. G. C., 252
Martov, Yu. O., 50
Marx, K., 21, 93, 205, 211, 217, 219 f.; Sov. historians on, 78, 200, 202, 207, 216, 264 n.
Marxism, 39, 45, 87, 89, 97, 110, 201, 205, 207 f.; and Asia, 156, 170, 178; and diplomacy, 248, 254
Marx-Engels-Lenin Institute (Moscow), 119
Marxism and Questions of Linguistics (Stalin), 122
Masaryk, President T. G., 295–8
Maslennikov, V. A., 163 n.
Matyushkin, N. I., 122
Mavrodin, V. V., 13
Mayorov, S., 245
McLane, C., 64, 85, 196
Meadows, T., 187
medicine, history of, 128
Medvedev, V. K., 30, 36
Meijer, J. M., 35, 41, 153
Meinecke, F., 148
Mekhlis, L. Z., 227
Melchin, A. I., 299
memoirs, historical, 24, 37, 127; distortion and suppression of, 22, 51, 53, 82, 146
Mendeleyev, D. I., 128
Mensheviks, Menshevism: role in 1905 and 1917 re-assessed, 22, 24, 26 f., 69, 72–6, 79, 202, 204; suppression and trial of, 57, 80, 84; reasons for continued attacks on, 80, 83 f., 85 f.
Merkalov, 262
Mezhdunarodnaya Zhizn, 244, 247 f., 265

Mikoyan, A. I., 21, 34, 42, 54, 202, 244 n., 264 n.
Mileikovsky, A. G., 107, 213
Miller, D. H., 298 f.
Milyukov, P. N., 296
Ministry of Defence, 224 n., 227, 241
Ministry of Education, 72
Ministry of Foreign Affairs, 243 f., 248, 275; Commission for Publication of Diplomatic Documents, 131, 133
Ministry of Internal Affairs, 118, 130; see also police (political), Main Archives Administration
Ministry of State Control, 227 n.
Mints, I. I., 52, 71, 75
Mirbach, Count R. von, 142 f.
Mirbach, Count W. von, 142
Mirovaya Ekonomika i Mezhdunarodnye Otnosheniya, 248 n.
Mirovoe Khozyaistvo i Mirovaya Politika, 248 n.
Modern History of Countries of Non-Soviet Asia and Africa (1959), 158 f.
Modern History of Countries of Non-Soviet East (1952), 158, 188
Molotov, V. M., 172, 262; upgrading of, 201; downgrading of, 53 f., 58, 77, 207, 262 ff., 275
Mongolia, 157, 189
monopolies, in West, 92; Sov. historians on, 97 ff.
Monroe doctrine, 309
Moscow, 163 n., 201, 289; battle of (1941), 229; trials at (1936–8), 53, 57, 80, 84; University of, 25, 69 f., 119, 188, 200, 246, 287
Moskalev, M. A., 24 f.
Mudyug, Island of, 301
Munich, agreement of (1938), Sov. historians on, 235, 238 f., 259 ff., 275
Muslim Brotherhood (Egypt), 167
Mussolini, B., 61, 167, 264 n.
myth, element of, in Sov. histories of Communist Party, 27, 36, 39, 54, 74, 84, 87, 111 ff., 127; of West, 95, 102, 106, 108 f., 110; of Asia, 194 f., of socialism, 219;
— , versus reality, in minds of Sov. historians, 15 ff., 83 f., 86, 88, 307

Naida, S. F., 122, 287–305
Nakhichevan, 132
Narochnitsky, A. L., 191
Narodnaya Volya, narodnichestvo: see Populism
Nasser, President G., 159, 162, 166 f., 173, 280
Nasyrin, V. P., 203 f., 205, 215
'national bourgeoisie', in colonial and ex-colonial countries: definition of, 155, 160 f., 174; Sov. attitude to, 158, 162–9, 171 ff., 175 f., 276
National Committee of Soviet Historians, 121
'national democracy', 168
nationalism, Asian, Sov. attitude to: before 1953, 155–8, 163, 164 f., 170 f., 174; since 1953, 158–169, 170 f., 172, 173 f.; Western attitude to, 172 ff.
nationalism, Russian, 27, 36, 128, 154, 255
nationalities, non-Russian, in USSR, Sov. historians on, 21 f., 27 f., 32, 36, 124
NATO, 106, 109
Nauchnye Doklady Vysshei Shkoly, 119 f.
navy, Soviet, history of, 132, 139 f.
Naydenov, M. E., 129 n.
Near and Middle East, 162 f., 166 f., 173, 175; Sov. historians on, 159 f., 162, 165; see also *individual countries*
Nechkina, M. V., 39
Negroes, in USA, 115 f., 308 f.
Nehru, J., 158
Nekrasov, V. P., 241
Nenni, P., 212 f.
Neue Zürcher Zeitung, 147
neutralism, 168
Nevsky, V. I., 47 f.
New Deal (in USA), 312 f.
New Times (Moscow), 276
Nicolson, Sir H., 250, 270, 275 f.
Nikhamin, V. P., 263 n.
Nikiforov, V. N., 187 f.
Nikolaevsky, B. I., 40, 64 f., 66, 207 f.
NKVD: see police (political), Ministry of Internal Affairs
Novaya i Noveyshaya Istoriya, 28, 119
Novyi Vostok, 170

Obichkin, G. D., 71
Obolensky, Prince, 50
Ocherki Istorii VChK (1956), 143
October Armed Insurrection in Petrograd (1957), 140
Odessa, University of, 200
Ogarev, N. P., 128
Oktyabr, 37, 40
Opposition, in CPSU: left-wing, 46, 55, 57; right-wing, 26, 31 f., 55, 57, 73
Ordzhonikidze, G. K., 264 n.
Orenburg, 132
Oriental studies: in Russia to 1917, 181 f.; in USSR to 1953, 171, 178–87, 194 f., 196 ff.; since 1953, 11, 18, 28, 155, 182 f., 189—92, 197 f.; in West, 174, 192 f.; congress on (Moscow, 1960), 169; *see also* China (historiography in)
Oxenstierna, A., 257

Pankratova, A. M., 121, 129; and crisis of 1955–7, 21 f., 25 f., 34, 40, 69 ff., 73, 244; death of, 26, 70
Paris Commune (1871), 204, 208; Peace Conference (1918–9), 293
Partiinaya Zhizn, 22, 24 ff., 34, 40 ff., 71, 151
partiinost, 13, 26 f., 43, 61, 73 ff., 95, 180
partisanship: *see partiinost*
Pashkov, A. I., 129
Paulus, Field-Marshal F. von, 230
Pavlodar, 132
Pavlov, I. P., 128
Pavlovich-Veltman, M., 155 n., 170
'Pedders, Major J.', 302 ff.
people's commissariats: *see* ministries
'periodization', Sov. historians on, 45 f., 73, 86, 178, 183, 187 f., 195, 264 f.
Persia, 156, 160 n., 167
personalities, role of, Sov. historians on, 53 f., 123, 149, 151, 275; cf. Stalin, Khrushchev
Peter the Great, 41
Petlyura, S. V., 290 f.
Petrashevsky, M. V., 128
Philipp, W., 117 n.
Philippines, 310, 314
Pikman, A. M., 21 f., 25
Pisarev, D. I., 128
Platonov, S. P., 237, 241

Plekhanov, G. V., 50, 73, 199 f., 209, 215
Pod Znamenem Marksizma, 219
Pokrovsky, M. N., 62, 120, 144 f., 205; rehabilitation of, 21, 39, 48 n., 129
Poland, communism in, 39, 207, 209, 212, 216–20; historiography in, 39, 64, 205; and Russia 133; (1918–20), 279, 298; (1939–45), 235, 261, 263; (1956–), 25, 34, 70, 206, 211
Polevoy, Yu. Z., 73, 78, 87, 146
police, political, 30 f., 43, 65, 142 f.
Political Dictionary (1958), 161
Ponomarev, B. N., 12 f., 49, 52, 65, 71
Popov, 143
Popov, F., 297 n.
Popov, N. N., 47
Populism, 63, 146, 156, 213; and origins of Bolshevism, 36, 38, 40, 44, 73, 86 f.
Pospelov, P. N., 81
Postyshev, P. P., 21
Potekhin, I. I., 159 n.
Potemkin, V. P., 250, 264 n.
Pravda, 31, 50, 55 f., 61, 73, 81, 87, 115, 123, 231
Prinkipo, 291
Problemy Vostokovedeniya, 182, 184, 196
Proletarskaya Revolyutsiya, 139
Proudhon, P.-J., 200, 220
Pskov, 228
Publishing House of Eastern Literature (Moscow), 155, 169
Pugwash conference, 277
purges, 31; of Sov. historians, 48 f., 243; Sov. historians on, 53, 77

Radek, K., 155 n.
Radishchev, A. N., 128
Raeff, M., 38, **148 f.**, 150, **153**, 153
Rakovsky, Kh. G., 238, 247
Rapallo, treaty of (1922), 152, 260
Raskolnikov, F. F., 140, 143, 150
Rathenau, W., 152
Red Book of the VChK, 142
Red Guards, 75 f., 191
Red Professors' Institute of Party History, 47, 49
Reed, J., 37, 84
Republican party (USA), 104
research, organization of: see historiography (Soviet), organization of

revisionism, 39, 109, 205–14, 217 f.,
219 f.; attacked, 26 f., 80 f., 84, 87,
122, 125, 206 f., 209, 216; condoned,
22, 26, 202
revolution, American, 308, 312; Russian,
of 1905, 44, 49; Sov. historians on,
22, 26, 29, 69, 73 f., 76, 87, 119, 122,
147, 153, 190, 201; Russian, of 1917,
204, 268; Sov. historians on, 22, 25,
29, 54, 74 ff., 79, 87, 119, 122, 131 f.,
133 f., 138 ff., 182, 184, 186 f., 191,
203 f., 211, 288–94
Reza Khan, 160 n.
Ribbentrop, J., 262, 263 n., 264 n.
Rogachevskaya, L. S., 128
Romodin, 188
Roosevelt, President F. D., 264 n., 312
Roshal, 140
Rothstein, T., 170
Roy, M. N., 157, 170
Rozhkov, B. A., 205
Rubel, M., 207 f., 219
Rubinstein, A. Z., 113, 114, **115, 173 f.,
276 f.,** 284
Rules for Publication of Documents on
Soviet Period (RPDSP), Rules for
Publication of Historical Documents
(RPHD): see documents
Rumania, 57, 133, 238, 261, 293, 297
Russia, history of (to 1917), 281; Sov.
historians on, 20 f., 29, 120, 149, 191;
(since 1917), 25, 29 ff., 32, 127 f.,
132 f., 146; see also Communist
Party, economic development, foreign
policy, revolution, social thought,
World War II
Russo-Polish War (1920), 279
Ryazanov, D. B., 219
Rykov, A. I., 204

Sabanin, A. V., 151
Sablukov, G. S., 182
Saburov, M. Z., 54, 58
Safarov, G. I., 155 n., 170
Safronov, 145, 153
St. Petersburg: see Leningrad
Saint-Simon, Count H. de, 217
Samsonov, A. M., 229 f.
Satow, Sir E., 270
Saudi Arabia, 160
Savelev, M. A., 31

Schaff, A., 39
Schapiro, L. B., 15, **37, 42, 63,** 64, 65,
68–82, 82 ff., 84, 85, 86, **90 f.,** 113,
139 n., **153,** 153, **240 f.**
Scheibert, P., 38 f., 115, 149 f., 150, 153,
153, **217,** 217, 219, **281 f.,** 284
Schnurre, E., 262
**Schram, S. R., 66, 87 f., 151 f., 196 f.,
238 f.**
Schulenberg, Count F. W. von, 262
science, history of, 128
Sechenov, I. M., 128
Second World War (1948), 241
Semennikov, V. P., 147
Semipalatinsk, 132
Shamil, Sov. historians on, 21 f., 25, 32,
35 f., 154, 182
Shchadenko, E. A., 227
Shchors, N. A., 132
Shlyapnikov, A. M., 139, 147, 247
Shmidt, A. E., 145
Short Course of History of VKP(b)
(Stalin), 36, 47, 50 f., 54, 62–5, 71 f.,
74, 76–9, 81–6, 88 f., 203; revaluation
of, 21, 42, 55, 69, 124
Shulgin, V. N., 291
Shumyatsky, B., 190
Siberia and Far East, 27, 131 f., 180,
190; in civil war, 292 ff., 296, 301–4
Sidorov, A. L., 118, 120 f., 123 f., 129
Simonov, K., 224
Sinkiang, 184
Sino-Polish Friendship Society, 183
Sino-Soviet Friendship Society, 133, 183
Sketches from History of Cheka: cf.
Ocherki Istorii VChK
Šmeral, B., 297 n.
Smith, F. W., 289 f.
Smolensk, archive of, 31, 36, 78, 144
Smirnov, N. A., 26
Smirnov, V., 25
social conditions, in West, Sov. histo-
rians on, 99, 101
Social Democracy, German, 48, 209 ff.,
213, 216, 218; Russian, 24, 29, 40, 47,
73, 78, 80, 146; cf. CPSU, Menshevism
Socialist-Revolutionaries, 44, 46, 50, 57,
69, 142 f.; see also Populism
socialist thought, history of, 218; Sov.
historians on, 123, 128 f., 145, 153,
200, 205–13, 214–21; cf. Populism,
Marxism, Leninism

Society of Historians (projected, in USSR), 121
Sofinov, P. G., 143
Sokolnikov, G. Yu., 247
Solovyov, S. M., 29, 39
South-east Asia, 159, 162, 174, 195 f.; see also individual countries
Sovetskoe Kitaevedenie, 182 ff., 197
soviets of workers' deputies: (1905), 44, 201; (1917), 74 f., 76, 139 f., 264; congresses of: II (1917), 76; IV (1918), 294; 137
Spartakists, 211
Stalin, J. V.: in 1905, 201; in 1917, 22, 75 f., 204; succeeds Lenin, 77; and Opposition (1928–9), 31 f.; and collectivization, 30; and purges, 53, 77, 181; and foreign policy, 48, 239, 261, 278; and Asia, 163, 183, 196; and World War II, 222, 226, 233, 240 f.;
— —, on equality, 90; on diplomacy, 254–7; on world revolution, 278; on strategy, 223 f., 229, 236 f.; on war, 255; on parliament, 309;
— —, as historian, 47 f., 50 f., 54, 62, 63 ff., 67, 72, 117, 147, (see also Short Course); and Soviet historiography, 14, 43, 47–51, 118, 126 f., 150, 201, 222, 243–6;
— —, in Soviet historiography: cult of (to 1953), 83, 88, 128, 201, 226; downgrading of, 10, 16, 20 f., 26, 51–8, 71, 73 f., 77, 123 f., 223 f., 263, 264 n.; cf. historiography (crisis in, 1955–7)
Stalingrad, battle of, 229 ff., 240 f.
State Institute of Historical and Archive Research, 134
State Pedagogical Institute (Moscow), 14
State Publishing House of Political Literature, 244 ff.
statistics, 11, 95, 101 n., 119
Stein, B. E., 25
Stevenson, A., 252
Strachey, J., 93, 213
strategy, Soviet military, 223 f., 228 f., 236 f.
Styer, Col. H. D., 302
Suchan, mines at, 302 ff.
Summers, M., 289 f.
Sun Yat-sen, 156, 158, 192
Suslov, M. A., 52, 202

Syria, 167
Syromyatnikov, P. E., 41

Taft-Hartley Act, 310
Taiping rebellion, 187
Talensky, Maj.-Gen. N. A., 228
Tarle, E. V., 41, 129, 237, 250, 257
Tatishchev, V. N., 29
Telpukhovsky, B. S., 232
Teodorovich, I. A., 154
Tiflis (Tbilisi), 289
Tikhomirov, M. N., 121, 123, 145
Tilak, B. G., 158
Tillett, L. R., 36
Timiryazev, K. A., 128
Timoshenko, Marshal S. K., 227, 238, 264 n.
Tito, President J. B., 207, 209, 212, 216, 257
Tochisky, P. V., 146
Tocqueville, A. de, 282
Toiling Peasant party, 57
Tolstoy, Count L. N., 187
totalitarianism, legitimation of, 61, 63 f., 66 f., 85, 88, 202, 219
trade unions, in West, 92; Sov. historians on, 104, 311, 313
Transcaucasia, 27, 32, 40, 66, 124, 131, 147, 230, 289 f., 298
Tretyakov, P. N., 121
trials: see Moscow, Mensheviks
Trifonov, I. Ya., 128
Trotsky, L. D., 30, 37, 47, 49, 62, 248; Sov. historians on, 54, 76 ff., 80, 85, 136, 150–3, 201, 247
Trotskyism, 26, 55, 57, 73, 183
Trukhanovsky, V. G., 13, 95, 99, 122
Truman, President H., 252
Tsagolov, N. A., 129
Tukhachevsky, Marshal M. N., 54
Turkey, 156, 280, 289, 294; Sov. historians on, 159 f., 170
Tvardovskaya, V. A., 36, 63, 146
Tvardovsky, A. T., 224 n.
Tyulenev, Gen. I. V., 231

U Nu, 159
Uchenye Zapiski Tikheokeanskovo Instituta, 196
Uglanov, N. A., 31

Uighurs, 184
Ukraine, 122; in civil war, 132, 238, 289–92, 295 f., 298; in World War II, 229 f., 232, 263
Ukrainskyi Istorychnyi Zhurnal, 119
Ulam, A. B., 16, 34, **38, 87,** 89, **199–214,** 214–7, 217, 219, **220 f.**
United Arab Republic: *see* Egypt, Syria
United Nations, 60, 281; Sov. historians on, 243 f., 276
United States, 88, 111, 113, 115; Sov. historians on, 94 ff., 98, 101, 104 f., 115 f., 235, 306–14;
— —, and USSR, Sov. historians on, 184; (1917–20), 192, 286–305; cf. Grand Alliance
'Unity and Progress' (Turkey), 156
Ushinsky, K. D., 128
Utechin, S. V., **35 f.,** 39, **40,** 66, 86, 117–29, 144 ff., 148, **153 f.**
Uzbekistan: *see* Central Asia

Vaganov, F. M., 31 f.
Varga, E., 39, 41, 94, 108, 111, 162, 248 n.
Vasiliev, V. P., 182
Vasilevsky, Marshal A. M., 242
Vatolina, L., 165
Vestnik Drevnei Istorii, 119
Vestnik Istorii Mirovoi Kultury, 119
Vestnik Leningradskovo Universiteta, 119
Vestnik Moskovskovo Universiteta, 119
Vladimirov, L. S., 314
Vladivostok, 180, 302 f.
Vlasov, Gen. A. A., 240 f.
Voennaya Mysl, 224, 236
Voenno-istoricheskii Zhurnal, 119, 230 f.
Voennyi Vestnik, 225, 226, 229
Voitinsky, G., 184
Volga region, 30, 34
Volkhov river, battle of, 240 f.
Volkov, I. M., 71
Volosevich, V., 47
Vollmar, G. von, 209
Voprosy Istorii, 11 f., 29, 61, 119, 184–92, 196 f., 199, 214, 222 n.; editors of, 13, 21, 70 f., 121, 287; in historical crisis (1955–7), 14, 20–8, 33 f., 40, 69–74, 120, 122 ff., 200; quoted, 12 f., 59, 131, 133, 180, 237

Voprosy Istorii KPSS, 28, 60, 71 f., 74, 119; editors of, 71; quoted, 31, 37, 46
Voroshilov, Marshal K. E., 31, 54, 264 n.
Voznesensky, N. A., 264 n.
Vyshinsky, A. I., 264 n.

wages, in West: *see* living standards
Weizsäcker, Baron E. von, 236, 262
Wilson, Sir H., 241
Wilson, President W., 294, 296
Wirth, J., 152
Wohltat, H., 241
Wolfe, B. D., **38,** 43–61, 61 f., 64, 66 ff., 84, **85 f.,** 90, 113, **114 f.,** 151, **217 f.,** 280 f.
Workers' Opposition, 55
World War II, Sov. historians on, 133, 223–42; on character of, 233 ff.; eastern front: (campaign of 1941), 77, 222, 223 ff., 226–9, 231 f., 237 f., 240 ; (1942), 229 f., 240; (1943), 229; (1944) 224 n.; other fronts, 111
Wright, J. B., 290

Yalta, conference of (1945), 256
Yaroslavsky, E., 31, 47 f., 62, 201
Yefimov, A. V., 308
Yefimov, G. V., 185 f., 191
Yemelyanov, V. S., 277
Yemen, 160
Yeremenko, Marshal A. I., 230 f., 237, 241
Yevzerov, R. E., 24, 200
Yezhov, N. I., 53, 63, 77
Yugoslavia: communism in, 175, 210 ff., 216 f.; historiography in, 64; and USSR (to 1953), 257, 272; (1953–), 26, 80, 206, 211, 278

Zenkovsky, V. V., 121
Zetkin, C., 279
Zhdanov, A. A., 88, 118, 122, 160, 264 n.
Zhilin, P. A., 224 n.
Zhukov, E. M., 16, 121, 126, 197, 312 f.
Zhukov, G. D., 54, 77, 225 ff., 240, 242
Zimin, A. A., 145
Zinoviev, G. E., as historian, 47, 49 f., 62, 79; Sov. historians on, 22, 26, 30, 37, 40, 204
Zueva, F. G., 263

Programme of the Conference on Contemporary History in the Soviet Mirror

held under the joint auspices of **Survey** and
L'Institut Universitaire de Hautes
Études Internationales,
Geneva, July 16—23, 1961

JULY 17

MORNING
SESSION
Marxism and Soviet Historiography
Leopold Labedz

AFTERNOON
SESSION
Soviet Historiography and the Problem of Change
Merle Fainsod

JULY 18

MORNING
SESSION
Soviet Party Histories from Lenin to Khrushchev
Bertram D. Wolfe

AFTERNOON
SESSION
Continuity and Change in the New Party History
Leonard Schapiro

JULY 19

MORNING
SESSION
The Post-War History of the Western World in the
Soviet Mirror
John Keep

JULY 20

MORNING
SESSION
Soviet Historiography after Stalin
S. V. Utechin

Soviet Historical Sources in the Post-Stalin Era
George Katkov

AFTERNOON
SESSION
The National Bourgeoisie in Soviet Historical Writings
Walter Z. Laqueur

Soviet Historians and the Sino-Soviet Alliance
Mark Mancall

JULY 21

MORNING   Socialism in Current Soviet Historiography
SESSION   *Adam B. Ulam*

The Moscow Institute of Marxism-Leninism
Boris I. Nikolaevsky

JULY 22

MORNING   Contemporary Soviet Sources on the Civil War
SESSION   *Jan Meijer*

Soviet Historiography of World War II
Matthew Gallagher

AFTERNOON   Soviet Historiography and Soviet Foreign Policy
SESSION   *Alvin Z. Rubinstein*

Diplomacy in the Mirror of Soviet Scholarship
Vernon V. Aspaturian

BACKGROUND PAPERS

Soviet Historians and American History
Max Beloff

Comintern in Soviet Historiography
Jane Degras

Soviet Historiography and America's Rôle in the
Intervention
George F. Kennan

Soviet Historiography between the Thaw and the Freeze
Leopold Labedz

India and Pakistan 1935-1960: The Soviet Version
G. B. Morris

PARTICIPANTS

Chairman of the Conference:

SIR ISAIAH BERLIN   All Souls College, Oxford   *England*

Organization of the Conference:

JACQUES FREYMOND   Institut Universitaire de   *Switzerland*
                          Hautes Études Inter-
                          nationales, Geneva

LEOPOLD LABEDZ   *Survey*, Ilford House,   *England*
                          135 Oxford St., London,
                          W.1

YVES COLLART   Institut Universitaire de   *Switzerland*
                          Hautes Études Inter-
                          nationales, Geneva

VERNON V. ASPATURIAN   Pennsylvania State Univer-   *U.S.A.*
                          sity, Pennsylvania

GEORGE BOLSOVER   School of Slavonic Studies,   *England*
                          University of London,
                          London

JANE DEGRAS   Royal Institute of Inter-   *England*
                          national Affairs, London

MERLE FAINSOD   Russian Research Center,   *U.S.A.*
                          Harvard University,
                          Cambridge, Mass.

MATTHEW GALLAGHER   802 Shelby Lane, Falls   *U.S.A.*
                          Church, Virginia

LOUIS HALLE   Institut Universitaire de   *Switzerland*
                          Hautes Études Inter-
                          nationales, Geneva

WALTHER HOFER   University of Berne, Berne   *Switzerland*

GEORGE KATKOV   St. Antony's College,   *England*
                          Oxford

JOHN KEEP   School of Slavonic Studies,   *England*
                          University of London,
                          London

WALTER Z. LAQUEUR   *Survey*, Ilford House,   *England*
                          135 Oxford St., London,
                          W.1

PARTICIPANTS (*continued*)

RICHARD LOWENTHAL	Freie Universität, Berlin	*Germany*
MARK MANCALL	Center for East Asian Studies, Harvard University Cambridge, Mass.	*U.S.A.*
CHARLES MCLANE	Institut Universitaire de Hautes Études Internationales, Geneva	*Switzerland*
JAN MEIJER	Internationaale Instituut voor Sociale Geschiedenis, Amsterdam	*Netherlands*
BORIS I. NIKOLAEVSKY	417 West 120 Street, New York 27, N.Y.	*U.S.A.*
MARC RAEFF	Columbia University, New York	*U.S.A.*
ALVIN Z. RUBINSTEIN	Wharton School of Finance and Commerce, University of Pennsylvania, Philadelphia	*U.S.A.*
LEONARD SCHAPIRO	London School of Economics and Political Science, London	*England*
PETER SCHEIBERT	University of Marburg, Marburg	*Germany*
STUART R. SCHRAM	Centre d'Études des Relations Internationales, Paris	*France*
BORIS SOUVARINE	Institut d'Histoire Sociale, Paris	*France*
ADAM B. ULAM	Russian Research Center, Harvard University, Cambridge, Mass.	*U.S.A.*
S. V. UTECHIN	St. Antony's College, Oxford	*England*
BERTRAM D. WOLFE	68 Montague Street, Brooklyn 1, N.Y.	*U.S.A.*

For Product Safety Concerns and Information please contact our EU
representative GPSR@taylorandfrancis.com
Taylor & Francis Verlag GmbH, Kaufingerstraße 24, 80331 München, Germany

www.ingramcontent.com/pod-product-compliance
Lightning Source LLC
Chambersburg PA
CBHW060144280326
41932CB00012B/1631

*9 7 8 1 0 3 2 8 7 2 1 5 5 *